THE
CIVIL JURISDICTION AND
JUDGMENTS ACT 1982

LAWRENCE COLLINS

MA, LLB (Cantab.), LLM (Columbia Univ., NY);
Solicitor, London; Fellow, Wolfson College, Cambridge;
Visiting Professor, Queen Mary College, London

LONDON
BUTTERWORTHS
1983

This book is also available as part of Butterworths Annotated Legislation Service

England	Butterworth & Co (Publishers) Ltd, 88 Kingsway, LONDON WC2B 6AB
Australia	Butterworths Pty Ltd, SYDNEY, MELBOURNE, BRISBANE, ADELAIDE and PERTH
Canada	Butterworth & Co (Canada) Ltd, TORONTO Butterworth & Co (Western Canada) Ltd, VANCOUVER
New Zealand	Butterworths of New Zealand Ltd, WELLINGTON
Singapore	Butterworth & Co (Asia Pte Ltd, SINGAPORE
South Africa	Butterworth Publishers (Pty) Ltd, DURBAN
USA	Mason Publishing Co, ST PAUL, Minnesota Butterworth Legal Publishers, SEATTLE, Washington; BOSTON, D & S Publishers, CLEARWATER, Florida

©
Butterworth & Co (Publishers) Ltd
1983

ISBN 0 406 00530 3

Typeset by CCC,
printed and bound in Great Britain
by William Clowes Limited,
Beccles and London

PREFACE

"... there still appears to be considerable ignorance about the consequences which this Convention will soon have for the jurisdiction of our Courts, and ... these deserve study and preparation in advance" (Lord Justice Kerr in *Citadel Insurance Co v Atlantic Union Insurance Co SA* [1982] 2 Lloyd's Rep 543 at 549).

The Civil Jurisdiction and Judgments Act 1982 is perhaps the most important piece of legislation relating to civil procedure enacted in this country this century. It, together with the amendments to the Rules of the Supreme Court, will effect fundamental changes in the law relating to jurisdiction and judgments in the United Kingdom. The primary purpose of the 1982 Act is to give effect in the law of the United Kingdom to the Brussels Convention of 1968 on jurisdiction and the enforcement of judgments in civil and commercial matters. It introduces a new concept of domicile for the purposes of jurisdiction. The 1968 Convention is given the force of law and similar (but not identical) rules of jurisdiction for intra-United Kingdom cases are applied. There are new provisions for the enforcement of intra-United Kingdom judgments. For the first time non-money judgments given by courts in other Contracting States will be enforceable, and non-money judgments rendered in one part of the United Kingdom will be enforceable in other parts. It cannot be said that the new system will be simple. Thus the jurisdictional rules of the English courts will differ depending on whether the defendant is domiciled in another part of the United Kingdom (1982 Act, Schedule 4), or is domiciled in another Contracting State (1982 Act, Schedule 1), or is domiciled in a non-Contracting State (Ord. 11, r. 1(1)). Foreign judgments will be enforceable under Part I of the 1982 Act (judgments of Contracting States), Part II of the 1982 Act (judgments of UK courts), the Foreign Judgments (Reciprocal Enforcement) Act 1933 (the Isle of Man, Guernsey, Jersey and some eight foreign and Commonwealth countries), the Administration of Justice Act 1920 (most Commonwealth countries) and at common law (particularly those countries with whom there are no reciprocal arrangements, such as the United States).

The object of this book is to provide a commentary on the Act and the Convention, to indicate some of the main areas of difficulty and offer some solutions to them, and to deal with the main changes to the Rules of the Supreme Court. There have now been over 30 judgments of the European Court of Justice on the Convention and I have endeavoured to take account of them, together with some of the more important judgments in the original Contracting States. The European Court has not made any use of decisions of national courts and it is well to bear in mind that "the persuasive value of a particular court's decision must depend on its reputation and status, the extent to which its decisions are binding on courts of co-ordinate and inferior jurisdiction in its own country and the coverage of the national law reporting system" (*Fothergill v Monarch Airlines* [1981] AC 251, at 284, per Lord Diplock).

iii

Dr. J H C Morris QC very kindly read a draft of the manuscript and made many helpful comments and suggestions, and his ideas were as valuable as one would expect from one whose contribution to the conflict of laws has been so great (see *The Hollandia* [1982] QB 872, at 884, per Lord Denning MR). Mr. Ulrich Stahl helped me with the German material to which I refer and raised a number of useful points for inclusion. Maureen Higgins, my secretary, dealt excellently, as always, with a difficult manuscript. This book is dedicated to my wife, Sarah.

London, August 1983   Lawrence Collins

NOTE

At the time this book went to press, the provisions of the Civil Jurisdiction and Judgments Act 1982 relating to the 1968 Convention and to intra-United Kingdom jurisdiction and enforcement of judgments had not been brought into force. But some of the changes to the general law came into force on 24 August 1982, most notably s. 24(1)(*a*), (2)(*a*) and (3) (interim relief and protective measures in cases of doubtful jurisdiction); s. 30 (proceedings for torts to foreign immovable property); s. 32 (foreign judgments given in breach of agreement for settlement of disputes); s. 33 (abolition of the rule in *Harris v Taylor* [1915] 2 KB 580 and *Henry v Geoprosco International Ltd* [1976] QB 726 on what constitutes a submission to the jurisdiction of a foreign court); s. 34 (abolition of non-merger rule).

The amendments to the Rules of the Supreme Court were made in July 1983 (S.I. 1983 No. 1181). The amendments which fall within the scope of this book will not come into force until s. 2 of the 1982 Act comes into force, except for the amendment to Ord. 12, r. 8, which came into force on 1 October 1983.

CONTENTS

Contents

Contents

CHAPTER 5 RECOGNITION AND ENFORCEMENT OF JUDG-
MENTS UNDER THE CONVENTION 105

CHAPTER 6 INTRA-UNITED KINGDOM JURISDICTION AND
ENFORCEMENT OF JUDGMENTS. JURISDICTION IN
SCOTLAND 127

Contents

REFERENCES AND ABBREVIATIONS

1933 Act	The Foreign Judgments (Reciprocal Enforcement) Act 1933
1968 Convention . .	The Convention on jurisdiction and the enforcement of judgments in civil and commercial matters signed at Brussels on 27 September 1968
1968 Protocol . . .	The Protocol annexed to the 1968 Convention
1971 Protocol . . .	The Protocol on the interpretation of the 1968 Convention by the European Court signed at Luxembourg on 3 June 1971
1982 Act	The Civil Jurisdiction and Judgments Act 1982
Accession Convention .	The Convention on the accession to the 1968 Convention and the 1971 Protocol of Denmark, the Republic of Ireland and the United Kingdom signed at Luxembourg on 9 October 1978
Am J Comp L	American Journal of Comparative Law
Anton	Anton *Private International Law* (1967)
BYIL	British Yearbook of International Law
Clunet	Journal du droit international (Clunet)
Collins	Collins *European Community Law in the United Kingdom* (2nd edn, 1980)
Dicey & Morris . . .	Dicey & Morris *Conflict of Laws* (10th edn, 1980)
Droz	Droz *La compétence judiciaire et l'effet des jugements dans la CEE* (1972)
Eur Comm Cas . . .	European Commercial Cases
Eur Court Digest . . .	Court of Justice of the European Communities *Digest of case-law relating to the European Communities*, D Series
Eur L Dig	European Law Digest
Eur L Rev	European Law Review
I C L Q	International and Comparative Law Quarterly
Jenard	Report by Mr. P. Jenard on the 1968 Convention and the 1971 Protocol, Official Journal of the European Communities, OJ C59, 5 March 1979, pp 1, 66
Maxwell Report . . .	Report of the Scottish Committee on Jurisdiction and Enforcement-Scottish Courts Administration (1980)
Mustill and Boyd . . .	Mustill and Boyd *Commercial Arbitration* (1982)
Neths Int L Rev . . .	Netherlands International Law Review
RIW/AWD	Recht der Internationalen Wirtschaft/Aussenwirtschaftdienst des Betriebs-Beraters
Rev Crit	Revue critique de droit international privé
Schlosser	Report by Professor Dr. Peter Schlosser on the Accession Convention, Official Journal of the European Communities, OJ C 59, 5 March 1979, p 71
Weser	Weser *Convention communautaire sur la compétence judiciaire et l'exécution des décisions* (1975)
Yb Eur L	Yearbook of European Law

TABLE OF STATUTES

References in this Table to *Statutes* are to Halsbury's Statutes of England (Third Edition) showing the volume and page at which the annotated text of the Act will be found.

Page references printed in bold type indicate where the Act is set out in part or in full.

xi

TABLE OF 1968 CONVENTION, ANNEXED PROTOCOL, 1971 PROTOCOL AND ACCESSION CONVENTION

Page references in bold type indicate where the Convention or Protocol is set out in part or in full.

TABLE OF CASES

Decisions of the European Court of Justice are listed below numerically. These decisions are also included in the preceding alphabetical table.

CHAPTER 1

INTRODUCTORY OUTLINE
INTERPRETATION AND REFERENCES
TO THE EUROPEAN COURT

Introduction

The European Community has adhered consistently to the notion, expressed in the EEC Treaty of 1957, that the ideals of a common market would be furthered by a convention between the Member States for the recognition and enforcement of judgments. Thus the original Member States agreed, in Art. 220 of the EEC Treaty, that they should, so far as was necessary, enter into negotiations with each other with a view to securing for the benefit of their nationals (inter alia) the simplification of formalities governing the reciprocal recognition and enforcement of judgments of courts or tribunals and of arbitration awards. There is room for some scepticism about the views expressed by the Commission when, in 1959, it invited Member States to commence negotiations in the area of recognition and enforcement of judgments; the Commission thought it would promote the true internal market between the Member States by mitigating the effect of differences between the legal effects of judicial acts in the States involved. The reasons for this belief were never fully articulated, but in response to this invitation the Committee of Permanent Representatives to the Community set up a Committee of Experts in 1960. The Committee, under the chairmanship of Professor Bülow and with Mr. Jenard, of the Belgian Ministry for Foreign Affairs, as rapporteur, went beyond the task of preparing a Convention on judgments and adopted, in 1964, a preliminary draft Convention which extended to rules on jurisdiction as well as on the recognition and enforcement of judgments. It met with considerable hostility from the United States because it contained rules which worked to the detriment of defendants not domiciled in Contracting States but with assets there.[1] Following the submission of the preliminary draft to governments, industry and other parties, a draft Convention was adopted in 1966. It was signed in 1968 and entered into force in 1973. In 1971 the Contracting States entered into a Protocol on the interpretation by the European Court of the 1968 Convention which entered into force in 1975. Since 1976 the European Court has delivered opinions on the Convention in more than thirty cases, some of the greatest importance, and there have been many decisions of national courts.[2]

The parties to the 1968 Convention recognised (in Art. 63) that any State

---

[1] See p. 50, post.
[2] See Court of Justice of the European Communities, *Digest of case-law relating to the European Communities*, D Series (hereinafter "Eur Court Digest"); Pocar, *Codice delle Convenzioni sulla Giurisdizione e l'Esecuzione delle Sentenze Straniere nella CEE* (1980). The decisions of the European Court on the Conventions will be controlling in the United Kingdom: Civil Jurisdiction and Judgments 1982 Act, s. 3(1), p. 7, post. As to the value of national decisions, cf. *Fothergill v Monarch Airlines Ltd* [1981] AC 251 at 284, 295.

which subsequently became a member of the EEC would be required to accept the Convention as a basis for the negotiations between the new member and the original members necessary to ensure the accession of the new member to the treaties contemplated by Art. 220 of the EEC Treaty, which included the 1968 Convention. Article 63(2) of the 1968 Convention contemplated that "the necessary adjustments" might be the subject of a special Convention between a new member and the original Contracting States. When the United Kingdom and the other two new Member States acceded to the European Communities in 1972 they agreed, by Art. 3 of the Act of Accession, to accede to the Conventions provided for in Art. 220 of the EEC Treaty (and the associated Protocol on interpretation by the European Court) signed by the original Member States and to this end they undertook "to enter into negotiations with the original Member States in order to make the necessary adjustments thereto". Following the accession of the new Member States to the Communities, the Committee of Permanent Representatives set up a Working Party composed of delegates of the original and the new Member States of the Communities and of a representative of the Commission. The Working Party was chaired by Mr. Jenard with Professor Schlosser as its rapporteur. After prolonged negotiations, an Accession Convention was signed by the original Member States and by representatives of the United Kingdom, the Republic of Ireland and Denmark on 9th October 1978,[1] making the necessary adjustments to the 1968 Convention and to the 1971 Protocol on interpretation. Both the 1968 Convention and the Accession Convention were the subject of substantial reports by Mr. Jenard and Professor Schlosser respectively. These reports were sent to the governments concerned at the same time as the draft Conventions and have a special status in relation to their interpretation.[2]

As Lord Justice Kerr has pointed out,[3] it was "very regrettable" that the United Kingdom "was not concerned with the original scheme and formulation of the Convention and that we only came on the scene after the original six had adhered to it". But during the accession negotiations the "necessary adjustments" went considerably beyond those changes which were necessary to accommodate the legal systems of the new Member States and included some improvements to the original Convention as well as purely formal changes required to adapt it to the legal systems of the new Contracting States.

The 1968 Convention extends far beyond matters relating to recognition and

---

[1] A Convention providing for the accession of Greece was signed on 25 October 1982: see Official Journal of the European Communities OJ L388, 31 December 1982, and Appendix 3, post.

[2] See p. 10, post. The Jenard reports on the 1968 Convention and the 1971 Protocol and the Schlosser report on the Accession Convention are published in the Official Journal of the European Communities, OJ C59, 5 March 1979, and are hereinafter cited as "Jenard" and "Schlosser". The Scottish Committee on Jurisdiction and Enforcement under the Chairmanship of Lord Maxwell published a report ("the Maxwell Report") in 1980 on (inter alia) the practical aspects of the implementation of the 1968 Convention. On the history of the Conventions see Jenard, p. 3; Schlosser, para. 1–3; Maxwell Report, paras. 1.9–1.15; Droz *La compétence judiciaire et l'effet des jugements dans la CEE* (1972) (hereinafter cited as "Droz"), paras. 11–15. See also Weser *Convention communautaire sur la compétence judiciaire et l'exécution des décisions* (1975) (hereinafter cited as "Weser").

[3] (1978) 75 L.S. Gaz. 1190.

enforcement of judgments, and lays down uniform rules of jurisdiction which will involve fundamental changes to the existing rules of jurisdiction in the United Kingdom. Its approach is quite different from that of the existing United Kingdom bilateral conventions governing recognition and enforcement of foreign judgments. Those conventions, which are given effect in the United Kingdom by the Foreign Judgments (Reciprocal Enforcement) Act 1933 ("the 1933 Act") do not regulate the circumstances in which the court which is originally seised may exercise jurisdiction: they merely tell the enforcing court in which circumstances the jurisdiction of the original court must be recognised, and they allow the enforcing court to investigate whether the original court had jurisidiction within the meaning of the 1933 Act or the convention. This is frequently called a system of "indirect" rules of jurisdiction, which do not affect the courts of the State in which the action is originally brought, and only become relevant at the stage of enforcement. The 1968 Convention lays down a very elaborate system of jurisdictional rules, to which the court in which the action is originally brought must adhere—this is a system of "direct" rules of jurisdiction. Once the court in which the action has been brought has decided that it can exercise jurisdiction under the Convention rules, a court in another State which is asked to enforce it has much more limited power than under the bilateral conventions to question the jurisdiction of the court which gave the original judgment.

The distinction may be illustrated by the following case. A, a French national, has a claim against B, an Englishman, who has an address in Paris and has assets in England. Before the 1968 Convention comes into force for the United Kingdom, A will be able to sue B in France because, under Art. 14 of the French Civil Code, A's French nationality will give the court jurisdiction. If B does not defend the action and A seeks to enforce the resulting French judgment in England under the 1933 Act, the French judgment will be enforceable (inter alia) if B was resident in France when the proceedings were instituted. It is irrelevant whether the French court took jurisdiction on the basis of B's residence; and the English court will have to consider afresh whether B was in fact resident in France; if he was, the French court will be regarded as having had international jurisdiction in the case, irrespective of the basis on which it took jurisdiction. But after the 1968 Convention comes into force the position will be quite different: A will not be able to seise the French courts on the basis of his nationality, because as regards defendants domiciled (in the sense of the 1968 Convention) in Contracting States that basis of jurisdiction is outlawed as exorbitant, but he will be able to seise the French court if (among other grounds) B is domiciled in France. If the French court determines that B is domiciled in France within the meaning of French law, and A seeks to enforce a resulting judgment in England, the English court will not be able to examine whether the original court properly took jurisdiction under the Convention, except in very limited cases (and even then cannot re-examine findings of fact). The judgment will be enforceable because the French court found that it had jurisdiction under the 1968 Convention because of B's domicile, and the English court will not be able to refuse enforcement because it would have come to a different view, under English law or on the facts, of B's domicile.

There is nothing unique in United Kingdom law about rules of direct jurisdiction or about enforcement of judgments without the chance to investigate the jurisdiction of the original court. Thus the Warsaw Convention on carriage by air and the Geneva Convention on carriage by road contain rules of direct jurisdiction, and United Kingdom courts cannot entertain actions falling within the scope of legislation giving effect to them unless the jurisdictional requirements of the conventions are fulfilled.[1] The enforcement of judgments without investigation of the jurisdiction of the original court is the basis (with limited exceptions) of the system of intra-United Kingdom enforcement introduced by the Judgments Extension Act 1868. But the 1968 Convention will be revolutionary for the United Kingdom because of the extent to which it takes these two features.

It is not only the technique of the 1968 Convention which will be revolutionary. The primary basis of jurisdiction under the Convention over those "domiciled" in a Contracting State is the "domicile" of the defendant. "Domicile" for the purposes of the Convention is to be equated with, broadly, residence (in the case of the individuals) and incorporation or place of central management and control (in the case of corporations). In addition to the courts of the domicile of the defendant, there are other special bases of jurisdiction, and to the exclusion of domicile and other special bases there are certain areas of exclusive jurisdiction. Provision is also made for submission to jurisdiction by contract or by appearance, and for certain other procedural matters, including *lis alibi pendens* and jurisdiction to order provisional measures. The Convention rules on jurisdiction and judgments will introduce major changes into the law and practice of the United Kingdom. Thus as regards defendants domiciled in another Contracting State or in another part of the United Kingdom, English courts will not be able to exercise jurisdiction merely by virtue of the defendant's temporary presence in England at the time of service of the writ; secondly, where a defendant is outside England at the time of service of the writ and the case falls within the jurisdiction of the United Kingdom court, service of the proceedings will not be (as it presently is in England under RSC Ord. 11, r. 1(1)) a matter for the discretion of the court but a matter of right; thirdly, where a case falls within the jurisdiction of a United Kingdom court under the Convention, there will be no discretion to stay the proceedings on the ground that some other court is more appropriate unless that other court has been first seised of the proceedings or related proceedings. This lack of flexibility in the exercise of jurisdiction under the Convention has given rise to considerable misgiving in the United Kingdom, whose efforts to introduce a degree of discretion or flexibility into the Convention failed; another area in which the Convention rules are open to criticism is that of insurance, where the draftsmen of the original Convention took it upon themselves to introduce rules supposedly designed to protect the insured, but which may allow "forum-shopping" of the most unfortunate kind; the accession negotiations led to some limited improvement in this area, as they also did in mitigating the effects of the very restrictive rules on exclusive jurisdiction clauses in the Convention.[2]

---

[1] Dicey & Morris *Conflict of Laws* (10th edn, 1980) p. 241.
[2] See Kerr, p. 2, n. 3 ante, for a good account of the main issues in the negotiations.

Judgments within the scope of the Convention given by courts of Contracting States will be entitled to recognition and enforcement in other Contracting States under the Convention. The judgments to which it applies are more extensive than under the existing United Kingdom bilateral treaties; it is not limited to "final" judgments, or to judgments of "superior courts" and it extends also to non-money judgments. The grounds for refusing recognition and enforcement are much more limited than under existing bilateral treaties: in particular the court in which enforcement is sought has only very limited powers to investigate the jurisdiction of the court which gave the judgment. In practice, this will make it easier to enforce judgments of the United Kingdom courts in other Contracting States, and will (as compared with the existing bilateral treaties) make it easier for judgments of courts of those States to be enforced in the United Kingdom.

The Civil Jurisdiction and Judgments Act 1982 ("the 1982 Act"), inter alia, brings into effect for the United Kingdom the rules of jurisdiction provided for by the 1968 Convention, as amended by the Accession Convention of 1978, and applies similar (but not identical) rules for allocating jurisdiction as between the constituent parts of the United Kingdom. It also provides for the recognition and enforcement of judgments emanating from other Contracting States, and introduces a revised system for the enforcement of judgments given by courts of one part of the United Kingdom in other parts. One consequence of the introduction of the Convention system in the United Kingdom is that there will be three sets of basic rules of jurisdiction in the United Kingdom: one set for cases within the Convention (mainly, but not only, where the defendant is domiciled in another Contracting State); a second set, similar but not identical to the first, where the defendant is domiciled in another part of the United Kingdom; and a third set, substantially different from the first two, where the defendant is not domiciled in a Contracting State.

The 1982 Act effects the following main changes in the law of the United Kingdom:

(a) it gives the 1968 Convention (as amended by the Accession Convention) the force of law;[1]

(b) as a result, the rules of jurisdiction of the United Kingdom courts are radically changed as regards defendants "domiciled" in other Contracting States (and in certain other cases);

(c) it introduces definitions of "domicile" for the purposes of the Conventions which differ considerably from the traditional rules of domicile;[2]

(d) it makes provision for the recognition and enforcement of judgments emanating from the other Contracting States;[3]

(e) it introduces new rules on jurisdiction of the courts of the constituent parts of the United Kingdom in cases where the defendant is "domiciled" in another part of the United Kingdom;[4]

(f) it introduces new rules for jurisdiction in Scottish cases involving foreign defendants;[5]

---

[1] 1982 Act, s. 2(1) and Schs. 1 to 3.
[2] 1982 Act, ss. 41 and 42.
[3] 1982 Act, ss. 4 and 5.
[4] 1982 Act, s. 16 and Sch. 4.
[5] 1982 Act, s. 20 and Sch. 8.

(*g*) it provides a new system of recognition and enforcement of judgments as between the constituent parts of the United Kingdom;[1]

(*h*) it makes considerable changes in the general rules of jurisdiction in the United Kingdom, in particular:

  (i) the rule in *The Siskina*[2] that interim relief is not available in England unless the English court has jurisdiction over the substantive dispute is to be abrogated;[3]

  (ii) the rule that the English courts have no jurisdiction to entertain proceedings for trespass to immovable property is abolished except to the extent that the proceedings are principally concerned with a question of title.[4]

(*i*) it makes major changes in the general law relating to the recognition and enforcement of judgments, and in particular:

  (i) abolishes the rule in *Harris v Taylor*[5] and *Henry v Geoprosco International Ltd*[6] that an appearance solely to protest the jurisdiction might nevertheless be a voluntary submission;[7]

  (ii) abolishes the rule that a foreign judgment does not, of itself, extinguish the original cause of action in respect of which the judgment was given.[8]

The provisions relating to the Conventions and to jurisdiction and enforcement of judgments as between the constituent parts of the United Kingdom are not yet in force, and will require detailed rules of court[9] for their implementation,[10] but important parts of the Act relating to the general law of jurisdiction and general law relating to recognition and enforcement of judgments are already in force.[11]

The Conventions in United Kingdom law. "Force of law"

Section 2(1) of the 1982 Act provides that:

"The Conventions shall have the force of law in the United Kingdom, and judicial notice shall be taken of them."

---

[1] 1982 Act, ss. 18 and 19, and Schs. 6 and 7.
[2] [1979] AC 210, [1977] 3 All ER 803.
[3] 1982 Act, s. 25.
[4] 1982 Act, s. 30.
[5] [1915] 2 KB 580 CA.
[6] [1976] QB 726, [1975] 2 All ER 702 CA.
[7] 1982 Act, s. 33.
[8] 1982 Act, s. 34.
[9] In particular, revisions to RSC Ord. 11, as well as changes to the county court rules and the matrimonial causes rules. See Chapter 7 and Appendix 2, post, on the new RSC which go considerably beyond merely implementing the Convention rules.
[10] See 1982 Act, s. 48; cf. ss. 4(4), 7(2) and 12.
[11] 1982 Act, s. 53(1) and Sch. 13, Part I; for transitional provisions see s. 53(2) and Sch. 13, Part II.

The "Conventions" are:[1]

(1) The Convention on jurisdiction and the enforcement of judgments in civil and commercial matters (including its Protocol) signed on 27th September 1968 ("the 1968 Convention");

(2) The Protocol on the interpretation of the 1968 Convention by the European Court signed on 3rd June 1971 ("the 1971 Protocol"); and

(3) The Convention on the accession to the 1968 Convention and the 1971 Protocol of Denmark, the Republic of Ireland and the United Kingdom signed on 9th October 1978 ("the Accession Convention").[2]

For "convenience of reference"[3] Schedules 1, 2 and 3 of the 1982 Act set out the English texts of the 1968 Convention as amended by the Accession Convention; the 1971 Protocol as amended by the Accession Convention; and the transitional and final provisions of the Accession Convention.

By s. 3:

(a) if any question of interpretation is not referred to the European Court under the 1971 Protocol, it shall be determined in accordance with the principles laid down by, and any relevant decision of, the European Court;

(b) the United Kingdom court may consider the reports of M. Jenard on the 1968 Convention and the 1971 Protocol and the report by Professor Schlosser on the Accession Convention in ascertaining the meaning or effect of any provision of the Conventions and give them such weight as is appropriate in the circumstances.

The effect of ss. 2 and 3 is that many problems which have arisen in the United Kingdom with regard to the interpretation of international conventions will not arise in the case of the Conventions incorporated by the 1982 Act. These problems have included: (1) whether it is permissible to consider the foreign language text of a Convention in interpreting it if only the English text is scheduled to the United Kingdom legislation;[4] (2) whether "travaux préparatoires" and official reports may be resorted to for the purpose of interpretation.[5] The expression "force of law" was considered in the recent decision of the House of Lords in *The Hollandia*,[6] where Lord Diplock, discussing the Carriage of Goods by Sea Act 1971, said:

"... the provisions in section 1 of the Act ... appear to me to be free from any ambiguity perceptible to even the most ingenious of legal minds. The Hague-Visby Rules, or rather all those of them that are included in the

---

[1] See the definitions in 1982 Act, s. 1(1). "Contracting State" means one of the parties to the 1968 Convention or one of the parties to the Accession Convention, provided that the Accession Convention has entered into force for it: 1982 Act, s. 1(3).

[2] S. 14 of the 1982 Act gives power for the Act to be modified by Order in Council to deal with (inter alia) the accession of further states to the Conventions. For Greece, see p. 2, n. 1, ante.

[3] 1982 Act, s. 2(2).

[4] As in *James Buchanan & Co Ltd v Babco Forwarding and Shipping (UK) Ltd* [1978] AC 141, [1977] 3 All ER 1048; cf. *Fothergill v Monarch Airlines Ltd* [1981] AC 251, [1980] 2 All ER 696.

[5] As in *Fothergill v Monarch Airlines Ltd* [1981] AC 251, [1980] 2 All ER 696; cf. *Black-Clawson International Ltd v Papierwerke Waldhof-Aschaffenburg AG* [1975] AC 591, [1975] 1 All ER 810.

[6] [1982] 3 WLR 1111, at 1116.

Schedule, are to have the force of law in the United Kingdom: they are to be treated as if they were part of directly enacted statute law. But since they form part of an international convention which must come under the consideration of foreign as well as English courts, it is, as Lord MacMillan said of the Hague Rules themselves in *Stag Line Ltd v Foscolo, Mango & Co* [1932] AC 328, 350 'desirable in the interests of uniformity that their interpretation should not be rigidly controlled by domestic precedents of antecedent date, but rather that the language of the rules should be construed on broad principles of general acceptation.' They should be given a purposive rather than a narrow literalistic construction ..."

The direct method of incorporation of the Conventions by the 1982 Act makes it unnecessary to consider in the United Kingdom context whether they have "direct effect", i.e. whether they could be relied on directly in the face of legislation inconsistent with it.[1] The 1982 Act and the Conventions will take precedence over any inconsistent prior legislation. This may have some unexpected results going beyond amendment of the existing general rules relating to jurisdiction and judgments. Thus Art. 17 of the 1968 Convention provides that where parties, one of whom is domiciled in a Contracting State, agree that a court in a Contracting State is to have exclusive jurisdiction, that court shall have exclusive jurisdiction. That provision will be discussed in detail below[2] but for present purposes it is sufficient to point out that where it applies the jurisdiction of the courts of the defendant's domicile will be wholly ousted, if another court has been chosen. The law of the United Kingdom contains provisions which prevent parties from contracting out of the jurisdiction of United Kingdom courts. Thus s 140 of the Employment Protection (Consolidation) Act 1978 would prevent an English employee of a German company from effectively agreeing that any claims brought by the employee should be brought in a German court. There are similar laws in other countries. But in *Sanicentral GmbH v Collin*[3] the European Court held that employment disputes came within the 1968 Convention, and that a jurisdiction clause in a contract between a French worker and a German employee conferring jurisdiction on a German court deprived the French courts of jurisdiction, notwithstanding that the jurisdiction clause was void by French law when it was entered into (before the Convention came into force in 1973). The effect of the decision is far-reaching. The Court disclaimed any intention on the part of the Convention to affect rules of substantive law, but held that "in matters of civil jurisdiction, the national procedural laws applicable to the cases concerned are set aside in the matters governed by the Convention in favour of the provisions thereof".[4]

In the case of the 1982 Act, it is "the Conventions" which are given the force of law and it is only "for convenience of reference" that the English texts are set out in the Schedules. The United Kingdom court is entitled, and bound, to look

---

[1] Cf. Collins *European Community Law in the United Kingdom* (2nd edn. 1980) Chap. 2; the question was touched on in argument in Case 42/76: *De Wolf v Cox BV* [1976] ECR 1759, [1977] 2 CMLR 43. See also Fletcher *Conflict of Laws and European Community Law* (1982) p. 110.
[2] Pp. 83–90.
[3] Case 25/79: [1979] ECR 3423.
[4] At 3429; cf. Case 150/80: *Elefanten Schuh GmbH v Jacqmain* [1981] ECR 1671, [1982] 3 CMLR 1.

at the texts in other languages where a problem of interpretation arises. There is no room for a rule in this context that the other language versions may be resorted to only in the case of ambiguity in the English text;[1] in resorting to the foreign language texts the United Kingdom judge may use his own knowledge, or consult a dictionary, and the parties may call expert evidence to supplement the judge's resources.[2] All language texts of the Conventions are equally authentic. Articles 68 and 14 of the 1968 Convention and 1971 Protocol respectively provided that the Dutch, French, German and Italian versions should be "equally authentic"; and by Art. 37(2) of the Accession Convention the English, Irish and Danish versions of the original 1968 Convention were annexed to the Accession Convention and are to be authentic under the same conditions as the original language texts.[3] Article 41 of the Accession Convention makes all language versions of the Accession Convention equally authentic in the same way. The effect of these provisions is that the English version of the Conventions in Schedules 1–3 to the 1982 Act is "authentic" but is only one of the authentic versions, and resort may be had to the others for the purposes of interpretation. In the context of the EEC Treaty, both the House of Lords and the European Court have recently warned national judges about the danger of concluding that the interpretation of a provision is clear merely on the basis of consideration of one language version.[4]

Thus Art. 18 of the 1968 Convention provides, in the English version, that an appearance entered *solely* to contest the jurisdiction, is not to be regarded as a submission to the jurisdiction of the court. The French version, unlike the English, German, Italian and Dutch texts, did not expressly refer to the requirement that the appearance must be *solely* to contest the jurisdiction if it was to escape being a voluntary submission. But the European Court, in basing its decision on the French text, said:

> "Although differences between the different language versions of Article 18 of the Convention appear when it is sought to determine whether, in order to exclude the jurisdiction of the court seised, a defendant must confine himself to contesting that jurisdiction, or whether he may on the contrary still achieve the same purpose by contesting the jurisdiction of the court as well as the substance of the claim, the second interpretation is more in keeping with the objectives and spirit of the Convention."[5]

Article 5(1) gives jurisdiction to the place of performance of the obligation "in matters relating to a contract". In considering whether this applied where the existence of the contract was disputed the European Court said, in deciding that it did so apply:

> "It is established that the wording of Article 5(1) of the Convention does not resolve this question unequivocally. Whilst the German version of that

---

[1] Cf. *James Buchanan & Co Ltd v Babco Forwarding and Shipping (UK) Ltd* [1978] AC 141, [1977] 3 All ER 1048.

[2] Cf. *Fothergill v Monarch Airlines Ltd* [1981] AC 251 at 273, 286, 293, 300.

[3] See also Greek Accession Convention, Art. 13(2).

[4] See *Henn and Darby v DPP* [1981] AC 850 at 906; Case 283/81: *CILFIT Srl v Minister of Health* [1983] 1 CMLR 472.

[5] Case 150/80: *Elefanten Schuh GmbH v Jacqmain* [1981] ECR 1671 at 1685.

provision contains the words "Vertrag oder Ansprüche aus einem Vertrag", the French and Italian versions contain the expressions "en matière contractuelle" and "in materia contrattuale" respectively. Under these circumstances, in view of the lack of uniformity between the different language versions of the provision in question, it is advisable, in order to arrive at the interpretation requested by the national court, to have regard both to the context of Article 5(1) and to the purpose of the Convention."[1]

Section 3(3) of the 1982 Act provides that the court may consider the Jenard and Schlosser reports "in ascertaining the meaning or effect of any provision of the Conventions" and that the reports "shall be given such weight as is appropriate in the circumstances". Thus the much-criticised rule that reports of this kind may only be resorted to find the "mischief" the law was intended to remove (and not to find the meaning of law)[2] is neatly avoided. The importance of the Jenard and Schlosser reports is that they were written by persons who were closely involved in the negotiations over the Conventions. M. Jenard was the rapporteur of the committee of governmental experts which drafted the Convention. Professor Schlosser was the rapporteur of the Council working party on the draft Accession Convention; the working party consisted of governmental and Commission representatives. Both reports were submitted to the Contracting States with the draft Convention. They are a valuable source on the background and meaning of many provisions; and there are passages in the Schlosser report which were inserted as interpretations after discussions between the governmental representatives; although these may not be conclusive in the European Court they will be of great weight. Thus far the European Court has increasingly made direct reference to the Jenard report (the only one strictly relevant to date).[3] The Jenard and Schlosser reports are also to be considered in interpreting those parts of the Convention which have been adopted for intra-United Kingdom and Scottish jurisdictional rules.[4]

References to the European Court

Section 3 of the 1982 Act provides as follows:

"(1) Any question as to the meaning or effect of any provision of the Conventions shall, if not referred to the European Court in accordance with the 1971 Protocol, be determined in accordance with the principles laid down by and any relevant decision of the European Court.
(2) Judicial notice shall be taken of any decision of, or expression of opinion by, the European Court on any such question."

---

[1] Case 38/81: *Effer SpA v Kantner* [1982] ECR 825 at 834.
[2] See *Black-Clawson International Ltd v Papierwerke Waldhof-Aschaffenburg AG* [1975] AC 591, [1975] 1 All ER 810.
[3] E.g. Case 150/80: *Elefanten Schuh GmbH v Jacqmain* [1981] ECR 1671 at 1685; Case 157/80: *Rinkau* [1981] ECR 1391 at 1399; Case 133/81: *Ivenel v Schwab* [1982] ECR 1891, [1983] 1 CMLR 538.
[4] 1982 Act, ss. 16(3)(b), 20(5)(b).

The 1971 Protocol, as amended by the Accession Convention, is set out in Sch. 2 to the 1982 Act. The power of national courts to make references to the European Court for preliminary rulings on interpretation bears some resemblance to the procedure of Art. 177 of the EEC Treaty, under which United Kingdom courts have made many references.[1]

For the purposes of proceedings in the United Kingdom the 1971 Protocol must be read together with s. 6 of the 1982 Act which identifies the appellate courts in the United Kingdom in proceedings relating to the recognition and enforcement of judgments from other Contracting States. The combined effect of the 1971 Protocol and s. 6 is as follows:

(1) Jurisdiction is conferred on the European Court to give rulings on the interpretation of the 1968 Convention, the 1971 Protocol and the Accession Convention (1971 Protocol, Art. 1).

(2) Where a question of interpretation of the Conventions is raised in a case before one of certain specified courts "that court *shall*, if it considers that a decision on the question is necessary to enable it to give judgment" request the European Court to give a ruling. If such a question is raised before any of the other courts entitled to make references that court *may*, if it considers that a decision on the question is necessary to enable it to give judgment, request the court to give a ruling thereon. (1971 Protocol, Art. 3).

(3) The English courts which *must* make a request in appropriate cases for a preliminary ruling are:

(i) the House of Lords (1971 Protocol, Arts. 2(1) and 3(1), and s. 6(1));

(ii) the Court of Appeal on appeal from a decision of the High Court on an appeal against an order registering or refusing to register a judgment (1971 Protocol, Arts. 2(1), 3(1); 1968 Convention, Arts. 37(2) and 41; and s. 6(1));[2]

(iii) the High Court in relation to recognition or enforcement of a maintenance order by way of case stated in accordance with s. 111 of the Magistrates' Court Act 1980 (1971 Protocol, Arts. 2(1), 3(1); 1968 Convention, Arts. 37(2) and 41; and s. 6(3)).[3]

(4) The English courts which *may* make a request are:

(i) the High Court when hearing an appeal against registration of a judgment (1971 Protocol, Arts. 2(3), 3(2); 1968 Convention, Art. 37);[4]

(ii) a magistrates' court when hearing an application to set aside registration of a maintenance order (1971 Protocol, Arts. 2(3), 3(2); 1968 Convention, Art. 37).[5]

(iii) any other court sitting in an appellate capacity other than those above (1971 Protocol, Arts. 2(2) and 3(2));

---

[1] For the procedure see RSC Ord. 114 as amended. On Art. 177 see Collins *European Community Law in the United Kingdom* (2nd edn. 1980) Chap. 3.

[2] In Scotland, the Inner House of the Court of Session; in Northern Ireland, the Court of Appeal.

[3] In Scotland, the Inner House of the Court of Session; in Northern Ireland, the Court of Appeal.

[4] In Scotland, the Court of Session; in Northern Ireland, the High Court.

[5] In Scotland, the Sheriff Court; in Northern Ireland, the Magistrates' Court.

(5) The competent authority of a Contracting State may request a ruling from the European Court if judgments given by courts of that State conflict with the interpretation given either by the European Court or in a judgment of one of the courts of another Contracting State referred to in Art. 2(1) or (2) of the 1971 Protocol, i.e. in effect other appellate courts (1971 Protocol, Art. 4). The competent authority may be designated by a Contracting State. The judgment of the European Court in such cases will have a purely advisory effect (1971 Protocol, Art. 4(2)).

There are two main differences between the system under the 1971 Protocol and under Art. 177 of the EEC Treaty as regards preliminary rulings on interpretation. First, under the 1971 Protocol only courts sitting in "an appellate capacity"[1] may request a preliminary ruling, whereas under Art. 177 any court or tribunal[2] may make a reference. A more restrictive system was used under the 1971 Protocol to prevent applications for preliminary rulings being used as a delaying tactic or as a means of putting pressure on an opponent of modest financial means; and to prevent the interpretation system being requested in too many cases, and particularly in trivial matters.[3] The second main difference between the 1971 Protocol and Art. 177 of the EEC Treaty is the provision in Art. 4 of the 1971 Protocol for the power of an authority of a Contracting State to request rulings in cases where their national court has given a ruling which is inconsistent with a ruling given by the European Court or by an appellate court in another Contracting State. Its purpose is to avoid perpetuating an erroneous interpretation of the law where the parties do not appeal against the decision which includes that interpretation.[4]

The 1971 Protocol and Art. 177 of the EEC Treaty have some important features in common, as a result of which decisions on the latter may be of relevance. In each case a question of "interpretation" must arise. Thus the mere fact that one of the parties contends that the dispute gives rise to a question of interpretation does not mean that the national court is bound to consider that a true question of interpretation arises; if the national court considers that there is no room for reasonable doubt as to the interpretation and that the matter would be equally obvious in the courts of the other States it need not make a reference; the national court must bear in mind that the different language versions are equally authentic and that interpretation involves a comparison of the different language versions; but in such a clear case the national court may refrain from making a reference.[5] But the House of Lords has emphasized, in the context of Art. 177 of the EEC Treaty, that English judges must:

"not be too ready to hold that because the meaning of the English text

---

[1] Which means sitting in any case involving a challenge before a higher jurisdiction: Schlosser, para. 255.

[2] Which includes magistrates courts and administrative tribunals: see Collins *European Community Law in the United Kingdom* (2nd edn. 1980) p. 87.

[3] Jenard, p. 69.

[4] Jenard, p. 69. See also Kohler (1982) 7 Eur L Rev 3, at 5–6.

[5] Case 283/81: *CILFIT Srl v Minister of Health* [1983] 1 CMLR 472. For a similar approach by the Italian Court of Cassation in relation to the 1971 Protocol see *Les Assurances Nationales v Levy* [1980] I Foro It 1861; [1981] ELD 80; and *Soc Cotonfil v Società Chemitex* [1980] I Foro It 1860, [1983] ECC 8.

(which is one of six of equal authority) seems plain to them no question of interpretation can be involved."[1]

The European Court will not question the discretion of the national court to decide whether, and at what stage, to refer a question to it[2] subject to two important matters: first, the national court must be one which is empowered to request a ruling under the relevant Treaty; the courts which may request rulings under the 1971 Protocol are limited to courts sitting in an appellate capacity; a request by any other court would be inadmissible, just as a request under Art. 177 from an ordinary arbitral tribunal would be;[3] secondly, the European Court will not give preliminary rulings on general or hypothetical questions: there must be a real dispute in which "a decision on the question is necessary to enable it to give judgment".[4] In one case on the 1968 Convention, Advocate General Warner invited the European Court not to answer a question from a German court because it was at that stage only hypothetical but the Court did give a ruling on the question of interpretation put to it.[5] Nor will the Court interpret Conventions other than those referred to in the 1971 Protocol.[6]

Thus a reference to the European Court or the application of its decisions are therefore likely to be relevant in the United Kingdom in the following circumstances:

(a) where a question of interpretation of the Conventions arises United Kingdom courts should decide it in accordance with the principles laid down by, and any relevant decision of, the European Court;[7]

(b) where such a question arises before an appellate court, the court may (and in certain circumstances, must) refer the question to the European Court;[8]

(c) the United Kingdom court need not make a reference if it is established (i) that the question raised is irrelevant; or (ii) that the Convention provision in question has already been interpreted by the European Court; or (iii) that the correct application of the Convention is so obvious as to leave no scope for any reasonable doubt[9] but it is not debarred from so doing, if it still entertains a doubt as to the answer, or if it wishes to find if the European Court still adheres to its decision;[10]

(d) it should also be noted that in those cases where the 1982 Act has made extensive use of the Convention scheme even though it is not applicable as such, namely intra-United Kingdom jurisdiction and Scottish rules of

---

[1] *Henn and Darby v DPP* [1981] AC 850 at 906, per Lord Diplock. See also on the acte clair doctrine Collins, pp. 101–3.
[2] See Collins, p. 133; Joined Cases 36 and 71/80: *Irish Creamery Milk Suppliers Association v Government of Ireland* and *Boyle v Taoiseach* [1981] ECR 735, [1981] 2 CMLR 455.
[3] Case 102/81: *Nordsee v Reederei Mond* [1982] ECR 1095.
[4] 1971 Protocol, Art. 2(1); cf. Case 104/79: *Foglia v Novello (No. 1)* [1980] ECR 745, [1981] 1 CMLR 45; Case 244/80: *Foglia v Novello (No. 2)* [1981] ECR 3045, [1982] 1 CMLR 585.
[5] Case 120/79: *De Cavel v De Cavel (No. 2)* [1980] ECR 731, [1980] 3 CMLR 1.
[6] Joined Cases 9 and 10/77: *Bavaria & Co KG and Germanair GmbH & Co KG v Eurocontrol* [1977] ECR 1517, [1980] 1 CMLR 566.
[7] 1982 Act, s. 3(1).
[8] 1971 Protocol, Art. 2; 1982 Act, s. 6.
[9] Cf. Case 283/81: *CILFIT Srl v Minister of Health* [1983] 1 CMLR 472.
[10] The European Court is not in any sense bound by its own decisions, although (for obvious reasons) it normally follows its previous decisions.

jurisdiction, the Act provides[1] that in determining any question as to the meaning or effect of any provision in Schedule 4 and of any provision in Schedule 8 derived to any extent from Title II of the 1968 Convention:

> "regard shall be had to any relevant principles laid down by the European Court in connection with Title II of the 1968 Convention and to any relevant decision of that court as to the meaning or effect of any provision of that Title."

(e) section 47 of the 1982 Act empowers Orders in Council to be made making provision:

   (i) to bring the law of any part of the United Kingdom into accord with the Conventions as affected by any principle laid down by, or any decision of, the European Court;
   (ii) to modify Schedules 4 or 8 (or any other affected statutory provision) in the light of any principles laid down by, or any decision of, the European Court: the modifications may bring them into line with the jurisprudence of the European Court or diverge from them.

The former provision is designed to implement decisions of the European Court where the Conventions are applicable; the latter provision allows a departure from its decisions where the Conventions are not applicable and the jurisprudence is not regarded by the United Kingdom as acceptable.

Art. 5 of the 1971 Protocol provides that the Statute of the European Court and its rules of procedure shall apply to preliminary rulings under the Conventions. The Rules of Procedure of the Court[2] provide (inter alia) that (a) as regards the representation and attendance of the parties to the main proceedings in the preliminary ruling procedure, the European Court shall take account of the rules of procedure of the national court which made the reference; (b) it is for the national court to decide as to the costs of the reference; (c) in special circumstances the Court may grant, as legal aid, assistance for the purpose of facilitating the representation or attendance of a party.[3] Copies of the references are sent to the Contracting States,[4] who have a right to present written and oral submissions; their costs are not recoverable from the parties to the national litigation.

The European Court has given judgment in some 30 cases on the 1968 Convention. It is of course dangerous to extrapolate from its decisions "principles" of interpretation which could frequently justify opposing interpretations of the same text.[5] The Court has emphasized that the 1968 Convention must be interpreted by reference to its principles and objectives in the light of its

---

[1] 1982 Act, ss. 16(3) and 20(5).
[2] See Official Journal of the European Communities, 1982, C 39, 15th February 1982.
[3] Art. 104, Rules of Procedure.
[4] The United Kingdom and the Republic of Ireland have been permitted to submit observations to the Court from the very first cases on the Convention notwithstanding that they were not yet parties: they had an interest in expressing their views when the Court was called upon to interpret a convention to which they were required to accede: Case 12/76: *Industrie Tessili Italiana Como v Dunlop AG* [1976] ECR 1473 at 1481–2.
[5] On the principles applied by the Court see Kohler (1982) 7 Eur L Rev 3, at 7–18.

preamble and Art. 220 of the EEC Treaty: thus the Court has to take into account the purposes of the simplification of formalities regarding the reciprocal recognition and enforcement of judgments and of strengthening the legal protection of persons within the European Communities.[1] The Court has encouraged uniformity in the Contracting States by interpreting most provisions of the 1968 Convention which have come before it according to a Convention interpretation, rather than by a purely national interpretation. A common problem has been whether terms in the Convention are to be interpreted according to national law (usually that of the *lex fori*) or according to an independent Convention concept. In a few cases the Convention itself supplies the answer by referring to national law,[2] or by supplying a Convention definition.[3] But more commonly the Convention is silent, and the strong tendency[4] of the Court has been to interpret terms in the Convention in accordance with an independent concept: e.g. "civil and commercial matters" in Art. 1;[5] "bankruptcy" in Art. 1;[6] "contract" in Art. 5(1);[7] "sale of goods on instalment credit terms" in Art. 13;[8] "place where the harmful event occurred" in Art. 5(3);[9] "branch, agency or other establishment" in Art. 5(5);[10] "tenancies of immovable property" in Art. 16(1);[11] "document which instituted the proceedings" in Art. 27(2);[12] "ordinary appeal" in Arts. 30 and 38.[13]

The European Court has also emphasized the desirability of interpretations which avoid increasing the multiplicity of jurisdictions under the Convention: this has justified a narrow interpretation of Art. 5(1) on the meaning of "the obligation in question";[14] and it has justified a Convention, rather than a national interpretation of Art. 5(5), on the meaning of "branch, agency or other establishment".[15] The Convention rules in Arts. 16 (exclusive jurisdiction) and 17 (prorogation) which altogether exclude the court of the domicile, the basic jurisdictional rule of the Convention, are to be interpreted strictly.[16] Those

---

[1] E.g. Case 12/76: *Industrie Tessili Italiana Como v Dunlop KG* [1976] ECR 1473, [1977] 1 CMLR 26; Case 42/76: *De Wolf v Cox BV* [1976] ECR 1759, [1977] 2 CMLR 43; Joined Cases 9 and 10/77: *Bavaria & Co KG and Germanair GmbH & Co KG v Eurocontrol* [1977] ECR 1517, [1980] 1 CMLR 566; Case 33/78: *Somafer SA v Saar-Ferngas AG* [1978] ECR 2183, [1979] 1 CMLR 490.

[2] E.g. 1968 Convention, Arts. 52 and 53 in relation to domicile.

[3] E.g. 1968 Convention Art. 25, definition of "judgment".

[4] But cf. Case 12/76: *Industrie Tessili Italiana Como v Dunlop AG* [1976] ECR 1473, [1977] 1 CMLR 26. See also Advocate General Warner in Case 814/79: *Netherlands State v Rüffer* [1980] ECR 3807, at 3833; Kohler (1982) 7 Eur L Rev 3, at 7–13.

[5] Case 29/76: *LTU GmbH & Co KG v Eurocontrol* [1976] ECR 1541, [1977] 1 CMLR 88; Joined Cases 9 and 10/77: *Bavaria & Co KG and Germanair GmbH & Co KG v Eurocontrol* [1977] ECR 1517, [1980] 1 CMLR 566; Case 814/79: *Netherlands State v Rüffer* [1980] ECR 3807, [1981] 3 CMLR 293.

[6] Case 133/78: *Gourdain v Nadler* [1979] ECR 733, [1979] 3 CMLR 180.

[7] Case 34/82: *Peters v ZNAV* [1983] ECR.

[8] Case 150/77: *Societe Bertrand v Paul Ott KG* [1978] ECR 1431, [1978] 3 CMLR 499.

[9] Case 21/76: *Handelskwekerij GJ Bier BV v Mines de Potasse d'Alsace SA* [1978] QB 708, [1976] ECR 1735, [1977] 1 CMLR 284.

[10] Case 33/78: *Somafer SA v Saar-Ferngas AG* [1978] ECR 2183, [1979] 1 CMLR 490.

[11] Case 73/77: *Sanders v Van der Putte* [1977] ECR 2383, [1978] 1 CMLR 331.

[12] Case 166/80: *Klomps v Michel* [1981] ECR 1593, [1982] 2 CMLR 773.

[13] Case 43/77: *Industrial Diamond Supplies v Riva* [1977] ECR 2175, [1978] 1 CMLR 349.

[14] Case 14/76: *De Bloos Sprl v Bouyer SA* [1976] ECR 1497, [1977] 1 CMLR 60.

[15] Case 33/78: *Somafer SA v Saar-Ferngas AG* [1978] ECR 2183, [1979] 1 CMLR 490.

[16] Case 24/76: *Estasis Salotti v RÜWA GmbH* [1976] ECR 1831, [1977] 1 CMLR 345; Case 25/76: *Galeries Segoura Sprl v Bonakdarian* [1976] ECR 1851, [1977] 1 CMLR 361; Case 73/77: *Sanders v Van der Putte* [1977] ECR 2383, [1978] 1 CMLR 331.

provisions which safeguard the procedural rights of the defendant are to be interpreted liberally.[1]

---

[1] Case 150/80: *Elefanten Schuh GmbH v Jacqmain* [1981] ECR 1671, [1982] 3 CMLR 1; Case 166/80: *Klomps v Michel* [1981] ECR 1593, [1982] 2 CMLR 773; cf. Case 125/79: *Denilauler v Snc Couchet Frères* [1980] ECR 1553, [1981] 1 CMLR 62.

CHAPTER 2

THE SPHERE OF APPLICATION OF THE CONVENTION

It is often said that the Convention applies only in cases involving "international legal relationships"[1] but in practice all this means is that like the rules of private international law it comes to the surface only in cases with a foreign element.[2] Thus an action by one Englishman against another in an English court only involves the Convention by implication (since it confers jurisdiction on United Kingdom courts if the defendant is domiciled in the United Kingdom); but if the defendant has assets in France, the enforcement rules of the Convention will certainly be applicable if the plaintiff seeks to enforce a judgment in France.

Civil and Commercial Matters

Article 1 provides:

"This Convention shall apply in civil and commercial matters whatever the nature of the court or tribunal. It shall not extend, in particular, to revenue, customs or administrative matters.

The Convention shall not apply to:

(1) the status or legal capacity of natural persons, rights in property arising out of a matrimonial relationship, wills and succession;
(2) bankruptcy, proceedings relating to the winding-up of insolvent companies or other legal persons, judicial arrangements, compositions and analogous proceedings;
(3) social security;
(4) arbitration."

The Convention thus applies only to "civil and commercial matters".

The system of law by which the term is to be defined

In civil law countries "civil" law (which includes commercial law) is generally contrasted with "public" law. In the United Kingdom, as Lord Diplock pointed out in *O'Reilly v Mackman*,[3] the appreciation of the distinction between what is

---

[1] Jenard, p. 8; Schlosser, para. 21.
[2] Cf. Droz, para. 29; Weser, p. 215.
[3] [1982] 3 WLR 1096 at 1102. See also *Davy v Spelthorne Borough Council* (1983) Times, 10 February, CA.

private law and what is public law has been a latecomer. The term "civil and commercial" is not a term of art in the United Kingdom, although it appears as early as the Foreign Tribunals Evidence Act 1856 and the United Kingdom is party to several bilateral treaties with some of the original Contracting States for the recognition and enforcement of judgments in "civil and commercial matters"[1] and to Hague Conventions which are similarly limited.[2] The scope of the expression "civil and commercial matters" arose in the context of the UK-Belgian Convention in *Vervaeke v Smith*[3] where the Court of Appeal was divided on the question whether it included matrimonial proceedings, and the point was not decided by the House of Lords.[4] The European Court has recognised that the expression when used in a bilateral treaty may bear a different meaning from that in the 1968 Convention.[5]

In the original Contracting States, there is a well-developed separate corpus of law dealing with the activities of public bodies acting in the exercise of public functions. It is claims by and against these authorities in relation to those functions which are effectively excluded by the general words of Art. 1. But the precise boundaries of civil and public law differ even in the civil law countries and therefore the question arose at an early stage as to what system of law was to be applied to solve any difficulties of interpretation. Three solutions were possible: the classification could be made by the court which gave the original judgment, or by the court in which enforcement was sought according to the law of the court which gave the original judgment; the classification could be made by the court in which enforcement was sought according to its own law; or each court would have to apply the expression as an independent Convention concept. It was the third solution which prevailed in a consistent series of decisions of the European Court commencing with its decision in 1976 in the *Eurocontrol* case.[6] Eurocontrol, the European Organisation for the Safety of Air Navigation, was set up in 1960 by an international agreement, to which most (but not all) of the original parties to the 1968 Convention were party, as an international organisation with its seat in Brussels. Route charges were levied by Eurocontrol on aircraft owners who wished to make use of the air safety devices provided by Eurocontrol. The charges were established by the agreement setting up Eurocontrol, supplemented by bilateral and multilateral agreements; the detailed rates and procedures (including place of payment and jurisdiction for collection) were set out in orders made by the executive organ of Eurocontrol. Eurocontrol issued bills for charges payable by LTU, a German air carrier; the bills conferred jurisdiction on the Belgian courts. LTU contested the charges, but was ordered to pay them by the Brussels Tribunal de Commerce. The Brussels court held that the case was not governed by public law because the sums due were not taxes

---

[1] With Belgium (SR & O 1936 No. 1169); France (SR & O 1936 No. 609); Germany (SI 1961 No. 1199); Italy (SI 1973 No. 1894).

[2] Service Abroad of Judicial and Extrajudicial Documents in Civil or Commercial Matters (1965); Taking of Evidence Abroad in Civil or Commercial Matters (1970); cf *Re Gross, ex p Treasury Solicitor* [1968] 3 All ER 804, [1969] 1 WLR 12.

[3] [1981] Fam 77, [1981] 1 All ER 55, CA; affd [1983] AC 145, [1982] 2 All ER 144, HL.

[4] The 1968 Convention does not apply to matters relating to status: see p. 23, post.

[5] See Joined Cases 9 and 10/77: *Bavaria & Co KG and Germanair GmbH & Co KG v Eurocontrol* [1977] ECR 1517, [1980] 1 CMLR 566.

[6] Case 29/76: *LTU GmbH & Co KG v Eurocontrol* [1976] ECR 1541, [1977] 1 CMLR 88.

but payments for commercial services. Eurocontrol sought to enforce the judgment in Germany under the 1968 Convention. The Düsseldorf court referred to the European Court the question whether, in the interpretation of the expression "civil and commercial matters" in Art. 1, the law to be applied was the law of the State in which the judgment was given (Belgium) or the law of the State in which enforcement was sought (Germany). Rejecting Advocate General Reischl's view that the classification depended on the national law of the court of origin, the Court held that the concept must be given an independent Convention meaning. It said:[1]

> "Apart from providing that the Convention shall apply whatever the nature of the court or tribunal to which the matter is referred and excluding certain matters from its area of application, Article 1 gives no further details as to the meaning of the concept in question.
> As Article 1 serves to indicate the area of application of the Convention it is necessary, in order to ensure, as far as possible, that the rights and obligations which derive from it for the Contracting States and the persons to whom it applies are equal and uniform, that the terms of that provision should not be interpreted as a mere reference to the internal law of one or other of the States concerned.
> By providing that the Convention shall apply 'whatever the nature of the court or tribunal' Article 1 shows that the concept 'civil and commercial matters' cannot be interpreted solely in the light of the division of jurisdiction between the various types of courts existing in certain States.
> The concept in question must therefore be regarded as independent and must be interpreted by reference, first, to the objectives and scheme of the Convention and, secondly, to the general principles which stem from the corpus of the national legal systems."[2]

The decisions establish that the task of interpretation and application must be approached from two angles: the first is to look to "the objectives and scheme of the Convention"; and the second is to look to "the general principles which stem from the corpus of the national legal systems".[3] The overriding aim which caused the European Court to adopt the Convention approach to interpretation was that it was necessary to ensure, so far as possible, that the rights and obligations which derive from it were "equal and uniform". The approach to the general principles which stem from the corpus of the national legal systems is not so easily stated. The Court has indicated that certain types of judicial decision must be regarded as excluded (in particular for enforcement purposes) "either by reason of the legal relationships between the parties to the action or of the subject matter of the action."[4]

As the European Court has emphasised, Art. 1 itself expressly states that the question is not determined by the nature of the court or tribunal. The Convention

---

[1] At 1550–1.
[2] See also Joined Cases 9 and 10/77: *Bavaria & Co KG and Germanair GmbH & Co KG v Eurocontrol* [1977] ECR 1517, [1980] 1 CMLR 566; Case 133/78: *Gourdain v Nadler* [1979] ECR 733, [1979] 3 CMLR 180; Case 814/79: *Netherlands State v Rüffer* [1980] ECR 3807, [1981] 3 CMLR 293.
[3] [1976] ECR at 1552.
[4] [1976] ECR at 1551.

will, therefore, cover civil and commercial claims in administrative tribunals,[1] and will not include public claims in commercial tribunals.[2] Thus it will apply, e.g. to the Lands Tribunal and industrial tribunals.[3]

In practice it has been claims by public authorities in the sphere of public law which have been the main object of judicial discussion in relation to the ambit of the expression "civil and commercial matters". In *LTU GmbH & Co KG v Eurocontrol* the Court indicated that certain judgments in actions between a public authority and a person governed by private law might be within the scope of the Convention, but not where "the public authority acts in the exercise of its powers".[4] In that case the Court emphasised the following features of the claim by Eurocontrol against LTU:

(a) the dispute concerned the recovery of charges payable by a person governed by private law to a national or international body governed by public law;

(b) the charges were for the use of equipment and services, where the use was obligatory and exclusive;

(c) the rate of charges, the methods of calculation and the procedures for collection were fixed unilaterally in relation to the users, and the public authority unilaterally fixed the place of performance of the obligation at its registered office and selected the national courts with jurisdiction to adjudicate upon the performance of the obligation.

Netherlands State v Rüffer[5] concerned a collision in a public waterway located in an area over which both Netherlands and Germany claim sovereign rights. By a 1960 treaty the two States instituted a working arrangement in the area without prejudice to the issue of sovereignty; the Netherlands was to be responsible for the administration of the waterways involving, inter alia, the removal of the wrecks and in regard to the administration of the waterways each State was to apply its own law. The collision was between a vessel owned by the defendant, who was a German resident, and a Dutch vessel. The Netherlands State had the wreck of the vessel removed and what was left of the vessel and its cargo were sold through the Mayor of a Dutch town and the proceeds remitted to the Netherlands State. The Netherlands State claimed a balance due to it for the costs of removing the wreck and brought proceedings in the Dutch courts against the German defendant. The Supreme Court of the Netherlands referred the question (among others) to the European Court, whether the concept "civil and commercial matters" in Article 1 included such a claim. The Court re-affirmed that whilst certain judgments given in an action between a public authority and a person governed by private law might come within the area of application of the Convention that was not the case if the public authority was acting in the exercise of its public authority powers. This was such a case because it was an action for the recovery of the costs involved in the removal of a wreck in a public waterway, administered by the State responsible in

---

[1] Jenard, p. 9.
[2] Case 29/76: *LTU GmbH & Co KG v Eurocontrol* [1976] ECR 1541, [1977] 1 CMLR 88.
[3] Cf. Maxwell Report, para. 4.3.
[4] [1976] ECR at 1551.
[5] Case 814/79: [1980] ECR 3807.

performance of an international obligation and on the basis of provisions of national law which, in the administration of that waterway, conferred on it the status of public authority in regard to private persons. It said:[1]

"The granting of such status to the agent responsible for policing public waterways, for the purpose of removing wrecks located in those waterways, is furthermore in keeping with the general principles which stem from the corpus of the national legal systems of the Member States whose provisions on the administration of public waterways precisely show that the agent administering those waterways does so, when removing wrecks, in the exercise of public authority. In view of those factors the action brought by the Netherlands State before the national court must be regarded as being outside the ambit of the Brussels Convention, as defined by the concept of 'civil and commercial matters' within the meaning of the first paragraph of Article 1 of that Convention, since it is established that the Netherlands State acted in the instant case in the exercise of public authority."

The case was therefore outside the Convention, despite the fact that the action pending before the national court did not concern the actual removal of the wreck but the costs involved in that removal and that the Netherlands State was seeking to recover those costs by means of a claim for redress and not by administrative process as provided for by the national law of other Member States, because:[2]

"the fact that in recovering those costs the administering agent acts pursuant to a duty which arises from an act of public authority is sufficient for its action, whatever the nature of the proceedings afforded by national law for the purpose, to be treated as being outside the ambit of the Brussels Convention."

Advocate General Warner had pointed out that Dutch law was unique among the original Contracting States in affording to a harbour waterway authority an action of that kind in tort (although the laws of Ireland and the United Kingdom were broadly in line with Dutch law, giving a harbour or waterway authority a right to sue in tort for the cost of removing a wreck); in the other States the action was in the administrative courts and not through ordinary civil proceedings.

In addition to the case-law relating to actions by public authorities, the second sentence of Art. 1, para. 1, provides expressly that the Convention "shall not extend, in particular, to revenue, customs or administrative matters". This provision was added by the Accession Convention, Art. 3, following the request of the United Kingdom in the accession negotiations. The exclusion of revenue and customs matters reflects the general principle found in most countries that foreign tax laws will not be enforced.[3] The exclusion of "administrative matters" relates, not to the tribunal in which the claim is brought or by which the

---

[1] At 3820.
[2] At 3821.
[3] See Dicey & Morris, pp. 92 and 1093; for jurisdiction of English courts in tax matters see RSC Ord 11, r (1)(o) (para. (n) under the revised Ord 11) and *IRC v Stype Investments (Jersey) Ltd* [1982] Ch 456, [1982] 3 All ER 419, CA.

judgment is given, but to the nature of the legal relationship between the parties or the subject matter of the action[1] and is little more than a re-affirmation of the case law.

There are a number of areas which have given rise to questions whether they are included in the Convention. First, it is settled that maintenance claims are covered by the Convention. They are within the concept of "civil matters", they are not excluded by Art. 1, para. 2, and Art. 5(2) makes specific provision for such claims.[2] Secondly, it is likely that claims for damages caused by restrictive practices or unfair competition,[3] which often have public law elements, come within the scope of the Convention. Thirdly, the Convention applies to labour or employment law claims, at least to the extent that they are not claims by or against public authorities in some capacity other than as employer. The question had arisen because in the laws of most of the original Contracting States, labour matters were dealt (as they are, at least in part, in the United Kingdom) by special courts under a separate corpus of law. The Convention was intended to apply to labour law.[4] In *Sanicentral GmbH v Collin*[5] the French Cour de Cassation (Social Chamber) had referred to the European Court a question on the effect of Art. 17 in relation to an employment contract, entered into before the Convention came into force, assigning exclusive jurisdiction to a German court, where under French law the exclusive jurisdiction clause was void. Advocate General Capotorti said that it was not open to question that the Convention applied to contracts of employment, even though the field of employment presented particular aspects which differentiated it considerably from other fields of private law and endowed it with numerous elements of public law, especially with regard to the composition and procedure of the tribunals dealing with labour questions; but traditionally a contract of employment was regarded as falling within the field of private law obligation. The European Court pointed out that the French court "rightly accepts that employment law comes within the substantive field of application of the Convention".[6]

The Convention does not apply to criminal judgments[7] but it applies to civil claims made before criminal courts. This is the position also at common law and under the 1933 Act.[8] Article II of the 1968 Protocol makes special provision with regard to the representation and defence of persons prosecuted in the courts of States in which they are not domiciled and the effect of their failure to appear upon civil judgments given in those proceedings.[9] As Jenard points out,[10] civil claims in road accident prosecutions may prove a major source of judgments in this area.

---

[1] *LTU v Eurocontrol*, ante; *Netherlands v Rüffer*, ante.
[2] See Case 120/79: *De Cavel v De Cavel (No. 2)* [1980] ECR 731, [1980] 3 CMLR 1.
[3] Cf. Restrictive Trade Practices Act 1976, s. 35(2), or the type of action in *Garden Cottage Foods Ltd v Milk Marketing Board* [1983] 2 All ER 770, [1983] 3 WLR 143, HL.
[4] Jenard, p. 9.
[5] Case 25/79: [1979] ECR 3423.
[6] At 3429. See also Case 133/81: *Ivenel v Schwab* [1982] ECR 1891, [1983] 1 CMLR 538.
[7] See 1968 Convention, Art. 5(4), p. 61, post; Jenard, p. 9; Schlosser, para. 29.
[8] See Dicey & Morris, pp. 1094 and 1108.
[9] See p. 61, post, and Case 157/80: *Rinkau* [1981] ECR 1391, [1983] 1 CMLR 205.
[10] At p. 9.

Penalties awarded in favour of private persons are within the scope of civil law and thus within the Convention. At common law and under the 1933 Act a foreign award of punitive or exemplary damages is enforceable,[1] but awards of multiple damages may be unenforceable at common law[2] and are made unenforceable by the Protection of Trading Interests Act 1980, s. 5. The position under the Convention is that penalties awarded in favour of a private plaintiff fall within its scope.[3]

Matters expressly excluded from the scope of the Convention

Article 1, para. 2, excludes four general categories from the scope of the Convention: (1) status; (2) bankruptcy; (3) social security; and (4) arbitration. These categories are excluded for two main reasons: the first was to exclude one category which fell within the borderland of civil and public law, namely social security; the second was to exclude those cases where there was a great disparity between the States in relation both to substantive law and private international law, particularly where there were other conventions in force or in draft; it was thought that to bring these areas within the scope of the Brussels Convention might interfere with the unification process being pursued elsewhere.[4] Matters relating to status in particular were excluded because of the great disparities between the different systems of law, and particularly in their rules of private international law; Jenard indicates that it would not have been possible to obtain agreement on their inclusion without allowing the court in which enforcement is sought to re-examine the basis of jurisdiction of the court of origin.[5]

(i) *Status or legal capacity of natural persons.* The most important area excluded by this provision is divorce, but it also excludes judgments relating to voidability and nullity of marriage, judicial separation, death, status and legal capacity of minors, legal representation of mental patients, nationality or domicile of individuals, custody and adoption of children, guardianship.[6] But they are only excluded if the proceedings deal directly with these questions. If they arise only in an incidental fashion the case will not be excluded from the scope of the Convention.[7] The fact that a proceeding or judgment deals with matters which fall outside the scope of the Convention will not prevent orders which do fall

---

[1] Cf *Consortium General Textiles SA v Sun and Sand Agencies Ltd* [1978] QB 279, [1978] 2 All ER 339, CA; Dicey & Morris, p. 1094.

[2] See Dicey & Morris, p. 1094.

[3] See 1968 Convention, Art. 43 and cf. Schlosser, para. 29.

[4] See Jenard, p. 10.

[5] Ibid.

[6] See Schlosser, para. 51. On the English rules in relation to these matters, which will be unchanged by the legislation, see Dicey & Morris pp. 332–391 (divorce, judicial separation, nullity, presumption of death, declarations as to status), 424–443 (guardianship and custody), 453–511 (legitimacy, legitimation and adoption), 512–518 (mentally disordered persons).

[7] Schlosser, ibid.

within it from being enforced.[1] Maintenance orders, in relation both to spouses and to children, are within the Convention.[2]

(ii) *Rights in property arising out of a matrimonial relationship* ("régimes matrimoniaux"). Although this expression is a term of art in civil law countries, it does not have the same implications in each and it has no clear meaning in United Kingdom law. It was considered by the European Court in *De Cavel v De Cavel (No. 1)*.[3] This was a reference by the German Federal Supreme Court in connection with the attempted enforcement in Germany of a French judgment. Divorce proceedings were pending before a Paris Court; the husband requested protective measures, and the family court authorised the putting under seal of the furniture and other effects in the couple's flat in Frankfurt and in a safe in the wife's name in a bank in Frankfurt. The court also authorised the freezing of the wife's bank account and, in addition, declared that in the event of difficulties the wife should have the right to apply for the adoption of interim measures to the court dealing with the order for enforcement in Germany. The Federal Supreme Court asked whether the Convention was applicable to an order made by a French judge in family matters, simultaneously with proceedings for the dissolution of marriage, for putting under seal and freezing assets, in view of the fact that the order related to proceedings incidental to an action concerning personal status or rights in property arising out of a matrimonial relationship.

The Court held that provisional measures of the kind in question did not fall within the scope of the Convention if they were designed to protect rights in respect of which proceedings fell outside the Convention. As regards rights in property arising out of a matrimonial relationship, the Court said:[4]

"The enforced settlement on a provisional basis of proprietary legal relationships between spouses in the course of proceedings for divorce is closely linked to the grounds for divorce and the personal situation of the spouses or any children of the marriage and is, for that reason, inseparable from questions relating to the status of persons raised by the dissolution of the matrimonial relationship and from the settlement of rights in property arising out of the matrimonial relationship.

Consequently, the term 'rights in property arising out of a matrimonial relationship' includes not only property arrangements specifically and exclusively envisaged by certain national legal systems in the case of marriage but also any proprietary relationships resulting directly from the matrimonial relationship or the dissolution thereof.

Disputes relating to the assets of spouses in the course of proceedings for divorce may therefore, depending on the circumstances, concern or be closely connected with:

(1) questions relating to the status of persons; or
(2) proprietary legal relationships between spouses resulting directly from the matrimonial relationship or the dissolution thereof; or

---

[1] See Case 120/79: *De Cavel v De Cavel (No. 2)* [1980] ECR 731, [1980] 3 CMLR 1.
[2] Ibid; 1968 Convention, Art. 5(2).
[3] Case 143/78: [1979] ECR 1055, [1979] 2 CMLR 547; Droz, 1980 Rev Crit 614.
[4] At 1066.

(3) proprietary legal relations existing between them which have no connection with the marriage.

Whereas disputes of the latter category fall within the scope of the Convention, those relating to the first two categories must be excluded therefrom.

The foregoing considerations are applicable to measures relating to the property of spouses whether they are provisional or definitive in nature."

Thus the Court's holding was that the question depended upon whether disputes relating to assets were concerned with status or proprietary legal relationships resulting directly from the matrimonial relationship, on the one hand, or proprietary legal relations existing between them without connection with the marriage, on the other. The solution of the Court seems to be close to interpreting the phrase, quite literally, as excluding any rights subsisting between spouses as would have existed between them even if they had not been married, although Advocate General Warner said of that argument that "no one, as I understood the arguments, actually supported that solution. Its adoption would be incompatible with the purpose of the Convention as a whole for the reason ... that it would require in each case an enquiry by the enforcing court into the sources of the rights to which the judgment was intended to give effect".[1]

The decision in *De Cavel v De Cavel (No 1)* was applied in *CHW v GJH*[2] where there were proceedings in the Netherlands between two spouses of Netherlands nationality, domiciled in Belgium, regarding the husband's management of his wife's property. The wife sought to produce in evidence a document drawn up by the husband bearing the word "codicil", the provisions of which were intended to exempt the wife's property from any charges resulting from management of it by the husband; the husband applied to the court for an order that the document should be returned to him and that its use in evidence should be prohibited. The Dutch court asked, essentially, whether an application for a provisional measure concerning the return of a document bearing the word "codicil" likely to be used in evidence in proceedings relating to a husband's management of property owned by his wife must be excluded from the application of the Convention as relating either to "wills and succession" or to "rights in property arising out of a matrimonial relationship". The Court held that an application for provisional measures intended to secure the return of a document in order to preclude its use as evidence in proceedings concerning a husband's management of his wife's property did not fall within the field of application of the Convention if the management was closely connected with property relationships directly resulting from the marriage bond.

In the United Kingdom, subject to a number of special statutory provisions, there is a general doctrine of separation of the spouses' property.[3] But marriage may make substantial changes in the property rights of spouses, and the effect of marriage on these rights differs widely in various countries.[4] Where the rights

---

[1] At 1074.
[2] Case 25/81: [1982] ECR 1189, [1983] 2 CMLR 125.
[3] See Bromley *Family Law* (6th edn. 1981) p. 418.
[4] See Dicey & Morris, p 656; Jenard, p. 11; Schlosser, para. 43.

between spouses depend upon such provisions as the Matrimonial Homes Act 1983[1] the Convention will have no application, but where they depend on the general law of contract or equity, more difficult problems of application will arise. A purely contractual dispute will by its nature be rare, not only because relations between spouses are not normally covered by contracts but also because, even if they were, the court would tend to regard them (except for cases such as marriage settlements and separation and maintenance agreements) as not giving rise to legal relations.[2] Much of the modern law relating to matrimonial property in England is an application of general principles of trust law.[3] Schlosser suggests that where relations affecting rights between spouses are governed by the general law of contract or tort, rather than by matrimonial law, they will fall within the scope of the Convention, even where there are special rules designed to govern cases where such transactions occur between spouses.[4]

This is an unrealistic distinction in the United Kingdom context, where many disputes relating to matrimonial property may depend on the general law of trusts. The test laid down by the European Court in *De Cavel v De Cavel (No 1)* is more realistic and, moreover, in line with the statement in Schlosser (agreed between the States during the negotiations) as follows:[5]

> "The Convention does not apply to the assumption of jurisdiction by United Kingdom and Irish courts, nor to the recognition and enforcement of foreign judgments by those courts, if the subject matter of the proceedings concerns issues which have arisen between spouses, or exceptionally between a spouse and a third party, during or after dissolution of their marriage, and which affect rights in property arising out of the matrimonial relationship. The expression 'rights in property' includes all rights of administration and disposal—whether by marriage contract or by statute—of property belonging to the spouses."

The case of lump-sum settlements is also controversial. Maintenance is within the Convention[6] and it is probable that a lump sum in lieu of a periodical order for maintenance would be within the Convention, but there is scope for doubt.[7]

(iii) *Wills and succession.* Matters relating to wills and succession were excluded because it was thought that the divergences in laws, especially the relevant rules of private international law, among the original Member States was so great that it would be premature to include them before the rules of private international law had been unified.[8] They diverge in such matters of substance as the compulsory portion for heirs, and the relative succession rights of spouses; in their private international law, some states (Germany, Italy and the Netherlands) apply the law of nationality, others (including England, Belgium and France)

---

[1] See Bromley, pp. 459–60.
[2] See Bromley, p. 151.
[3] See Bromley, pp. 442 et seq.
[4] Schlosser, para. 46.
[5] Para. 50.
[6] See 1968 Convention, Art. 5(2).
[7] See p. 57, post.
[8] See Jenard, p. 11.

the law of domicile to movable property and the lex situs to immovables, and in Luxembourg, the lex situs is applied to immovables, but the law of nationality to movables.[1] The expression "wills and succession" covers all claims to testate or intestate succession, including disputes as to validity or interpretation of wills setting up trusts; but disputes concerning the relations of the trustee with persons other than beneficiaries may come within the scope of the Convention.[2]

(iv) *Bankruptcy etc.* The second sub-paragraph of Art. 1, para. 2 excludes from the scope of application of the Convention the following matters relating to bankruptcy or analogous proceedings:

  (i) bankruptcy;
 (ii) proceedings relating to the winding-up of insolvent companies or other legal persons;
(iii) judicial arrangements, compositions and analogous proceedings.

Bankruptcy was excluded because of the great disparities in national practice, because of its proximity to public law, and because of the draft Bankruptcy Convention being considered by the Community.[3] The English wording relating to companies was clarified to make it clear that it related only to insolvent companies and also that it included creditors' voluntary winding up—the French text, for example, refers only to "faillites, concordats et autres procédures analogues". In the United Kingdom the following institutions are within the scope of the draft Bankruptcy Convention: England, Wales and Northern Ireland: bankruptcy; administration in bankruptcy of estates of persons dying insolvent; compulsory winding up; winding up under the supervision of the court; compositions and schemes of arrangement; creditors' voluntary winding up; Scotland: sequestration and judicial compositions.[4] There is an overlap between the 1968 Convention and the draft Bankruptcy Convention in the case of the compulsory winding-up of solvent companies.[5] There is not likely to be a conflict because in such cases Art. 16(2) of the 1968 Convention assigns exclusive jurisdiction to courts of the State in which the "seat" of the company is situate[6] and the draft Bankruptcy Convention assigns it to the courts of the place of "the centre of administration":[7] it is not easy to envisage cases in the United Kingdom where these two places would not coincide in view of the United Kingdom definition of "seat".[8]

---

[1] See Jenard, p. 11.

[2] Under 1968 Convention, Art. 5(6): see Schlosser, para. 52. See also Case 25/81: *CHW v GJH* [1982] ECR 1189, [1983] 2 CMLR 125, where a question was raised (but not decided) as to whether an application for the return of a "codicil" was excluded from the scope of the Convention as relating to wills and succession.

[3] See Draft Convention on bankruptcy, winding-up, arrangements, compositions and similar proceedings, with Report by Lemontey, Bulletin of the European Communities, Supplement 2/82.

[4] Protocol, in Bulletin 2/82, p. 30.

[5] To which both apply: see 1968 Convention, Art. 16(2); and Protocol to draft Bankruptcy Convention.

[6] See p. 80, post.

[7] Art. 3.

[8] See p. 41, post.

There will inevitably be borderline cases.[1] In *Gourdain v Nadler*[2] a German company incorporated a French subsidiary, and when the German company was wound up, the French court appointed Mr. G. as the syndic (a kind of trustee in bankruptcy) of the French company. Mr. N. the manager of the company was deprived of his right to manage and was ordered by the Paris court to be responsible for part of the company's debts on the basis of imprudence or dishonesty, and Mr. G. sought to enforce the judgment in Germany. The question was whether the judgment was given by the French courts on the basis of the French law against the de facto manager of a legal person for payment into the assets of the company in liquidation was to be regarded as having been given in bankruptcy etc. proceedings, or whether was it a decision given in a civil and commercial matter.

The Court held that for proceedings to be excluded on the basis that they concerned bankruptcy, etc., it was necessary that "they must derive directly from the bankruptcy or winding up and be closely connected with the proceedings for the 'liquidation des biens' or the 'règlement judiciaire'."[3] It was therefore necessary to ascertain whether the legal foundation of the application such as that provided for in the French law was based on the law relating to bankruptcy and winding-up; it was so based because (i) the application was made only to the court which made the order for the règlement judiciaire or the liquidation des biens; (ii) it was only the syndics (apart from the court) who could make this application in the interest of the general body of creditors; (iii) the managers were presumed to be liable and they could only discharge the burden by proving that they managed the affairs of the company with all energy and diligence; (iv) the period of limitation ran from the date when the final list of claims was drawn up and was suspended for the duration of any scheme of arrangement; (v) if the application succeeded it was the general body of creditors which benefited. Thus a claim by an English liquidator against the directors of a company for fraudulent trading under s. 332 of the Companies Act 1948 would be outside the scope of the Convention. But an action by a liquidator to recover debts due to the insolvent company will not be excluded, since the claim in no sense relates to bankruptcy.[4]

(v) *Social security.* The third sub-paragraph of Art. 1, para. 2 excludes social security. According to Jenard[5] social security was excluded because in some countries it was a matter of public law and in others it fell within the borderline area between private law and public law; in some countries it was within the jurisdiction of the ordinary courts, and in others within the jurisdiction of administrative tribunals, and sometimes both; social security had not given rise to conflicts of jurisdiction, since judicial jurisdiction had coincided with legislative jursidiction, although the recovery of contributions due to social security bodies

---

[1] See Jenard, p. 12.

[2] Case 133/78: [1979] ECR 733, [1979] 3 CMLR 180.

[3] At 744.

[4] See *Société France International Représentation v Héritiers Baas*, Paris, 1979, affd Cour de Cassation, 1981, 1980 Rev Crit 121 and 1981 Rev Crit 553, note Mezger; *Van Rolleghem v Roth*, Brussels, March 1977, Eur Court Digest D I–1.2 B5, note.

[5] At 12.

raised problems of enforcement. The concept of social security was not defined because it was in a state of development. The litigation on social security which is excluded is confined to disputes arising from relationships between the administrative authorities concerned and employers or employees, but the Convention is applicable when the authority concerned relies on a right of direct recourse against a third party responsible for injury or damage, or is subrogated as against a third party to the rights of an injured party insured by it, since, in doing so, it is acting in accordance with the ordinary legal rules.[1]

(vi) *Arbitration.* The final subject excluded in Art. 1 is "arbitration". Arbitration was excluded from the Convention because of the other international instruments in force or in contemplation dealing with the subject.[2] The scope of the exclusion is in one important respect a matter of controversy. It is clear that the effect of the exclusion is to render the Convention inapplicable to such matters as proceedings to set aside an arbitral award or to enforce an award[3] or to proceedings ancillary to arbitration such as applications to appoint or dismiss arbitrators or to judgments concerning the validity of an arbitration agreement.[4] During the negotiations on the Accession Convention the United Kingdom took the view that the effect of the exclusion was also to remove from the ambit of the Convention all disputes which the parties had effectively agreed should be settled by arbitration, including any secondary disputes connected with the agreed arbitration; the original Contracting States only regarded proceedings before national courts as part of "arbitration" if they referred to arbitration proceedings, whether concluded, in progress or to be started. It was agreed that no amendment should be made to the text, so that the new Contracting States could deal with this problem of interpretation in their implementing legislation.[5] The question still remains whether recognition and enforcement of a judgment may be refused under the Convention on the ground that it was given notwithstanding a valid arbitration agreement. The view that such a judgment need not be enforced rests on the basis that the court in which enforcement is sought is entitled to consider whether a judgment is within the scope of the Convention, and that it may legitimately take the view that a judgment given by a court notwithstanding a valid arbitration agreement relates to arbitration and so is outside its scope. The other view is that the meaning of the exclusion cannot be extended beyond proceedings which literally relate to the arbitration, such as proceedings to set aside or enforce an award.[6]

Section 32 of the 1982 Act expressly provides that foreign judgments given in breach of (inter alia) arbitration agreements will not be enforceable.[7] Should the United Kingdom interpretation of "arbitration" in Art. 1 not ultimately prevail in the European Court, it is expressly provided that nothing in the

---

[1] Jenard, ibid.
[2] Jenard, p. 13.
[3] Ibid.
[4] Schlosser, paras. 64 & 65.
[5] Schlosser, para. 61.
[6] See Schlosser, para. 62; see also Maxwell Report, paras. 4.12–4.14.
[7] See further pp. 141–3, post, and *Tracomin SA v Sudan Oil Seeds Co Ltd* [1983] 1 All ER 404, [1983] 1 WLR 662, affd. (1983) Times, 2 July.

section shall affect the recognition or enforcement of a judgment which is required to be recognised or enforced under the Convention.[1] It was not necessary to provide for cases where a court in the United Kingdom is the court of origin, because the Arbitration Act 1979 provides for a mandatory stay in almost all cases with a foreign element where there is a valid arbitration clause.

Ancillary claims and provisional measures

It is clear that applications for provisional measures, such as preservation of property or interim injunctions, are within the scope of the Convention, both as regards jurisdiction and enforcement;[2] and it is equally clear that provisional orders for interim payments, e.g. in respect of damages or of maintenance are within it.[3] The European Court has emphasised that procedures authorising provisional and protective measures are found in the legal systems of the Contracting States; but the grant of these measures requires special care on the part of the national court and detailed knowledge of the actual circumstances in which the measures are to take effect; the courts of the Contracting State where the assets subject to the measures sought are located are those best able to assess the need for the measures and the conditions on which they are to be granted; it was for this reason that Art. 24 of the Convention allows applications for provisional and protective measures to be made to the courts of a Contracting State even if, under the Convention, the courts of another Contracting State have jurisdiction as to the substance of the matter.[4]

Where a case involves some aspects which are within the Convention and others which are not, those aspects which are within the Convention are severable.[5] But if the ancillary claims are concerned essentially with a matter which is excluded from the scope of the Convention, the ancillary claims themselves are outside its scope. The distinction is illustrated by three decisions of the European Court: in *De Cavel v De Cavel (No. 1)*[6] divorce proceedings were pending in France, and in the course of those proceedings the husband obtained a protective order freezing matrimonial assets in Germany. The Court held that the order was not enforceable under the Convention in Germany because it concerned or was closely connected with a matter excluded from the scope of the Convention, namely status and proprietary rights arising out of the matrimonial relationship. Similarly, in *CHW v GJH*[7] a wife made a claim in a Dutch court for the delivery up of a document intended to exempt her separate property from the liabilities arising from her husband's management of that property: it was held that the Dutch court would not have jurisdiction under the Convention if the question of management was closely connected with the proprietary relationship resulting from the marriage bond: if that was so, the

[1] 1982 Act, s. 32(4)(a).
[2] See 1968 Convention, Art. 24, p. 98, post; Case 143/78: *De Cavel v De Cavel (No. 1)* [1979] ECR 1055, [1979] 2 CMLR 547.
[3] Case 120/79: *De Cavel v De Cavel (No. 2)* [1980] ECR 731, [1980] 3 CMLR 1.
[4] Case 125/79: *Denilauler v SNC Couchet Frères* [1980] ECR 1553 at 1570.
[5] Cf. 1968 Convention, Art. 42.
[6] Case 143/78: [1979] ECR 1055, [1979] 2 CMLR 547.
[7] Case 25/81: [1982] ECR 1189, [1983] 2 CMLR 125.

application for provisional measures would also be outside the Convention. On the other hand, in *De Cavel v De Cavel (No. 2)*[1] the Court held that a maintenance claim, even though ancillary to a divorce proceeding, was within the Convention: this was so because the test was the subject matter of the ancillary claim and not that of the principal claim: the subject matter of the ancillary claim was maintenance, which was within the Convention.[2] The consequence of these decisions is that provisional and protective measures are within the scope of the Convention, provided that they are used to protect rights which are within its scope; and that ancillary claims are within the scope of the Convention, provided that they are concerned with a subject matter within its scope.

Where a claim or judgment is outside the scope of the Convention, jurisdiction and enforcement will depend on the respective national laws of the court of origin and of the court in which enforcement is sought, subject to the operation of any relevant bilateral or multilateral conventions.[3]

Transitional Provisions

The combined effect in the United Kingdom of the transitional and final provisions in the Accession Convention[4] and of the commencement provisions of the 1982 Act[5] is as follows:

(1) The Convention, as amended, will enter into force for the United Kingdom after it has been ratified by all the original Contracting States and by the United Kingdom, whether or not the other new Contracting States have by then ratified it;[6]

(2) its provisions will enter into force in the United Kingdom on a day to be appointed;[7]

(3) the Convention will apply to legal proceedings instituted in the United Kingdom after the entry into force of the Convention;[8]

(4) as regards the enforcement in the United Kingdom of judgments of courts of other Contracting States, they will be enforceable in the United Kingdom if the Convention is in force in the United Kingdom *and* either (*a*) the proceedings in the court which gave the judgment were commenced after the Convention entered into force for the United Kingdom,[9] or (*b*) where the proceedings were commenced before, and the judgment was given after, the Convention entered into force for the United Kingdom, the jurisdiction of the court which gave the judgment was founded upon rules which accorded with (i) the provisions of Title II of the Convention

---

[1] Case 120/79: [1980] ECR 731, [1980] 3 CMLR 1; Droz, 1980 Rev Crit 614.

[2] This was a decision on the original version of Art. 5(2) of the 1968 Convention. The scope of the new version is wider, and puts the matter beyond doubt.

[3] See e.g. Joined Cases 9 and 10/77: *Bavaria & Co KG and Germanair GmbH & Co KG v Eurocontrol* [1977] ECR 1517, [1980] 1 CMLR 566.

[4] Accession Convention, Arts. 34, 35, 39. See also Greek Accession Convention, Arts. 12 and 15.

[5] 1982 Act, s. 53(1) and Sch. 13.

[6] Accession Convention, Art. 39.

[7] 1982 Act, Sch. 13, Part I, para. 3.

[8] Accession Convention, Art. 34(1).

[9] Accession Convention, Art. 34(1).

or (ii) the provisions of a bilateral Convention between the United Kingdom and the country concerned;[1]

(5) if the parties to a dispute concerning a contract had agreed in writing before the entry into force of the Convention that the contract was to be governed by the law of a part of the United Kingdom, the courts of that part will retain the right to exercise jurisdiction in the dispute, whether or not the claim falls within the ambit of Art. 5(1) of the Convention.[2]

These transitional provisions primarily relate to the dates of court proceedings. Once their conditions are fulfilled it does not matter (except in the special case of contracts expressed to be governed by the law of England or Northern Ireland) when the cause of action arose or when (where relevant) a contract was entered into. Thus in *Sanicentral GmbH v Collin*[3] a contract of employment, containing a German jurisdiction clause, was entered into before the Convention came into effect for France (1st January 1973). The question was whether the French courts could take jurisdiction on the basis of the prior law, which made such clauses invalid, or whether Art. 17 of the Convention operated so as to give the German courts exclusive jurisdiction. The European Court held that the Convention did not affect rules of substantive law, but the national procedural laws applicable to the cases concerned were set aside in the matters governed by the Convention in favour of its provisions; the only essential for the rules of the Convention to be applicable to litigation relating to legal relationships created before the date of the coming into force of the Convention was that the legal proceedings should have been instituted subsequently to that date, which was the position in that case. As a result, in legal proceedings instituted after the coming into force of the Convention, clauses conferring jurisdiction included in contracts of employment concluded prior to that date were to be regarded as valid even in cases in which they would have been regarded as void under the national law in force at the time when the contract was entered into.

Relationship with Other Conventions

Title VII of the 1968 Convention deals with its relationship with other conventions: first, with the existing treaties (all bilateral, except for the Benelux Treaty 1961) between the Contracting States; second, with other international conventions (mainly multilateral); and third, with treaties to be entered into with third States by individual Contracting States. Section 9(1) of the 1982 Act provides that the provisions of Title VII shall have effect in relation to (*a*) any statutory provision, whenever passed or made, implementing any such other convention in the United Kingdom; and (*b*) any rule of law so far as it has the effect of so implementing any such other convention, as they have effect in relation to that other convention itself.

By Art. 55, as amended, the Convention supersedes the conventions listed

---

[1] Accession Convention, Art. 34(3); see Schlosser, paras. 228 et seq.

[2] Accession Convention, Art. 35. In practice this will apply only to England and Northern Ireland, since Scotland does not exercise jurisdiction on the basis of the contract being governed by Scots law. This provision applies also to the Republic of Ireland.

[3] Case 25/79: [1979] ECR 3423, [1980] 2 CMLR 164.

there. They include those which the United Kingdom has entered into with France, Belgium, Federal Republic of Germany, Italy and the Netherlands.[1] But by Art. 56 these conventions are to continue to have effect (*a*) in relation to matters to which the 1968 Convention does not apply; and (*b*) in respect of judgments given and documents formally drawn up before the entry into force of the Convention. Further, by Art. 54(2) judgments given after the date of entry into force of the 1968 Convention in proceedings instituted before then are to be recognised and enforced in accordance with the 1968 Convention if jurisdiction was founded upon rules which accorded with those in Title II of the 1968 Convention or in a bilateral convention concluded between the State in which the judgment was given and the State in which enforcement is sought.

Articles 55 and 56 of the Convention were considered by the European court in *Bavaria & Co KG and Germanair GmbH & Co KG v Eurocontrol*.[2] In *LTU GmbH & Co KG v Eurocontrol*[3] the European Court had held, on a reference from a German Court, that a Belgian judgment for landing charges was excluded from the area of application of the Convention. The Court held in the *Bavaria* case that although a national court could not apply the Brussels Convention so as to recognise or enforce judgments which were excluded from its scope because they were not "civil and commercial" within the meaning of the 1968 Convention, nevertheless they could apply to the same judgments one of the special agreements referred to in Art. 55, in this case the Belgian-German Convention of 1958, which continued to have effect in relation to judgments to which the Brussels Convention does not apply. The oddity was that the bilateral convention also applied only to "civil and commercial" matters, and thus could result in the same expression in the Brussels Convention and in a bilateral agreement being interpreted differently; this was because in German law the question whether a case concerns a civil or commercial matter has traditionally been decided according to the law of the State in which the judgment was originally given.

The practical consequence as regards the United Kingdom bilateral treaties is that they will continue to be of relevance in the following cases:

(1) where a judgment has been given after the date of entry into force of the 1968 Convention for the United Kingdom but in relation to proceedings which were instituted before it came into force, the judgment can be recognised and enforced under the 1968 Convention if the jurisdiction of the court which gave it was founded upon rules which accorded with those in the 1968 Convention or in the bilateral convention.[4] United Kingdom bilateral treaties do not contain rules of direct jurisdiction, i.e. they do not determine what jurisdiction (say) the German court may actually exercise; they merely indicate the cases in which a German judgment will be recognised as having been rendered with international jurisdiction. But if a German judgment is given in any of the circumstances

---

[1] SR & O 1936 Nos. 609, 1169; SI 1961 No. 1199; SI 1973 No. 1894; SI 1969 No. 1063, as amended by SI 1977 No. 2149.
[2] Joined Cases 9 and 10/77: [1977] ECR 1517, [1980] 1 CMLR 566.
[3] Case 29/76: [1976] ECR 1541.
[4] 1968 Convention, Art. 54(2).

mentioned in the bilateral treaty[1]—all of which have a counterpart in the jurisdictional provisions of the 1968 Convention, although the test of residence/principal place of business in the bilateral conventions is somewhat different—then it is likely that it could be enforced in the United Kingdom either under the bilateral treaty or (in most cases) under the 1968 Convention;

(2) if the judgment was rendered prior to the entry into force of the 1968 Convention for the United Kingdom, then it may only be enforced under the bilateral convention;

(3) if the 1968 Convention does not apply because the case is not within the scope of the Convention, the bilateral treaties may continue to operate in certain very limited spheres. All of the United Kingdom bilateral conventions with other Contracting States relate to judgments in civil or commercial matters, or, in the case of the Netherlands convention, to civil matters; all exclude taxes and penalties from their ambit; all except those with Belgium and Italy exclude matters relating to family law and status, succession, bankruptcy and winding-up. But even in the case of the conventions with Belgium and Italy there is very little scope for their continued operation in the field of status, succession and bankruptcy because their enforcement provisions relate only to money judgments. It would therefore seem that in practice the only likely continued relevance of the bilateral treaties is in the recognition (as distinct from enforcement) provisions of the conventions with Belgium and Italy; but even here there is some doubt as to whether the recognition provisions of the 1933 Act will be effective in the case of matrimonial proceedings.[2]

Article 57(1) deals with other treaties governing jurisdiction or the recognition and enforcement of judgments. It does so in a way which has given rise to much difficulty.[3] It provides that:

"This Convention shall not affect any conventions to which the Contracting States are or will be parties and which, in relation to particular matters, govern jurisdiction or the recognition or enforcement of judgments."

Following discussions in the accession negotiations, it was agreed that Art. 57(1) should be interpreted[4] so that:

(a) the 1968 Convention is not to prevent a court of a Contracting State which is a party to a convention on a particular matter from assuming jurisdiction in accordance with it, even if the defendant is domiciled in another Contracting State which is not a party;

(b) but where the defendant is domiciled in another Contracting State and does not enter an appearance, the court must examine whether it has

---

[1] SI 1961 No. 1199.

[2] Differing views were expressed by Waterhouse J and the Court of Appeal in *Vervaeke v Smith* [1981] Fam 77, [1981] 1 All ER 55, but the point was left open in the House of Lords [1983] AC 145, [1982] 2 All ER 144.

[3] See Schlosser, paras. 238–245, who gives a list in Annex II to his Report.

[4] Accession Convention, Art. 25(2), which is set out in Art. 57 of the 1968 Convention: see 1982 Act, Sch. 1.

jurisdiction and whether the defendant has had an opportunity to arrange for his defence;[1]

(c) a judgment given in a Contracting State in the exercise of jurisdiction provided for in a convention on a particular matter shall be recognised and enforced in the other Contracting States in accordance with the 1968 Convention;

(d) where such a convention, to which the State in which the judgment was given and the State in which it is to be enforced are both parties, lays down conditions for the recognition or enforcement of judgments, those conditions shall apply; but in any event the procedures of the 1968 Convention for the recognition and enforcement of judgments may be applied.

The United Kingdom is a party to several such conventions, the most important of which are the Warsaw Convention of 1929 for the unification of certain rules relating to international carriage by air (Carriage by Air Act 1961, Carriage by Air (Supplementary Provisions) Act 1962 and Carriage by Air and Road Act 1979); the Brussels International Convention of 1952 on arrest (Supreme Court Act 1981, s. 20); the Brussels International Convention of 1952 on collision (Supreme Court Act 1981, s. 22); the Geneva Convention of 1956 on the Contract for the International Carriage of Goods by Road (Carriage of Goods by Road Act 1965); the New York Convention of 1956 on the Recovery Abroad of Maintenance (Maintenance Orders (Reciprocal Enforcement) Act 1972, Part II); and the Hague Convention of 1973 on the Recognition and Enforcement of Decisions Relating to Maintenance Obligations (Maintenance Orders (Reciprocal Enforcement) Act 1972, Part I).

No problem arises in the case of a convention for the reciprocal enforcement of judgments such as the Hague Convention of 1973, which is without prejudice to the operation of any other convention (Art. 33). But some of the other Conventions lay down direct rules of jurisdiction which are different from those of the 1968 Convention, including such bases as diverse as that of the court of the place of destination under the Warsaw Convention or the arrest of a ship under the Brussels Convention. The effect of the agreed interpretation of Art. 57(1) is that in these cases the court which is entitled to exercise jurisdiction under the treaty may do so[2] and its judgment will be enforced in another Contracting State under the 1968 Act even if the defendant is domiciled in that other State and that other State is not a party to the relevant international convention.[3] If on its true construction the international convention does not lay down exclusive rules of jurisdiction, then the parties may also invoke those of the 1968 Convention.[4]

Article 59 (which is designed to accommodate, to a limited extent, the fears of

---

[1] Under 1968 Convention, Art 20, p. 94, post.

[2] See *The Netty* [1981] 2 Lloyd's Rep 57.

[3] See also Nuclear Installations Act 1965, s. 17 and cf. Schlosser, para. 246.

[4] This point was raised, but not decided, in Case 814/79: *Netherlands State v Rüffer* [1980] ECR 3807, [1981] 3 CMLR 293.

the United States as to the effects of the Convention on its nationals)[1] allows Contracting States to enter into conventions with third States by which they agree not to recognise judgments given in other Contracting States against defendants domiciled or habitually resident in the third State, where the judgment can only be founded on a ground of jurisdiction branded as "exorbitant" by Art. 3. This would allow the United Kingdom to enter into a judgments convention with the United States whereby, e.g. the United Kingdom would agree not to enforce French judgments against U.S. residents with assets in England where the French court took jurisdiction on the basis of the French nationality of the plaintiff. But where the "exorbitant" basis of jurisdiction is the possession of property (as in Scotland) Art. 59(2), added by the Accession Convention, limits the extent to which a Contracting State may exclude its enforcement vis-a-vis the residents of third States. It provides that a Contracting State may not assume an obligation towards a third State not to recognise a judgment given in another Contracting State by a court basing its jurisdiction on the presence within that State of property belonging to the defendant or seizure by the plaintiff of property situate there: (a) if the action is brought to assert or declare proprietary or possessory rights in that property, seeks to obtain authority to dispose of it, or arises from another issue relating to such property; or (b) if the property constitutes the security for a debt which is the subject matter of the action.[2]

---

[1] See p. 50, post. See 1982 Act, s. 9(2), for Orders in Council to provide for the implementation of 1968 Convention, Art. 59. There have been negotiations with the United States, Australia and Canada.

[2] It would seem that the bilateral convention may limit enforcement of the judgment to the value of the security in the latter case. Cf. 1982 Act, Sch. 4, Art. 5(8) where there is no such limitation.

CHAPTER 3

THE CONCEPT OF DOMICILE IN THE 1968 CONVENTION AND UNDER THE 1982 ACT

Introduction

The basic jurisdictional rule of the 1968 Convention is that individuals and corporations domiciled in a Contracting State are, subject to certain important exceptions, to be sued in the courts of their domicile.[1] The concept of domicile under the Convention and the 1982 Act is relevant in several different contexts, for determining, e.g.:

(1) whether a person is domiciled in one of the Contracting States[2] or in a particular Contracting State;[3]
(2) whether a person is domiciled outside the Contracting States;[4]
(3) whether a person is domiciled outside a particular Contracting State;[5]
(4) whether a person is domiciled in a particular place;[6]
(5) whether a person is domiciled in a part of the United Kingdom, and, if so, which part.[7]

"Domicile" is not defined in the 1968 Convention. This was so because among other reasons it was thought that a new uniform definition of domicile properly belonged in a Convention on uniform law rather than in a jurisdiction and judgments convention.[8] In the original Contracting States the domicile of an individual was close to the notion of habitual residence, although its meaning differed somewhat as between the States.[9] In the case of corporations, the 1968 Convention assimilated domicile to the "seat", but the original Contracting States had differing approaches to the determination of the seat, some preferring the "siège réel" or effective seat, and others the "siège statutaire" or law of incorporation.[10]

Consequently the 1968 Convention limited itself to providing, in Arts. 52 and 53, rules regulating what law would determine the domicile of an individual or corporation for the purposes of the Convention.

---

[1] 1968 Convention, Art. 2(1).
[2] 1968 Convention, Arts. 2(1); 3; 4(2); 5; 6; 8(1); 11; 12(3); 13(1)(3); 14; 15; 17; 20; 36.
[3] 1968 Protocol, Art. I.
[4] 1968 Convention, Arts. 4(1); 8(2); 12(4); 13(2); 17.
[5] 1968 Convention, Arts. 32; 45.
[6] 1968 Convention, Arts. 5(2); 6(1); 8(1)(2); 32(2).
[7] 1982 Act, Sch 4.
[8] Jenard, pp. 15–16
[9] Schlosser, para. 71; Droz, paras. 344–352. Very confusingly, some English versions of decisions of the European Court translate "domicile" as habitual residence: see e.g. Case 166/80: *Klomps v Michel* [1981] ECR 1593, [1982] 2 CMLR 773.
[10] See Droz, paras. 386–392; Weser, pp. 115–117.

Individuals

Article 52 deals with individuals, and provides:

> "In order to determine whether a party is domiciled in the Contracting State whose courts are seised of the matter, the court shall apply its internal law. If a party is not domiciled in the State whose courts are seised of the matter, then, in order to determine whether the party is domiciled in another Contracting State, the court shall apply the law of that State.
> The domicile of a party shall, however, be determined in accordance with his national law if, by that law, his domicile depends on that of another person or on the seat of an authority."

The application of Art. 52 to the law of domicile in the United Kingdom as it stood prior to the 1982 Act would have produced a serious imbalance, because the traditional concept of domicile with its emphasis on permanent home would have excluded many persons settled, but not domiciled, in the United Kingdom from the provisions of the Convention, and included many persons settled outside, but domiciled within, the United Kingdom. Accordingly, it was agreed in the negotiations for accession that the United Kingdom (and the Republic of Ireland) would include in their legislation for the purposes of the 1968 Convention a definition of domicile which would reflect more the concept of domicile as understood in the original Contracting States.[1] This has been effected by a definition of domicile of individuals based on a combination of residence in, and substantial connection with, the United Kingdom.[2] The main differences between the concept of domicile in the 1982 Act and at common law[3] are that there is no question of the need for a "permanent home" under the 1982 Act; the concepts of domicile of origin and domicile of dependancy have no role under the 1982 Act; under the 1982 Act it will be possible for a person to have more than one domicile, whereas in the common law concept only one domicile is possible. At common law the question where a person is domiciled depends on the lex fori,[4] whereas under the Convention scheme the United Kingdom court must apply the law of another Contracting State to determine whether a party is domiciled in that State.

The first principle in Art. 52 is that in order to determine whether an individual is domiciled in the Contracting State whose courts are seised of the matter, the court shall apply its internal law.[5] When a court in the United Kingdom is the court seised, the relevant internal law is to be found in s. 41 of the 1982 Act, which provides that an individual is domiciled in the United Kingdom if and only if he is resident in the United Kingdom and the nature and circumstances of his residence indicate that he has a substantial connection with

---

[1] Schlosser, para. 73. The Convention concept of domicile is also to be adopted for non-Convention Cases under RSC Ord. 11 r. 1: see the new RSC Ord. 11, r. 1(4), Chapter 7 and Appendix 2, post.

[2] 1982 Act, s. 41.

[3] See Dicey & Morris, pp. 100–141.

[4] Dicey & Morris, p. 106.

[5] 1968 Convention, Art. 52(1). For an example of the application of this principle in relation to 1968 Convention, Art. 20 see Case 166/80: *Klomps v Michel* [1981] ECR 1593, [1982] 2 CMLR 773.

the United Kingdom;[1] in the case of an individual who is resident in the United Kingdom and has been so for the last three months or more, the requirement of substantial connection is presumed to be fulfilled unless the contrary is proved.[2] "Residence" is not defined in the 1982 Act but it probably indicates some degree of continuity.[3]

If a party is not domiciled in the State whose courts are seised of the matter, then, in order to determine whether the party is domiciled in another Contracting State, the court shall apply the law of that State.[4] This provision did not require specific treatment in the 1982 Act because under the Convention rules in Schedule 1 the United Kingdom court will apply the law of the relevant Contracting State. Since the Convention lays down no rule for determining the domicile of a person who is not domiciled in a Contracting State, s. 41(7) of the 1982 Act provides that an individual is domiciled in a State other than a Contracting State if and only if he is resident in that State and the nature and circumstances of his residence indicate that he has a substantial connection with the State.

Article 52(3) provides that the domicile of a party shall be determined in accordance with his national law if, by that law, his domicile depends on that of another person or on the seat of an authority.[5] The 1982 Act does not import the concept of domicile of dependency into the Convention regime. The question of a domicile of dependency will only arise therefore in the case of foreign nationals. It is not clear from its terms whether Art. 52(3) qualifies the whole of Art. 52 or merely Art. 52(2). The difference can be illustrated thus: the question arises whether a young Frenchman settled in England is domiciled in the United Kingdom: if Art. 52(3) qualifies the whole of Art. 52, then if by French law his domicile depends on that of another person, French law will be applied to determine his domicile without regard to s. 41 of the 1982 Act (which is expressly "subject to Article 52");[6] if Art. 52(3) qualifies only Art. 52(2) then the question of the domicile of dependency would be irrelevant unless the United Kingdom court is called upon to decide whether the Frenchman is domiciled in another Contracting State. The latter solution would be more practicable,[7] but Jenard[8] and Schlosser[9] appear to support the former. Article 52(3) provides no solution to the problems of dual nationality.[10]

As indicated above,[11] it is frequently necessary to determine the "place" of an individual's domicile, or the part of the United Kingdom in which he is domiciled. An individual is domiciled in a particular place in the United Kingdom if, and only if, he is (a) domiciled in the part of the United Kingdom in which that place

---

[1] 1982 Act, s. 41(2).
[2] 1982 Act, s. 41(6).
[3] See Dicey & Morris, p. 142; cf. *Shah v Barnet London Borough Council* [1983] 1 All ER 226; [1983] 2 WLR 16, HL on "ordinary residence".
[4] 1968 Convention, art. 52(2).
[5] See Droz, p. 350; Weser, pp. 363–4.
[6] 1982 Act, s. 41(1).
[7] Maxwell Report, para. 5.12.
[8] P. 17.
[9] Para. 74
[10] Jenard, p. 18.
[11] P. 37.

is situated; and (*b*) is resident in that place.[1] He is domiciled in a particular part of the United Kingdom if, and only if, (*a*) he is resident in that part; and (*b*) the nature and circumstances of his residence indicate that he has a substantial connection with that part;[2] but if he is domiciled in the United Kingdom but has no substantial connection with any particular part, he is to be treated as domiciled in the part of the United Kingdom in which he is resident.[3] The latter provision deals with the case where a person has ties with the United Kingdom but does not stay long at any place.[4]

It will be apparent from the above that a person may be domiciled in more than one Contracting State. Section 41 seeks to answer the questions (*a*) whether an individual is domiciled in the United Kingdom or (*b*) whether an individual is domiciled in a State other than a Contracting State. It does not answer the question whether he is domiciled in another Contracting State, since that question depends, by Art. 52(2), on the law of that other State.

This may be illustrated by the case of a person who is from New York by origin, and who lives both in Paris and London. He is on a visit to New York. May he be sued in a contract dispute in England (*a*) on the basis of service on him out of the jurisdiction under RSC Ord 11, r. 1(1), on the theory that the contract is governed by English law, or (*b*) on the basis of the Convention rules by virtue of his domicile in the United Kingdom? If he is domiciled in a Contracting State, the provisions of RSC Ord 11, r. 1(1), allowing service on him on the theory that the contract is governed by English law cannot be applied under the Convention.[5] The English court will have first to decide whether he is domiciled in the United Kingdom; this will turn on whether he is resident in the United Kingdom and whether the nature and circumstances of his residence indicate that he has a substantial connection with the United Kingdom and, in particular, with England (which will be presumed in each case from three months residence).[6] If he is so domiciled, then he may be sued in England on the basis of the Convention and intra-United Kingdom rules. If he is not so domiciled, then he may object to the jurisdiction on the basis that he is domiciled in France and must be sued there: in that case the court will apply French law to determine his domicile.[7] If he is not domiciled in the United Kingdom or in France, then the English court may exercise jurisdiction under RSC Ord 11, r. 1(1).[8] But if he is domiciled in the United Kingdom under the 1982 Act, it will be no answer for him to say that he is also domiciled in France under French law, because the English court will be able to exercise jurisdiction unless a French court is first seised.[9]

Corporations

Article 53(1) provides:
"For the purposes of this Convention, the seat of a company or other legal

[1] 1982 Act, s. 41(4).
[2] 1982 Act, s. 41(3).
[3] 1982 Act, s. 41(5).
[4] Maxwell Report, para. 5.5.
[5] Subject to Accession Convention, Art. 35: see 1982 Act, Sch. 3.
[6] 1982 Act, s. 41(2) and (6).
[7] 1968 Convention, Art. 52(2).
[8] It will probably not be necessary for it to apply s. 41(7) in such a case to find that he is domiciled in New York.
[9] 1968 Convention, Arts. 21 and 22.

person or association of natural or legal persons shall be treated as its domicile. However, in order to determine that seat, the court shall apply its rules of private international law."

Thus although the Convention refers to the "seat" of a corporation as its domicile, it does not define seat, but instead provides a choice of law rule for its determination. The concept of "seat" of a corporation has no precise equivalent in the law of the United Kingdom (where the domicile of a corporation is the place of its incorporation)[1] and it was necessary to provide expressly in the 1982 Act for the determination of the domicile of corporations and associations.

This has been effected in s 42 of the 1982 Act, which provides that a corporation or association has its seat in the United Kingdom if and only if (*a*) it was incorporated or formed under the law of a part of the United Kingdom and has its registered office or some other official address in the United Kingdom or (*b*) its central management and control is exercised in the United Kingdom.[2] In order to determine the seat of a corporation or association which does not have its seat in the United Kingdom, a corporation or association has its seat in a State other than the United Kingdom if and only if (*a*) it was incorporated or formed under the law of that State and has its registered office or some other official address there or (*b*) its central management or control is exercised in that State.[3] But it is not to be regarded as having its seat in a Contracting State under s. 42(6) if the courts of that State would not regard it as having its seat there.[4]

Thus if the question arises whether a Bermuda company with Dutch directors and which holds board meetings in Amsterdam and Paris can be sued in England otherwise than in accordance with the Convention, the English court will first find that it was not formed under the law of, and does not have its central management and control in, the United Kingdom; it will then consider whether its central management and control is in the Netherlands or France; if it finds that its central management and control is in the Netherlands and not in France, the English court will only be able to exercise jurisdiction under the Convention, if by the law of the Netherlands the seat of a company depends, not on its place of management, but on its registered office;[5] in that event, as a result of the rules in the 1982 Act the company will not be domiciled in a Contracting State and the Convention rules of jurisdiction will not normally apply.

At present a foreign company with a place of business in Great Britain must file with the Registrar of Companies the name and address of a person authorised to accept service of process on its behalf; such a company may be sued in England or Scotland, as the case may be, even on a transaction which was not effected through the branch in Great Britain.[6] But under the Convention scheme, as implemented by the 1982 Act, such a company will not be domiciled in the United Kingdom unless its central management and control is conducted

---

[1] See Dicey & Morris, p. 727.

[2] 1982 Act, s. 42(2). On the meaning of "central management and control" see Dicey & Morris, p. 728 and e.g. *Unit Construction Co Ltd v Bullock* [1960] AC 351, [1959] 3 All ER 831.

[3] 1982 Act, s. 42(6).

[4] 1982 Act, s. 42(7).

[5] Dutch law does in fact consider the place of incorporation as the domicile of a company: see *Tropical Shipping Co v Dammers and Van der Heide* [1982] ECC 353 (Hague 1980).

[6] Although in such a case the defendant company may apply for a stay: see Dicey & Morris, p. 189.

there. Thus for a French company to be capable of being sued in England or Scotland one of the other heads of jurisdiction will have to be applicable, especially Art. 5(5) which confers jurisdiction, in relation to disputes arising out of the operations of a branch, on the courts of the place of the branch. But if a corporation has its seat in the United Kingdom, then it will be regarded as having a seat in each part of the United Kingdom in which it has a place of business.[1]

Where it is necessary to determine the "place" of domicile of a corporation or association, it has its seat in a particular place in the United Kingdom if and only if it has its seat in the part of the United Kingdom in which that place is situated and has its registered office or some other official address in that place or its central management and control is exercised in that place.[2] For the purposes of allocation of jurisdiction within the United Kingdom, a corporation or association has its seat in a particular part of the United Kingdom if, and only if, it has its seat in the United Kingdom and it has its registered office or some other official address in that part, or its central management and control is exercised in that part, or it has a place of business in that part.[3]

The Convention does not indicate what corporate bodies are included within the expression "or other legal person or association of natural or legal persons" in Art. 53(1). Schlosser[4] suggests that the similar expression in Art. 16(2) applies to partnerships established under United Kingdom law, but although s. 50 of the Act defines corporation to include a Scottish partnership, there must be room for doubt as regards English partnerships, since in English law the expression "unincorporated association" normally connotes such bodies as clubs and charitable and social organisations;[5] and s. 50 of the Act defines "association" as an unincorporated body of persons. But other language versions of the Convention use expressions which are apt to include partnerships. Whether the expression must be given a national or a Community interpretation has not been decided.[6]

Articles 8(2) and 13(2) provide that in the case of insurance and consumer contracts, a person who is not domiciled in a Contracting State may be deemed to be domiciled in a Contracting State in which it has a branch in connection with disputes arising out of the operations of that branch. Although it applies both to individuals and companies it is likely to be of practical relevance mainly in relation to corporate defendants. Section 44 of the Act confirms that for the purposes of proceedings arising out of the operations of a branch, agency or other establishment in the United Kingdom, a person who is deemed for the purposes of the 1968 Convention to be domiciled in the United Kingdom by virtue of Art. 8(2) and Art. 13(2) shall, for the purposes of those proceedings, be

---

[1] 1982 Act, s. 42(4)(c).

[2] 1982 Act, s. 42(5).

[3] 1982 Act, s. 42(4). "Place" of business connotes some degree of permanence; *cf. The Theodohos* [1977] 2 Lloyd's Rep 428.

[4] Para. 162.

[5] 9 Halsbury's Laws (4th edn), para. 344.

[6] Jenard, p. 57, suggests that a national interpretation might be appropriate, but his report was written before the case-law of the European Court which has established Convention interpretations in the majority of cases: see p. 15, ante: see also EEC Convention on the Mutual Recognition of Companies and Bodies Corporate, 1968; Dicey & Morris, p. 725.

treated for the purposes of the 1982 Act as so domiciled and as domiciled in the part of the United Kingdom in which the branch, agency or establishment in question is situated.

Under Art. 16(2) the courts of a Contracting State in which a company, legal person or association has its seat have exclusive jurisdiction (regardless of domicile) in proceedings which have as their object the validity of the constitution, the nullity or the dissolution of the company, legal person or association. Section 43 provides that for the purpose of this provision[1] a corporation or association has its seat in the United Kingdom if, and only if, (a) it was incorporated or formed under the law of a part of the United Kingdom or (b) its central management and control is exercised in the United Kingdom.[2] A corporation or association has its seat in a particular part of the United Kingdom if, and only if, it has its seat in the United Kingdom and (a) it was incorporated or formed under the law of that part or (b) being incorporated or formed under the law of a State other than the United Kingdom, its central management and control is exercised in that part;[3] a corporation or association incorporated or formed under an enactment forming part of the law of more than one part of the United Kingdom or an instrument having effect in the domestic law of more than one part of the United Kingdom shall, if it has a registered office, be taken to have its seat in the part of the United Kingdom in which that office is situated, and not in any other part of the United Kingdom.[4] A corporation or association is to be regarded as having its seat in a Contracting State other than the United Kingdom if, and only if, (a) it was incorporated or formed under the law of that State or (b) its central management and control is exercised in that State;[5] but a corporation or association shall not be regarded as having its seat in a Contracting State other than the United Kingdom if (a) it has its seat in the United Kingdom by virtue of incorporation or formation under the law of a particular part of the United Kingdom or (b) it is shown that the courts of that other State would not regard it for the purposes of Art. 16(2) as having its seat there.[6]

For the purposes of ss. 42 and 43 "official address" means, in relation to a corporation or association, an address which it is required by law to register, notify or maintain for the purposes of receiving notices or other communications.[7] For the purposes of s. 42 "business" includes any activity carried on by a corporation or association, and "place of business" is to be construed accordingly.[8]

Trusts

Article 53(2), which was added by the Accession Convention, provides that in order to determine whether a trust is domiciled in the Contracting State whose

---

[1] And similar provisions in Schs. 4 and 8.
[2] 1982 Act, s. 43(2).
[3] 1982 Act, s. 43(3).
[4] 1982 Act, s. 43(5).
[5] 1982 Act, s. 43(6).
[6] 1982 Act, s. 43(7).
[7] 1982 Act, ss. 42(8), 43(8).
[8] 1982 Act, s. 42(8).

courts are seised of the matter[1] the court shall apply its rules of private international law. The relevant rule of private international law is enacted by s. 45, which provides that a trust is domiciled in the United Kingdom if and only if it is domiciled in a part of the United Kingdom. It is domiciled in a part of the United Kingdom if and only if the system of law of that part is the system of law with which the trust has its closest and most real connection.[2]

The Crown

Section 46 contains provision for the domicile and seat of the Crown.

---

[1] See 1968 Convention, Art. 5(6).

[2] 1982 Act, s. 45(3). This test is derived from the common law: see Dicey & Morris, p. 678; *Iveagh v IRC* [1954] Ch 364, [1954] 1 All ER 609.

CHAPTER 4

THE JURISDICTIONAL RULES UNDER THE 1968 CONVENTION

Introduction

Title II of the Convention sets out the rules relating to jurisdiction in cases within the scope of the Convention: (*a*) the general provisions in Section 1, which establish domicile as the primary basis of jurisdiction and which bar certain "exorbitant" bases of jurisdiction against defendants domiciled in Contracting States; (*b*) the special rules in Section 2 relating to such matters as jurisdiction in matters of contract, maintenance, tort, and to joinder of co-defendants and third parties; and those in Sections 3 and 4 relating to insurance and consumer contracts; (*c*) the exclusive jurisdiction provisions in Section 5; (*e*) the provisions relating to jurisdiction agreements and submission in Section 6; (*f*) the procedure in Section 7 for consideration by the court seised whether it has jurisdiction; (*g*) the provisions in Section 8 dealing with actions pending in more than one Contracting State; and (*h*) in Section 9, jurisdiction to order provisional and protective measures.

The most important changes in the law of the United Kingdom which these provisions will introduce (where they apply) will be the abolition of the jurisdiction of the English courts derived from the service of a writ on an individual only temporarily present in England; the abolition of the Scottish jurisdiction based on the arrest or ownership of assets within the jurisdiction; and major modifications to the other rules relating to jurisdiction over non-residents such as those in RSC Ord 11, r. 1(1).

Where the Convention confers jurisdiction on United Kingdom courts, there is no question of a discretion whether or not to exercise it. Where a defendant is to be served outside the jurisdiction under RSC Ord 11, r. 1(1), the court has a discretion whether to exercise jurisdiction, but no such discretion exists under the 1968 Convention, except in the very limited case where related proceedings have been begun in some other State.[1] Therefore if the defendant is outside the United Kingdom, service of English proceedings on him will be as of right when under the Convention rules the English court has jurisdiction.[2] Nor is it likely that the United Kingdom courts will be able to stay proceedings merely because some other court is the more appropriate one, on the basis of forum non conveniens;[3] nor, if a court in another Contracting State has jurisdiction, will

---

[1] 1968 Convention, Art. 22.

[2] See the new Ord. 11, r 1(2), Chapter 7 and Appendix 2, post.

[3] Maxwell Report, para. 1.26; cf. Dicey & Morris, p. 247; *MacShannon v Rockware Glass Ltd* [1978] AC 795, [1978] 1 All ER 625. For the Scots rule see Anton *Private International Law* (1967) pp. 148–154, and for a recent example *Crédit Chimique v James Scott Engineering Group Ltd* 1982 SLT 131.

the United Kingdom court have power to enjoin the foreign proceedings.[1] Section 49 of the 1982 Act provides that nothing in the Act is to prevent any court in the United Kingdom from staying any proceedings on the ground of forum non conveniens or otherwise "where to do so is not inconsistent with the 1968 Convention". This would certainly apply to the intra-United Kingdom jurisdictional provisions discussed below[2] but its application to Convention cases is limited. But the English rule is sufficiently wide to allow stays of English proceedings (or injunctions to restrain foreign proceedings) in the case of (to use the older expressions) vexation and oppression,[3] and there may be cases where the power to stay or to enjoin may be exercised, not because of the doctrine of forum non conveniens, but because of oppressive behaviour by a party.[4] In such cases the power could be exercised even in Convention cases.

General Provisions

Section 1 of Title II of the Convention sets out the general provisions of jurisdiction of the Convention, which, with the special jurisdictions of Section 2, will be the most important in practice. The essential provisions of this section are as follows:—

(i) subject to the special provisions of the Convention, persons domiciled in a Contracting State must be sued in that State, whatever their nationality;[5]

(ii) persons domiciled in a Contracting State may be sued in another Contracting State only by virtue of the rules in Sections 2 (special jurisdiction), 3 and 4 (insurance and consumer contracts), 5 (exclusive jurisdiction) and 6 (prorogation of jurisdiction); in particular, certain specific rules of jurisdiction classified by the Convention as exorbitant may not be applied as against domiciliaries of Contracting States;[6]

(iii) persons who are domiciled in, but not nationals of, a Contracting State shall have the benefit and burden of the rules of jurisdiction in that State applying to nationals;[7]

(iv) if a defendant is not domiciled in a Contracting State, then (subject to the rules of exclusive jurisdiction set out in Art. 16) jurisdiction of the courts of each Contracting State shall be determined by the law of that State; and, as against any such defendant, any person domiciled in a Contracting State may, whatever his nationality, avail himself of the rules of jurisdiction there in force, including the rules of exorbitant jurisdiction set out in Art. 3(2).[8]

---

[1] Cf. *Castanho v Brown & Root (UK) Ltd* [1981] AC 577, [1981] 1 All ER 143.

[2] Pp. 127–130.

[3] As to which see *MacShannon v Rockware Glass Ltd*, cited above.

[4] See e.g. *Smith Kline and French Laboratories Ltd v Bloch* [1983] 2 All ER 72, [1983] 1 WLR 730 CA.

[5] 1968 Convention, Art. 2(1).

[6] 1968 Convention, Art. 3.

[7] 1968 Convention, Art. 2(2).

[8] 1968 Convention, Art. 4.

The primary rule of domicile as the basis of jurisdiction is set out in Art. 2, which provides that "persons domiciled in a Contracting State shall, whatever their nationality, be sued in the courts of that State". Article 2 is expressly subject to the other provisions of the Convention; but the over-riding importance of the principal rule of domicile has been the starting point of the European Court's interpretation of the scope of the special jurisdictions under Art. 5 because the basis of the system of jurisdiction under Title II of the Convention "is the general conferment of jurisdiction on the court of the defendant's domicile"[1] and "it is in accord with the objective of the Convention to avoid a wide and multifarious interpretation of the exceptions to the general rule of jurisdiction contained in Article 2".[2] It is the domicile of the defendant which is crucial for the purposes of jurisdiction. Only rarely is the domicile of the plaintiff relevant to the jurisdiction of the court.[3] Article 2 expressly applies whatever the nationality of the defendant, although this provision is of no practical importance in the United Kingdom where the rules of civil jurisdiction are in no way related to nationality—but it is of practical importance in countries such as France where important rules of jurisdiction depend on the French nationality of the plaintiff or defendant.[4] This is also the explanation of the third feature of Art. 2, the provision that persons who are not nationals of the State in which they are domiciled shall be governed by the rules of jurisdiction applicable to nationals of that State—this provision will have no practical importance in the United Kingdom.

Article 3(1) provides that persons domiciled in a Contracting State may be sued in the courts of another Contracting State only by virtue of the rules set out in Sections 2 to 6.[5] The effect of this is that a person domiciled in a Contracting State may *always* be sued in that State unless

(a) the courts of another Contracting State have exclusive jurisdiction under Art. 16;

(b) the parties have agreed under Art. 17 that the courts of another Contracting State shall have exclusive jurisdiction; or

(c) proceedings involving the same cause of action have already been brought in the courts of another Contracting State with jurisdiction under Sections 2, 3 or 4.

Article 3(2) contains a (non-exhaustive) catalogue of jurisdictional rules in various Contracting States which may not be invoked against domiciliaries.[6] Strictly, this provision is not necessary and is merely declaratory, because Art. 3(1) makes it clear that domiciliaries may only be sued in the circumstances set out in the Convention, but the catalogue is of considerable importance in relation to jurisdiction over non-domiciliaries under Art. 4(2). As amended by the

---

[1] Case 12/76: *Industrie Tessili Italiana Como v Dunlop AG* [1976] ECR 1473 at 1485.

[2] Case 33/78: *Somafer SA v Saar-Ferngas AG* [1978] ECR 2183 at 2191.

[3] See 1968 Convention, Art. 5(2) (domicile of maintenance creditor); Art. 8(1) (2) (domicile of policyholder); Art. 14(1) (domicile of consumer).

[4] French Civil Code, Arts. 14 and 15.

[5] 1968 Convention, section 2: special jurisdiction; Section 3: insurance; Section 4: consumer contracts; Section 5: exclusive jurisdiction; Section 6: prorogation of jurisdiction.

[6] Cf. the approach of the Supplementary Protocol of the Hague Convention on the Recognition and Enforcement of Foreign Judgments (1971) to exorbitant jurisdiction.

Accession Convention the provisions which are deemed to be exorbitant are as follows:

(1) Belgium: Art. 15 of the Civil Code, which gives jurisdiction to the Belgian courts whenever a Belgian national is defendant, and is equivalent to Article 15 of the French Civil Code; and Art. 638 of the Judicial Code, which provides that where Belgian courts do not possess jurisdiction based on other provisions, a plaintiff resident in Belgium may sue any person before the court of the plaintiff's place of residence.[1]

(2) Denmark: Art. 248(2) of the Law on Civil Procedure and Chapter 3 (Art. 3) of the Greenland Law on Civil Procedure provide that a foreigner may be sued before any Danish court in whose district he is resident or has property when the document instituting proceedings is served.

(3) Federal Republic of Germany: Art. 23 of the Code of Civil Procedure, which provides that, where no other German court has jurisdiction, actions relating to property instituted against a person who is not domiciled in the national territory are under the jurisdiction of the court for the place where the property or subject of the dispute is situated.[2]

(4) France: Arts. 14 and 15 of the Civil Code: the former provides that any French plaintiff may sue a foreigner or another Frenchman in the French courts, even if there is no connection between the cause of action and those courts; Art. 15 provides that a Frenchman may always be sued in the French courts by a Frenchman or by a foreigner.

(5) Ireland: the rules which enable jurisdiction to be founded on the document instituting the proceedings having been served on the defendant during his temporary presence.

(6) Italy: Art. 2 and Art. 4, (1) and (2) of the Code of Civil Procedure: Art. 2 severely limits the enforceability of agreements providing for the jurisdiction of a foreign court or arbitral tribunal as against Italian citizens. Art. 4 contains jurisdictional provisions in relation to Italian citizens and foreigners which are much wider than the Convention will allow.

(7) Luxembourg: Arts. 14 and 15 of the Civil Code, which correspond to Arts. 14 and 15 of the French Civil Code.

(8) Netherlands: Art. 126(3) and Art. 127 of the Code of Civil Procedure: the former provides that in personal matters or matters concerning movable property, a defendant who has no known domicile or residence in the Netherlands shall be sued in the court for the domicile of the plaintiff; this applies whether or not the plaintiff is a Netherlands national. Art. 127 provides that a foreigner, even if he does not reside in the Netherlands, may be sued in the Netherlands court for the performance of obligations contracted towards a Netherlands national, either in the Netherlands or abroad.

(9) United Kingdom: the rules which enable jurisdiction to be founded upon:
 (a) the document instituting the proceedings having been served on the defendant during his temporary presence in the United Kingdom;

---

[1] The previous version of Art. 3 erroneously classified the jurisdiction based on Arts. 52 and 52 Bis of the Law of 1876 as exorbitant: see Schlosser, para. 83.

[2] Art. 3 of the Greek Accession Convention adds the similar Art. 40 of the Greek Code of Civil Procedure to the list of exorbitant jurisdictions.

(b) the presence within the United Kingdom of property belonging to the defendant; or

(c) the seizure by the plaintiff of property situated in the United Kingdom.

(*a*) relates to England and Northern Ireland; and (*b*) and (*c*) primarily to Scotland.

The rule in English law which is in effect branded as exorbitant is the rule allowing the exercise of jurisdiction over an individual by virtue of his mere presence at the time of the service of the writ.[1] But in practice the operation of this much-criticised rule of jurisdiction does not work inconvenience or injustice, since in the case of a genuinely contested claim, the defendant may seek a stay of the proceedings if they have no real connection with England.[2] The Scottish rules referred to are those which allow jurisdiction based on arrestment of movable property or on the possession of immovable property.[3]

Because the philosophy of the Convention is against the exercise of jurisdiction based on the presence of property, it has been suggested[4] that interpleader actions are no longer permissible in the United Kingdom in respect of persons domiciled in another Contracting State, in so far as the international jurisdiction of the United Kingdom courts does not result from other provisions of the 1968 Convention. On this view, the English court would not have jurisdiction in an action by an auctioneer to establish whether ownership of an article sent to him for sale belongs to his customer or a third party claiming it if the defendant were domiciled in another Contracting State and did not submit. But it is likely that the court could use its powers under Art. 24 to provide protection to persons faced with conflicting legal claims, e.g. a court order authorising an article to be temporarily withdrawn from auction.[5]

Article 4 relates to actions against persons who are not domiciled in a Contracting State. In relation to non-domiciliaries, Art. 4 provides for two things: first, it provides that the rules of internal law (i.e. those existing apart from the Convention rules) will apply, including the rules of exorbitant jurisdiction set out in Art. 3(2); secondly, it extends those rules by providing that a plaintiff domiciled in a Contracting State may avail himself of those rules as against a person not domiciled in a Contracting State, whatever his nationality. In some Contracting States the second provision adds nothing to the first. Thus in England a French plaintiff will be able to assert jurisdiction over an individual, domiciled in New York, who is temporarily present in London:[6] the English rule on jurisdiction and service does not discriminate in favour of British citizens. But in France (and the other countries where there are jurisdictional rules based

---

[1] See *Colt Industries Inc v Sarlie* [1966] 1 All ER 673, [1966] 1 WLR 440; *Maharanee of Baroda v Wildenstein* [1972] 2 QB 283, [1972] 2 All ER 689, CA. Dicey & Morris, p. 182. The rule for corporations is different, presence being treated as equivalent to place of business: Dicey & Morris, pp. 186–188. For the Scottish rule on itinerant defenders, which is of more limited scope see Anton, p. 105. It does not apply if the defender has a fixed residence, and so would not in any event apply to persons domiciled in other Contracting States.

[2] See e.g. *MacShannon v Rockware Glass Ltd* [1978] AC 795, [1978] 1 All ER 625; Dicey & Morris, pp. 247–253.

[3] See Anton, pp. 102–114.

[4] Schlosser, para. 88.

[5] Ibid. See 1968 Convention, Art. 24; 1982 Act, s. 25: see pp. 98–102, post.

[6] Subject to the defendant's right to apply to have the action stayed: see above, n.2.

on the nationality of the plaintiff, Luxembourg and Netherlands) the impact on United States defendants will be very considerable. Article 14 of the French Civil Code provides that any French plaintiff may sue a foreigner (or another Frenchman) in the French courts, irrespective of whether the case has any other connection with France. In relation to United States defendants the effect of Art. 4(2) is to extend this power to all plaintiffs with their domicile in France, irrespective of their nationality. Judgments rendered in such actions will be automatically enforceable under the Convention in other Contracting States. It was this extension of the rules of exorbitant jurisdiction that was regarded in the United States as outrageous[1] and ill-conceived.[2] But Art. 59, which was introduced after protests from the United States, allows a Contracting State to assume, in a convention on the recognition and enforcement of judgments, an obligation towards a third State not to recognise judgments given in Contracting States against defendants domiciled or habitually resident in the third State where, in cases provided for in Art. 4, the judgment could only be founded on one of the grounds of exorbitant jurisdiction specified in Art. 3(2). The United States has therefore, for the first time in its history, been anxious to conclude treaties with Contracting States to avoid the extension throughout the Community of judgments against United States nationals based on these rules of jurisdiction.[3] Their interest is obvious. The problem may be illustrated by this example: a United States company has assets (e.g. a branch or shares in a subsidiary) in England, but none in France; X, a French national, and Y, a German national domiciled in France, have separate claims against it; both of the claims arose in the United States and have no connection with France. X and Y sue in France: the French courts have jurisdiction because (a) Art. 4 provides that where the defendant is not domiciled in a Contracting State, internal law, i.e. French law, applies; (b) Art. 14 of the French Civil Code allows any Frenchman to sue any foreigner before the French court, and so X may sue in France; (c) Art. 4(2) of the Convention provides that any domiciliary of a Contracting State may avail himself of the rules of jurisdiction of that State, irrespective of nationality, and so Y may sue in France. If the United States defendant does not defend the proceedings, i.e. does not submit to the French jurisdiction, the French court will give a default judgment against it. Such a judgment will not be enforceable against the United States defendant's assets under the present United Kingdom-France Judgments Convention, because (in summary) Art. 14 jurisdiction is not a sufficient basis under that Convention, but it will be enforceable in England (and in other Contracting States) under the 1968 Convention, unless the United States concludes a convention with the United Kingdom under Art. 59.

The much-criticised rule in Art. 4(2) is defended by Jenard[4] on the ground that it is justified by the principle of equality of treatment and on economic grounds: since rules of exorbitant jurisdiction may be invoked against foreigners

---

[1] Hay (1968) Am J Comp L 149, 172.

[2] See Nadelmann *Conflict of Laws: International and Interstate* (1972) p. 245.

[3] Negotiations between the United States and the United Kingdom for a bilateral treaty broke down because of opposition to the enforcement in the United Kingdom of the huge damages awarded by American juries: see HL Debs, vol 410, col 1864, 26 June 1980; (1980) 51 BYIL 449.

[4] P. 21.

domiciled outside the EEC, persons who are domiciled in the Member State concerned and who thus contribute to the economic life of the Community should be able to invoke such rules in the same way as nationals. In practice it is really likely only to be of practical importance in relation to Art. 14 of the Civil Codes of France and Luxembourg. There are certain cases where, even if the defendant is not domiciled in any Contracting State, Art. 4(2) has no application. First, it does not apply when the exclusive jurisdiction provisions of Art. 16 are applicable. Thus even as against a United States national or domiciliary English courts may not assume jurisdiction in proceedings relating to immovables in other Contracting States caught by Art. 16(1).[1] Secondly, the provisions of Art. 4 can have no application to non-domiciliaries if there is a valid jurisdiction agreement under Arts. 12, 15 or 17: Arts. 12 and 17 both expressly contemplate cases where only one of the parties to the jurisdiction agreement is a domiciliary of a Contracting State. If there is such an agreement, the chosen court will have jurisdiction, and no other court: the same consequence should apply also where a plaintiff has sued in the courts of one Contracting State and the defendant has submitted: those courts will have jurisdiction under Art. 18, and it will not be open for the plaintiff to rely on the law of some other Contracting State to start a second action.[2]

Special Jurisdiction

Article 5 of the 1968 Convention, as amended, sets out seven categories of disputes in which, in addition to the court of the domicile, a court in one of the other Contracting States may exercise jurisdiction. These heads of jurisdiction are relevant only when the defendant is domiciled in another Contracting State. If he is domiciled in the State of the court in which the plaintiff seeks to sue, jurisdiction will be derived from his domicile under Art. 2. If he is not domiciled in a Contracting State, jurisdiction in the matters dealt with by Art. 5 will depend on national law, e.g. the provisions of RSC Ord. 11, r. 1(1).[3] They are all cases where the Convention seeks to ascribe jurisdiction to the court of a State which has a close connection with the case. Article 6 deals with jurisdiction (*a*) over co-defendants; (*b*) in third party claims; and (*c*) in relation to counterclaims. Article 6A deals with actions for limitation of liability in shipping cases. It must be borne in mind that where a court has jurisdiction under one of these heads over a defendant, there is no question of a discretion whether or not to exercise it.[4]

Article 5(1): Contract

Article 5(1) confers jurisdiction "in matters relating to a contract, in the courts for the place of performance of the obligation in question". This provision relates

---

[1] Even if they would not be prohibited by the *Mocambique* rule: see Dicey & Morris, pp. 538–545, and post on Art. 16(1), 1968 Convention, p. 78 and 1982 Act, s. 30, p. 139.
[2] See 1968 Convention, Art. 21.
[3] 1968 Convention, Art. 4(1).
[4] See p. 46, ante.

to contractual claims ("en matière contractuelle") and, in conferring jurisdiction on the courts of the place of performance, represented a compromise between various national laws.[1] In England, jurisdiction over persons not present, domiciled or resident within England may be exercised at present in contractual matters (*a*) where the contract was made within the jurisdiction, or (*b*) where the contract was made by or through an agent trading or residing within the jurisdiction, or (*c*) where the contract is by its terms, or by implication, governed by English law or (*d*) for a breach of contract committed within the jurisdiction; and (*e*) where there is a contractual choice of English jurisdiction.[2] The Convention rules are significantly different; there is no provision corresponding to (*a*), (*b*) or (*c*), and (*d*) which, although it has some superficial similarity, differs from the Convention rules in at least one important respect. Under RSC Ord. 11 it is possible to envisage a breach in England of a contractual obligation to be performed elsewhere, e.g. by express or implied repudiation.[3] Under the Convention, however, jurisdiction is conferred on the place of performance of the obligation in question.

Article 5(1) must be read subject to three other provisions. First, Art. 35 of the Accession Convention[4] provides that if the parties to a dispute concerning a contract had agreed in writing before the entry into force of the Accession Convention that it was to be governed by the law of a part of the United Kingdom or by the law of the Republic of Ireland, the courts of the United Kingdom and the Republic of Ireland shall retain the right to exercise jurisdiction in the dispute.[5] This means that, in addition to the place of performance jurisdiction under Art. 5(1) the English courts will retain the right to exercise jurisdiction under what will be RSC Ord. 11, r. 1(1)(*d*)(iii).[6] It should be noted that: (*a*) this jurisdiction will remain discretionary; (*b*) it will apply only if there is an express choice of law in writing; and (*c*) it will apply only if the choice of law is made before the Accession Convention comes into force.

Secondly, Art. I of the 1968 Protocol provides that a person domiciled in Luxembourg who is sued in a court of another Contracting State pursuant to Art. 5(1) may refuse to submit to the jurisdiction of the court; if the defendant does not enter an appearance, the court shall declare of its own motion that it has no jurisdiction. This provision was originally designed to protect Luxembourg domiciliaries from the jurisdiction of Belgian courts[7] and it is not easy to understand its continued justification,[8] but its implications are wide and must be borne in mind in any case in the United Kingdom involving Luxembourg.[9] Thirdly, it should be noted that under Art. VB of the 1968 Protocol, inserted by

---

[1] Jenard, p. 23, gives an account of the differing national approaches.
[2] RSC Ord. 11, r. 1(1)(*f*) and (*g*), which do not apply if the defendant is domiciled or ordinarily resident in Scotland, or under (*g*), in Northern Ireland; RSC Ord. 11, r. 2. See also the new paras. (*d*) and (*e*), Appendix 2, post.
[3] See Dicey & Morris, p. 208.
[4] 1982 Act, Sch. 3.
[5] This provision is not relevant in Scotland, where courts do not exercise jurisdiction on the basis of the law governing the contract.
[6] Where there is a choice of English *jurisdiction* Art. 17 will apply.
[7] Jenard, p. 63.
[8] Cf. Lagarde, 1981 Rev Crit 339.
[9] See also under 1968 Convention, Art. 17, p 87, post.

the Accession Convention, there are special provisions relating to disputes involving the terms of service of crews of ships registered in Denmark or Ireland.[1]

Whether a matter relates to a contract will not usually give rise to difficulty. There is a sufficiently common core on the meaning of contract to result in the term being given a Community interpretation.[2] Thus the fact that in English law a contract must be supported by consideration has not been an obstacle to the enforcement in England of contracts of agreements not so supported.[3] There will be borderline cases, such as quasi-contractual claims, which have also given rise to difficulty under RSC Ord. 11.[4] Such claims are probably included under Art. 5(1), at least where they are very close in nature to contractual claims or where they arise out of a contract.[5] Thus there can be little doubt that claims arising out of an ineffective contract[6] or claims for necessary goods supplied to a person under incapacity are covered by Art. 5(1); other claims may be closer to tort claims, and included, if at all, under Art. 5(3).[7]

This jurisdiction may be invoked even if the existence of the contract is denied by the defendant. In *Effer SpA v Kantner*[8] the plaintiff, a German patent agent, sued an Italian company in a German court for payment of a fee for investigating certain patent rights. The Italian company said it had not authorised its distributor to engage the plaintiff; that there was therefore no jurisdiction in the German court because there was no contract which was to be performed in Germany. The European Court held that this argument was unacceptable, for otherwise Art. 5(1) would have no useful effect if a defendant could oust the jurisdiction of a court seised under Art. 5(1) by denying the existence of a contract. Instead, Art. 5(1) should be construed as meaning that the court called upon to decide a dispute arising out of a contract might examine the essential preconditions for its jurisdiction, having regard to the evidence adduced with regard to the existence or non-existence of the contract. The dispositive holding was that the plaintiff may invoke Art. 5(1) jurisdiction "even when the existence of the contract on which the claim is based is in dispute between the parties". Taken together, these two statements would seem to indicate that the national court may decide on the existence of the contract at the jurisdictional phase (in which event it probably does not give rise to a judgment requiring recognition in other States), or, at its option, it may decide to assume jurisdiction if the plaintiff adduces prima facie proof of the existence of a contract.[9] It is suggested

---

[1] And in Greece: Greek Accession Convention, Art. 9.

[2] See Case 34/82 *Peters v ZNAV* [1983] ECR which gives little guidance.

[3] See *Re Bonacina, Le Brasseur v Bonacina* [1912] 2 Ch 394, CA.

[4] See Dicey & Morris, p. 204 and *McFee Engineering Pty Ltd v CBS Constructions Pty Ltd* (1980) 44 FLR 340, 28 ALR 339.

[5] Cf. OLG Frankfurt, 9 January 1979, RIW/AWD 1979, 204; [1979] ELD 375.

[6] Total failure of consideration and similar claims: see, e.g. Cheshire & Fifoot *Law of Contract* (10th edn 1981) pp. 588 et seq.

[7] E.g. the type of claim in *United Australia Ltd v Barclays Bank Ltd* [1941] AC 1, [1940] 4 All ER 20.

[8] Case 38/81: [1982] ECR 825. For subsequent proceedings in Germany see [1983] ECC 1.

[9] As the United Kingdom urged in its submissions. This is the position under RSC Ord. 11: see Dicey & Morris, p. 204. For the position in France see Gaudemet-Tallon, 1982 Rev Crit 570; Huet, 1982 Clunet 473, where a similar problem has arisen in various contexts.

that English courts should adopt the latter course, because it is manifestly inconvenient and often impractical to decide on the existence of a contract at the interlocutory stage.

"The obligation in question" whose place of performance must be in the State which assumes jurisdiction is the obligation which is the basis of the action.[1] In *De Bloos Sprl v Bouyer SA*[2] there was an agreement between Bouyer, a French company, and de Bloos, a Belgian company, for the exclusive distribution of Bouyer's goods in Belgium, Luxembourg and Zaire. De Bloos brought proceedings in Belgium for a declaration that the contract be dissolved because of Bouyer's conduct and for damages for unilateral revocation of the exclusive sales concession. Under Belgian law there was a division of case law on the nature of the compensation for termination of such a concession, some decisions holding that the obligation to pay compensation was an obligation under the contract and others that it was an independent obligation. The Belgian court asked the European Court to what "obligations" Art. 5(1) applied. The European Court held that the "obligation" in Art. 5(1) was the contractual obligation which formed the basis of the legal proceedings; where the plaintiff seeks damages for faulty performance or non-performance of a contractual obligation, it is the latter obligation which is the relevant obligation for the purposes of Art. 5(1). But as regards compensation for termination, it is for the national court to decide whether the obligation to pay it is a separate independent contractual obligation or whether it is merely replacing the unperformed contractual obligation to continue the distribution agreement.

This decision gave rise to considerable practical problems in cases of exclusive agency or distribution contracts where the defendant had repudiated a contract containing obligations to be performed in more than one country.[3] In *Ivenel v Schwab*[4] the Court modified the approach in *De Bloos Sprl v Bouyer SA* to deal with a case involving mutual obligations to be peformed in different countries. Ivenel was a French domiciliary employed by a German company to work in France as an exclusive representative. Ivenel sued the German company in France following the German company's termination of the agreement, claiming payment of commission, compensation for goodwill in lieu of notice, and holiday pay. The plaintiff had argued that the relevant obligations were the obligation for him to work and to be provided with work, in each case in France; the defendant argued that the relevant obligation was the duty to pay commission, which was payable, both under French law and German law at the address of the debtor, namely Germany. The European Court, much influenced by the doctrine of "characteristic performance" in the EEC Convention on the Law

---

[1] As a result of the decision in *De Bloos Sprl v Bouyer SA* discussed below, the French text of 1968 Convention, Art. 5(1) was modified by the Accession Convention to make this clear.

[2] Case 14/77: [1976] ECR 1497, [1977] 1 CMLR 60.

[3] Especially in France: see cases discussed by Holleaux, 1980 Clunet 333 and 889, 1981 Clunet 849; Gaudemet-Tallon, 1979 Rev Crit 816, 1981 Rev Crit 118; Huet, 1982 Rev Crit 383. A similar problem arose in Germany where the plaintiff sought a declaration that a contract containing obligations to be performed in more than one country was still subsisting: see OLG Frankfurt, 28 November 1979, RIW/AWD 1980, 585.

[4] Case 133/81: [1982] ECR 1891, [1983] 1 CMLR 538. See Hartley (1982) 7 Eur L Rev 328.

Applicable to Contractual Obligations[1] held that it was necessary to interpret the Convention so that there is a close connecting factor between the dispute and the court with jurisdiction to resolve it; in employment matters it was desirable, as far as possible, for disputes to be brought before the courts of the State whose law governed the contract. The EEC Convention on the Law Applicable to Contractual Obligations provided that a contract of employment was to be governed, in the absence of choice, by the law of the country in which the work was carried out, unless it appeared from the circumstances as a whole that the contract was more closely connected with another country; Art. 5(1) of the 1968 Convention was particularly concerned to attribute jurisdiction to the court of the country which had a close connection with a case, and in the case of a contract of employment, the connection was particularly with the law applicable to the contract; and the trend in conflict rules was towards determining the obligation characterising the contract in question, which was normally the obligation to carry out work; it was necessary to interpret Art. 5(1) in such a way that the national court was not compelled to find that it had jurisdiction to adjudicate upon certain claims but not on others, especially in employment matters, where the law applicable contained provisions protecting the worker and was normally that of the place where the work characterising the contract was carried out.

Once the relevant contractual obligation has been determined, the next question is what law determines where it is to be performed. Article 5(1) is silent on this question. In *Industrie Tessili Italiana Como v Dunlop AG*[2] the European Court held that it was for the national court, applying its own rules of private international law, to determine where the obligation was to be performed. In that case Dunlop AG, a German company, after negotiations in Como, Italy, ordered 310 ski suits from Tessili, an Italian company. Dunlop's letter contained conditions of purchase providing that a German court should have jurisdiction. Dunlop took delivery and received Tessili's invoice, the back of which provided that the courts of Como, Italy, should have jurisdiction. Dunlop complained of the quality of the goods and brought an action in Germany for annulment of the contract, and Tessili contested the jurisdiction of the German court. The Court of Appeal in Frankfurt, in the first reference under the 1971 Protocol, asked for guidance from the European Court. The Frankfurt Court thought, rightly[3] that there had been no agreement on choice of forum under Art. 17, and therefore the question was whether Germany was the place where the obligation had to be performed. The European Court held that it was for the national court which is asked to exercise jurisdiction to determine what the place of performance is, in accordance with the substantive law applicable according to the private international law of the lex fori.[4]

Subject to the validity of the agreement under national law, and perhaps also

---

[1] Not yet in force. It was opened for signature on June 19, 1980 and has been signed but not yet ratified by the United Kingdom. For text see Official Journal of the European Communities, OJ L266, 9 October 1980 and in North (ed.) *Contract Conflicts* (1982), p. 347, and report by Professors Giuliano and Lagarde OJ C282, 31 October 1980 and in North, op. cit., p. 355.

[2] Case 12/76: [1976] ECR 1473, [1977] 1 CMLR 26.

[3] See p. 86, post.

[4] See also Case 133/81: *Ivenel v Schwab* [1982] ECR 1891, [1983] 1 CMLR 538.

its not being a sham,[1] there is no reason in principle why the parties should not in practice confer (non-exclusive) jurisdiction on the courts of a particular State by specifying that the performance of the obligation is to be deemed to be due there. In *Zelger v Salinitri*[2] it held that if the parties to the contract are permitted by the law applicable to the contract, subject to any conditions imposed by that law, to specify the place of performance of an obligation without satisfying any special condition of form, an agreement (even an oral agreement) on the place of performance of the obligation is sufficient to found jurisdiction in that place within the meaning of Art. 5(1).[3]

Thus a court in the United Kingdom will have to determine what the relevant obligation is, what law governs it, and where it is to be performed. In sale of goods cases (subject to the special provisions relating to consumer contracts)[4] English courts will have jurisdiction over a French seller for damages for breach of warranty of quality if delivery was to be made in England.[5] Where the claim is for payment of the price it will be necessary to determine the due place of payment, "a matter in which it is especially difficult to determine the place of performance in the absence of an express term in the contract".[6] Where there is agreement as to the place of payment, there will be no difficulty.[7] Where there is no agreement, the normal English rule is that, in the absence of contrary indications, the debtor must seek out his creditor.[8] In practice, therefore, English courts will normally have jurisdiction in claims by the seller[9] where the seller is English, and will normally have jurisdiction in claims by the buyer where the goods were to be delivered in England.[10] The result will be different if the proper law of the contract is foreign, and if the foreign law has a different rule.[11]

---

[1] Cf. *Audi-NSU v Adelin Petit*, Belgian Cour de Cassation 1979 [1980] ECC 235.

[2] Case 56/79: [1980] ECR 89, [1980] 2 CMLR 635. See, post, p. 87, on the relationship between this decision and the requirements of Art. 17.

[3] See Mezger, 1980 Rev Crit 385; Huet, 1980 Clunet 435; *Société Gotz v Barsaghian*, Lyons, 1979, 1980 Clunet 888, note Holleaux. See also *Créations Davos Sprl v Katag Gruppe Top Textil AG*, Brussels, 1977, Eur Court Digest D I-5.1.2-B12.

[4] As to which see pp. 74–77, post.

[5] Cf. Dicey & Morris, p. 210: see also various national decisions, including *Vaccaro v Abitbol*, Aix 1977, Eur Court Digest D I-5.1.1-B5; *Italconf v Andreae*, Florence 1976, ibid., D I-5.1.2-B7; *Manheim & Zoon v Tasselli*, Amsterdam 1977, ibid., B14; 1978 Neths Int L Rev 82.

[6] Dicey & Morris, p. 209. See also Law Commission, Report on Council of Europe Conventions on Foreign Money Liabilities (1967) and the Place of Payment of Money Liabilities (1972), Cmnd 8318, 1981, p. 28.

[7] Cf. on 1968 Convention, Art. 5(1), *Zelger v Salinitri*, ante.

[8] Dicey & Morris, p. 209.

[9] Provided the consumer contract provisions of 1968 Convention, Section 4, Arts. 13–15, do not apply.

[10] In the original Contracting States the strong (but not universal tendency) has been to give jurisdiction to the courts of the seller in actions for the price, especially where Art. 59 of the Uniform Law on the International Sale of Goods is applicable, notwithstanding that the normal rule in several of the original Contracting States is that the price is payable at the establishment of the buyer. See, e.g. *Société Julia v Société Sodevoc*, Rennes and Cour de Cassation, 1978, 1980 Clunet 351, note Holleaux; German Federal Supreme Court, 4 April 1979 RIW/AWD 1979, 639; LG Waldshut-Tiengen, 28 June 1979, RIW/AWD 1979, 784; *Klöchner v Societá Tazzetti*, Italian Ct of Cass 1980, [1980] I Foro It 1687; [1981] ELD 71.

[11] Dicey & Morris, p. 211.

Article 5(2): Maintenance

The adjusted Art. 5(2) provides that a person domiciled in a Contracting State may be sued in another Contracting State in matters relating to maintenance, in the courts for the place where the maintenance creditor is domiciled or habitually resident or, if the matter is ancillary to proceedings concerning the status of a person, in the court which, according to its own law, has jurisdiction to entertain those proceedings, unless that jurisdiction is based solely on the nationality of one of the parties. Prior to the Accession Convention, the only maintenance jurisdiction under the Convention was in the courts of the place where the maintenance creditor was domiciled or habitually resident.[1] The adjustment to bring in maintenance orders ancillary to status proceedings (although the Convention does not itself apply to proceedings concerning status) was made because the laws of the new Contracting States—as was also by then the case with the laws of many of the original Contracting States—allowed status proceedings to be combined with proceedings concerning maintenance claims.[2] There may be some difficulty in distinguishing claims for maintenance and which are therefore within Art. 5(2) and those which are in the nature of a division of matrimonial property and thus excluded by Art. 1(2) (1).[3] In *De Cavel v De Cavel (No. 1)*[4] it was held that the judicial division of matrimonial property was closely linked to the grounds for divorce and was inseparable from questions relating to status; but in *De Cavel v De Cavel (No. 2)*[5] the court held that the compensatory payments provided for in the French Civil Code were concerned with financial obligations between spouses after divorce fixed on the basis of their respective needs and resources and were in the nature of maintenance. The fact that the maintenance claim was linked with that of divorce (not covered by the Convention) did not mean that the judgment was not enforceable since ancillary claims came within the scope of the Convention according to the subject matter with which they were concerned and not according to the subject matter involved in the principal claim. It would seem that a claim for maintenance payable under an agreement is not within Art. 5(2) but falls within the contract head of Art. 5(1) unless perhaps it merely reflects an already existing maintenance obligation imposed by law.[6] A claim may be a maintenance claim even if it is not for periodic payments but is a lump sum order, provided probably that it is not intended as a division of matrimonial property.[7] Maintenance orders are within Art. 5(2) whether they are of an interim or final nature.[8] Contribution orders[9] are not, it seems, "matters relating to maintenance"[10] but it is likely that affiliation orders are within the scope of

---

[1] Cf. Hague Convention on maintenance obligations in respect of children (1958).
[2] Schlosser, para. 90. See Dicey & Morris, p. 391.
[3] The Hague Convention of 1973 is more explicit.
[4] Case 143/78: [1979] ECR 1055, [1979] 2 CMLR 547.
[5] Case 120/79: [1980] ECR 731, [1980] 3 CMLR 1.
[6] Schlosser, para. 92.
[7] Schlosser, paras. 93–95. See also Maxwell Report, para. 4.11.
[8] *De Cavel (No 2), supra.*
[9] E.g. under the Child Care Act 1980.
[10] Schlosser, para. 97.

Art. 5(2).[1] According to both Jenard[2] and Schlosser[3] a court which has made a maintenance order is only competent to vary or revoke it if at the time of the application to vary or revoke it is still a competent court under Art. 5(2); if the court which made the original order no longer has jurisdiction (e.g. because the maintenance creditor is no longer domiciled or habitually resident in that State), it cannot adjust the order, and must recognise the variation order made by a court which does have jurisdiction.[4]

The effect of Art. 5(2) in England[5] will be that English courts will continue to have jurisdiction to make maintenance orders against respondents domiciled in other Contracting States where they have jurisdiction under English law to grant a decree of divorce, nullity or judicial separation;[6] and that their other powers to make maintenance orders will be exercisable if (*a*) the respondent is domiciled in England for the purposes of the 1982 Act; (*b*) the respondent is domiciled in another Contracting State and the court is a court for the place where the maintenance creditor is domiciled or habitually resident; or (*c*) the respondent submits to the jurisdiction.[7] Where a country to which Part II of the Maintenance Orders (Reciprocal Enforcement) Act 1972 extends is also a party to the 1968 Convention, magistrates' courts in the United Kingdom may take jurisdiction under that Act to make provisional maintenance orders notwithstanding that the domicile of the respondent is in that country.[8] All of the original and new Contracting States are countries to which Part II of the 1972 Act extends.

Article 5(3): Torts

By Art. 5(3) jurisdiction is conferred in matters "relating to tort, delict or quasi-delict" on the courts of the place where "the harmful event occurred".[9] Whether the expression, "tort, delict or quasi-delict" should be interpreted according to the lex fori or according to an independent Convention meaning has been raised but not decided. In *Netherlands State v Rüffer*[10] the European Court held that a claim by a public authority for compensation for the removal of a wreck was not within the Convention because it was not a civil or commercial matter. It was, therefore, not necessary for the Court to rule on the question raised by the Dutch Supreme Court, whether a claim of the kind made by the public authority was within the concept of tort, delict or quasi-delict. The opinion of Advocate General Warner argued strongly for a Community interpretation. He pointed out[11] that the corresponding phrase in the authentic

---

[1] Maxwell Report, para. 5.48.
[2] P. 25.
[3] Paras. 107–108.
[4] Jenard, p. 25. See also Maxwell Report, paras. 5.52–5.55.
[5] See also 1982 Act, s. 48(3) for provision for rules of court to deal with maintenance problems.
[6] The exception at the end of 1968 Convention, Art. 5(2) for the case where jurisdiction is based solely on the nationality of the parties has no significance for the United Kingdom because its courts do not exercise jurisdiction in matrimonial causes on the basis of nationality.
[7] 1968 Convention, Art. 18, see p. 91, post.
[8] 1968 Convention, Art. 57, in conjunction with the New York Convention of 1956 on the Recovery of Maintenance Abroad, or (in the case of Ireland) with the bilateral arrangements.
[9] "le fait dommageable s'est produit".
[10] Case 814/79: [1980] ECR 3807, [1981] 3 CMLR 293.
[11] Pp. 3832–5.

text of the official languages of each Member State did not in each case connote a concept known to the law of that State, which suggested that the expression had an independent meaning; "like the proverbial elephant, tort is easier to recognise than to define" and it was not necessary to attempt a definition. It is likely that the concept would be given an independent meaning, especially in view of the decision on the "place" of the tort discussed below.

Most of the original Contracting States had a form of jurisdiction in tort matters equivalent to Art. 5(3);[1] the draftsmen deliberately left open the question whether the "place" was the place where the wrongful act occurred or the place where the damage was suffered, if they were in different places.[2] This is a question which, under the present RSC Ord. 11, r. 1(1) (*h*), is not finally settled.[3] The tendency of some recent decisions has been to look to the place where in substance the act or omission occurred which gave rise to the cause of action.[4] The point arose for decision under Art. 5(3) in the European Court in *Handelskwekerij GJ Bier BV v Mines de Potasse d'Alsace*.[5] Bier, a company engaged in the business of nursery gardening, and the Reinwater Foundation, which exists to promote improvements in the quality of water in the Rhine, brought an action in the Rotterdam court against a French company, whose registered office was at Mulhouse and which worked mines in Alsace. The defendant was alleged to have discharged more than 10,000 tonnes of chloride every 24 hours through a waste flow into the Rhine. The Appeal Court of the Hague, in an appeal against a judgment denying Dutch jurisdiction, asked the European Court whether Art. 5(3) applied to the place where the damage occurred or the place where the event having the damage as its sequel occurred. The European Court held that the "place" was to be determined, not by the diverging solutions of national law, but by a Convention rule that both places had jurisdiction. It said:[6]

> "The form of words 'place where the harmful event occurred', used in all the language versions of the Convention, leaves open the question whether, in the situation described, it is necessary, in determining jurisdiction, to choose as the connecting factor the place of the event giving rise to the damage, or the place where the damage occurred, or to accept that the plaintiff has an option between the one and the other of those two connecting factors. As regards this, it is well to point out that the place of the event giving rise to the damage no less than the place where the damage occurred can, depending on the case, constitute a significant connecting factor from the point of view of jurisdiction. Liability in tort, delict or quasi-delict can only arise provided that a causal connexion can be established between the damage and the event in which that damage

---

[1] See Advocate General Capotorti in Case 21/76: *Handelskwekerij GJ Bier BV v Mines de Potasse d'Alsace* [1976] ECR 1735, at 1751–4 for a discussion of national provisions.

[2] Ibid.

[3] Dicey & Morris, p. 213. The new version of this head of jurisdiction in Ord. 11, r. 1(1)(*f*) will adopt a solution similar to that under Art. 5(3): see Chapter 7, post.

[4] See e.g. *Distillers Co (Biochemicals) Ltd v Thompson* [1971] AC 458, [1971] 1 All ER 694, PC, on a differently worded rule; *Castree v ER Squibb & Sons Ltd* [1980] 2 All ER 589, [1980] 1 WLR 1248 CA; *Multinational Gas and Petrochemical Co v Multinational and Petrochemical Services Ltd* [1983] 2 All ER 563 [1983] 3 WLR 492, CA.

[5] Case 21/76: [1978] QB 708, [1976] ECR 1735, [1977] 1 CMLR 284.

[6] At 1746–1747.

originates. Taking into account the close connexion between the component parts of every sort of liability, it does not appear appropriate to opt for one of the two connecting factors mentioned to the exclusion of the other, since each of them can, depending on the circumstances, be particularly helpful from the point of view of the evidence and of the conduct of the proceedings. To exclude one option appears all the more undesirable in that, by its comprehensive form of words, Article 5(3) of the Convention covers a wide diversity of kinds of liability. Thus the meaning of the expression 'place where the harmful event occurred' in Article 5(3) must be interpreted in such a way as to acknowledge that the plaintiff has an option to commence proceedings either at the place where the damage occurred or the place of the event giving rise to it."

Thus the plaintiff has an option to sue either in the place where the wrongful act occurred or in the place where the damage arose. But if he sues in one, he cannot subsequently sue in the other.[1]

The place of damage connotes the place where the physical damage is done or the economic loss is actually suffered. Even though in one sense a plaintiff may suffer economic loss at the place of its business, that is not sufficient to confer jurisdiction on that place, for otherwise the place of business of the plaintiff would almost automatically become another basis of jurisdiction.[2]

An important question which has not been settled is whether Art. 5(3) justifies the assumption of jurisdiction to grant injunctions against *threatened* torts which have not been committed, e.g. defamation, passing off, patent infringement. Where the tort has been committed within the jurisdiction, there is no doubt that the national court may grant an injunction restraining future commission.[3] Schlosser[4] notes that the courts of the United Kingdom exercise preventive jurisdiction of this kind, and that Art. 24[5] would allow them to grant provisional measures which might, in practice if not in law, have final effect. He gives hesitant support to the view that Art. 5(3) would also provide a basis of jurisdiction in proceedings where the main object was to prevent the imminent commission of a tort. This might require a somewhat strained interpretation to be given to the word "occurred" but would clearly arrive at a practical and sensible result. The other view would require provisional measures to be taken under Art. 24 in the State where the threatened wrong might occur, and for the merits of the case to be fought at the place of the defendant's domicile.[6]

There are many cases in English law (as in other systems) where a claim may be based alternatively in contract and in tort;[7] in such cases a plaintiff may invoke the RSC Ord. 11 jurisdictional rules relating to either head, but he may

---

[1] 1968 Convention, Art. 21; *Geobra Brandstätter GmbH v Big Spielwarenfabrik*, Netherlands, 1977 Eur Court Digest D 1-5.3-B5; 1978 Neths Int L Rev 86.
[2] Cf. Advocate General Warner in Case 814/79: *Netherlands State v Rüffer* [1980] ECR at 3836; *Mecoma v Stahlhandel*, Netherlands, 1978, Eur Court Digest D 1-5.3-B7; 1981 Neths Int L Rev 72.
[3] Cf. *Forge v Fantu Food*, Netherlands, 1975, Eur Court Digest D 1-5.3-B1.
[4] Para. 134.
[5] See p. 98, post.
[6] The point has been put beyond doubt in the former sense in the version of Art. 5(3) in Sch. 4 to the 1982 Act: see p. 129, post.
[7] See, e.g., *Matthews v Kuwait Bechtel Corpn* [1959] 2 QB 57, [1959] 2 All ER 345, CA.

Jurisdictional Rules under the Convention

not litigate a claim in relation to which Ord. 11 does not confer jurisdiction.[1] The position under the Convention will be similar. The plaintiff may base his claim under either head; whether it is appropriately tort or contract will be a matter for the lex fori—although there are limits to what a national court may treat as a tort case;[2] once the court is seised under the Convention, it will not have jurisdiction to litigate claims which under the Convention have to be litigated in another state.

Article 5(4): Civil claims in criminal proceedings

Article 5(4) confers jurisdiction, in relation to civil claims for damages or restitution based on an act giving rise to criminal proceedings, on the court seised of those proceedings if it has jurisdiction under its own law to entertain civil proceedings. This is of considerable practical importance in the original Contracting States especially in cases involving road accidents, and will also sometimes be relevant to the United Kingdom, not only in relation to recognition of judgments, but to the occasional cases where foreign defendants in criminal proceedings are ordered to give restitution.[3] Article II of the 1968 Protocol contains special provisions relating to the enforcement of default judgments of a civil nature given in criminal proceedings. These need not be enforced if (a) the court which gave the judgment was of a State in which the defendant was neither a national or a domiciliary; (b) the criminal offence was "not intentionally committed";[4] and (c) the defendant did not have an opportunity to arrange for his defence. This provision, which is intended to apply mainly to civil judgments in road traffic accident cases,[5] is not likely to have any practical importance in the United Kingdom.

Article 5(5): Branches and agencies

Article 5(5) confers jurisdiction in relation to a "dispute arising out of the operations of a branch, agency or other establishment" on the courts of the place where the branch, agency or other establishment is situated. It relates only to defendants domiciled in a Contracting State, i.e. companies or firms with their seat in one Contracting State and a branch in another Contracting State; companies with their seats outside the Contracting States but with a branch within them come within Art. 4, i.e. the internal jurisdictional rules of the place where the branch is situated apply.[6] By Art. 8(2), however, an insurer not domiciled in a Contracting State but which has a branch, agency or other establishment in a Contracting State is, in disputes arising out of the operations

---

[1] Dicey & Morris, p. 199.
[2] Cf. *Netherlands State v Rüffer*, ante.
[3] See Theft Act 1968, s. 28; Criminal Justice Act 1972, s. 6. This is so even though the victim-applicant is not technically a party to the proceedings, as he is in civil law countries. Several bilateral United Kingdom treaties, e.g. with France, Belgium and the Federal Republic of Germany, apply to judgments for restitution or damages in criminal proceedings.
[4] On the meaning of which see Case 157/80: *Rinkau* [1981] ECR 1391, [1983] 1 CMLR 205.
[5] See Jenard, p. 63.
[6] See Jenard, p. 26.

of the branch, agency or establishment, deemed to be domiciled in that State; by Art. 13(2), similar provision is made in relation to suppliers of goods and services in consumer contracts.[1]

Two main questions arise. First, what is a "branch, agency or other establishment"? Second, what disputes arise out of its operations? On the first question, it is clear that the concept must be interpreted by Convention standards and not by purely national notions.[2] The obvious case of a branch bearing the same business name and staffed by the employees of the main undertaking needs no comment. In two cases the European Court has declined to extend the concept of a branch to distributors or sales agents for the goods of foreign companies. *De Bloos Sprl v Bouyer SA*[3] was a reference by a Belgian court in an action by a Belgian company against a French company for a declaration that a contract for the exclusive distribution by the Belgian company of the French company's goods in Belgium, Luxembourg and Zaire be dissolved because of the French company's repudiation, together with damages for unilateral revocation of the exclusive sales concession. The defendant objected to the jurisdiction of the Belgian court, which therefore asked the European Court (inter alia) whether the grantee of a sales concession who cannot negotiate in the name of the grantor and is not subject to the control of the grantor is at the head of a branch etc. of the grantor within the meaning of Art. 5(5). The Court held, as was indeed obvious, that one of the essential characteristics of the concept of branch or agency was the fact of being subject to the direction and control of the parent body; that the concept of "establishment" should be interpreted in a similar way, and that an exclusive distributor was therefore not a "branch" etc. of the manufacturer. *Blanckaert and Willems PVBA v Trost*[4] involved an action in Germany against a Belgian company by a German undertaking allegedly acting as its sales representative. The dispute was concerned with the plaintiffs' appointment as a kind of sub-agent by another German company which had agreed to set up a sales network in Germany for the Belgian company. The German Federal Supreme Court referred to the European Court the question whether a commercial agent who is a business negotiator is an "agency" or "other establishment" within Art. 5(5). The European Court held that an independent commercial agent who merely negotiates business, who is free to arrange his own work and decide what proportion of his time to devote to the interests of the undertaking which he agrees to represent, who may represent at the same time several firms competing in the same manufacturing or marketing sector, and who merely transmits orders to the parent undertaking without being involved in either their terms or their execution does not have the character of a branch, agency, or other establishment within the meaning of Art. 5(5).

In addition to the element of direction and control the Court has required the element of the "appearance of permanency", which may rise to practical problems, in view of the many "representative" offices of foreign companies in the United Kingdom. *Somafer SA v Saar-Ferngas AG*[5] was a reference by a

---

[1] See pp. 71 and 76, post, and 1982 Act, s. 44.
[2] See Case 33/78: *Somafer SA v Saar-Ferngas AG* [1978] ECR 2183 at 2190.
[3] Case 14/76: [1976] ECR 1497, [1977] 1 CMLR 60.
[4] Case 139/80: [1981] ECR 819, [1982] 2 CMLR 1.
[5] Case 33/78: [1978] ECR 2183, [1979] 1 CMLR 490.

German court. The defendant, Somafer, had its principal place of business in France and was involved in the business of demolition and blasting. It blew up a bunker in the Saarland, and Saar-Ferngas took steps to protect its gas mains and sought reimbursement of the expense. The letterhead of Somafer indicated that it had an office or place of contact in Germany described on its notepaper as "representation for Germany", with a telephone number, but its central administration was in France and in Germany it had no accommodation or furniture, no separate accounting and was not entered into the commercial register as a branch; but its letterhead stated that its bankers were Credit Lyonnais, Saarbrücken; and a representative or employee of Somafer stayed in Germany occasionally and it was with him that Ferngas alleged that it agreed the security measures to be taken. The European Court said:[1]

> "... the concept of branch, agency or other establishment implies a place of business which has the appearance of permanency, such as the extension of a parent body, has a management and is materially equipped to negotiate business with third parties so that the latter, although knowing that there will if necessary be a legal link with the parent body, the head office of which is abroad, do not have to deal directly with such parent body but may transact business at the place of business constituting the extension."

It was for the court seised to find the facts on which it could be established that an "effective place of business" existed.[2]

An important point which was raised but not decided in the *Somafer* case was whether the defendants were estopped from denying that they had an establishment in Germany by virtue of their letterhead which indicated that they had an office there. Advocate General Mayras said that, having regard to the special nature of the jurisdiction under Art. 5(5), appearances should be disregarded and the realities considered; it was for third parties who wished to rely on Art. 5(5) to adduce evidence that the entity which they wished to bring before the national court was in fact subject to the control and direction of the parent company. This does seem somewhat impractical and unfair on a third party, who should be entitled to rely on the representations openly made by the defendant.

The second question will be whether the claim arises out of the operations of the branch, agency or other establishment. In *Somafer SA v Saar-Ferngas AG* the European Court explained:[3]

> "This concept of operations comprises on the one hand actions relating to rights and contractual or non-contractual obligations concerning the management properly so-called of the agency, branch or other establishment itself, such as those concerning the situation of the building where such entity is established or the local engagement of staff to work there. Further it also comprises those relating to undertakings which have been entered into at the above-mentioned place of business in the name of the

---

[1] At 2192.

[2] The German court did ultimately hold that the defendant had a branch and that 1968 Convention Art. 5(5) applied: OLG Saarbrucken, 3 April 1979 RIW/AWD 1980, 796.

[3] At 2192-3.

parent body and which must be performed in the Contracting State where the place of business is established and also actions concerning non-contractual obligations arising from the activities in which the branch, agency or other establishment ... has engaged at the place in which it is established on behalf of the parent body."

The wording of Art. 5(5) suggests that it grants jurisdiction to the courts of the place of the branch in relation to *any* contract entered into by it; but the Court, in the passage quoted above, has limited such a jurisdiction to cases where performance is to take place in the same State as the branch.[1] If this is right, and it must be open to question, then in contract matters Art. 5(5) would add little to Art. 5(1). Such a limitation would also deprive Art. 8(2) of much of its effectiveness.[2] It may be that an essential element of this jurisdiction is that it is designed for the benefit of third parties, and not for intra-company or intra-firm disputes.[3]

Article 5(6): Trusts

This is a new provision introduced by the Accession Convention providing for jurisdiction over a settlor, trustee or beneficiary of a trust created by the operation of a statute, or by a written instrument, or created orally and evidenced in writing, in the courts of the Contracting State in which the trust is domiciled.[4] The phrase "created by the operation of a statute, or by a written instrument, or created orally and evidenced in writing" is intended to indicate clearly that the new rules apply only to cases in which a trust has been expressly constituted or for which provision is made by statute—it does not include "constructive" or "implied" trusts.[5] Nor will it apply to testamentary trusts or to trustees in bankruptcy.[6] Article 5(6) is intended, it seems, only to deal with disputes relating to the internal relationships of the trust, e.g. disputes between beneficiaries and trustees, and not to its external relations, e.g. the enforcement by third parties of contracts made by trustee.[7]

To determine whether a trust is domiciled in the Contracting State whose courts are seised, the court is to apply its rules of private international law. The 1982 Act provides that a trust is domiciled in the United Kingdom if the trust has its closest and most real connection with a system of law of one of the constituent parts of the United Kingdom, and that any proceedings which are

---

[1] E.g. see LG Köln, 23 March 1979, RIW/AWD 1980, 215, negligent collection of cheque by German branch of Belgian bank.

[2] P. 271, post.

[3] Cf. Advocate General Reischl in case 14/76: *De Bloos Sprl v Bouyer SA* [1976] ECR at 1519 and in Case 139/80: *Blanckaert and Willems PVBA v Trost* [1981] ECR at 838, [1982] 2 CMLR 1.

[4] Cf. RSC Ord. 11, r. 1(1)(e), which applies only where the action is for the execution of trusts relating to property in England; only to trusts constituted by a written instrument; and only to actions against trustees. See *Official Solicitor v Stype Investments (Jersey) Ltd* [1983] 1 All ER 629, [1983] 1 WLR 214. The new para (*j*) does not require that the property be in England: see Chapter 7, post.

[5] Schlosser, para. 117.

[6] 1968 Convention, Art. 1, exclusion of wills and succession, bankruptcy. On trust deeds for creditors and marriage contract trusts see Maxwell Report, para. 5.63.

[7] Schlosser, para. 120.

brought in the United Kingdom by virtue of Art. 5(6) shall be brought in the part of the United Kingdom in which the trust is domiciled.[1]

Article 5(7): Salvage

Article 5(7), added by the Accession Convention, provides for jurisdiction in cases concerning remuneration for salvage, in the court in which (*a*) the cargo or freight has been arrested to secure such payment or (*b*) the court in which it could have been so arrested, but bail or other security has been given; but Art. 5(7) only applies if it is claimed that the defendant has an interest in the cargo or freight or had such an interest at the time of salvage.[2] The reason for this provision was to preserve for the United Kingdom the jurisdiction in rem in salvage claims, not only against the ship (as the Brussels Convention of 1952 on the Arrest of Seagoing Ships allows) but also against cargo and freight. If no adjustment had been made to the 1968 Convention the United Kingdom would "have suffered an unacceptable loss of jurisdiction."[3]

Article 6: Co-defendants; Third Party Claims; Counterclaims

Co-defendants

Article 6(1) provides that a person domiciled in a Contracting State may also be sued, where he is one of a number of defendants, in the courts for the place where any one of them is domiciled. A similar jurisdiction is found in the law of most of the original Contracting States[4] and is analogous to the "necessary and proper party" provisions of RSC Ord. 11,[5] r. 1(1). Article 6(1) refers to the "courts for the place" of the primary defendant's domicile, and not to the court of the State of the domicile.[6] This is especially important in those States where courts have local jurisdiction based on local domicile. In the context of the United Kingdom, it seems that because (except for County Courts and Sheriff Courts) jurisdiction is not local, Art. 6(1) will normally apply wherever the main defendant is domiciled in the part of the United Kingdom in which the court exercises jurisdiction.[7] This jurisdiction is clearly open to potential abuse, since a plaintiff is able to sue the main defendant at the domicile of another, less important, defendant. Thus by framing what is essentially a claim for breach of contract as a claim for conspiracy or inducement to break a contract, and suing a third party alleged to be guilty of conspiracy to break the contract, jurisdiction

---

[1] 1982 Act, ss. 10 and 45.
[2] On Admiralty matters generally see Schlosser, para. 121.
[3] Schlosser, para. 122. For other shipping problems cf. 1968 Convention, Art. 6A (actions for limitation of liability); Art. 36 of the Accession Convention (maritime jurisdiction in Denmark and Ireland); Art. VB of the 1968 Protocol (remuneration and conditions of service of crews of ships registered in Denmark and Ireland).
[4] Jenard, p. 26; Droz, para. 83.
[5] RSC Ord. 11, r. 1(1)(*j*); para. (*c*) in the new version: see Chapter 7, post.
[6] See Maxwell Report, para. 568; Droz, para. 86.
[7] It is not likely that 1982 Act, s. 41(4) has any bearing on this question.

over the original party may be created at the domicile of the third party. According to Jenard[1] there must be a connection between the claims made against each of the defendants, as, for example, in the case of joint debtors, and an action cannot be brought solely with the object of ousting the jurisdiction of the courts of the State in which the defendant is domiciled, but it is not clear how abuse can easily be prevented.[2] It may be possible to imply something similar to what is expressed in Art. 6(2), namely that Art. 6(1) should not apply if the proceedings were instituted with the object of removing the defendant from the jurisdiction of the court which would otherwise be competent. But Art. 6(1) is not limited to claims which are strictly "joint"; it also applies to separate causes of action which have a genuine relationship with each other.[3] The court of the domicile must be validly seised of the claim. Thus if X is domiciled in England, but has agreed with Y that the courts of France are to have exclusive jurisdiction over disputes between them, Y cannot use Art. 6(1) to justify bringing an action in England against X and adding A and B, domiciled in Germany, as additional defendants. If the additional defendant has a contract with the plaintiff providing for the exclusive jurisdiction of another court, then the provisions of Art. 17 would supersede those of Art. 6(1) and the chosen court would continue to have exclusive jurisdiction.[4]

Third parties

Article 6(2) provides for jurisdiction in an action on a warranty or guarantee or other third party proceeding[5] in the court seised of the original proceedings unless they were instituted solely with the object of removing the third party from the jurisdiction of the court which would otherwise be competent. The "demande en garantie" is equivalent to a claim for indemnity, and this provision deals with what in England is regulated by third party procedure.[6] In the case of third parties (as distinct from additional defendants) in English law it is not sufficient for there to be jurisdiction in the main claim for there also to be jurisdiction over a foreign third party. In the case of third parties, the rule is that service out of the jurisdiction may only be authorised if service would have been authorised against the third party if the third party claim had been the subject of an independent claim.[7] It follows from Art. 6(2) that a third party may be sued in a court which has little connection with the claim against the third party, if its jurisdiction is derived from a contract between the plaintiff and defendant. Thus if A in England has supplied goods to B in France, and B sells them under a contract to C in Italy providing for the exclusive jurisdiction of the Italian courts, then B may add A in proceedings brought in Italy by C against B, unless

---

[1] P. 26.
[2] See Maxwell Report, para. 5.73. The Court of Appeal of Paris held that a defendant could not be "artificially" joined under the provision; *Banque Nationale de Paris v Société Felk*, [1978] Eur Court Digest D I-6-B4, 1979 Rev Crit 444, note Santa-Croce.
[3] Cf. *Ruffino v Fornaro*, Milan 1979 [1981] ECC 541.
[4] See Droz, para. 92.
[5] "une demande en garantie ou . . . une demande en intervention".
[6] See RSC Ord. 16.
[7] See Dicey & Morris, pp. 227–8. But the position will be different under the new RSC: see Chapter 7, post.

the contract between A and B provides for the exclusive jurisdiction of some other court.[1] This underlines the importance to vendors of protecting themselves from being joined in such actions by stipulating for the exclusive jurisdiction of their own courts. An attempt is made to prevent abuse of this head of jurisdiction by providing that it is not to apply if the original proceedings were brought solely with the object of removing the third party from the jurisdiction which would otherwise have been competent. But the subjective element in this exception will make it extremely difficult for the third party to be in a position to show that the sole purpose of the proceedings was to achieve the object of bringing in the third party.[2]

Counterclaims

Article 6(3) provides that a person domiciled in a Contracting State may be sued on a counterclaim[3] arising from the same contract or facts on which the original claim was based, in the court in which the original claim is pending. This is similar to the English rule of jurisdiction that a plaintiff submits to counterclaims in related matters.[4] In Art. 6(3) the requirement that the claims be related is expressed in the following way: the counterclaim must (*a*) "arise", from (*b*) the same contract or (*c*) the same facts, (*d*) on which the original claim was "based". These requirements are stricter than a requirement that the matters merely be "related".

Article 6A: Limitation of Liability

An action for limitation of liability allows a shipowner (and others who incur liability in connection with a ship) to limit their liability to a specific amount based on the tonnage of a ship in the case of claims arising without their fault. In some countries, as in England, the claim is brought against a potential claimant, or by way of counterclaim; in others, as in Germany, the claim is not made against a person, but instead leads to the setting up of a fund.[5] The purpose of Art. 6A, added by the Accession Convention, is to ensure that an original action for limitation of liability may be brought, not only in the courts which would have jurisdiction over the potential claimants under Arts. 2 to 6, but also in the court of the domicile of the shipowner and any other courts which have

---

[1] Cf. Jenard, p. 27.

[2] The special position of German law is covered by Art. V of the 1968 Protocol, whereby the jurisdiction under Art. 6(2) in actions on a warranty or guarantee may not be resorted to in Germany, but any person domiciled in another Contracting State may be summoned before the German courts on the basis of Arts. 72 and 74 of the Code of Civil Procedure. The effect of these is that no money judgment is given against the third party but only a declaratory judgment binding in subsequent proceedings: see Jenard, p. 27.

[3] "une demande reconventionnelle"—which is not quite the same as a counterclaim since it does not have to be brought in the same action: see Maxwell Report, para. 5.90 and Anton, p. 132, for the Scots procedure of reconvention.

[4] Dicey & Morris, p. 191; for Scotland see Anton, p. 132.

[5] Schlosser, para. 125.

jurisdiction by virtue of the Brussels Arrest and Collision Conventions of 1952. If the claimants have already brought an action, then Art. 22 applies and the claim for limitation might have to be brought by way of counterclaim in the court where the original action was brought.[1]

Articles 7 to 12A: Jurisdiction in Matters relating to Insurance

The draftsmen of the Convention made special provision for insurance and consumer contracts in order to protect policyholders and consumers. In the negotiations for accession, the United Kingdom sought to adapt the Convention to meet the needs of the London insurance market; in particular, the United Kingdom stressed that the nature of the London market was such that a large proportion of its business was with policyholders outside the Community; and that a large proportion was insurance of "large risks" with substantial industrial and commercial concerns; neither of these groups needed the special protection of the Convention rules.[2] As the House of Lords Select Committee on the European Communities[3] put it:

> "The opportunities of shopping around which these arrangements offer to the policyholder or the injured person derive, so it is understood, from a theory that the policyholder is at a disadvantage compared with the insurer which needs to be compensated for by giving him a choice of forum. This accords with what appears to be a general policy of the Community at the present time to try to protect people who it seems are thought to be at some disadvantage in business affairs. There seems little reason to suppose that this sort of disadvantage prevails in international insurance transactions."

The special position of the United Kingdom did result in some changes to the Convention, but these were not of a very far-reaching character, and did not much mitigate the problems of forum-shopping to which the insurance provisions give rise.[4] The main changes were:

(1) where there are co-insurers, they can only be added in other proceedings if those proceedings are against the leading insurer;
(2) the jurisdiction based on the domicile of intermediaries such as brokers was removed;
(3) exclusive jurisdiction clauses are to be given full effect (*a*) where (subject to certain exceptions) the policyholder is not domiciled in a Contracting State; and (*b*) where the risk relates, broadly, to loss of or damage to ships, aircraft or cargoes.

---

[1] See 1968 Convention, Art. 6(3). On Art. 22, see pp. 97–98, post.
[2] See Schlosser, para. 136.
[3] Session 1976–7, 45th Report, para. 12, page 6.
[4] See Kerr (1978) 75 Law Soc Gaz 1190.

Summary

The broad effect of Arts. 7 to 12A is that the following courts will have jurisdiction[1] in insurance matters:[2]

A *Actions against insurer domiciled in a Contracting State*
   (1) the courts of the State of the insurer's domicile;[3]
   (2) the courts of the place of its branch, agency or other establishment in the case of a dispute arising out of the operations of the branch etc.;[4]
   (3) the courts of the place where the policy-holder is domiciled;[5]
   (4) if he is a co-insurer, the courts of the State in which proceedings are brought against the leading insurer;[6]
   (5) in respect of liability insurance and insurance of immovable property, the courts of the place where the harmful event occurred,[7] which as a result of the decision in Case 21/76: *Handelskwekerij GJ Bier BV v Mines de Potasse d'Alsace*[8] will be, at the option of the plaintiff (*a*) the place where the damage occurred or (*b*) the place of the event giving rise to the damage;
   (6) in third party claims by the insured in the case of liability insurance, the courts of the place where the insured has been sued, if the law of that place permits it;[9]
   (7) in the case of a counterclaim against the insurer, any court in which it has brought an action arising from the same contract or facts;[10]
   (8) the court on which exclusive jurisdiction has been conferred in favour of the policy-holder by agreement.[11]

B *Actions against insurer not domiciled in a Contracting State*
   The courts of any Contracting State which has jurisdiction under its own law;[12] unless the insurer has a branch, agency or other establishment and the dispute arises out of its operations, in which event the action must be brought in the State of the branch etc.[13]

---

[1] It is probable that the defendant can also confer jurisdiction on a court of Contracting State by submission under 1968 Convention, Art. 18, although it is not certain that the latter applies to cases covered by Section 3 of the Convention.

[2] Which do not include reinsurance contracts, see p. 71, n.1, post.

[3] 1968 Convention, Art. 8(1) (1). Here and elsewhere the date of determination of domicile is at the date of proceedings, except in Art. 12(3).

[4] 1968 Convention, Arts. 7, 5(5).

[5] 1968 Convention, Art. 8(1) (2).

[6] 1968 Convention, Art. 8(1) (3).

[7] 1968 Convention, Art. 9.

[8] Case 21/76: [1978] QB 708, [1976] ECR 1735, [1977] 1 CMLR 284.

[9] 1968 Convention, Art. 10(1).

[10] 1968 Convention, Arts. 11(2), 6(3).

[11] 1968 Convention, Art. 12(2).

[12] 1968 Convention, Arts. 7, 4(1).

[13] 1968 Convention, Art. 8(2).

C *Actions against policy-holder or insured domiciled in a Contracting State*
(1) the courts of his domicile;[1]
(2) in the case of a counterclaim against him, the courts of the place where the action is brought by him;[2]
(3) the courts of the place where a direct action has been brought against the insurer;[3]
(4) the courts of the place on which exclusive jurisdiction has been conferred by agreement:

    (a) if the agreement was entered into after the dispute arose;[4] or
    (b) if the policy-holder and insurer are both domiciled or habitually resident in that State at the time of conclusion of the contract;[5] or
    (c) if it relates to insurance relating to loss of or damage to ships, aircraft or cargoes.[6]

D *Actions against policy-holder or insured not domiciled in a Contracting State*
The courts of any Contracting State which has jurisdiction under its own law[7] or to which the parties have agreed to submit.[8]

Commentary

Policy-holder, insured and beneficiary. Section 3 of the Convention distinguishes between policy-holder, insured and beneficiary, so that (a) "policy-holder" is referred to alone in Arts. 8(1)(2), 12(3) and 12(4); (b) "insured" is referred to alone in Art. 10(1); (c) "policy-holder" and "insured" are referred to together in Art. 10(3); and (d) "policy-holder", "insured" and "beneficiary" are referred to together in Arts. 11 and 12(2). The purpose of these expressions is to distinguish between the original party to the contract of insurance ("preneur d'assurance") who may not necessarily be the same person as the insured or beneficiary.[9] The practical effect of these distinctions is considerable, particularly when the benefit of the policy is assigned or transmitted with goods, or when the beneficiary is different from the person who takes out the policy.

General scope. Article 7 provides that in insurance matters jurisdiction shall be determined by Section 3, without prejudice to Art. 4 (non-EEC domiciliaries) and Art. 5(5) (disputes arising out of the operations of a branch, etc.). "Insurance" is not defined, and there may be borderline areas in which, under the Convention,[10] whether a contract is one of insurance will be in doubt. In such cases, national courts (and ultimately, the European Court) will have to seek a

---

[1] 1968 Convention, Art. 11(1).
[2] 1968 Convention, Art. 11(2).
[3] 1968 Convention, Art. 10(3).
[4] 1968 Convention, Art. 12(1).
[5] 1968 Convention, Art. 12(3).
[6] 1968 Convention, Art. 12(5).
[7] 1968 Convention, Arts. 7, 4(1).
[8] 1968 Convention, Art. 12(4).
[9] Jenard, p. 31; Schlosser, para. 152.
[10] As under English law, see MacGillivray and Partington *Insurance Law* (7th edn. 1981), pp. 3 and 901; *Medical Defence Union v Department of Trade* [1980] Ch 82, [1979] 2 All ER 421.

Convention, rather than a national, definition. Reinsurance is not within the provisions of Section 3.[1] The effect of the reference in Art. 7 to Art. 4 is that where the *defendant* is not domiciled in a Contracting State, then national rules of jurisdiction apply, except where the defendant is an insurer and has a branch etc. in a Contracting State, and the dispute arises out of the operations of that branch.[2]

Article 8 provides that an insurer domiciled in a Contracting State may be sued: (1) in the courts of the State where he is domiciled, or (2) in another Contracting State, in the courts for the place where the policy-holder is domiciled, or (3) if he is a co-insurer, in the courts of a Contracting State in which proceedings are brought against the leading insurer. An insurer who is not domiciled in a Contracting State but has a branch, etc. in one of the Contracting States shall, in disputes arising out of the operations of the branch, etc. be deemed to be domiciled in that State. Section 44 of the 1982 Act provides that a person who, for the purposes of proceedings arising out of the operations of a branch, agency or other establishment in the United Kingdom, is deemed to be domiciled in the United Kingdom by virtue of Art. 8(2) shall be treated as domiciled in the United Kingdom, and as domiciled in the part of the United Kingdom in which the branch etc. is situate. The main changes made by the Accession Convention in Art. 8 were that: (1) previously if there were two or more insurers, the action could be brought where any one of them was domiciled and (2) an insurer could be sued in the Contracting State where the intermediary (such as a broker) was domiciled. The jurisdiction in favour of the policy-holder's domicile will allow an action in that place by the policy-holder but not also by the insured and the beneficiary if they are different from the policy-holder.[3] Article 8(1)(3) does not define leading insurer, and it does not impose an obligation for proceedings to be concentrated in one court, and there is nothing to prevent a policy-holder from suing the various co-insurers in different courts.[4] The effect of Arts. 7 and 8(2) is that an insurer may normally be sued at any place where it has a branch if the dispute arises from an insurance contract entered into at that branch, whether or not the insurer is domiciled in a Contracting State.

Arts. 9 and 10 confer additional bases of jurisdiction against insurers. In the case of liability insurance (i.e. insurance against legal liability to third parties), jurisdiction is conferred on the courts of the State where the harmful event occurred.[5] The relevant harmful event is the event which gives rise to the cause of action against the insured party—that place will be, at the option of the plaintiff, (i) the place where the damage occurred or (ii) the place of the event giving rise to the damage.[6] Jurisdiction is also conferred on the courts of the place in which the injured party has brought an action against the insured, if the lex fori permits joinder of the insurer.[7] This is designed to deal with third party

---

[1] Schlosser, para. 151; *Citadel Insurance Co v Atlantic Union Insurance Co SA* [1982] 2 Lloyd's Rep 543, CA at 549, per Kerr LJ.
[2] 1968 Convention, Art. 8(2).
[3] Cf. German Federal Supreme Court, May 2 1979 RIW/AWD 1979, 494.
[4] Schlosser, para. 149.
[5] 1968 Convention, Art. 9.
[6] Case 21/76: *Handelskwekerij GJ Bier BV v Mines de Potasse d'Alsace* [1978] QB 708, [1976] ECR 1735, [1977] 1 CMLR 284.
[7] 1968 Convention, Art. 10(1).

claims by the insured against the insurer;[1] it would apply even if the insurer and insured were domiciled in the same Contracting State, but it does not apply if the insurer and insured are bound by an exclusive jurisdiction clause validly conferring jurisdiction on another court under Art. 12. In the case of insurance of immovable property, jurisdiction is conferred on the courts of the State where the harmful event occurred.[2] This applies if movable and immovable property are covered by the same policy and both are affected by the same contingency, e.g. if a building and property in it are covered by the same policy.[3]

Article 10(2)–(3) deals with direct actions against insurers, which are found, at least to a limited extent, in most of the Contracting States.[4] The effect of Art. 10(2) is that these actions may only be brought in those places where the policy-holder could have brought proceedings pursuant to Arts. 7, 8 and 9. Jurisdiction is not therefore extended to the places where the injured party is domiciled, unless, for example, that is also the place where the policy-holder is domiciled.[5] Article 10(2) applies only "where such direct actions are permitted" under the lex fori, including its rules of private international law.[6] The policy-holder or insured may be joined "if the law governing such direct actions" provides for such joinder. The governing law in this context means, it seems, the law to which the private international law rules of the lex fori point. In England there is no clear answer to the applicable law. The view expressed in Dicey & Morris[7] and supported by Australian authority[8] is that the question of direct liability depends on the law governing the contract of insurance rather than on the rules applicable to torts. But what law governs the joinder of the policy-holder or insured to such proceedings may be a question purely of procedure for the lex fori. Where there is a jurisdiction agreement valid under Art. 12, Art. 10 (as between the parties to the agreement) is superseded by the agreement.[9]

Article 11, which is unchanged, provides that, without prejudice to the right granted by Art. 10(3) to join the policy-holder or insured in a direct action, an insurer may bring proceedings only in the courts of the Contracting State in which the defendant is domiciled, irrespective of whether the defendant is the policy-holder, the insured or a beneficiary, without prejudice to the right to bring a counterclaim in the court in which the original claim against the insurer is pending. This provision does not apply where the defendant is domiciled outside the Contracting States.[10]

Jurisdiction clauses. Clauses attributing jurisdiction to courts receive special treatment in Arts. 12 and 12A in the case of insurance contracts, and the general provisions of Art. 17 do not apply, although it is possible that the formal

---

[1] Jenard, p. 32. For the special position in Germany see Art. V of the 1968 Protocol: p. 67, n.2, ante.
[2] 1968 Convention, Art. 9.
[3] Jenard, p. 32.
[4] For the United Kingdom see Third Parties (Rights Against Insurers) Act 1930.
[5] Jenard, p. 32.
[6] Ibid.
[7] P. 960.
[8] *Plozza v South Australian Insurance Co Ltd* [1963] SASR 122.
[9] Schlosser, para. 148.
[10] Jenard, p. 33.

requirements of Art. 17 are applicable.[1] The position with regard to insurance contracts may be summarised as follows:

(1) if there is an *arbitration* agreement between the parties the case will be outside the scope of the Convention;[2]
(2) if there is a jurisdiction clause conferring jurisdiction on the courts of a particular State (perhaps even a non-Contracting State) then it will be given effect

    (*a*) in favour of a policy-holder, insured or beneficiary generally;[3]
    (*b*) in favour of the insurer only if

        (i) it is entered into after the dispute has arisen, or[4]
        (ii) the agreement is between a policy-holder and an insurer both domiciled[5] or habitually resident in the same Contracting State and which confers jurisdiction on the courts of that State,[6] or
        (iii) the agreement was concluded with a policy-holder not domiciled in a Contracting State, unless the insurance is compulsory or relates to immovable property in a Contracting State,[7] or
        (iv) it relates to one of the risks in Art. 12A.[8]

The main changes introduced by the Accession Convention in this Article were in the provisions concerning policyholders domiciled outside the Contracting States, and those concerning marine and aviation insurance, which were altered as a result of the concerns of the UK insurance industry. The following points are worthy of note: first, express agreements on choice of court after a dispute has arisen will not be common practice; second, the effect of Art. 12(2) is that an exclusive jurisdiction clause will always be effective for the benefit of a policy-holder, insured or beneficiary; third, the relevant time for testing the domicile or habitual residence of the insurer and the policy-holder under Art. 12(3) is the date of the contract, and not (as under the previous version) the date of commencement of the proceedings; fourth, Art. 12(4) applies where the policy-holder is not domiciled in a Contracting State, but there is an action by or against an insured or beneficiary in a Contracting State on a policy containing an exclusive jurisdiction clause. The conferment of jurisdiction is to be effective unless one of two exceptions is applicable: the first is where the insurance is compulsory, in which case no departure from the provisions of Arts. 8 to 11 is permitted, even if the policy-holder is domiciled outside the Contracting States.[9] The second exception is for insurance relating to immovable property, where the other applicable provisions (especially Art. 9) will continue to apply even if

---

[1] Cf. Maxwell Report, para. 5.93.
[2] 1968 Convention, Art. 1(2) (4).
[3] 1968 Convention, Art. 12(2).
[4] 1968 Convention, Art. 12(1).
[5] This may include an insurer not domiciled in a Contracting State but with a branch in a Contracting State in relation to a policy issued through that branch: 1968 Convention, Art. 8(2).
[6] 1968 Convention, Art. 12(3).
[7] 1968 Convention, Art. 12(4).
[8] 1968 Convention, Art. 12(5).
[9] See Schlosser, para. 138; e.g. aviation and motor vehicle insurance.

the national law of the State in which the immovable property is situated allows jurisdiction agreements.[1]

The risks set out in Art. 12A are (1) any loss of or damage to (*a*) ships,[2] offshore installations or aircraft, arising from perils relating to their use for commercial purposes or (*b*) goods in transit, other than passengers' baggage, where the transit consists of or includes carriage by ships or aircraft; (2) any liability, other than for bodily injury to passengers or loss of or damage to their baggage (*a*) arising out of the use or operation of ships, etc., (*b*) for loss or damage caused by goods in transit as above; (3) any financial loss connected with the use or operation of ships, etc., in particular loss of freight or charter hire; (4) any ancillary risk or interest connected with any of those referred to in (1) to (3) above.[3]

The practical effect of Art. 12 is that a United Kingdom insurer can effectively confer exclusive jurisdiction on the courts of the United Kingdom by the original insurance contract only in the following cases:

(1) where the policy-holder is domiciled in the United Kingdom at the time the insurance contract is entered into;[4] or

(2) where the policy-holder is not domiciled in any of the Contracting States at the time the insurance contract is entered into; or

(3) the insurance relates to one of the major risks set out in Art. 12A.

Articles 13 to 15: Jurisdiction over Consumer Contracts

Special provision was made in favour of consumers because there was special protection from them in the law of the original Contracting States.[5] The objectives of Section 4 of the Convention were inspired by a desire to protect consumers; national laws, by contrast, were designed partly to protect the "weaker" party, but also to serve economic, monetary and savings policy.[6] The European Court has emphasized[7] that "the compulsory jurisdiction provided for in the second paragraph of Article 14 of the Convention must, because it derogates from the general principles of the system laid down by the Convention in matters of contract, such as may be derived in particular from Articles 2 and 5(1), be strictly limited to the objectives proper to Section 4 of the said Convention. Those objectives, as enshrined in Article 13 and 14 of the Convention, were inspired solely by a desire to protect certain categories of buyers...".

The main change introduced into Section 4 by the Accession Convention was to make it clear that it applied only to consumer contracts, and not to all instalment sales and financing contracts irrespective of whether the buyer was

---

[1] Schlosser, para. 139: sed quaere.

[2] See Schlosser , para. 141 for the scope of this expression.

[3] See also Schlosser, paras. 141 to 147 for a discussion of 1968 Convention, Art. 12A, including its application to ships in the course of construction.

[4] But see Maxwell Report, para. 5.118 and Droz, para. 130.

[5] Jenard, p. 33.

[6] Case 150/77: *Société Bertrand v Paul Ott KG* [1978] ECR 1431, [1978] 3 CMLR 499.

[7] [1978] ECR at 1445.

a businessman rather than a private consumer. In *Société Bertrand v Paul Ott KG*[1] the European Court held, on the original wording of Section 4, that it applied only to private final consumers and not to those who were engaged, while buying the product, in trade or professional activities. This is confirmed by the new wording of Art. 13, which was influenced by the drafts of the European Obligations Convention, which makes special provision for choice of law in consumer contracts.[2]

Section 4 relates to proceedings concerning a contract concluded by a person for a purpose which can be regarded as being outside his trade or profession, "the consumer".[3] The Section applies to (1) contracts for the sale of goods on instalment credit terms; or (2) contracts for a loan repayable by instalments, or for any other form of credit, made to finance the sale of goods; or (3) any other contract for the supply of goods or a contract for the supply of services and where, in the State of the consumer's domicile, the conclusion of the contract was preceded by a specific invitation addressed to him or by advertising and the consumer took in that State the steps necessary for the conclusion of the contract.[4]

The meaning of sale of goods on "instalment credit terms" was considered in *Société Bertrand v Paul Ott KG*[5] where the European Court held that it was necessary to give the expression a Convention interpretation. It said:[6]

"... an attempt must be made to elaborate an independent concept of the contract of sale on instalment credit terms in view of the general principles which are apparent in this field from the body of laws of the Member States and bearing in mind the objective of the protection of a certain category of buyers. It is clear from the rules common to the laws of the Member States that the sale of goods on instalment credit terms is to be understood as a transaction in which the price is discharged by way of several payments or which is linked to a financing contract."

But the Section is not limited to instalment sales and instalment loans to finance them, and applies also to contracts for the supply of goods or services where there was an invitation to purchase (either specific or by advertising) and the consumer took the steps necessary to conclude the contract in the State of his domicile. The steps necessary to conclude the contract would seem to include buying by mail order (although in English law it is probable that it is the consumer who makes the offer and the seller who accepts) since Art. 13(1) (3) was intended to cover mail order and door-step selling[7] but may have much

---

[1] Case 150/77: [1978] ECR 1431, [1978] 3 CMLR 499.
[2] For text see Convention on the Law Applicable to Contractual Obligations, 19 June 1980, OJ L 266, 9 October 1980, and North (ed.) *Contract Conflicts* (1982), p. 347, and Giuliano—Lagarde Report, ibid., esp. at p. 377. See also Hague Convention of 1980 on the law applicable to certain consumer sales.
[3] 1968 Convention, Art. 13(1).
[4] 1968 Convention, Art. 13(1).
[5] Case 150/77: [1978] ECR 1431, [1978] 3 CMLR 499.
[6] At 1446.
[7] Cf. Giuliano-Lagarde, on the Obligations Convention, in *Contract Conflicts* (1982) (ed. North) at p. 378.

wider effects, e.g. where a French company places an advertisement in a United States publication which circulates in the United Kingdom.

The result of these provisions is that the following courts will have jurisdiction:[1]

A *Actions by consumer against supplier of goods or lender or supplier of services:*

    (1) the courts of the State of the defendant's domicile[2]

    (2) the courts of the State of the plaintiff's domicile;[3]

    (3) if the defendant is domiciled in a Contracting State and has a branch etc. within another Contracting State and the dispute arises out of its operations, the courts of the State in which the branch is situated;[4]

    (4) if the defendant is domiciled outside the Contracting States, but has a branch etc. within a Contracting State and the dispute arises out of its operations, the courts of the State where the branch etc. is situate;[5]

    (5) if the defendant is domiciled outside the Contracting States and has no branch etc. within them[6] then any court which has jurisdiction under national law;[7]

    (6) in the case of a counterclaim against the supplier etc., any court in which it has brought an action arising from the same contract or facts;[8]

    (7) a court chosen by a jurisdiction agreement allowed under Art. 15.

B *Actions by supplier etc. or lender against consumer:*

    (1) the courts of the consumer's domicile (Art. 14(2));

    (2) a court chosen by a jurisdiction agreement allowed under Art. 15;

    (3) if the consumer is domiciled outside the Contracting States, any court which has jurisdiction under national law;[9]

    (4) in the case of a counterclaim against the consumer, any court in which it has brought an action arising from the same contract or facts.[10]

Jurisdiction Agreements

The jurisdiction provisions of Section 4 may be departed from only by an agreement[11] (1) which is entered into after the dispute has arisen or (2) which

---

[1] It is probable that the defendant can also confer jurisdiction on a court of a Contracting State by submission under 1968 Convention, Art. 18, although it is not certain that the latter applies to Section 4 of the Convention.

[2] 1968 Convention, Art. 14(1).

[3] 1968 Convention, Art. 14(1). If the consumer is domiciled in the United Kingdom, then action must be brought in the courts of that part of the United Kingdom in which he is domiciled: 1982 Act, s. 10(3).

[4] 1968 Convention, Art. 13(1), Art. 5(5).

[5] 1968 Convention, Art. 13(2). See 1982 Act, s. 44(2), which gives effect to Art. 13(2).

[6] Or it has a branch but the dispute does not relate to its operations.

[7] 1968 Convention, Art. 13(1), Art. 4.

[8] 1968 Convention, Art. 14(3); cf. Art. 6(3).

[9] 1968 Convention, Art. 13(1), Art. 4.

[10] 1968 Convention, Art. 14(3), Art. 6(3).

[11] Which must, it seems, comply with the formal requirements of 1968 Convention, Art. 17: see Schlosser, para. 161a.

allows the consumer to bring proceedings in courts other than those indicated in the Section or (3) which is entered into when the consumer and the other party are both domiciled or habitually resident in the same Contracting State and which confers jurisdiction on the courts of that State, provided that such an agreement is not contrary to the law of that State.[1] The relevant date for testing domicile is that of the commencement of proceedings, subject to two points: first, if the Section applies because of Art. 13(1) (3) (advertising in the State of the consumer's domicile) then it will also be necessary to determine the consumer's domicile at the time of the conclusion of the contract; second, if there is a jurisdiction agreement which is to be upheld under Art. 15(3) it will be necessary to consider the party's domicile at the date of the conclusion of the contract.

Although the conferment of jurisdiction on the courts of the plaintiff-consumer's domicile may appear at first sight very far-reaching, the practical effect of these provisions in the United Kingdom is not likely to be very marked; except perhaps in relation to the Republic of Ireland, sales of goods to consumers in other Contracting States (or purchases by United Kingdom consumers from other Contracting States) must rarely be on the credit terms which Art. 13 contemplates. Only the provisions relating to cross-frontier advertising are likely to be of any practical importance, and even they will only be applicable to confer jurisdiction on the courts of the plaintiff-consumer in another Contracting State in actions against United Kingdom companies in the case where the United Kingdom company advertises abroad, contracts directly with the consumer in that country, and yet has no branch there: this must be an unusual situation.[2] Where, however, the Convention applies it will supersede any national law, such as s. 141 of the Consumer Credit Act 1974.[3]

Article 16: Exclusive Jurisdiction

Article 16 grants exclusive jurisdiction to specified courts in relation to certain subject matters. Article 4, which remits questions of jurisdiction to national law if the defendant is not domiciled in a Contracting State, is expressly subject to Art. 16, and these heads of exclusive jurisdiction apply whether or not the defendant is domiciled in a Contracting State. These rules of exclusive jurisdiction apply even if the parties have purported by agreement to grant jurisdiction to another court or have submitted to the jurisdiction of another court. Their importance is underlined by the fact that failure to observe these rules is a ground for non-recognition (under Arts. 28 and 34) of any resulting judgment. Because it is an exception to the general domicile rule of the Convention, Art. 16 is to be construed strictly. The European Court said:[4]

"... the assignment, in the interests of the proper administration of justice,

---

[1] 1968 Convention, Art. 15.
[2] Where the defendant has a branch in that other Contracting State 1968 Convention, Art. 5(5) applies.
[3] Not yet in force. See Case 25/79: *Sanicentral GmbH v Collin* [1979] ECR 3423, [1980] 2 CMLR 164.
[4] In Case 73/77: *Sanders v Van Der Putte* [1977] ECR 2383 at 2391.

of exclusive jurisdiction to the courts of one Contracting State in accordance with Article 16 of the Convention results in depriving the parties of the choice of the forum which would otherwise be theirs, and, in certain cases, results in their being brought before a court which is not that of the domicile of any of them. Having regard to that consideration the provisions of Article 16 must not be given a wider interpretation than is required by their objective."

It should be noted that there are circumstances in which it is possible that the courts of more than one Contracting State will have exclusive jurisdiction. This may arise particularly under Art. 16(2) where exclusive jurisdiction is given to the courts of the seat of a company; because of the differing approaches to the "seat" of a company, its seat may be situated in more than one Contracting State. In such cases Art. 23 provides that where actions come within the exclusive jurisdiction of several courts, any court other than the first seised shall decline jurisdiction.

Immovable property

Article 16(1) provides that in proceedings which have as their object rights in rem in, or tenancies of, immovable property, the courts of the Contracting State in which the property is situated have exclusive jurisdiction. The basic principle of Art. 16(1) is found in the law of most countries.[1] Thus in French law actions relating to immovable property situated abroad are recognised exceptions to the provisions in Arts. 14 and 15 of the French Civil Code, with the result that the French courts cannot take jurisdiction on the basis of the French nationality of the plaintiff or the defendant if the action relates to land in the United States.[2] Adopting Jenard[3] the European Court justified Art. 16(1):[4]

"... actions concerning rights *in rem* in immovable property are to be judged according to the rules of the State in which the immovable property is situated since the disputes which arise result frequently in checks, inquiries and expert assessments which must be carried out on the spot, with the result that the assignment of exclusive jurisdiction satisfies the need for the proper administration of justice. Tenancies of immovable property are generally governed by special rules and it is preferable, in the light of their complexity, that they be applied only by the courts of the States in which they are in force."

Put shortly, the lex situs is paramount both from the point of view of convenience of evidence and from the fact that its law will apply.

It is clear that the way in which Art. 16(1) is worded will not make it easy to apply in the United Kingdom context. The expression "proceedings which have as their object rights in rem in, or tenancies of, immovable property" does not fit with any existing concepts of property law in the United Kingdom. Its origin

---

[1] See Dicey v Morris, p. 538; Wolff *Private International Law* (2nd edn. 1950), p. 92.
[2] Loussouarn & Bourel *Droit International Privé* (2nd edn. 1980), para. 464.
[3] P. 35.
[4] Case 73/77: *Sanders v Van Der Putte* [1977] ECR 2383, at 2390–1.

owes more to French law[1] which has a well-established notion of "actions réels immobiliers", actions involving title to immovables (but not actions of a contractual nature which involve title to land).[2] Leases of immovables were specifically included in Art 16(1) because in French law a lease is a personal and not a real right. But what are immovables, or what actions have as their object rights in rem in, or tenancies of, immovable property will not be a matter for national law, but must be determined by interpretation of a uniform concept.[3] This is implicit in the decision of the European Court in *Sanders v Van der Putte*[4] where it was held that a dispute over the lease of a florist business in a shop was not within Art. 16(1), because the principal aim of the lease was the operation of the business. There are several questions with regard to category of "proceedings which have as their object rights in rem in .... immovable property". The expression is clearly aimed at actions involving title or possession. Thus, it does not include an action for damages caused to an immovable.[5] Nor is it concerned, it seems, with an action concerning the purely contractual aspects of a property transaction, e.g. an action for the payment of damages for failure to complete a purchase[6] or even an action for specific performance.[7] Thus if two Englishmen agree on the sale of a house in France from one to the other, one could sue the other in England for failure to complete or for an order requiring completion, but they would have to go to the French courts if an order for possession was required. It is not easy to fit equitable rights into the scheme of Art. 16(1), but equitable interests equivalent to property rights in immovables will fall within Art. 16(1) if the action is designed to vindicate them as against the world.[8]

As regards leases, which have contractual as well as proprietary aspects, in *Sanders v Van der Putte*[9] the European Court held that the fact that there is a dispute as to the existence of a lease did not of itself prevent the application of Art. 16. As to the scope of the application of Art. 16(1) to leases, it is clear that Art. 16(1) would include actions for forfeiture or possession by landlords but there is considerable doubt as to whether it gives exclusive jurisdiction where the claim is of a contractual rather than a proprietary nature. It includes disputes between landlord and tenant over the existence and interpretation of tenancy

---

[1] In the French version of 1968 Convention, Art. 16 the expression reads, "en matière de droits réels immobiliers et de baux d'immeubles".

[2] Cf. *Intpro Properties (UK) Ltd v Sauvel* [1983] 2 All ER 495, [1983] 2 WLR 908, CA, for meaning of "real actions" in the context of the Vienna Convention on Diplomatic Relations.

[3] Schlosser, para. 168, expresses a different view.

[4] Case 73/77 [1977] ECR 2383, [1978] 1 CMLR 331.

[5] Schlosser, para. 163; cf. 1982 Act, s. 30, abolishing the rule (except where the proceedings are principally concerned with a question of title or possession) that English courts have no jurisdiction to entertain actions for trespass to, or any other tort affecting, foreign land: see Chapter 7, p. 139, post.

[6] Cf. *Société Civile Immobilière de Bourgogne v Raat*, Amsterdam 1975, Eur Court Digest D I-16.1-B2.

[7] According to Schlosser, paras. 169–172, in cases where there is a distinction between contract and conveyance, such as England and Germany (in contrast to France, Belgium and Italy), an action based on contracts for the transfer of ownership would not have as their object rights in rem. Cf. the rule that actions to enforce a contract relating to foreign land may be heard in English courts: Dicey & Morris, p. 541. But the Italian Court of Cassation appears to have proceeded on the basis that an action concerning a contract to exchange land was not within the scope of 1968 Convention, Art. 16(1): *Theunissen v Luz* [1981] I Foro It 1607; [1981] ELD 440.

[8] Schlosser, para. 167.

[9] Case 73/77: [1977] ECR 2383; cf. Case 38/81: *Effer SpA v Kantner* [1982] ECR 825.

agreements and claims for compensation for damage caused by a tenant,[1] but the position with regard to actions purely for rent is unclear. The view that an action purely for rent is not within Art. 16(1) is expressed by Jenard[2] and was supported in the submissions of the UK Government and of the European Commission in *Sanders v Van der Putte*, but the point was not discussed by the Court, and Advocate General Mayras took a different view.[3] The point was not resolved in the accession negotiations because of disagreement on it in the Working Party.[4] Schlosser[5] suggests that the underlying principle of Art. 16(1) does not require its application to short-term agreements for use and occupation such as, for example, holiday accommodation. Whether it will apply to disputes relating to "time-sharing" of properties will depend on the nature of the arrangements, which vary from co-ownership at one end to company share schemes at the other: the former may fall within Art. 16(1), but probably not the latter.

If the defendant is not domiciled in one of the Contracting States and the immovable is situated outside the Contracting States, Art. 16 probably has no application and the national courts may apply their own jurisdictional rules.[6] But if the land is situate outside the Contracting States and the defendant is domiciled in a Contracting State, then it would seem that the defendant can be sued in that Contracting State pursuant to Art. 2 despite the policy in most national systems and expressed in Art. 16 that cases involving title to property must be brought in the courts of the place where the property is situate. To avoid this result it has been suggested[7] that the court of the Contracting State should decline to exercise jurisdiction in such a case, but, although desirable, it is not easy to justify this result under the present Convention scheme.

Companies

Article 16(2) provides that in proceedings which have as their object the validity of the constitution, the nullity or the dissolution of companies or other legal persons or associations of natural or legal persons, or the decisions of their organs, the courts of the Contracting State in which the company, legal person or association has its seat shall have exclusive jurisdiction. Article 16(2) does not itself indicate how the seat is to be determined, but Art. 53[8] provides that in order to determine the seat of a company, the court seised shall apply its rules of private international law. In the United Kingdom this is effected by s. 43 of the

---

[1] *Sanders v Van der Putte* at 2391.

[2] P. 35. A similar problem arose in relation to RSC Ord. 11, r. 1(1)(*b*) (to be replaced by para. (*g*)): see Dicey & Morris, p. 200.

[3] [1978] ECR at 2397; see also Droz, para. 150; LG Aachen, 1975, Eur Court Digest D I-16.1-B1.

[4] Schlosser, para. 164.

[5] Ibid.

[6] Pursuant to 1968 Convention, Art. 4.

[7] Droz, paras. 165–169; Maxwell Report, para. 5.159–160. Cf. Rotterdam 1978, 1981 Neths Int L Rev 75.

[8] Which primarily concerns the seat of a company for the purposes of its domicile, but applies also to the determination of a seat for the purposes of 1968 Convention, Art. 16(2): Jenard, p. 57; Schlosser, para. 162.

1982 Act, which provides for the purposes of Art. 16(2) that a corporation or association has its seat in the United Kingdom if, and only if, (a) it was incorporated or formed under the law of a part of the United Kingdom or (b) its central management and control is exercised in the United Kingdom (s. 43(2)).[1] By s. 43(6) it will have its seat in a Contracting State other than the United Kingdom if and only if (a) it was incorporated or formed under the law of that State or (b) its central management and control is exercised in that State; but it will not be regarded as having its seat in another Contracting State if (a) it was incorporated or formed under the law of the United Kingdom; or (b) that other Contracting State would not regard it as having its seat there.[2] Thus under the 1982 Act:

(1) a company incorporated under the Companies Acts 1948 to 1981 with its registered office in England, but with its central management and control in France, will be regarded in the United Kingdom as having its seat exclusively in England;[3]

(2) a company incorporated in the Netherlands with its central management and control in England will be regarded as having its seat in England, and also in the Netherlands if by Netherlands law its seat is in the Netherlands;[4]

(3) a French company with its central management and control in the Netherlands, will be regarded as having its seat both in France and in the Netherlands, provided that by the laws of France and the Netherlands respectively it has its seat in that country;[5]

(4) a Bermudian company with its central management and control in England will be regarded as having its seat in England;[6]

(5) a Bermudian company with its central management and control in France will be regarded as having its seat in France, if by French law its seat is situate there.[7]

The purpose of Art. 16(2) is to avoid conflicting judgments being given as regards the existence of a company or with regard to the validity of the decisions of its organs, and it is therefore preferable that all proceedings should take place in the courts of the State in which the company has its seat, where information about the company will have been notified and made public.[8] Schlosser suggests that it applies to partnerships established under United Kingdom law,[9] but there is room for doubt as regards English partnerships.[10]

Problems relating to the dissolution of insolvent companies are part of the law of bankruptcy and are outside the scope of Art. 16(2); but problems relating to

---

[1] Provision is made for allocation within the United Kingdom of jurisdiction in 1982 Act, s. 43(3)–(5). "Association" means an unincorporated body of persons, and corporation means a body corporate, and includes a partnership subsisting under Scots law: 1982 Act, s. 50.
[2] 1982 Act, s. 43(7).
[3] 1982 Act, ss. 43(2), (3), (7).
[4] 1982 Act, ss. 43(2), (3), (6), (7).
[5] 1982 Act, ss. 43(6), (7).
[6] 1982 Act, ss. 43(2), (3).
[7] 1982 Act, ss. 43(6), (7).
[8] Jenard, p. 35.
[9] Para. 162.
[10] P. 42, ante.

the dissolution of solvent companies, including the rights of contributories, would be within Art. 16(2).[1] But an action for negligence against directors, even if it involved the decisions of the board, would not be subject to the special rules of Art. 16(2) but to the general Convention rules; a proceeding by a liquidator against directors for misfeasance would be excluded by Art. 1.[2] Actions concerning the interpretation of Articles of Association, such as those relating to restrictions on transfer of shares, would not be within Art. 16(2),[3] unless perhaps the action related to the validity of a board decision to refuse to register a transfer. But an action to declare a contract void on the ground that it was outside the powers of the board[4] might be within Art. 16(2).

Public registers

Article 16(3) deals with proceedings which have as their object the validity of entries in public registers, and assigns exclusive jurisdiction to the courts of the Contracting State in which the register is kept. It corresponds to the provisions which appear in the internal laws of the original Contracting States and covers entries in land registers, land charges registers and commercial registers.[5] In the United Kingdom it is not likely to be of practical significance except in connection with problems relating to registered land, which would in any event come within the provisions of Art. 16(1).

Industrial property rights

Article 16(4) assigns exclusive jurisdiction in proceedings concerned with registration or validity of patents, trademarks, designs or other similar rights required to be deposited or registered, to the courts of the Contracting State in which the deposit or registration has been applied for, has taken place or is under the terms of an international convention deemed to have taken place. Article VD of the Protocol, which was added by the Accession Convention, provides, broadly, that the courts of each Contracting State are to have jurisdiction in proceedings concerned with the registration or validity of any European patent granted for that State, provided it is not a "Community patent" which, if instituted, will be valid for the whole Community.[6]

Article 16(4)[7] applies to proceedings concerned with the registration or validity of patents and other industrial property rights (including applications

---

[1] Schlosser, paras. 57–58. See Art. 1, pp. 27–28, ante.

[2] See p. 28, ante.

[3] Cf. Maxwell Report, para. 5. 169.

[4] E.g. as in *Rolled Steel Products (Holdings) Ltd v British Steel Corpn* [1982] Ch 478, [1982] 3 All ER 1057.

[5] Jenard, p. 35.

[6] For the system of European Patents and Community Patents, see Terrell, *Patents* (13th edn. 1982), pp. 6–10.

[7] The terms used in 1968 Convention, Art. 16(4), should, it seems, be given a Convention, rather than a purely national, interpretation; the question arises in Case 288/82: *Duijnstee v Goderbauer*, pending.

for revocation), but other actions, including those for infringement[1] are governed by the general rules of the Convention, e.g. the domicile of the defendant or the place of the wrong.[2] Similarly, with regard to trade marks, Art. 16(4) does not apply to passing off actions nor does it apply to actions concerning licence agreements.[3]

Enforcement of judgments

Article 16(5) assigns jurisdiction, in proceedings concerned with the enforcement of judgments, exclusively to the courts of the Contracting State in which judgment has been or is to be enforced.[4] This is not as restrictive as the French notion that all matters relating to execution are within the exclusive jurisdiction of the State where enforcement is to take place.[5] Thus, for example, where execution in France is contemplated, an English court may examine an Englishman against whom an English judgment has been given on his assets in France under RSC Ord. 48, r. 1.[6] It is therefore not likely to be of great practical importance in England, but it may have the effect of preventing an English court from enjoining the enforcement of a judgment in the courts of another Contracting State.[7]

Articles 17 and 18: Prorogation of Jurisdiction

Exclusive jurisdiction agreements

Article 17 sets out the circumstances in which a contractual agreement on jurisdiction will be effective to confer exclusive jurisdiction on the courts of a Contracting State. The effect of the present version of Art. 17, substituted by the Accession Convention, is as follows:

(a) There must be an agreement between the parties, one or more of whom is domiciled in a Contracting State. A sentence added by the Accession Convention provides that where the agreement is between parties none of whom is domiciled in the Contracting State, the courts of other Contracting States have no jurisdiction over their disputes unless the court or courts chosen have declined jurisdiction.

(b) There must be an agreement that a court or the courts of a Contracting State are to have jurisdiction to settle any disputes which have arisen, or which may arise, in connection with a particular legal relationship—in such cases that court or those courts shall have exclusive jurisdiction.

(c) There must be an agreement in writing or evidenced in writing or, in international trade or commerce, in a form which accords with the practices in that trade or commerce of which the parties are or ought to

---

[1] Which in the United Kingdom often involve questions of validity.
[2] See Jenard, p. 36; Schlosser, para. 173; Maxwell Report, para. 5.173.
[3] *Contra, Société Salik v Martin*, Paris 1980, 1982 Rev Crit 135, note Bonet.
[4] See Jenard, p. 36.
[5] On which see Loussouarn & Bourel, para. 448, op. cit. p. 78, n.2.
[6] Cf. OLG Nürnberg, 1974 and 1976. Eur Court Digest D I-16.5-B1 & B2.
[7] Cf. *Ellerman Lines Ltd v Read* [1928] 2 KB 144, CA.

have been aware. The previous version merely referred to an agreement in writing or an oral agreement evidenced in writing.

(d) Agreements conferring jurisdiction have no legal force if they are contrary to the provisions of Art. 12 or 15 (insurance and consumer contracts) or if the courts whose jurisdiction they purport to exclude have exclusive jurisdiction by virtue of Art. 16.

(e) If an agreement conferring jurisdiction was concluded for the benefit of only one of the parties, that party shall retain the right to bring proceedings in any other court which has jurisdiction by virtue of the Convention.

Special provision is made for trust instruments, and Art 17(2), which is entirely new, provides that the court or courts of a Contracting State on which a trust instrument has conferred jurisdiction shall have exclusive jurisdiction in any proceedings brought against a settlor, trustee or beneficiary, if relations between these persons or their rights or obligations under the trust are involved. This was added because they need not be contained in bilateral agreements.

Where a jurisdiction clause is effective under Art. 17, the court chosen does not have a discretion whether to exercise its discretion, and other courts cannot override the choice of that court. In English law, a clause conferring jurisdiction on the English courts will be effective to give them jurisdiction[1] and a question of discretion will normally only arise if the contract does not provide for service in England.[2] Where a clause confers jurisdiction on a foreign tribunal, English proceedings in breach of the agreement will be stayed, unless the plaintiff proves that it is just for them to continue.[3]

The scope of Article 17

There has been much discussion of the question whether Art. 17 applies in a case where two persons domiciled in the same Contracting State choose the courts of that State as the exclusive forum for their disputes. According to Jenard, this is a purely domestic case without international character and Art. 17 (and indeed the Convention as a whole) has no application.[4] But the better view is that it does apply[5] at least if there is some foreign element in the case.[6] This is the better view because the domicile of the parties is only one of several bases of jurisdiction and the domicile of the parties may change so as to cause the original choice of jurisdiction to have a real practical effect. A similar problem arises when two persons domiciled in one Contracting State seek to confer exclusive jurisdiction on the courts of another State, e.g. two Frenchmen agree that the English courts shall have exclusive jurisdiction. According to

---

[1] Dicey & Morris, p. 191.

[2] Dicey & Morris, p. 225. But it is difficult to imagine circumstances in which the court would exercise its discretion not to assume jurisdiction in such a case.

[3] Dicey & Morris, p. 255; *Evans Marshall & Co Ltd v Bertola SA* [1973] 1 All ER 992, [1973] 1 WLR 349, CA. The position is similar in the United States: *M/S Bremen v Zapata Off-Shore Co.* (1972) 407 US 1, discussed by Collins (1971) 20 ICLQ 550, (1973) 22 ICLQ 332.

[4] Pp. 37–38. Cf. Schlosser, para. 174.

[5] Weser, p. 314.

[6] Droz, paras. 187 to 191.

Jenard, Art. 17 applies to this case[1] but this is not free from doubt; nor is the question whether there must be a genuine link with the chosen court.

Special provision has now been made in Art. 17 for jurisdiction agreements concluded by parties none of whom is domiciled in a Contracting State but which confer jurisdiction on the courts of a Contracting State. The effect is to be that other courts will have no jurisdiction unless the court or courts chosen decline jurisdiction. This will be of considerable practical importance in relation to the United Kingdom, on whose courts foreigners commonly confer jurisdiction. It will not require United Kingdom courts to take jurisdiction but if they are prepared to, then courts of other Contracting States will not have jurisdiction and any resulting judgment will be enforceable throughout the Contracting States.[2] Where parties domiciled within the Contracting States purport to confer jurisdiction on the courts of a non-Contracting State, the position is uncertain. If an English company and a German company confer jurisdiction on the courts of New York, plainly the New York court may take jurisdiction, but will (say) the English court be prevented from taking jurisdiction if the German company sues in England (as the English company's domicile) or the English company sues there (as e.g. the place of performance)? It seems that the English court may apply its normal rules and either give effect to the choice of New York jurisdiction or override it according to whether the plaintiff is able to show that it is just and convenient that the proceedings should be fought in England.[3]

Although Art. 17 speaks of submission to "a court or courts of *a* Contracting State" it also applies if the courts of more than one Contracting State are contemplated by the contract. In *Meeth v Glacetal Sarl*[4] a contract provided that if a German buyer were to sue a French seller, the French courts alone should have jurisdiction, and if the French seller were to sue the German buyer the German courts alone would have jurisdiction. The French seller sued the German buyer in Germany, in accordance with the jurisdiction clause, for failure to pay for deliveries. The European Court held, in response to a request from the German Federal Supreme Court, that, although Art. 17 referred to a court in the singular, it could not be interpreted as intended to exclude the right to agree on two or more courts in a form which was based on widespread commercial practice.[5] It is not clear whether this decision would justify the effectiveness of such clauses as "the parties agree to the jurisdiction of the courts of England and France" or "the parties agree to the non-exclusive jurisdiction of the courts of England". Both of these are "non-exclusive" in the sense that they allow actions in more than one State, and they do not fit easily into the framework of Art. 17. Art. 17(4) provides that if the jurisdiction agreement has been concluded for the benefit of only one of the parties, that party retains the right to sue in any other court which has jurisdiction under the Convention. So that if a contract provides

---

[1] P. 38; Maxwell Report, para. 5.181.
[2] Schlosser, para. 177.
[3] Cf. Schlosser, para. 176.
[4] Case 23/78: [1978] ECR 2133, [1979] 1 CMLR 520.
[5] See also *Société Schumacher v Société Technic-Equipement*, French Cour de Cassation 1980, 1981 Rev Crit 131, note Gaudemet-Tallon.

that all claims by A against B shall be brought in the courts of B's domicile, B may sue A in the courts of A's domicile under the general rules.[1]

Formal requirements

The main change in Art. 17 introduced by the Accession Convention was the amendment of the requirement that the jurisdiction agreement be "in writing or evidenced in writing" by the addition of "or, in international trade or commerce, in a form which accords with practices in that trade or commerce of which the parties are or ought to have been aware". This change was introduced because the requirement of writing, particularly as interpreted by the European Court, was contrary to the needs and practices of international commerce, where communication by telex and the use of printed conditions are everyday practice; in particular, the original wording had led to several German and Belgian decisions that bills of lading incorporating jurisdiction clauses in charterparties were ineffective under Art. 17,[2] and to many decisions refusing to give effect to printed conditions of sale or purchase which had not been signed by the defendant. The new wording will render largely obsolete two decisions of the European Court;[3] in the former it was held that general conditions of sale containing a jurisdiction clause on the back of a contract signed by both parties were not sufficient without an express reference in the contract to the general conditions to give jurisdiction under Art. 17; and that in the case of a contract concluded by reference to earlier offers, which were themselves made with reference to the general conditions of one of the parties including a clause conferring jurisdiction, the requirement of writing was satisfied only if the reference was *express*. In the latter case it was held that in the case of an oral contract the requirements of Art. 17(1) were satisfied only if the vendor's confirmation in writing accompanied by notification of the general conditions of sale had been accepted *in writing* by the purchaser; and that the fact that the purchaser did not raise any objection against the confirmation issued unilaterally by the vendor did not amount to acceptance on the purchaser's part of the clause conferring jurisdiction, unless the oral agreement came within the framework of a continuing trading relationship between the parties which was based on the general conditions of one of them, and those conditions contained a clause conferring jurisdiction.[4] Although the expressions in Art. 17 discussed in these cases are still in Art. 17, each of these cases is typically a case of international trade where forms were used in accordance with practices of which the parties would be aware. Problems of general conditions may still arise in relation to

---

[1] See on this provision OLG München, January 29, 1980 RIW/AWD 1982, 281.
[2] See, e.g. OLG Düsseldorf, 1975, Eur Court Digest D-I.17.1.2-B3; German Federal Supreme Court, 26 October 1981 NJW 1982, 1228; *NV R v A* Antwerp, 1979 [1981] ELD 461.
[3] Case 24/76: *Estasis Salotti v RÜWA* [1976] ECR 1831, [1977] 1 CMLR 345 and Case 25/76: *Galeries Segoura Sprl v Bonakdarian* [1976] ECR 1851, [1977] 1 CMLR 361. These decisions have been applied in many national decisions.
[4] See Collins, *The Jurisdiction and Judgments Convention—Practical Aspects of United Kingdom Accession, with particular reference to jurisdiction, in Harmonisation of Private International Law by the EEC* (ed. Lipstein, 1978), p. 91.

non-traders but many of them would fall within the very restrictive provisions of Art. 15 rather than Art. 17.

It seems that the parties by agreeing orally the place of performance can achieve an object very similar to that of a choice of court under Art. 17. In *Zelger v Salinitri*[1] the plaintiff was a Munich merchant and the defendant was a merchant in Sicily. The plaintiff alleged an express oral agreement that Munich was to be the place of performance for repayment, and the German Federal Supreme Court asked whether the informal agreement was sufficient to found jurisdiction under Art. 5(1) or whether the form in Art. 17 was necessary. It was held that an informal agreement was sufficient. The European Court contrasted Art. 5(1) and Art. 17, and held that the jurisdiction of the court for the place of performance and that of the selected court were two distinct concepts and only agreements selecting a court were subject to the requirements of form prescribed by Art. 17 of the Convention. It is possible that such an agreement will only be effective under Art. 5(1) if it is not a sham.[2]

In relation to Luxembourg domiciliaries there is a special provision which is more restrictive than Art. 17. Art. 1 of the Protocol annexed to the 1968 Convention provides that an agreement conferring jurisdiction, within the meaning of Art. 17, shall be valid with respect to a person domiciled in Luxembourg "only if that person has expressly and specifically so agreed". In *Porta-Leasing GmbH v Prestige International SA*[3] the European Court held that the aim of the Protocol could only be achieved if the clause had been accepted both expressly and specifically, and it therefore must be contained in a provision which is specially and exclusively devoted to jurisdiction, and the clause itself must be signed. It is difficult to justify the continued special treatment of Luxembourg domiciliaries.[4] This decision shows that special care has to be taken in the preparation and execution of contracts with Luxembourg domiciliaries.

Consensus, choice of law and validity

Article 17 requires that there be a consensus in a particular form, but it gives no guidance[5] to the national court as to how to determine whether a consensus exists. The problem can arise in a number of contexts: there may be conflicting conditions of sale and purchase, each specifying a different court as the court of exclusive jurisdiction; or one party may claim that the agreement, including the jurisdiction clause, is not binding on it because of mistake or uncertainty of terms; or because it was entered into because of the other party's misrepresentation or through duress. The solution may be different in each of these contexts.

Where there are conflicting conditions, e.g. of purchase and sale, each providing for the exclusive jurisdiction of the courts of a different country, the *lex fori* will have to apply its own rules, including its rules of private international law, to

---

[1] Case 56/79: [1980] ECR 89, [1980] 2 CMLR 635.
[2] See p. 56, ante.
[3] Case 784/79: [1980] ECR 1517, [1981] 1 CMLR 135.
[4] See Lagarde, 1981 Rev Crit 339.
[5] Nor does Schlosser, para. 179.

determine which (if either) of the conflicting conditions is to be regarded as the contractual term. If England is the *lex fori*, and is also one of the chosen fora, then it would seem that the question will be answered by the law which would be the proper law of the contract if it had been validly concluded,[1] although the determination of that law would be particularly difficult in the case of conflicting conditions.

An even more difficult problem arises if an alleged agreement contains a jurisdiction clause and one of the parties denies that it is binding on him, on the ground of (say) mistake, or misrepresentation. Thus England may be the forum in one of two different situations: the parties may have chosen the English courts as the courts with exclusive jurisdiction, but the defendant may deny the validity of the jurisdiction clause; or the parties may have chosen the courts of another Contracting State, and the plaintiff may be suing in England in breach of the jurisdiction clause, claiming that the contract is void. In each case it is plain that the English court, as the forum, must decide the question of the validity of the clause. Where the chosen court is a foreign court, and where the issue relates, not to a question of consensus, but to the continued existence of a contract, the authorities on arbitration clauses and jurisdiction clauses suggest that the English court would decline jurisdiction and leave the question to the chosen tribunal, in effect treating the jurisdiction clause as an independent agreement.[2] Where the issue is one of consensus, the English court will probably apply the putative proper law, although the question is not free from doubt.[3]

In *Eléfanten Schuh GmbH v Jacqmain*[4] Advocate General Slynn suggested that these questions should be decided, not by the private international law rules of the *lex fori* (which may point to the law of the forum, or to the law of the chosen court, or to some other law) but by the internal law of the chosen forum. It is submitted that this solution will not give an answer where there are conflicting clauses; nor would it be just to apply the law of the chosen court in all cases where one of the parties is vigorously protesting that it has not agreed to that jurisdiction. The only solution which is capable of supplying a general answer is that questions of validity must be determined by the law of the court seised with the problem of validity, including its rules of private international law.

It is clear, however, that national law cannot invalidate agreements which would otherwise come within Art. 17. *Sanicentral GmbH v Collin*[5] was an action in a French court by a French employee against a German employer. The contract had been entered into in October 1971 and terminated in December 1971. The work was to be done in Germany, and the defendant argued that the contract of employment contained an exclusive jurisdiction clause conferring jurisdiction on the local German court. By French law[6] a clause in an employment contract of this kind was invalid. The French Cour de Cassation

---

[1] Dicey & Morris, p. 775. Perhaps only on a prima facie basis: see pp. 53–54, ante.

[2] See Mustill & Boyd, *Commercial Arbitration* (1982) pp. 78–81; *Heyman v Darwins Ltd* [1942] AC 356, [1942] 1 All ER 337; *Mackender v Feldia AG* [1967] 2 QB 590, [1966] 3 All ER 847, CA.

[3] Dicey & Morris, p. 775.

[4] Case 150/80: [1980] ECR 1671, at 1697–9. See also Hartley (1980) 5 Eur L Rev 73. Cf. *Cotonfil v Chemitex*, Italian Ct Cass 1980 [1983] ECC 8.

[5] Case 25/79: [1979] ECR 3423, [1980] 2 CMLR 164.

[6] As under United Kingdom law; see Employment Protection (Consolidation) Act 1978, s. 140.

asked whether the jurisdiction clause was valid under the Convention even if void under French law prior to 1st January 1973, when the 1968 Convention came into force for France. The European Court pointed out that the Convention did not affect rules of substantive law, but that national procedural law relevant to cases concerned would be set aside in the matters governed by the Convention in favour of its provisions. It held that Art. 17.[1]

> "must be interpreted to mean that, in judicial proceedings instituted after the coming into force of the Convention, clauses conferring jurisdiction included in contracts of employment concluded prior to that date, must be considered valid even in cases in which they would have been regarded as void under the national law in force at the time when the contract was entered into."

In *Elefanten Schuh GmbH v Jacqmain*[2] one of the issues arose out of the fact that under Belgian law a contract of employment should have been written in Flemish, as well as in its actual language, which was German, and therefore under Belgian law the contract of employment, including the clause conferring jurisdiction on a German court, was invalid under Belgian law. The European Court held that Contracting States were not free to lay down formal requirements other than those contained in the Convention, and in particular that the legislation of a Contracting State may not allow the validity of an agreement conferring jurisdiction to be called in question solely on the ground that the language used is not that prescribed by that legislation. These cases show that the Contracting States may not declare jurisdiction agreements void for some social purpose (such as in employment contracts) nor provide for requirements of form additional to those in Art. 17 (such as language).

Where a court of one Contracting State disregards a clause providing for the exclusive jurisdiction of the courts of another Contracting State, the disregard of the clause would not, it seems, be a ground for refusal to recognise or enforce a resulting judgment.[3]

Set-off

In *Meeth v Glacetal Sarl*[4] Glacetal, a French company, and Meeth, a German company, entered into a contract for the supply of glass by Glacetal to Meeth; as has been seen,[5] the contract provided that if Meeth were to sue Glacetal, the French courts alone were to have jurisdiction; but if Glacetal sued Meeth, the German courts alone would have jurisdiction; that is, each had to sue in the courts of the defendant's domicile. But when Glacetal sued Meeth in Germany for failure to pay for deliveries, Meeth raised a set-off for damages for delay or default, so that the French plaintiff in effect lost the protection of the contractual provision that claims against it should be brought in France. The German

---

[1] At 3431.
[2] Case 150/80: [1980] ECR 1671, [1982] 3 CMLR 1.
[3] See p. 112, post.
[4] Case 23/78: [1978] ECR 2133, [1979] 1 CMLR 520.
[5] P. 85, ante.

Federal Supreme Court asked whether such a clause was within Art. 17, and whether it permitted the defendant to raise a set-off. The European Court held that the clause was a jurisdiction agreement within the meaning of Art. 17, and that the German court was not prevented by the agreement to confer jurisdiction on the French court in claims against the plaintiff from taking the set-off into account if it was connected with the legal relationship.[1] Although the reciprocal clause in *Meeth v Glacetal Sarl* is not uncommon, it will still be the untypical case. In the usual case where the jurisdiction of only one court is chosen for disputes, it will normally have jurisdiction over set-off and counterclaims, either because the jurisdiction agreement applies to the claim for set-off or counterclaim, or because the plaintiff has submitted, by bringing the action, to claims for set-off or counterclaim.[2]

Waiver

Where the parties have agreed by contract to the exclusive jurisdiction of the courts of one Contracting State, there is no reason why the defendant should not submit to the jurisdiction of the courts of another State if the plaintiff chooses to sue there. In *Elefanten Schuh GmbH v Jacqmain*[3] the European Court said:

> "... neither the general scheme nor the objectives of the Convention provide grounds for the view that the parties to an agreement conferring jurisdiction within the meaning of Article 17 are prevented from voluntarily submitting their dispute to a court other than that stipulated in the agreement. It follows that Article 18 of the Convention applies even where the parties have by agreement designated a court which is to have jurisdiction within the meaning of Article 17."

Provisional Measures

Where the parties have concluded a valid agreement conferring exclusive jurisdiction on the courts of one Contracting State, it remains open to one party to resort to the courts of another Contracting State for provisional measures under Art. 24;[4] the court which is asked to grant the provisional measures is probably entitled, as a matter of national law, to refuse the relief if it considers that the parties intended that such measures should not be sought outside the chosen court.[5]

---

[1] See Gaudemet-Tallon, 1980 Rev Crit 127. In subsequent proceedings in Germany, it was held that the cross-claim had to be brought in France: [1979] ECC 455.

[2] See 1968 Convention, Art. 6(3).

[3] Case 150/80: [1981] ECR 1671, at 1684–5.

[4] See pp. 98–102, post; cf. *R v B*, Bruges, 1977 (1980) 5 Eur L Rev 420. This is also the position under the Hague Convention on Choice of Court (1965), Art. 6(4).

[5] Cf. *Mike Trading and Transport v R Pagnan & Fratelli, The Lisboa* [1980] 2 Lloyd's Rep 546, CA; Collins (1981) 1 Yb Eur L 249, 259–262.

Article 18: Submission

Article 18 provides that, in addition to jurisdiction derived from other provisions, a court of a Contracting State before whom a defendant enters an appearance shall have jurisdiction; but there is no submission "where appearance was entered solely to contest the jurisdiction", and the principle of submission does not apply where another court has exclusive jurisdiction by virtue of Art. 16. Article 18 applies only to cases within the scope of the Convention as a whole[1] so that it does not confer jurisdiction or require the enforcement of judgments in matters falling outside the Convention such as divorce.[2] But once a matter is within the scope of the Convention then appearance will confer jurisdiction even though without appearance jurisdiction could not have been taken: so that a defendant domiciled in a Contracting State who is sued in another Contracting State by virtue of one of the exorbitant bases of jurisdiction prohibited by Art. 3(2), may nevertheless by his appearance confer jurisdiction on the court of that State.[3]

Article 18 does not apply in a case which is covered by the exclusive jurisdiction provisions of Art. 16.[4] But it does apply where the parties have agreed to submit their disputes to the exclusive jurisdiction of the courts of a Contracting State under Art. 17. In such a case appearance by the defendant in the courts of another State will confer jurisdiction on the courts of the latter.[5]

The most difficult question which arises on Art. 18 is the scope and effect of the provision that appearance is not to confer jurisdiction if it "was entered solely to contest the jurisdiction". This is a problem which arose in England in connection with the recognition and enforcement of foreign judgments. Until 1982 the position at common law was that the default judgment of a foreign court would be recognised as the basis of jurisdiction obtained by voluntary appearance where the defendant appeared unsuccessfully before the foreign court to invite that court in its discretion not to exercise a jurisdiction which it had under its local law; and that there was also a voluntary appearance if the defendant merely protested against the jurisdiction of the foreign court and the protest took the form of a conditional appearance which was converted automatically by operation of law into an unconditional appearance if the decision on jurisdiction went against the defendant. The question whether an appearance the sole purpose and effect of which was to protest against the jurisdiction of the foreign court would be a voluntary appearance was left open.[6] This position was subject to heavy criticism[7] but by s. 33 of the 1982 Act[8] the common law was brought into line with the 1933 Act, which provided that appearance to contest the jurisdiction was not to amount to a submission.

---

[1] The question whether it applies if neither party is domiciled in a Contracting State has no practical significance: cf. Droz, para. 221; *The Atlantic Duke*, Rotterdam 1980 [1982] ECC 348.

[2] Cf. Case 25/81: *CHW v GJH* [1982] ECR 1189 at 1209, per Advocate General Rozes.

[3] Jenard, p. 38.

[4] It does however apply, it seems, in insurance and consumer contract cases.

[5] Case 150/80: *Elefanten Schuh GmbH v Jacqmain* [1981] ECR 1671, [1982] 3 CMLR 1, p. 90, ante.

[6] *Henry v Geoprosco International Ltd* [1976] QB 726, [1975] 2 All ER 702, CA, applying *Harris v Taylor* [1915] 2 KB 580, CA.

[7] See Dicey & Morris, p. 1049; Collins (1976) 92 LQR 268.

[8] See, p. 143, post.

The problem in England before the 1982 Act arose in the context of the enforcement of foreign judgments, because a foreign judgment in default of defence might be entitled to recognition in England if (inter alia) the appearance to contest the jurisdiction were regarded as a voluntary appearance. In the case of English domestic law of jurisdiction, the position before 1979 was that a defendant who wished to dispute the jurisdiction of the English court could apply by summons or motion to have the writ set aside without entering an appearance of any kind. If the challenge to the jurisdiction failed, and the defendant took no further steps, then judgment could be entered against him in default of appearance; but the more usual procedure was to enter a conditional appearance and then challenge the jurisdiction; if the challenge failed the appearance would stand as unconditional and if the defendant failed to take further steps, judgment could be given against him in default of defence, and he would not normally be allowed to withdraw his appearance.[1] But the position now is that a defendant who wishes to dispute the jurisdiction gives notice of intention to defend the proceedings and then applies to set aside the proceedings; RSC Ord. 12, r. 8(6), expressly provides that a defendant who follows this procedure shall not be treated as having submitted to the jurisdiction of the court and if the challenge to the jurisdiction fails, the original notice of intention to defend will cease to have effect.

Under the 1968 Convention the problem will normally arise in the court of origin at the stage of assumption of jurisdiction, because under the Convention scheme of direct jurisdiction it is the court of origin which will have to decide whether the appearance of itself gives jurisdiction. If, for example, the court of origin decides that it has jurisdiction on the basis of some other provision of the Convention, then it will not be the appearance under Art. 18 which will be regarded by other courts as the basis of recognition and enforcement but the fact that the court of origin has found that it has jurisdiction under the Convention. Except in the very limited circumstances set out in Arts. 27 and 28 the jurisdiction of the court of origin cannot be questioned at the enforcement stage. The applicability of Art. 18 will not therefore normally arise in enforcement proceedings.[2]

In *Elefanten Schuh GmbH v Jacqmain*[3] Jacqmain, a Belgian domiciliary, was employed as a sales agent by a German company, and was dismissed without notice. The contract of employment contained a jurisdiction clause providing for the exclusive jurisdiction of a German court. But Jacqmain brought an action before a Belgian court seeking damages from the German company and its Belgian subsidiary (for whom he actually worked). The German company put in its defence as to the substance of the claim, but by a further document almost a year later it invoked the exclusive jurisdiction clause in order to challenge the jurisdiction of the Belgian court. The Belgian court referred the following questions (inter alia) to the European Court: (i) whether the exception in Art. 18

---

[1] See *Somportex v Philadelphia Chewing Gum Corpn.* [1968] 3 All ER 26, CA.

[2] In Case 27/81: *Rohr SA v Ossberger* [1981] ECR 2431, [1982] 3 CMLR 29 the defendant tried to make it relevant to enforcement proceedings on the basis of public policy under 1968 Convention, Art. 27(1). See p. 108, post.

[3] Case 150/80: [1981] ECR 1671, [1982] 3 CMLR 1.

was applicable if the defendant had not only contested jurisdiction but had, in addition, made submissions on the merits; (ii) if it was to be applicable, whether the jurisdiction had to be contested at the outset of the litigation, *in limine litis*. The European Court drew attention to the fact that the French text (unlike the English, German, Italian and Dutch texts) did not have any requirement that only jurisdiction must be contested[1] and held that a defendant did not submit by pleading to the merits as well as contesting the jurisdiction, but "only if the plaintiff and the court seised of the matter are able to ascertain from the time of the defendant's first defence that it is intended to contest the jurisdiction".[2] If the challenge to jurisdiction was not a preliminary matter[3] then to avoid pleading to the merits being regarded as a submission, the challenge must not occur after the making of submissions which under national procedural law are considered to be the first defence put to the court.

This decision was followed in *Rohr SA v Ossberger*[4] which arose in the context of proceedings in France to enforce a German judgment. Ossberger, a German company, sued Rohr, a French company, in a German court, alleging that the parties had agreed on the jurisdiction of the German courts in Ossberger's conditions of sale. Rohr contested the jurisdiction of the German court but did not submit any defence on the substance of the case. The German courts held that they had jurisdiction, and because Rohr had not submitted a defence, gave judgment in default, and Ossberger sought to enforce the judgment in France. Rohr resisted enforcement on the ground that, because under Art. 18 it was impossible for it to lodge a defence without submitting to the jurisdiction of the German courts, it would be contrary to French public policy for the French courts to enforce the judgment. The French court asked whether Art. 18 permitted a defendant who contested the jurisdiction to submit at the same time a defence on the substance of the action without thereby losing the right to raise an objection of lack of jurisdiction. The European Court held, applying its ruling in the *Elefanten* case, that the defendant could, without submitting, put in a defence on the merits "in the alternative".[5] It followed therefore that there could be no bar to the enforcement of the judgment in France, and the question of public policy did not arise.[6]

For the reasons given above[7] the exception in Art. 18 for an appearance to contest the jurisdiction is not likely to give rise to problems in England because English law now allows a defendant to make a plea to the jurisdiction without being deemed to have submitted.[8] The English court may order interim measures in the case of doubtful jurisdiction,[9] and a defendant may put in

---

[1] "si la comparution a pour objet de contester la compétence".
[2] At 1685.
[3] As it is under English law.
[4] Case 27/81: [1981] ECR 2431, [1982] 3 CMLR 29.
[5] "à titre subsidiaire", on the meaning of which see Gaudemet-Tallon, 1982 Rev Crit 143; Huet, 1982 Clunet 482. Cf. Hague Convention on the Recognition and Enforcement of Foreign Judgments (1971), Art. 10(6).
[6] See also Case 25/81: *CHW v GJH* [1982] ECR 1189, [1983] 2 CMLR 125.
[7] P. 92, ante.
[8] In Scotland the rule is that it is necessary to file a defence on the merits at the same time as a plea to the jurisdiction: Maxwell Report, para. 5.194. Cf. 1982 Act, Sch. 8, para. 6(2).
[9] 1982 Act, s. 24.

evidence on the substance of an application for interim measures, such as an application for an interlocutory injunction, without submitting to the jurisdiction provided he makes it clear he is contesting the jurisdiction.[1]

Articles 19 and 20: Examination as to Jurisdiction

The effect of Arts 19 and 20 is that a court in a Contracting State seised of a claim must declare *of its own motion* that it has no jurisdiction in the following two cases:

(1) where the claim is principally concerned with a matter over which the courts of another Contracting State have exclusive jurisdiction by virtue of Art. 16;[2]

(2) where the defendant is domiciled in another Contracting State and does not enter an appearance, and the court seised does not derive its jurisdiction from the provisions of the Convention.[3]

The reason for the specific reference to Art. 16 in Art. 19 is that the exclusive jurisdiction provisions are matters of public policy, but they do not apply if the relevant issue is raised only as a preliminary or incidental matter.[4]

Article 20 deals with default of appearance and provides as follows:

(1) Where a defendant domiciled in one Contracting State is sued in a court of another Contracting State and does not enter an appearance, the court shall declare of its own motion that it has no jurisdiction unless its jurisdiction is derived from the provisions of the Convention.

(2) The court shall stay the proceedings so long as it is not shown that the defendant has been able to receive the document instituting the proceedings[5] in sufficient time to enable him to arrange for his defence, or that all necessary steps have been taken to this end: Art. 20(2).

(3) The provisions of Art. 20(2) are to be replaced by those of Art. 15 of the Hague Convention of 1965 on the Service Abroad of Judicial and Extrajudicial Documents in Civil or Commercial Matters if the document instituting the proceedings, or notice thereof, had to be transmitted abroad in accordance with that Convention. Article 15 of the Hague Convention provides that where a writ is transmitted abroad for service, and the defendant has not appeared, judgment in default is not to be given until it is established that service was effected abroad in accordance with the local

---

[1] See *Société Gotz v Barsaghian*, Lyons 1979, 1981 II JCP 19519, [1981] ELD 185. Cf. Dicey & Morris, p. 191, and *Obikoya v Silvernorth Ltd* (1983) Times, 6 July.

[2] 1968 Convention, Art. 19.

[3] 1968 Convention, Art. 20(1).

[4] Jenard, p. 39.

[5] Or an equivalent document, added by the Accession Convention to deal with the fact that in English proceedings it was not the writ, but notice of the writ, which was to be served abroad. But since 1980 it is the writ which is served.

law, or the writ was delivered to the defendant personally or to his residence, in each case in sufficient time to enable the defendant to defend.[1]

Article IV of the 1968 Protocol deals with service and provides that judicial and extrajudicial documents drawn up in one Contracting State, which have to be served on persons in another Contracting State, shall be transmitted in accordance with the procedures laid down in the conventions and agreements concluded between the Contracting States; unless the State in which service is to take place objects by declaration to the Secretary-General of the Council of the European Communities, such documents may also be sent by the appropriate public officers of the State in which the document has been drawn up directly to the appropriate public officers of the State in which the addressee is to be found; in that case the officer of the State of origin shall send a copy of the document to the officer of the State addressed who is competent to forward it to the addressee; the document shall be forwarded in the manner specified by the law of the State addressed; the forwarding shall be recorded by a certificate sent directly to the officer of the State of origin. The United Kingdom has Civil Procedure Conventions with all the Contracting States except Ireland and Luxembourg and the Hague Convention is in force between the United Kingdom, Belgium, Denmark, France, Germany, Italy, Luxembourg and the Netherlands.[2]

The practical effect of these provisions in England will be as follows:

(1) It is not for the court, but for the parties, to raise any question of jurisdiction, except in two cases.
(2) The first case is where the claim is principally concerned with a matter over which the courts of another Contracting State have exclusive jurisdiction by virtue of Art. 16.
(3) The second case is where the defendant is domiciled in another Contracting State and does not enter an appearance. Before entering a default judgment, the court must consider (*a*) whether it has jurisdiction under the Convention, and (*b*) whether the defendant has been able to receive the writ in sufficient time for him to arrange for his defence, or, where it is applicable, whether the defendant has been served pursuant to Art. 15 of the Hague Convention of 1965.
(4) The new Rules of the Supreme Court will contain provisions (*a*) requiring a writ which is to be served out of the jurisdiction in a Convention case to be endorsed with a statement that the court has jurisdiction under the 1982 Act to determine the claim and that no proceedings involving the same cause of action are pending in another Contracting State; and (*b*) requiring, before judgment in default is entered on a writ served out of the jurisdiction in a Convention case or served within the jurisdiction on a defendant domiciled in another Contracting State, an affidavit to the effect

---

[1] But each Contracting State is free to declare that the judge may nevertheless give judgment notwithstanding that no certificate of service or delivery has been received if the document was transmitted by one of the methods in the Hague Convention, at least six months have elapsed since transmission of the document and no certificate of service has been received even though every reasonable effort has been made to obtain it; the United Kingdom has made such a declaration.

[2] On the Conventions see Supreme Court Practice 1982, 11/5/3 (Hague) and 11/6/2 (bilateral).

that the Court has jurisdiction under the 1982 Act, no other court has exclusive jurisdiction under the Convention and the writ has been duly served.[1]

(5) The English rules as to time[2] for acknowledgement of service (failing which judgment in default may be entered) will be regarded by the English court as sufficient to enable the defendant to arrange for his defence, but they will not prevent the court of the State in which enforcement of the default judgment is sought from re-examining the question.[3]

Articles 21 to 23: Lis Pendens and Related Actions

These provisions deal with the related problems of actions pending in different Contracting States where, first, the cause of action is the same, and, second, where it is not the same but is related. The first problem is lis pendens in the strict sense ("litispendance") where the actions have "le même objet et la même cause") and the second is that of "connexité". In English law there is no hard distinction between the two in the context of jurisdiction.[4] In English law, apart from the Convention, the court has a discretion in the case where the same, or related proceedings are being taken elsewhere, either to stay its own proceedings[5] or to enjoin the continuance of the foreign proceedings.[6] In each case the jurisdiction to stay or grant an injunction is discretionary, and the discretion is to be exercised whenever it is necessary to prevent injustice.[7]

The Convention is silent as to the method of determining at what point in time a court is seised. Under English law proceedings are pending from the moment of the *issue* of the writ or other originating proceedings. In the law of the original Contracting Parties (and in Scottish law) proceedings are pending from the time of *service* upon the defendant. According to Schlosser[8] the moment at which proceedings become pending under the national procedural law concerned is the deciding factor for the application of Art. 21. If therefore proceedings are issued in France but are not served until after proceedings are subsequently commenced in England, it will be the French court which will have to decline jurisdiction. Each court would have to look to the procedural law of the other court to see whether the latter was seised first.

The Convention draws a distinction between those cases where a court seised *must* decline jurisdiction and those where it *may* decline jurisdiction. A court of

---

[1] RSC Ord. 6, r. 7(1); Ord. 13, r. 7B: see Chapter 7 and Appendix 2, post.

[2] See the new RSC Ord. 11, r. 1(3).

[3] 1968 Convention, Art. 27(2); Case 166/80: *Klomps v Michel* [1981] ECR 1593, [1982] 2 CMLR 773; Case 228/81: *Pendy Plastic Products BV v Pluspunkt Handelsgesellschaft mbH* [1983] 1 CMLR 665.

[4] But for res judicata, where the distinction may be important, see e.g. *Carl Zeiss Stiftung v Rayner & Keeler Ltd (No 3)* [1970] Ch 506, [1969] 3 All ER 897.

[5] See e.g. *MacShannon v Rockware Glass Ltd* [1978] AC 795, [1978] 1 All ER 625.

[6] See, e.g. *Smith, Kline & French Laboratories Ltd v Bloch* [1983] 2 All ER 72, [1983] 1 WLR 730, CA.

[7] Dicey & Morris, p. 247.

[8] Para. 182; cf. Jenard, p. 41.

a Contracting State *must*, of its own motion,[1] decline jurisdiction if the courts of another Contracting State have first been seised where the proceedings involve the same cause of action and are between the same parties.[2] If the jurisdiction of the court first seised is contested by the defendant, then the second court may stay its proceedings pending the outcome of the issue as to jurisdiction in the first court. In theory the second court could exercise its right not to stay the proceedings pending the outcome of the contest in the first court, but it would be an unnecessarily costly exercise and might result in a judgment irreconcilable with that of the court first seised which would be unenforceable as a result of Art. 27(3). One of the objects of Art. 21 is to prevent the courts of two Contracting States from giving judgment in the same case.[3] Another case where the stay is mandatory is where actions come within the exclusive jurisdiction of several courts, in which case any court other than that first seised must decline jurisdiction,[4] or stay the proceedings.[5] Such cases will by their nature be rare, but it is theoretically possible, e.g. where a company has its seat in more than one State and the action concerns the validity of its constitution.[6] In these cases, the court which is seised later has no discretion, and English courts will lose the flexibility which they have at present.[7] But Art. 21 does not apply if one of the actions is brought in a non-Contracting State. In that case the English court would retain its discretion to stay or grant an injunction.

For there to be a mandatory stay there must be an identical cause of action, and there are several national cases in which this condition of the operation of Art. 21 was held not to be met, e.g. where one case was for the payment of the purchase price of goods and the other for damages for their failure to be of the contractual quality[8] or where one action was for damages and the other for a declaration.[9] If a plaintiff brings an application for provisional measures in one State under Art. 24, he will not be precluded from pursuing a later action on the substance in another State.[10]

Because Art. 21 only relates to lis alibi pendens in a very strict sense, it is unlikely to be of much practical application except where a plaintiff brings the same proceedings in a number of courts. Article 22 is of more practical importance, although it does not seem to have been much used.[11] It provides for a discretionary stay in the following conditions: (1) where the court is not the court first seised; (2) where "related actions" have been brought in the courts of different States: (3) where the actions are still pending at first instance, i.e. where neither has gone to judgment. Actions are "related" for the purpose of Art. 22

---

[1] See the new RSC Ord. 6, r. 7(1), p. 96, ante.
[2] 1968 Convention, Art. 21.
[3] Case 42/76: *De Wolf v Cox BV* [1976] ECR 1759 at 1767.
[4] 1968 Convention, Art. 23.
[5] Weser, p. 336; Droz, para. 314.
[6] 1968 Convention, Art. 16(2). The question whether the court which declines jurisdiction must recognise the judgment of the court first seised is controversial: see Weser, p. 335; Droz, para. 312.
[7] See also Schlosser, para. 181. It is not likely that s. 49 of the 1982 Act will be of assistance.
[8] *Ferronato v Barth and Pohl*, Italy 1976, Eur Court Digest D I-21-B1.
[9] LG Cologne, ibid. B3.
[10] Cf. *Verhulst v Thovadec Plastics* Netherlands 1978, ibid. B2; 1981 Neths Int L Rev 78.
[11] See, for a case where no stay was ordered, e.g. *BvT v General Accident*, Netherlands 1977, Eur Court Digest D I-8-B1; 1978 Neths Int L Rev 82.

"where they are so closely connected that it is expedient to hear and determine them together to avoid the risk of irreconcilable judgments resulting from separate proceedings".[1] Article 22(1) only speaks of a *stay* of proceedings and therefore contemplates that the proceedings will remain alive. But Art. 22(2) deals with the possibility of the court declining jurisdiction. This requires the following conditions to be met: (1) the court which is to decline jurisdiction is not the court first seised; (2) "related actions" have been brought in the courts of different States; (3) the actions are still pending at first instance;[2] (4) one of the parties makes an application; (5) the law of the court first seised has jurisdiction over both actions under the Convention and its law[3] permits consolidation of related actions. It should be noted that Art. 22 does not confer any jurisdiction. It merely deals with problems arising out of related actions pending before courts of different Contracting States.[4]

Article 24: Provisional and Protective Measures

Article 24 provides:

"Application may be made to the courts of a Contracting State for such provisional measures, including protective, measures as may be available under the law of that State, even if, under this Convention, the courts of another Contracting State have jurisdiction as to the substance of the matter."

As has been seen above, the Convention as a whole applies to provisional measures.[5] Article 24 is designed to allow provisional measures to be taken in the place where assets are, even though the main action is pending elsewhere. As the European Court said in *Denilauler v Snc Couchet Frères*:[6]

"The courts of the place or, in any event, of the Contracting State, where the assets subject to the measures sought are located, are those best able to assess the circumstances which may lead to the grant or refusal of the measures sought or to the laying down of procedures and conditions which the plaintiff must observe in order to guarantee the provisional and protective character of the measures ordered."

The effect of Art. 24 is that a plaintiff (or in some cases a defendant) may apply for provisional measures in a Contracting State notwithstanding that the courts of that State are not entitled under the Convention to exercise jurisdiction over the substance of the case, because, for example, the parties conferred exclusive

---

[1] 1968 Convention, Art. 22(3).
[2] This is not express, but seems to follow: see Droz, para. 325.
[3] Jenard, p. 41; but other language texts and Droz, para. 326, suggest that the relevant law is that of the court seised second, although that does not make practical sense.
[4] See Case 150/80: *Elefanten Schuh GmbH v Jacqmain* [1981] ECR 1671, [1982] 3 CMLR 1.
[5] P. 30, ante; Case 143/78: *De Cavel v De Cavel (No. 1)* [1979] ECR 1055, [1979] 2 CMLR 547; Case 120/79: *De Cavel v De Cavel (No. 2)* [1980] ECR 731, [1980] 3 CMLR 1.
[6] Case 125/79: [1980] ECR 1553 at 1570.

jurisdiction on the courts of another State.[1] Article 24 applies whether or not proceedings are actually pending in another court. It does not create a system of provisional remedies in the Contracting State. It is merely permissive, enabling each Contracting State to grant its provisional remedies to a party even if the substance of the case is outside its jurisdiction.[2] National law may allow the power to be exercised even if the courts of another Contracting State have exclusive jurisdiction as a result of an agreement under Art. 17.[3] In the six original Contracting States there has been extensive use of the power to order provisional measures notwithstanding the lack of jurisdiction over the merits. In practice the power has been used in somewhat questionable cases. Thus in France, the Court of Appeal at Versailles made a provisional award of damages to an employee notwithstanding that the Belgian courts had jurisdiction over the substance.[4] Although the decision refers to the fact that the underlying claim was not seriously contested, it leads to results which are surely contrary to the spirit of the Convention, and one may doubt whether such an award is really a provisional or protective measure within the meaning of the Convention.[5] In Germany, there are conflicting decisions as to whether courts may make use of Art. 917(2) of the Code of Civil Procedure to order attachment as security for claims being pursued in foreign courts but the better view is that they may.[6]

In England, prior to the 1982 Act, the courts did not have power to grant provisional measures where they had no jurisdiction over the substance of the case. The question of the relationship between jurisdiction to order provisional measures and jurisdiction to hear the merits arose in a very simple form in a case involving a *Mareva* injunction: *The Siskina*.[7] The Siskina was carrying marble slabs originating in Italy and destined for Saudi Arabia. The Siskina was owned by a one-ship Panamanian company, but managed by Greeks in Piraeus. The ship owners, when the ship was near the entrance to the Suez Canal, alleged that the charterers had not paid the full freight due under the charter party, and ordered the master to turn back and go to Cyprus and unload the cargo, where the ship owners issued a writ in rem against the cargo. After discharge of the cargo (worth US $5 million) the vessel left Cyprus and sank on the way to Greece. The ship owners made a claim on London underwriters, and were likely to receive US $750,000. The cargo owners were anxious about these moneys, since the ship owners had no other assets; in particular the cargo owners were anxious that the money should not be paid to the ship owners, because they would then be beyond reach of their claim for compensation for the storage charges and additional expenses caused by what the cargo owners said was the wrongful arrest of the cargo in Cyprus. The cargo owners sought to have the insurance moneys of US $750,000 retained in England until their claim for damages was

---

[1] See p. 90, ante.
[2] See generally Collins (1981) 1 Yb Eur L p. 249.
[3] Cf. *Mike Trading and Transport v R Pagnan & Fratelli, The Lisboa* [1980] 2 Lloyd's Rep 546, CA, Collins, op. cit., pp. 259–262.
[4] *Tron v Verkor* 1980 Clunet 894, note Holleaux. Cf. *Wisseborn BV v Blome KG* Netherlands 1977, 1981 Neths Int L Rev 80.
[5] See Mezger, 1979 Rev Crit 128.
[6] Cf. OLG Frankfurt September 23, 1980, RIW/AWD 1980, 779; LG Bremen May 30 1978 RIW/AWD 1980, 366; Düsseldorf, May 18, 1977, Eur Court Digest D I-24-B4.
[7] [1979] AC 210, [1977] 3 All ER 803; see Kerr (1978) 41 MLR, 11–15; Lipstein 1978 CLJ 241.

settled. The bills of lading contained a clause giving exclusive jurisdiction to the Courts of Genoa. The only connection of the case with England was the location of the insurance money. If the plaintiffs were to have any hope of obtaining satisfaction it was essential for them to have the money frozen. As Kerr J. put it, the basic contention of the plaintiffs was that the *Mareva* jurisdiction could be extended to provide a general power of attachment even in cases in which English courts had no other basis of jurisdiction against the defendants, but he held that the court did not have such a power. The Court of Appeal held, by a majority (Lord Denning M.R. and Lawton L.J., Bridge L.J. dissenting) that the court did have the power. The view of the majority was that the *Mareva* injunction was an injunction which was "sought ordering the defendant to do or refrain from doing anything within the jurisdiction" within RSC Ord 11, r. 1(1). The view of Bridge L.J. and the first instance judge, Kerr J., was that, for a case to come within the relevant provision of RSC Ord. 11, the injunction had to be part of the substantive relief to which the plaintiff's cause of action entitled him; in the circumstances the plaintiffs had no actual claim to the insurance money, merely a claim to damages arising from a cause of action over which the English courts had no jurisdiction. Lord Denning M.R. invoked the 1968 Convention in support of his view that the injunction should be granted. He said:[1]

> "comity in this case is all in favour of granting an injunction seeing that it is a close parallel to 'saisie conservatoire' with which other countries are very familiar. I go further. Now that we are in the common market it is our duty to do our part in harmonising the laws of the countries of the nine. . . . Now under Article 220 it is the duty of the member states to seek to secure the 'reciprocal recognition' of the 'judgments of courts'. To do so in this case means that we should regard a determination by the Italian courts—one of the countries of the common market—with the same respect as a determination of the English courts: and that we should give our aid to the enforcement of it to the same extent as we would our own. In particular, we should take protective measures to see that the moneys here are not spirited away pending the decision of the Italian courts. In this context it is instructive to study the way in which article 220 has been implemented by the original six countries of the common market in the 1968 Convention on Jurisdiction and the Enforcement of Judgments. This will in due course be extended to cover all the nine countries which are now members. When the creditor and debtor live in different countries of the common market, the Convention adopts the principle that the creditor must seek out the debtor and sue him in the country in which the debtor lives: see article 2. The creditor cannot sue the debtor in his own (the creditor's) country so as to enforce the substance of the debt save in particular defined circumstances: see article 3. But meanwhile the creditor can apply to the courts of his own (the creditor's) country for protective measures to be taken against the assets of the debtor—when those assets are situate in the creditor's country—as as to prevent the debtor from disposing of them before the creditor obtained his judgment in the substantive case: see article 24. . . . In order to harmonise the laws of the

---

[1] [1979] AC at 233–5.

common market countries, it is therefore appropriate that we should apply protective measures here so as to prevent these insurance moneys being disposed of before judgment."

The decision of the Court of Appeal was reversed by the House of Lords in a decision which Lord Denning has described as the most disappointing reversal in his career.[1] The decision of the House of Lords was that the injunction provision of RSC Ord. 11, r. 1(1) could only be used if the injunction was in connection with an underlying dispute subject to the jurisdiction of the English court. Lord Diplock was highly critical of Lord Denning's appeal to the 1968 Convention. He said:[2]

"With regard to the alternative suggestion that the High Court should have jurisdiction to order the attachment of assets of a foreign defendant notwithstanding that it had no jurisdiction to adjudicate upon the merits of the claim, it is the fact that article 24 of the Convention of 1968 expressly preserves the jurisdiction of courts of member states in which the national law provides for this, to make orders of a protective or provisional character on the application of a claimant, notwithstanding that under the Convention jurisdiction to adjudicate on the merits of the claim in aid of which the protective or provisional orders are requested is vested in the courts of some other member state. It is also the fact that the codes of civil procedure of several of the original member states which provide for the provisional attachment (saisie conservatoire) of the assets of an alleged debtor within the territorial jurisdiction of the court do extend this general power to the attachment of assets of a non-resident defendant pending adjudication of the merits of a claim against him in an action brought in some foreign court; but as article 24 of the Convention indicates, this is a field of law in which it has not been considered necessary by member states or by the Council or Commission to embark upon a policy of harmonisation. . . . [T]here may be merits in Lord Denning M.R.'s alternative proposals for extending the jurisdiction of the High Court over foreign defendants but they cannot, in my view, be supported by considerations of comity, or by the Common Market treaties."[3]

The gap revealed by *The Siskina* has been filled by s. 25 of the 1982 Act, which provides that the High Court will have power to grant interim relief where proceedings have been or are to be commenced in a Contracting State other than the United Kingdom[4] and the proceedings fall within the scope of the 1968 Convention.[5] The effect of this will be that, when the Convention comes into force for the United Kingdom, provisional measures may be obtained pursuant to Art. 24 even if the courts of another Contracting State have jurisdiction over the substance. The absence of jurisdiction over the substance will continue to be

---

[1] Due Process of Law, 1980, p. 141.

[2] At 259–60.

[3] Cf. *Perry v Zissis* [1977] 1 Lloyd's Rep 607; but see *Chief Constable of Kent v V* [1983] QB 34, [1982] 3 All ER 36 for a view that *The Siskina* had been superseded by the Supreme Court Act 1981, s. 37.

[4] Or in another part of the United Kingdom.

[5] For Scotland, see 1982 Act, s. 27.

a factor in the exercise of discretion whether or not to order interim relief.[1] In practice the *Mareva* injunction is likely to be the most common exercise of this power. It seems that a *Mareva* injunction, which is normally granted ex parte, will not be granted in relation to assets abroad.[2] It is therefore unlikely that the problem which arose in *Denilauler v Snc Couchet Frères*[3] will have any practical importance in relation to the enforcement of English *Mareva* injunctions abroad, although the case remains relevant to the enforcement of foreign attachment orders in England. This case arose out of a reference by the Frankfurt Court. The plaintiff in the main action in France, Couchet, sued a German company, Denilauler, for the purchase price of goods; in the course of the French proceedings the court made an order authorising the freezing of Denilauler's bank assets in the Frankfurt branch of a French bank as security. The order was made ex parte, and the plaintiff sought to have it enforced in Germany. The basic thrust of the questions referred by the German Court concerned the applicability of the various provisions in the Convention which envisage the giving of notice of proceedings to the judgment debtor before judgment is given against him by the original court or notice of the judgment itself prior to enforcement.[4] The Court concluded that although Art. 24 did not preclude provisional or protective measures ordered in the State of origin pursuant to adversary proceedings—even though by default—from being the subject of recognition and an authorisation for enforcement on the conditions laid down in the Convention, the conditions imposed by the Convention on the recognition and the enforcement of judicial decisions were not fulfilled in the case of provisional or protective measures which were ordered or authorised by a court ex parte and which were intended to be enforced without prior service on that party. But it seems that if such measures are ordered and the party against whom they are made is given notice, then the resulting order will be enforceable in other Contracting States[5] provided that the case is within the scope of the Convention. This may lead to surprising results if the court which orders the provisional measures purports to affect property situated in other States.[6]

Security for costs

Although Art. 45 of the Convention prohibits the requirement of security for costs from an applicant for enforcement of a judgment, the jurisdictional provisions of the Convention do not deal with security for costs. The question therefore arises whether a person domiciled in a Contracting State who sues in England may be required to give security for costs under RSC Ord. 23. The

---

[1] 1982 Act, s. 25(2). The power may be extended to non-Convention cases (s. 25(3)). For cases of doubtful, rather than non-existent jurisdiction, 1982 Act, see s. 24.

[2] See *Intraco Ltd v Notis Shipping Corpn of Liberia, The Bhoja Trader* [1981] 2 Lloyd's Rep 256, CA. But in *Cook Industries Inc v Galliher* [1979] Ch 439, [1978] 3 All ER 945 the English court made an order for inspection of chattels in a flat in Paris: this may have been an excessive exercise of jurisdiction.

[3] Case 125/79: [1980] ECR 1553, [1981] 1 CMLR 62.

[4] See 1968 Convention, Arts. 27(2); 46(2); 47(1).

[5] Case 143/78: *De Cavel v De Cavel (No. 1)* [1979] ECR 1055, [1979] 2 CMLR 547.

[6] See Collins, op. cit., p. 99, n.2, ante, at p. 265.

position with regard to claimants from countries with whom the United Kingdom has bilateral treaties (which all allow costs orders to be enforced) is that the court has power to order security for costs because enforcement of costs under the relevant treaty would be difficult in practice;[1] but the court has a discretion, which may weigh against the making of an order, if the plaintiff is resident in a Member State of the EEC, although it is not discriminatory within the meaning of Art. 7 of the EEC Treaty to order security in such a case.[2] But the position may be different once the 1968 Convention is in force, since one of its objects is to facilitate the enforcement of procedural rights across the frontiers of the Contracting States.

---

[1] *Kohn v Rinson & Stafford (Brod) Ltd* [1948] 1 KB 327, [1947] 2 All ER 839; *Aeronave SpA v Westland Charters Ltd* [1971] 3 All ER 531, [1971] 1 WLR 1445 CA.

[2] *Landi den Hartog v Stopps* [1976] 2 CMLR 393, [1976] FSR 497; *Compagnie Francaise de Télévision v Thorn Consumer Electronics* [1981] 3 CMLR 414, [1981] FSR 306; cf. Case 22/80: *Boussac Saint-Frères SA v Gerstenmeier* [1980] ECR 3427, [1982] 1 CMLR 202. Nor, it seems, is the position affected by the bilateral treaties on legal proceedings which forbid discrimination on the basis of nationality in relation to security for costs.

CHAPTER 5

RECOGNITION AND ENFORCEMENT OF JUDGMENTS UNDER THE CONVENTION

Introduction

The recognition and enforcement provisions of the 1968 Convention are, like the jurisdiction provisions discussed in the previous chapter, given the force of law in the United Kingdom by s. 2 of the 1982 Act. The 1968 Convention differs in two important respects from the system of enforcement under the existing bilateral Conventions. First, it is not limited to money judgments or to final judgments; second, the court in which enforcement is sought has very much more limited powers under the 1968 Convention than under the bilateral Conventions to investigate the jurisdiction of the court which gave the judgment. It is also important to note that the effect of the Convention is that the enforcement procedures apply to all judgments within its scope, whether or not they are against persons domiciled in a Contracting State. Thus an English default judgment against a New York resident where the jurisdiction of the English court was based on the temporary presence of the defendant in England will be enforceable in France; and a French judgment against a New York resident where the jurisdiction of the French court was based on the French nationality of the plaintiff under Art. 14 of the Civil Code will be enforceable in England. But Art. 59 allows a Contracting State to assume in relation to a non-Contracting State the obligation not to recognise judgments given in other Contracting States against defendants domiciled or habitually resident in the third state where the basis of jurisdiction could only be one of the "exorbitant" bases of jurisdiction set out in Art. 3(2) (which include the jurisdiction in England based on temporary presence and the jurisdiction in France based on nationality).[1]

Article 25 of the 1968 Convention provides that "judgment" means any judgment given by a court or tribunal of a Contracting State, whatever the judgment may be called, including a decree, order, decision, or writ of execution, as well as the determination of costs by an officer of the court.[2] The Convention enforcement provisions apply to maintenance orders falling within the scope of the Convention. Special provision is made for maintenance orders in the 1982 Act, and they are dealt with below.[3]

---

[1] See p. 50, ante.
[2] S. 15(1) of the 1982 Act provides that judgment in Part I of the Act (which deals with the Convention) has the meaning given to it by 1968 Convention, Art. 25. Cf. s. 50 of the 1982 Act, which provides that, subject to s. 15(1), "judgment" means any judgment or order (by whatever name called) given or made by a court in any civil proceedings; that court includes a tribunal; and that tribunal means a tribunal of any description other than a court of law (and in relation to an overseas country, as regards matters relating to maintenance, any authority having power to give, enforce, vary or revoke a maintenance order, on which see also 1968 Protocol, Art. VA, dealing with the special case of Denmark).
[3] Pp. 123–125.

As regards the scope of the recognition and enforcement provisions:

(1) the judgment must be one given in a civil or commercial matter, and the court in which enforcement is sought is not bound by the determination of the court in which the judgment is given; what is a civil or commercial matter is to be given a Convention interpretation.[1] Where a judgment falls partly within the Convention, it will be recognised and enforced only as to that part;[2]

(2) they apply to any judgment given by a court or tribunal (including such statutory bodies as employment tribunals but not an administrative authority) of a Contracting State within the scope of the Convention, irrespective of the nationality or domicile of the parties. "Judgment" includes one made under the "Zahlungsbefehl" procedure of German law, or order to pay;[3]

(3) there is no requirement (as there is at common law and under the bilateral treaties) that the judgment be "final and conclusive": it may be an interim order providing for periodical payments or a provisional order freezing assets[4] and may include orders under 1968 Convention, Art. 24, even if the court granting the order had no jurisdiction over the substance of the case but not if they are granted ex parte and are intended to be executed without notice: *Denilauler v Snc Couchet Frères*;[5]

(4) it seems that orders for discovery or for the taking of evidence, which are of a procedural character and do not affect the legal relationship of the parties, are outside the scope of the Convention.[6] These would be dealt with through the existing machinery such as Hague Conventions on Civil Procedure (1954), on Service Abroad (1965), and on the Taking of Evidence Abroad in Civil or Commercial Matters (1970), and the bilateral conventions on judicial assistance;

(5) "judgments" do not include "judgments on judgments", i.e. judgments of Country A enforcing judgments of Country B;[7]

(6) the enforcement provisions apply to orders for costs[8] and to orders for interest.[9]

The effect of the recognition and enforcement provisions is, broadly, as follows: (1) a judgment of a Contracting State within the scope of the Convention must be recognised and enforced in other Contracting States; (2) the grounds for non-recognition or non-enforcement are limited to (i) public policy; (ii) lack of notice of proceedings; (iii) judgments irreconcilable with a judgment of the court

---

[1] See for cases in which enforcement was sought unsuccessfully, e.g. Case 29/76: *LTU v Eurocontrol* [1976] ECR 1541, [1977] 1 CMLR 88; Case 133/78: *Gourdain v Nadler* [1979] ECR 733, [1979] 3 CMLR 180, pp. 18–30, ante.

[2] 1968 Convention, Art. 42.

[3] Case 166/80: *Klomps v Michel* [1981] ECR 1593, [1982] 2 CMLR 773.

[4] Cf. Case 143/78: *De Cavel v De Cavel (No. 1)* [1979] ECR 1055, [1979] 2 CMLR 547; Case 123/79: *Denilauler v SNC Couchet Frères* [1980] ECR 1553, [1981] 1 CMLR 62.

[5] Ante.

[6] Schlosser, paras. 184–187.

[7] Droz, para. 437; cf. 1982 Act, s. 18(7).

[8] 1968 Convention, Art. 25.

[9] 1982 Act, s. 7.

of the State in which enforcement is sought or of a non-Contracting State; (iv) certain cases involving preliminary questions as to status etc.; (3) the jurisdiction of the court in which judgment was given may only be investigated by the court in which enforcement is sought if the case falls within Sections 3 (insurance), 4 (consumer contracts) or 5 (exclusive jurisdiction), but even in these cases the court in which enforcement is sought is bound by the findings of fact on which the original court based its judgment; public policy cannot be used by the court in which enforcement is sought to deny jurisdiction to the original court; (4) the judgment may not be reviewed as to its substance.

Grounds for refusal of recognition or enforcement

The grounds for non-recognition are set out in Arts. 27 and 28, which are applied to enforcement by Art. 34(2). There are other grounds not expressly mentioned such as (*a*) the judgment has been satisfied; (*b*) the judgment is not within the scope of the Convention; (*c*) the judgment is not enforceable in the state of origin; (*d*) the procedural formalities for enforcement have not been complied with.[1]

Public policy

The first is where the foreign judgment is contrary to public policy ("contraire à l'ordre public") in the State where its recognition or enforcement is sought. This was intended to operate only in exceptional cases.[2] In the United Kingdom, public policy is a ground for refusal of recognition or enforcement, but there have been very few examples.[3] It is plain that a mere difference between the substantive law (or the rules of private international law, except in the special case of Art. 27(4)) of the original court and that of the court in which enforcement is sought is not sufficient to justify non-recognition or non-enforcement,[4] although there may be cases where the court in which enforcement is sought regards the original judgment as so unfairly based that it will not be enforced.[5] The mere fact that the foreign judgment does not contain reasons should be insufficient to justify public policy being invoked.[6] Ultimately it is for the court

---

[1] See Jenard, p. 50; Schlosser, para. 220.

[2] Jenard, p. 44.

[3] See Dicey & Morris, p. 1087.

[4] Cf. *Almacoa SA v Moteurs Cérès*, France 1978, 1979 Clunet 623, note Huet and Kovar.

[5] Cf. LG Hamburg, 1977, Eur Court Digest D-I-27.1-B2, where a German court refused on the ground of public policy (inter alia) to enforce an Italian judgment against a German principal who under Italian law was deemed to be represented by his agent in the proceedings.

[6] E.g. an English summary judgment under RSC Ord. 14, which in simple cases contains no reasons. But cf. *Société France International Représentation v Héritiers Baas*, Paris and Cour de Cassation, 1979 and 1981, 1980 Rev Crit 121 and 1981 Rev Crit 553, note Mezger.

in which enforcement is sought to apply its own rules of public policy, subject to a possible check by the European Court on its abuse.[1]

In the United Kingdom fraud is a ground for refusal of recognition or enforcement of a foreign judgment, and in this context fraud has a very wide meaning.[2] In the original Contracting States fraud is not a separate reason for non-recognition, and the Convention does not contain a special provision for fraud. But in the original Contracting States a judgment procured by fraud may be refused recognition on grounds of public policy, and this is reflected in the United Kingdom bilateral treaties with France and the Federal Republic of Germany. Under the 1968 Convention it is likely that the procurement of a judgment by fraud (at least where it is no longer possible to raise it in the court of origin[3]) may be held to offend against the public policy of the court in which enforcement is sought.[4]

In *Rohr SA v Ossberger*[5] it was argued that a German judgment should be held contrary to public policy in France because German law did not allow an objection to jurisdiction to be made without at the same time putting in a defence on the merits, if a judgment in default of defence was to be avoided. This, it was said, was contrary to French public policy because the effect of Art. 18 would be that there would be an automatic submission to the jurisdiction of the German courts. The point on public policy did not in the event arise, because Art. 18 was held not to have the result of such a submission if the objection to the jurisdiction and the defence on the merits were made at the same time.[6] Article 28 expressly provides that public policy cannot be used to re-open the question of jurisdiction of the original court. This would prevent, e.g. an English court from refusing to recognise a French judgment based on Art. 14 of the Civil Code, in a case where the plaintiff was French, the defendant was domiciled in a non-Contracting State and the case had nothing to do with France;[7] and it has the general effect of making public policy inapplicable to procedural matters, which are dealt with in the special provisions of Art. 27(2).[8]

Right to defend

Article 27(2), which requires non-recognition or non-enforcement, applies if the following conditions are met: (1) the judgment is in default of appearance; (2) the defendant was not duly served with the document instituting the

---

[1] Cf. *Re A German Commercial Agent*, German Federal Supreme Court 1979 [1980] ECC 207. For a similar question in relation to the EEC Treaty see *Henn and Darby v DPP* [1981] AC 850; Case 34/79: *R v Henn* [1979] ECR 3795, [1980] 1 CMLR 246.
[2] Dicey & Morris, p. 1081.
[3] See Schlosser, para. 192; Droz, paras. 493–496.
[4] Cf. *Kendall v Kendall* [1977] Fam 208, [1977] 3 All ER 471 (foreign divorce obtained by fraud refused recognition on grounds of public policy). For the special problem of the Irish Constitution and maintenance orders see Schlosser, para. 193.
[5] Case 27/81: [1981] ECR 2431, [1982] 3 CMLR 29.
[6] See p. 92, ante.
[7] Jenard, p. 44.
[8] Droz, para. 489.

proceedings (or an equivalent document); and (3) the defendant did not have sufficient time to arrange for his defence. The purpose of Art. 27(2) is to safeguard the interests of the defendant and to ensure that he has sufficient time to defend himself.[1] It applies only to judgments in default of appearance; a judgment remains a judgment in default of appearance even if the defendant later seeks, unsuccessfully, to set it aside.[2] It applies whether or not the defendant is domiciled in the state of the court of origin.[3] But it has no application to ex parte orders granting interim relief which are intended to be executed without prior notice. These are outside the scope of the Convention.[4]

Article 20(2), as has been seen,[5] contains provisions relating to default judgments which are intended to safeguard, in the court in which the original judgment is given, the rights of a defendant. Article 20(2) is of more limited scope than Art. 27(2), because the former applies only to defendants domiciled in another Contracting State, whereas Art. 27(2) applies to all default judgments. In *Klomps v Michel*[6] the European Court held that it was for the court in which enforcement is sought to consider whether, following service, the defendant had sufficient time for his defence.[7] As a general rule the court in which enforcement is sought may confine its examination to ascertaining whether the period reckoned from the date on which service was duly effected allowed the defendant sufficient time to arrange for his defence. Nevertheless the court must consider whether, in the particular case, there are exceptional circumstances which warrant the conclusion that although service was duly effected, it was, however, inadequate for the purposes of enabling the defendant to take steps to arrange for his defence and accordingly could not cause the time stipulated by Art. 27(2) to begin to run. In considering whether it is confronted with such a case, the court in which enforcement is sought may take account of all the circumstances of the case, including the means employed for effecting service, the relations between the plaintiff and the defendant or the nature of the steps which had to be taken in order to prevent judgment from being given in default. If, for example, the dispute concerns commercial relations and if the document which instituted the proceedings was served at an address at which the defendant carries on his business activities, the mere fact that the defendant was absent at the time of service should not normally prevent him from arranging his defence, especially if the action necessary to avoid a judgment in default may be taken informally and by a representative.

It seems from *Klomps v Michel* and *Pendy Products v Pluspunkt* that the court in which enforcement is sought may re-open the question whether there has been due service under the law of the original court, including any applicable international conventions. If the original court has not been seised of the question in adversary proceedings, then the court in which enforcement is sought has no

---

[1] Case 166/80: *Klomps v Michel* [1981] ECR 1593 at 1605; Case 228/81: *Pendy Plastic Products BV v Pluspunkt Handelsgesellschaft mbH* [1982] ECR 2733, [1983] 1 CMLR 665.

[2] Ibid.

[3] Cf. Jenard, p. 44; Droz, para. 500; [1981] ECR at 1621 per Advocate General Reischl.

[4] Case 125/79: *Denilauler v SNC Couchet Frères* [1980] ECR 1553, [1981] 1 CMLR 62.

[5] P. 94, ante.

[6] Case 166/80: [1981] ECR 1593, [1982] 2 CMLR 773.

[7] The decision was applied in Case 228/81: *Pendy Plastic Products v Pluspunkt* [1982] ECR 2733, [1983] 1 CMLR 665.

choice but to consider it, although it will of course apply the law of the original court. In particular, the applicable provisions relating to translation of documents must be observed.[1] But the defendant must be served, and it seems that he would not lose his right to resist enforcement of a default judgment merely because he learned of the proceedings from other sources and deliberately refused to apply to set it aside in the original court.

A question which also arose in *Klomps v Michel* which has considerable practical importance with regard to certain forms of judgment was whether a Zahlungsbefehl, or order to pay, under German law was the document instituting the proceedings for the purposes of enforcement. The European Court ruled that a measure such as the order for payment in German law, service of which on the defendant enables the plaintiff, where no objection to the order is made, to obtain an enforceable decision was to be understood as being covered by the words "the document which instituted the proceedings". The enforcement order, issued following service of an order for payment and which is, in itself, enforceable under the Convention, is not the relevant document.[2]

Incompatibility with a judgment already given in the State in which recognition is sought[3]

Article 27(3) provides that a judgment irreconcilable with a judgment given in a dispute between the same parties in the State in which recognition is sought shall not be recognised. Its practical importance will be limited by Arts. 21 to 23, which in substance give priority to the court first seised. The second court seised must give up its jurisdiction or stay its proceedings, and must recognise the judgment of the first court under Art. 26. It is not necessary for the same cause of action to be involved: e.g., where a French court has given judgment in a dispute between parties in which a contract has been declared invalid, and is asked to enforce a Belgian judgment awarding damages for failure to perform the contract, the French court would be able to refuse recognition.[4] It probably applies also to the case where enforcement is sought in State A of a judgment given in State B which is irreconcilable with an earlier judgment in State C which is entitled to recognition in State A.[5]

Preliminary questions as to status

Article 27(4) provides that a judgment shall not be recognised if the original court, in order to arrive at its judgment, has decided a preliminary question concerning status or legal capacity of natural persons, rights in property arising

---

[1] See e.g. Art. 5 Hague Convention on service; Ord. 11, r 6(5), RSC.
[2] See also Mezger, 1981 Rev Crit 726; Huet, 1981 Clunet 893.
[3] See Droz, paras. 509–524.
[4] Jenard, p. 45. Cf. *Sofraco v Pluimvee Export*, French Cour de Cassation 1977, Eur Court Digest D I-27.3-Bl.
[5] Jenard, p. 45: see 1968 Convention, Art. 27(5), where State C is a non-Contracting State.

out of a matrimonial relationship, wills or succession in a way that conflicts with a rule of the private international law of the court in which recognition or enforcement is sought, unless the same result would have been reached by the application of the rules of private international law of the latter.[1] In several systems application by the court of origin of a rule of private international law different from that of the state addressed is a ground for non-recognition. This is a very limited example of that practice; it will be relevant where an English court is asked to enforce a maintenance order made in another Contracting State on the basis of a decision by the foreign court that the applicant was the spouse or child of the defendant in circumstances where the application of the English rules of private international law would have led to the result that the applicant was not the spouse or child. Thus a Dutch court refused to recognise a French judgment that a husband was not under a duty to maintain his wife, because under Dutch law (which is different from French law) the divorce would have been governed by Dutch law and the marriage would not have been regarded as dissolved.[2]

Conflicts with judgments given in non-Contracting States which qualify for recognition

The new Art. 27(5) provides that a judgment shall not be recognised if it is irreconcilable with an earlier judgment given in a non-Contracting State involving the same cause of action and between the same parties, provided that this latter judgment fulfils the conditions necessary for its recognition in the state addressed. It applies, for example, in the case of a decision dismissing an action against a person domiciled in a Contracting State which is given in non-Contracting State A; Contracting State B is obliged to recognise the judgment under a bilateral convention; the plaintiff brings fresh proceedings in another Contracting State, C, which is not obliged to recognise judgments given in a non-Contracting State. The text of Art. 27(3) had left it open to doubt which judgment had to be recognised in State B[3] and, therefore, the new version, which is based on Art. 5 of the 1971 Hague Convention, on Recognition and Enforcement of Foreign Judgments, is designed to ensure that a judgment given in a non-Contracting State takes priority where it has to be recognised not only by virtue of a multilateral or bilateral Convention, but also at common law.[4]

Insurance; consumer contracts; exclusive jurisdiction; conventions with third States

Article 28, in conjunction with Art. 34(2), provides that a judgment shall not be recognised or enforced if it conflicts with any of the following provisions:

---

[1] See Droz, paras. 525–533.
[2] *Onnen v Nielen*, 1976, Eur Court Digest D I-27.4-Bl.
[3] See Droz, para. 524.
[4] See Schlosser, para. 205.

(1) Section 3: insurance contracts.[1]
(2) Section 4: consumer contracts.
(3) Section 5: exclusive jurisdiction.
(4) Art. 59: Conventions with third states relating to claims against their domiciliaries.

But it is limited in scope, because in its examination of the grounds of jurisdiction referred to in Art. 28(1) the court or authority applied to is to be bound by the findings of fact on which the court in which the judgment was given based its jurisdiction. As indicated above[2] subject to these specific provisions, the jurisdiction of the court of the state in which the judgment was given may not be reviewed, and the test of public policy referred to in Art. 27(1) may not be applied to the rules relating to jurisdiction. Article 28 reflects the basic principle that the court in which recognition or enforcement is sought is not entitled to examine the jurisdiction of the original court, subject to limited exceptions. Even in the case of the limited exceptions, the court in which recognition or enforcement is sought is bound by the factual findings of the original court. But the court in which recognition or enforcement is sought is entitled to challenge the original court's finding that the case is within the Convention.[3] It is possible that this would entitle the United Kingdom court to disregard under s. 32 of the 1982 Act the judgment of the court of a Contracting State if it had been rendered despite a valid arbitration agreement between the parties. This would require the United Kingdom court to find that for this purpose the exclusion of arbitration from the ambit of the Convention extended not only to arbitration proceedings themselves but to judgments in disregard of them,[4] but the matter is not clear;[5] and s. 32(4) expressly provides that the section does not affect the recognition and enforcement in the United Kingdom of a judgment which is required to be recognised or enforced under the 1968 Convention. But there are no grounds for arguing that a judgment rendered in breach of a jurisdiction agreement under Art. 17 would not be enforceable. It will be for the court in which the proceedings are begun to rule on whether another court has exclusive jurisdiction by virtue of Art. 17. If it decides that the agreement is invalid or inoperative, or for any other reason, that the alleged jurisdiction agreement is inapplicable and that it has jurisdiction, then any resulting judgment will be enforceable in the United Kingdom. This is so notwithstanding the terms of s. 32 of the 1982 Act (which would otherwise entitle the United Kingdom court to disregard a foreign judgment given in disregard of a jurisdiction agreement) since that section is, as indicated above, expressly subject to the 1968 Convention.

Where the defendant has appeared to protest the jurisdiction of the foreign court of another Contracting State, the position is easier. Article 18 provides that it is not a submission, and if the foreign court holds that it has jurisdiction under the Convention (i.e. the defendant loses on the question of jurisdiction) and the

---

[1] For such a case in Germany see Federal Supreme Court, May 2, 1979, RIW/AWD 1979, 494.
[2] P. 107, ante.
[3] P. 106, ante.
[4] As in the case of the Swiss judgment in *Tracomin SA v Sudan Oil Seeds Co Ltd* [1983] 1 All ER 404, [1983] 1 WLR 662 affd. at (1983) Times, 2 July.
[5] See p. 29, ante; A German court enforced an Italian judgment which had held an arbitration clause ineffective: OLG Celle, December 8, 1977, RIW/AWD 1979, 131.

defendant then contests the proceedings, a resulting judgment will be enforceable in the United Kingdom because the court of the other Contracting State found that it had jurisdiction under the Convention and also the defendant submitted to the jurisdiction of the foreign court; if, however, the defendant takes no further steps in the proceedings and the foreign court enters a judgment in default of defence, it should only do so if it finds that it has jurisdiction under the Convention[1] and should not do so merely on the basis of the appearance to contest the jurisdiction; but if it finds it has jurisdiction the resulting judgment will be enforceable in the United Kingdom subject only to the strict exceptions in Arts. 27 and 28, as applied by Art. 34(2). There will be no room for refusal to enforce the judgment on the basis of s. 33 of the 1982 Act (which is not intended to affect enforcement under the 1968 Convention: s. 33(2)) on the theory that the defendant submitted only for the purpose of contesting the jurisdiction etc.[2]

Recognition

Article 26 which, like English law[3] and other systems, distinguishes between recognition and enforcement, provides that:

(1) a judgment given in a Contracting State shall be recognised in the other Contracting States without any special procedure being required. This was designed to abolish special procedures for recognition existing in some countries, such as Italy;

(2) any interested party who raises the recognition of a judgment as the principal issue in a dispute may apply for a decision that the judgment be recognised.[4] This is designed to deal with a situation where a person who is not a party to the action in which a judgment was given wishes to raise the judgment as a defence, e.g. a bank in State B presented with a bill of exchange which has already been declared invalid in State A.[5] In this case the jurisdiction of the court which gave the original judgment does not have to be verified by the court of the State in which the recognition is sought unless the matter in question falls within the scope of provisions relating to insurance, consumer contracts, or exclusive jurisdiction;

(3) if the outcome of the proceedings in a court of a Contracting State depends on the determination of an incidental question of recognition that court shall have jurisdiction over the question.

Neither the Convention nor the Official Reports try to solve the very difficult question of the scope of the estoppel arising from a foreign judgment or of the law on which it depends.[6] In particular, the Working Party in the accession negotiations did not try to find a general solution to the problem of the enforcement of judgments on issues regarded as substantive in the original court

---

[1] See 1968 Convention, Art. 20.
[2] See p. 92, ante, on 1968 Convention, Art. 18, and p. 143, post, on 1982 Act, s. 33.
[3] Dicey & Morris, pp. 1117–1120.
[4] See the new RSC Ord. 71, r. 35 for the procedure, Appendix 2, post.
[5] Jenard, p. 43.
[6] See Droz, para. 447.

but regarded as procedural in the court in which enforcement was sought.[1] It is difficult to see how issue estoppel as developed in England, with very uneven results,[2] can be fitted within the Convention framework, but it is likely that the court would apply analogous principles to determine whether the court which determined the issue had jurisdiction under the Convention.

Enforcement

Article 31 provides as follows:

"A judgment given in a Contracting State and enforceable in that State shall be enforced in another Contracting State when, on the application of any interested party, the order for its enforcement has been issued there.

However, in the United Kingdom, such a judgment shall be enforced in England and Wales, in Scotland, or in Northern Ireland when, on the application of any interested party, it has been registered for enforcement in that part of the United Kingdom."

This is the basic Article providing for enforcement of judgments of Contracting States within the scope of the Convention. The second paragraph was added by the Accession Convention to deal with registration in the separate "law districts" of the United Kingdom. "Any interested party" would seem to cover successors and assigns of the original party in whose favour the judgment was given. In the United Kingdom enforcement is to be by way of registration (1982 Act, s. 4(1)). The judgment creditor cannot bring an action on the original cause of action.[3] Nor, it seems, can he proceed by way of enforcement at common law; this would follow from the decision in *De Wolf v Cox BV*[4], where it was held that it would be incompatible with the enforcement provisions of the Convention to allow an action on the original cause of action, even though it might be cheaper to obtain summary judgment on the original cause of action than to enforce a foreign judgment. There would be no advantage, in any event, to a judgment creditor in attempting to enforce at common law.[5]

On the procedure for enforcement, the 1982 Act provides:

(1) A judgment which is the subject of an application under Art. 31 for its enforcement in any part of the United Kingdom (other than a maintenance order) shall, to the extent that its enforcement is authorised by the

---

[1] See Schlosser, para. 191; Dicey & Morris p. 1118; *Black-Clawson International v Papierwerke Waldhof-Aschaffenburg Aktiengesellschaft* [1975] AC 591, [1975] 1 All ER 810; Law Commission Working Paper on Statutes of Limitation in Private International Law (No. 75).

[2] See *Carl Zeiss Stiftung v Rayner & Keeler Ltd (No 2)* [1967] 1 AC 853, [1966] 2 All ER 536; *Tracomin SA v Sudan Oil Seeds Co Ltd* [1983] 1 All ER 404 at 413–14; affmd. (1983) Times, 2 July, CA; *Westfal-Larsen & Co AS v Ikerigi Compania Naviera SA, The Messiniaki Bergen* [1983] 1 All ER 382 at 388–9.

[3] Case 42/76: *De Wolf v Cox BV* [1976] ECR 1759, [1977] 2 CMLR 43; 1982 Act, s. 34.

[4] Supra. In this case the plaintiff brought an action on the original cause of action because it was cheaper than registering the foreign judgment. Dutch law was subsequently altered to remove this anomaly: (1979) 4 Eur L Rev 312.

[5] Cf. Jenard, p. 47.

appropriate court (normally the High Court or the Court of Session under Art. 32) be registered in the prescribed manner in that court.[1]

(2) Where a judgment is registered the reasonable costs or expenses of and incidental to its registration shall be recoverable as if they were sums recoverable under the judgment.[2]

(3) A judgment registered under s. 4 shall, for the purposes of its enforcement, be of the same force and effect, and the registering court shall have, in relation to its enforcement, the same powers, and proceedings for or with respect to its enforcement may be taken, as if the judgment had been originally given by the registering court and had (where relevant) been entered,[3] subject to Art. 39 (restriction on enforcement where appeal pending or time for appeal unexpired); to s. 7 (interest); and to any provision made by rules of court as to the manner in which the conditions subject to which a judgment registered under s. 4 may be enforced.[4]

(4) Interest on the judgment (as distinct from the interest on the underlying claim) is payable pursuant to s. 7. The applicant will have to show that the judgment provides for the payment of a sum of money and that in accordance with the law of the Contracting State in which the judgment was given interest on that sum is recoverable under the judgment from a particular date or time. In this event, the rate of interest and the date or time from which it is so recoverable is registered with the judgment and the resulting debt carries interest in accordance with the registered particulars.[5] Provision may be made by rules of court as to the manner in which and the periods by reference to which any interest payable is to be calculated and paid, including provision for such interest to cease to accrue as from a prescribed date. Costs or expenses recoverable by virtue of s. 4(2) carry interest as if they were the subject of an order for the payment of costs or expenses made by the registering court on the date of registration.[6] Debts under judgments registered under s. 4 carry interest only as provided by s. 7.[7] Under the 1933 Act and the bilateral Conventions with the Contracting States interest payable under the law of the original court is registrable at the time of registration of the judgment, but thereafter interest at the United Kingdom rate is payable on the total registered judgment.[8] The 1968 Convention is silent on interest, and courts in other Contracting States have taken differing views as to the applicable law on interest on judgment debts, but s. 7 clarifies the position in the United Kingdom.

---

[1] 1982 Act, s. 4(1). See the new RSC Ord. 71, rr. 25ff for the procedure in the High Court: Chapter 7 and Appendix 2, post.

[2] 1982 Act, s. 4(2). Cf. Foreign Judgments (Reciprocal Enforcement) Act 1933, s. 2(6). Art. III of the 1968 Protocol prohibits the charging of a court fee by reference to the value of the matter in issue: this will have no practical significance in the United Kingdom.

[3] 1982 Act, s. 4(3).

[4] 1982 Act, s. 4(4).

[5] See the new RSC Ord 71, r. 28(1)(b).

[6] 1982 Act, s. 7(3).

[7] 1982 Act, s. 7(5).

[8] 1933 Act, s. 2(2)(c); s. 2(6).

Currency of registered judgments

The Convention does not deal expressly with the currency in which judgments within its scope are to be enforced; but it is implicit in the system of the Convention that they should be registered in their original currency, as under the 1933 Act since the repeal of s. 2(3) in 1977.[1] There would have to be a conversion into sterling for the practical purposes of enforcement of execution.[2] For practical reasons, s. 8 of the 1982 Act makes special provision for the currency in which registered maintenance orders are payable.[3]

The Convention applies to non-money judgments, such as injunctions, including provisional measures (but not those granted and intended to be enforced ex parte).[4] This means that the English court may enforce German injunctions by sequestration or committal,[5] but the enforcement procedure of the English court will apply, including, it seems, the requirement of penal notices and including the discretion of the court as to whether or not to commit or fine. It will also be necessary for any order to be put into a form which will enable the object of the order to know precisely what it is that has to be done or not done. The court in which enforcement is sought must, it seems, apply the same sanctions as it would do in the case of one of its own orders.[6] This question may arise in practice if it is sought to enforce English orders in those countries which do not provide for fine or committal, but only for a fixed compensation to the plaintiff.[7] It is not likely that the courts of those countries will take power to imprison for breach of English orders; if an order of one of those countries is registered in England but disobeyed, it is not likely that the English court would in practice commit although it would have power to do so.[8] Schlosser[9] leaves open the question whether fines accruing to the State could be enforced under the Convention, but to enforce them would seem to be inconsistent with Art. 1.

Because of different private international law rules as to situs of debts, it is possible that garnishee or similar orders made by Contracting States may create problems where judgment debtors and third party debtors are situate in different States. In some countries the court of the third party debtor assumes jurisdiction;[10] in others the court of the domicile of the judgment debtor assumes jurisdiction. In these circumstances the judgment creditor should seek an order for enforcement in the country of the third party.[11]

Procedure

Article 32 sets out the authorities in each of the Contracting States to which the application for enforcement must be submitted. For the United Kingdom it

---

[1] Administration of Justice Act 1977, s. 4.
[2] Dicey & Morris, p. 1016.
[3] P. 125, post.
[4] See Case 125/79: *Denilauler v SNC Couchet Frères* [1980] ECR 1553, [1981] CMLR 62, p. 102, ante.
[5] RSC Ord. 45, r. 5.
[6] Schlosser, para. 212.
[7] E.g. Belgium and Luxembourg, and, to some extent, in France.
[8] See also 1968 Convention, Art. 43.
[9] Para. 213.
[10] This is broadly the position in England: Dicey & Morris, p. 530; cf. *Intraco v Notis Shipping Corpn of Liberia, The Bhoja Trader* [1981] 2 Lloyd's Rep 256, CA.
[11] Cf. Schlosser, para. 207, who points out that the Working Party abandoned attempts to deal with this problem in the Convention.

specifies in the case of England and Wales, the High Court of Justice; for Scotland, the Court of Session; and for Northern Ireland, the High Court of Justice. In each case special provision is made for maintenance judgments in the Magistrates' Court in England, the Sheriff Court in Scotland and the Magistrates' Court in Northern Ireland. These are the courts which are to be regarded as "the appropriate court" for registration.[1] The system follows that of the 1933 Act in giving jurisdiction to higher courts whatever the amount of the judgment debt in question. Article 32(2) allocates local jurisdiction where the system of law of the Contracting State provides for separate enforcement procedures. Separate registration procedures will have to be brought in each of the constituent parts of the United Kingdom; it will not be enough, for example, once registration of a judgment of another Contracting State has been effected in Scotland, to re-register the Scottish judgment in England: 1982 Act, s. 18(7).

The combined effect of Arts. 33 and 46 to 49 in the United Kingdom will be that (*a*) the procedure for registration will depend on the laws of England, Scotland and Northern Ireland;[2] (*b*) the applicant will have to give an address for service; (*c*) the application will have to be accompanied by:

(1) a copy of the judgment which satisfies the conditions necessary to establish its authenticity;

(2) in the case of a judgment given in default, the original or a certified true copy of the document which establishes that the party in default was served with the document instituting the proceedings or with an equivalent document;[3]

(3) documents which establish that, according to the law of the court in which judgment was given, the judgment is enforceable and has been served;

(4) where appropriate, a document showing that the applicant is in receipt of legal aid in the original court.

If the documents specified in (*c*) (2) and (4) above are not produced, the court may specify a time for their production, accept equivalent documents or, if it considers that it has sufficient information before it, dispense with their production; if the court so requires, a translation of the documents shall be produced, which shall be certified by a person qualified to do so in one of the Contracting States.[4] No legalisation or other similar formality will be required in respect of the documents referred to in (*c*) (1)–(4) above or in respect of a document appointing a representative ad litem.[5]

Section 11 of the 1982 Act supplements the provisions relating to the proof of judgments of courts of other Contracting States. It provides that for the purposes

---

[1] 1982 Act, s. 4(1); s. 5(1) deals with maintenance orders.
[2] The new RSC Ord. 71, r. 28 requires application for registration to be made by affidavit exhibiting the judgment or an authenticated copy and a document establishing that, according to the law of the State in which it was given, it is enforceable and has been duly served; where the judgment or document is not in English, a duly authenticated translation must be exhibited; in the case of a default judgment, the applicant must exhibit proof of service of the original proceedings; details of interest due under the law of the court of origin must be given.
[3] The reference to equivalent document was added because at that time under English procedure it was notice of writ which had to be served. See p. 108, ante under 1968 Convention, Art. 27(2).
[4] 1968 Convention, Art. 48. See the new RSC Ord. 71, r. 28.
[5] 1968 Convention, Art. 49.

of the 1968 Convention a document, duly authenticated, which purports to be a copy of a judgment given by a court of a Contracting State, other than the United Kingdom, shall without further proof be deemed to be a true copy, unless the contrary is shown[1]. A document purporting to be copy of a judgment given by any such court is duly authenticated for the purposes of the section if it purports (*a*) to bear the seal of that court or (*b*) to be certified by any person in his capacity as a judge or officer of that court to be a true copy of a judgment given by that court. The original or a copy of any such document as is mentioned in Art. 46(2) or 47 shall be evidence, and in Scotland sufficient evidence, of any matter to which it relates.[2] Nothing in s. 11 is to prejudice the admission in evidence of any document which is admissible apart from the section.[3]

Section 12 deals with the provision of certificates in connection with United Kingdom judgments. Rules of court[4] may make provision for enabling any interested party wishing to secure under the 1968 Convention the recognition or enforcement in another Contracting State of a judgment given by a court in the United Kingdom to obtain, subject to any conditions specified in the rules, (*a*) a copy of the judgment and (*b*) a certificate giving particulars relating to the judgment and the proceedings in which it was given.

Articles 34 to 41 set out the system of registration of judgments and appeals from registration and non-registration. Their broad effect in the United Kingdom, in conjunction with s. 6 of the 1982 Act, will be as follows:

(1) the first registration is to be made on an ex parte application;[5]
(2) the applicant is to be notified without delay of the registration after it has been effected;[6]
(3) the judgment debtor is notified of the registration, and may appeal against registration; the appeal must be made within one month (or two months, if he is domiciled in a Contracting State other than the United Kingdom) of service of notification of registration either personally or at the place of his residence;[7]
(4) the initial appeal is made in the United Kingdom to the High Court (England), the Court of Session (Scotland) and the High Court (Northern Ireland);[8]
(5) before the time limited for an appeal has expired or before such an appeal has been determined, execution of the judgment is not possible but the court may authorise protective measures to preserve the property or keep it within the jurisdiction;[9]

---

[1] See also the new RSC Ord. 71, r. 28(1)(*a*)(iv).
[2] 1982 Act, s. 11(1)(*b*).
[3] 1982 Act, s. 11(3).
[4] See the new RSC Ord. 71, r. 36, for the procedure in the High Court.
[5] 1968 Convention, Art. 34(1). This will in England be to a master of the Queen's Bench Division: RSC Ord. 71, rr. 26–27.
[6] 1968 Convention, Art. 35.
[7] 1968 Convention, Art. 36; it seems that the one month period should operate in relation to a French judgment against a U.S. resident: but see the new RSC Ord. 71, r. 33(2).
[8] 1968 Convention, Art. 37(1). The appeal will in England be to the judge in chambers: RSC Ord. 71, r. 33.
[9] 1968 Convention, Art. 39. See RSC Ord. 71, r. 34(4). If the applicant seeks a *Mareva* injunction, the application would be to the judge in Chambers.

(6) following the initial appeal, there is one further appeal on a point of law; the appeal is, in the case of England and Northern Ireland, to the Court of Appeal or the House of Lords;[1] and, in Scotland, to the Inner House of the Court of Session.[2]

(7) registration is only to be refused on one of the grounds set out in Arts. 27 and 28[3] and the merits of the judgment may not be reviewed;[4]

(8) if an appeal is pending against the decision of the court in which the original judgment was given, or if the time for appeal has not expired, the United Kingdom court may, on the application of the judgment debtor, stay the execution of the registered judgment or make its execution subject to the provision of security by the judgment creditor;[5]

(9) if the original application for registration is refused the applicant may appeal to the High Court (England[6] and Northern Ireland) or the Court of Session (Scotland); the judgment debtor will be given notice and if he fails to appear the court will have to be satisfied that he received notice in time to appear whether or not he is domiciled in a Contracting State;[7] if the registration is granted or refused on this inter partes application, the losing party may appeal once on a point of law.[8] The appeal system is the same as under (6) above.

The ex parte procedure required by Art. 34 is designed to produce a surprise effect to prevent the defendant from protecting his assets against the judgment creditor;[9] it gave rise to a question by the United Kingdom in the accession negotiations as to whether Art. 34 excluded the possibility of notifying the judgment debtor that an application for registration of a foreign judgment had been lodged. According to Schlosser,[10] since one of the aims of Art. 34 is to secure the element of surprise, although this provision does not expressly forbid notifying the debtor in the proceedings of the application for a grant of an enforcement order, such notification should be confined to very exceptional cases, such as where an application for registration is made a long time after the original judgment; in any case the court may not consider submissions from the judgment debtor, whether or not he was notified in advance.[11]

The effect of Arts. 37 and 41, which were adjusted to deal with (inter alia) the courts in the United Kingdom is that when registration is granted the judgment debtor (or, when refused, the judgment creditor) may appeal, to the High Court (England and Northern Ireland) or the Court of Session (Scotland).[12] Either party

---

[1] In cases covered by the system of "leap-frog" appeals under the Administration of Justice Act 1969.

[2] 1968 Convention, Art. 37(2); 1982 Act, s. 6. For maintenance orders see s. 6(3).

[3] But see also additional grounds, p. 107, ante.

[4] 1968 Convention, Art. 34(2)–(3).

[5] 1968 Convention, Art. 38.

[6] By appeal to the judge in chambers: RSC Ord. 71, r. 33.

[7] 1968 Convention, Art. 40.

[8] 1968 Convention, Art. 41 and 1982 Act, s. 6.

[9] See Case 125/79: *Denilauler v SNC Couchet Frères* [1980] ECR 1553, at 1569.

[10] Para. 219.

[11] The new provisions for Convention judgments do not contain a provision corresponding to RSC Ord. 71, r. 2(2), giving power to the court to direct a summons to be issued.

[12] Maintenance judgments: magistrates courts or Sheriff Court.

may appeal from these decisions by only "a single further appeal on a point of law". Section 6 of the 1982 Act provides that the single further appeal lies in England and Northern Ireland to the Court of Appeal or the House of Lords in accordance with the Administration of Justice Act 1969 ("leap-frog")[1] and in Scotland to the Inner House of the Court of Session. In the case of maintenance judgments the single appeal on a point of law lies in England to the High Court by way of case stated in accordance with the Magistrates' Courts Act 1980, s. 111, in Scotland to the Inner House of the Court of Session and in Northern Ireland to the Court of Appeal.

Effect of appeals

While an appeal is pending against the decision to enforce a judgment under the Convention, no measures of enforcement may be taken other than protective measures taken against the property of the judgment debtor: the decision authorising enforcement carries with it power to proceed to any protective measures.[2] The object of Art. 39 was to ensure at the enforcement stage a balance between the rights and interests of the parties concerned; the applicant is protected by the ex parte procedure and by the provision in Art. 39 that protective measures may be taken; to safeguard the rights of the judgment debtor it was necessary to delay enforcement to the end of the time specified for appeal under Art. 36, or if an appeal is lodged, until it has been determined.[3] There is no express power to grant protective measures while an appeal against non-registration is pending, but no doubt the court could grant them in exceptional cases.[4]

Articles 30 and 38 deal with applications for recognition or enforcement while appeals are pending in the foreign court in which the judgment was originally given. They provide as follows:

(1) a court of a Contracting State in which *recognition* is sought of a judgment given in another Contracting State may stay the proceedings if an "ordinary appeal" against the judgment has been lodged;

(2) a court of a Contracting State in which recognition is sought of a judgment given in the United Kingdom or Ireland may stay the proceedings if enforcement is suspended in the State in which the judgment was given by reason of an appeal;

(3) a court to which the judgment debtor has applied to set aside the registration may stay the enforcement proceedings if an ordinary appeal has been lodged against the judgment in the State in which the judgment was given; it may also stay the proceedings if the time for such appeal has

---

[1] Even though there is no appeal from the Court of Appeal to the House of Lords under the Convention scheme: 1982 Act, s. 6(2).

[2] 1968 Convention, Art. 39; 1982 Act, s. 4(4). See also the new RSC Ord. 71, r. 34. Cf. *Commerzbank v Giangrande*, Turin 1980 [1982] ECC 207.

[3] Jenard, p. 52.

[4] See the new RSC Ord. 71, r. 34(4) for reservation of this power.

not yet expired, but in that case the court in which enforcement is sought may specify the time within which an appeal is to be lodged;

(4) the court in which enforcement is sought is not bound to grant the stay, but if it does not do so it may make enforcement conditional on the provision of such security as it may determine.[1] This is to ensure that the judgment debtor does not find that he is unable to recover the judgment debt from the judgment creditor if the original judgment is overturned.[2]

The distinction between ordinary and extraordinary appeals has no counterpart in the United Kingdom, and although the distinction is found in the civil law Contracting States it is not applied uniformly.[3] In these circumstances the European Court in *Industrial Diamond Supplies v Riva*,[4] in answer to a Belgian court, held (in the context both of Art. 30 and of Art. 38) that (*a*) whether an appeal was ordinary or extraordinary depended on a Convention interpretation rather than on the procedural law of the court of origin; (*b*) the expression "ordinary appeal" must be understood as meaning any appeal which forms part of the normal course of an action and which, as such, constitutes a procedural development which any party must reasonably expect; (*c*) any appeal bound by the law to a specific period of time which starts to run by virtue of the actual decision whose enforcement is sought constitutes such a development. Consequently, any appeal which might be dependent on events which were unforeseeable at the date of the original judgment or upon action taken by persons who were extraneous to the judgment would not be an "ordinary appeal". The first case would include such matters as an application for a re-trial after new evidence had come to light or an application for a re-hearing. Article 38(2) provides that where the judgment is given in the United Kingdom or the Republic of Ireland any form of appeal available under their law shall be treated as an ordinary appeal for the purposes of Art. 38(1).[5] The special provisions relating to the United Kingdom and Ireland apply only to the enforcement of their judgments in other Contracting States. Therefore the United Kingdom courts may be required to consider whether an ordinary appeal is pending in another Contracting State in order to decide whether to grant a stay of enforcement proceedings.

Miscellaneous matters

Where a foreign judgment has been given in respect of several matters and enforcement cannot be authorised for all of them, the court shall authorise

---

[1] Cf. 1933 Act, s. 5; Dicey & Morris, p. 1108.

[2] E.g. OLG Celle, 1977, European Court Digest D I-27.1-Bl.

[3] See Schlosser, paras. 195–204; Gaudemet-Tallon, 1979 Rev Crit 426; Huet, 1978 Clunet 398.

[4] Case 43/77: [1977] ECR 2175, [1978] 1 CMLR 349.

[5] In relation to recognition of United Kingdom and Irish judgments, Art. 30(2) provides that the power to stay proceedings is only to be exercised if the United Kingdom or Irish court has granted a stay of execution pending appeal. In England, an appeal does not operate as a stay of execution or of proceedings under the decision unless the court below or the Court of Appeal so order (RSC Ord. 59, r. 13). It is not easy to see how Art. 30(2) would operate in the case of a judgment in favour of a defendant.

enforcement for those which may be enforced; an applicant may request partial enforcement of a judgment.[1] The former provision is intended to cover the case where a judgment deals with separate heads of claim and the decisions on some of them are contrary to the public policy of the court in which enforcement is sought (and perhaps also where parts of the claim are outside the Convention); the latter relates to such situations as where part of the judgment has been paid since the judgment was given.[2]

A foreign judgment which orders a periodic payment by way of a penalty is enforceable in the State in which enforcement is sought only if the amount of the payment has been finally determined by the courts of the State in which the judgment was given.[3] This deals with the enforcement of judgments originating from those countries which provide for a fixed penalty payable to the other party if one party fails to obey an order of the court.[4]

Legal Aid

By Art. 44, which was altered by the Accession Convention, an applicant who, in the State in which the judgment was given, has benefited from complete or partial legal aid or exemption for costs or expenses, shall be entitled, on the application for registration, to benefit from the most favourable legal aid or the most extensive exemption from costs or expenses provided for by the law of the State in which enforcement is sought.[5] The new version of Art. 44 applies to partial aid, as well as complete aid, but does not oblige States which do not at present have a system of legal aid in civil matters to introduce such a system. Section 40(1)(*b*) of the 1982 Act empowers the modification of legal aid provisions to deal with applications for registration of judgments under (inter alia) the 1968 Convention. Article 44, whose main practical application is likely to be in relation to maintenance orders, is of very limited scope because it applies only to the initial registration procedure under Arts. 32 to 35 and not to appeals.

Security for costs

No security, bond or deposit, however described, shall be required of a party who, in one Contracting State, applies for enforcement of a judgment given in another Contracting State on the ground that he is a foreign national or that he is not domiciled or resident in the State in which enforcement is sought.[6] This is

[1] 1968 Convention, Art. 42; by 1982 Act, s. 15(2), judgment includes a judgment registered to a limited extent only.
[2] Jenard, p. 53.
[3] 1968 Convention, Art. 43.
[4] Jenard, p. 53; Schlosser, para. 213.
[5] Special provision is made for the enforcement of a Danish maintenance order given by an administrative authority.
[6] 1968 Convention, Art. 45.

in line with the bilateral Conventions to which the United Kingdom is a party.[1] It does not prevent security being ordered on other grounds or (it seems) being ordered in relation to appeals.

Authentic instruments and court settlements

Article 50 deals with the enforcement of "authentic instruments", for which there is no equivalent in England and Ireland. In Scotland instruments establishing obligations to perform a contract can be entered in a public register, and an extract from the public register may then serve as a basis for enforcement in the same way as a court judgment.[2] Article 50 applies only to authentic instruments which have been drawn up or registered in matters falling within the scope of the Convention; they must be enforceable in the State in which they were drawn up or registered, and must satisfy the conditions necessary to establish authenticity in that State; their enforcement must not be contrary to public policy.[3] Settlements are dealt with by Art. 51, which provides that a settlement which has been approved[4] by a court in the course of proceedings and is enforceable in the State in which it was concluded shall be enforceable in the State in which enforcement is sought under the same conditions as authentic instruments. The normal forms of consent orders and judicial settlements in England are probably to be treated as judgments within Art. 25, rather than as settlements within Art. 51 but it probably makes no practical difference. The usual form of "Tomlin" order (i.e. that an action be stayed on terms agreed in a schedule, with liberty to apply to carry them into effect) would probably not qualify as a court settlement or a judgment for the purposes of enforcement in other Contracting States; this is because it cannot be enforced without a further order. Orders in Council may provide for statutory provisions (including the 1982 Act) dealing with recognition or enforcement of judgments within the scope of the 1968 Convention to be applied, with modifications, to authentic instruments and court settlements.[5]

Maintenance orders

The enforcement provisions of the Convention apply to maintenance orders within the scope of the Convention,[6] but it would seem that maintenance orders will continue to be enforceable under the Hague Convention of 1973 (to which the United Kingdom, Netherlands, Luxembourg, France and Italy are parties) and under the United Kingdom—Republic of Ireland bilateral arrangements.[7] A number of points in connection with the enforcement of maintenance orders

---

[1] See also RSC Ord. 71, r. 29.
[2] Schlosser, para. 226.
[3] Jenard, p. 56.
[4] Other language versions do not require that the settlement be "approved".
[5] 1982 Act, s. 13.
[6] On which see p. 57, ante.
[7] By virtue of Art. 57, under the Maintenance Orders (Reciprocal Enforcement) Act 1972, Part I.

made by courts of other Contracting States call for comment. A judgment is not to be recognised under the Convention if the court which gave it decided a preliminary question concerning the status or legal capacity of natural persons or rights in property arising out of a matrimonial relationship in a way which conflicts with a rule of the private international law of the State in which recognition or enforcement is sought, unless the same result would have been reached by the application of the rules of private international law of the latter State.[1] Thus an English court will not enforce a maintenance order made by a court in another Contracting State on the basis of the decision of that court that the applicant was the spouse or a legitimate or legitimated or illegitimate or adopted child of the defendant when the English court would not have reached the same result by applying the English rule of private international law.

The procedure under the 1982 Act for the enforcement of maintenance orders is similar to that under the 1972 Act.[2] The application under Art. 31 is transmitted to the magistrates' court or Sheriff Court for the place where the respondent is domiciled by the Secretary of State.[3] The person seeking enforcement must either give an address for service within the jurisdiction of the court applied to or appoint a representative ad litem.[4] The application is determined in the first instance by the prescribed officer of the court, who will probably be the clerk to the justices, and the order is then registered in the court; a registered order is to be, for the purposes of its enforcement, of the same force and effect, the registering court shall have in relation to its enforcement the same powers, and proceedings for or with respect to its enforcement may be taken, as if the order had originally been made by the registering court.[5] This is subject to the court's discretion under Art. 38 to stay enforcement if an appeal is pending in the country of origin and to Article 39, under which no measures of enforcement can be taken other than protective measures while an appeal is pending against the registration; the appeal must be made within one month, unless the respondent is domiciled in another Contracting State, in which case the period is two months; the initial appeal to set aside registration is to the magistrates' court or the Court of Session, with the possibility of a single further appeal on a point of law to the High Court by way of case stated under s. 111 of the Magistrates' Courts Act 1980.[6] If enforcement is refused by the prescribed officer of the court, the applicant may appeal to the magistrates' court or sheriff court with a single further appeal on a point of law as above.[7] The method of enforcement in England and Northern Ireland is the same as for an affiliation order, i.e. by a distress warrant, committal or attachment of earnings.[8]

Interest on arrears of sums payable under a registered order is not recoverable in the magistrates' court, and can only be recovered if the order is re-registered

---

[1] 1968 Convention, Art. 27(4). See p. 110, ante.

[2] See 1982 Act, s. 5.

[3] Or as respects Northern Ireland, by the Lord Chancellor.

[4] Schlosser, para. 218, suggests this will be the clerk to the justices.

[5] 1982 Act, s. 5(4).

[6] 1968 Convention, Arts. 36, 37; 1982 Act, s. 6(3). In Scotland, the Inner House of the Court of Session; in Northern Ireland, the Court of Appeal.

[7] 1968 Convention, Arts. 40, 41; 1982 Act, s. 6(3).

[8] 1982 Act, s. 5(6).

for enforcement in the High Court under the Maintenance Orders Act 1958, s. 2A, which was added by the 1982 Act[1] and provides for orders for interest made by the original court to be registrable in the High Court. Sums payable in the United Kingdom under a registered maintenance order are to be paid in sterling; where a maintenance order is expressed in a foreign currency, it is to be converted at the rate on the date of registration; a certificate of an officer of a bank is to be evidence of the rate.[2]

---

[1] 1982 Act, s. 37(1), Sch. 11, para. 6.
[2] 1982 Act, s. 8. Cf. Maintenance Orders (Reciprocal Enforcement) Act 1972, s. 16.

CHAPTER 6

INTRA-UNITED KINGDOM JURISDICTION AND ENFORCEMENT OF JUDGMENTS JURISDICTION IN SCOTLAND

Introduction

Part II of the 1982 Act deals with two matters regulating relations in the field of civil and commercial matters between the constituent parts of the United Kingdom. The first is entirely new, a system of jurisdictional rules for intra-United Kingdom cases, i.e. cases where the defendant is domiciled in the United Kingdom or where the proceedings are of a kind mentioned in Art. 16 of the 1968 Convention (exclusive jurisdiction); these rules are closely modelled on the 1968 Convention and will apply to allocate jurisdiction as between the parts of the United Kingdom, whether or not the 1968 Convention is actually applicable to the case. The second matter is a system of recognition and enforcement in one part of the United Kingdom of judgments rendered in another part; this is not new, but an improvement on the Judgments Extension Act 1868 and the Inferior Courts Judgments Extension Act 1882, which it will replace. Part III of the 1982 Act also provides for new jurisdictional rules in Scotland for cases with an international element which are not governed by the 1968 Convention or the intra-United Kingdom rules.

Jurisdiction

The primary rule of jurisdiction in the 1968 Convention is that a defendant domiciled in a Contracting State is to be sued in the courts of that State. Because the United Kingdom is not a unitary state for the purposes of civil jurisdiction it was necessary to allocate jurisdiction as between its constituent parts. But instead of confining itself to determining in which part of the United Kingdom a party is domiciled, the 1982 Act goes much further in laying down rules for determining jurisdiction in cases where the parties are domiciled in different parts of the United Kingdom. These rules (which are set out in Schedule 4 to the Act) are closely modelled on those in the 1968 Convention, but are not identical with them. They apply where (*a*) the subject-matter of the proceedings is within the scope of the 1968 Convention as determined by Art. 1 (whether or not the Convention has effect in relation to the proceedings) and (*b*) the defendant is domiciled in the United Kingdom or the proceedings are of a kind mentioned in Art. 16 (exclusive jurisdiction).[1]

Where, in a Convention case, Art. 2 applies and the courts of the United

---

[1] 1982 Act, s. 16(1).

Kingdom have jurisdiction as the Contracting State in which the defendant is domiciled, Schedule 4 determines in which part of the United Kingdom the defendant must be sued. Similarly, the reference in Art. 16 is to the courts of "the Contracting State" in which the property is situate, the company has its seat, the register is kept, etc. In these cases too it is necessary to allocate the resulting jurisdiction. Where the defendant is not domiciled in the United Kingdom and Art. 16 does not apply, the problem of intra-United Kingdom jurisdiction rarely arises in the Convention provisions set out in Schedule 1. Allocation is irrelevant in Arts. 3 and 4. Article 5(1), (2), (3), (5) and Art. 6(1) give jurisdiction to a "place" and it will be that part of the United Kingdom in which that place is situated which will be the relevant part of the United Kingdom for the purposes of jurisdiction. Article 5(4), (7) and Art. 6(2), (3), and Art. 6A refer to a "court" in which proceedings are pending and it will be the law district in which the relevant court is situated which will be the court with jurisdiction.

There are three further cases which do require allocation:

(1) Article 5(6) gives jurisdiction in actions against settlors, trustees or beneficiaries to the courts of the Contracting State in which the trust is domiciled, and s. 10(2) of the 1982 Act provides that any proceedings which by virtue of Art. 5(6) are brought in the United Kingdom shall be brought in the courts of the United Kingdom in which the trust is domiciled.[1]

(2) Article 14(1) allows a consumer to bring proceedings in the courts of the State in which he is domiciled, and s. 10(3) of the 1982 Act provides that any proceedings which, by virtue of Art. 14(1) are brought in the United Kingdom by a consumer on the ground that he is himself domiciled there, shall be brought in the court for the part of the United Kingdom in which he is domiciled.

(3) In Section 3 of the 1968 Convention (insurance) the only provision which requires an allocation is Art. 8(3). That provides that an insurer domiciled outside the Contracting States but with a branch, etc. in one of the Contracting States shall, in disputes arising out of the operations of that branch, etc., be deemed to be domiciled in that State. Article 13(2) (consumer contracts) requires a similar allocation. Section 44(2) of the 1982 Act provides for the purpose of those two provisions that, where the United Kingdom is deemed to be the place of domicile, the defendant is to be treated as domiciled in the part of the United Kingdom in which the branch, etc. is situated.

By s. 16(1), the provisions set out in Schedule 4 (which contains a modified version of Title II of the 1968 Convention) shall have effect for determining for each part of the United Kingdom, whether the courts of law of that part, or any particular court of law in that part, have or has jurisdiction in proceedings where:

(a) the subject matter of the proceedings is within the scope of the 1968 Convention as determined by Art. 1 (whether or not the Convention has effect in relation to the proceedings); and

---

[1] For the domicile of trusts see 1982 Act, s. 45.

(b) the defendant is domiciled in the United Kingdom or the proceedings are of a kind mentioned in Art. 16 (exclusive jurisdiction regardless of domicile).

Section 16(2) explains that in Schedule 4 modifications of Title II of the 1968 Convention are indicated by dots for the indication of modifications by way of omission and by heavy type for modifications by way of addition or substitution. In determining any question as to the meaning or effect of any provision contained in Schedule 4: (a) regard shall be had to any relevant principles laid down by the European Court in connection with Title II of the 1968 Convention and to any relevant decision of that Court as to the meaning or effect of any provision of that title; and (b) without prejudice to the generality of (a), the Jenard and Schlosser reports may be considered and shall, so far as relevant, be given such weight as is appropriate in the circumstances.

The primary rule of jurisdiction in Schedule 4 is, like that in the 1968 Convention, the domicile of the defendant, but there are differences between Schedule 4 and its 1968 Convention equivalent in the other heads of jurisdiction, the main ones being these:

(1) certain proceedings listed in Schedule 5 are excluded from the operation of Schedule 4.[1] Most of these are cases which would fall outside the Convention scheme, but there are others, such as (a) winding up of solvent companies or (b) proceedings concerned with registration of patents etc. which are within the Convention but outside Schedule 4. The former is excluded because it was not appropriate to apply the standard tests for seats of companies in the intra-United Kingdom context, where place of incorporation is the only appropriate test for winding up of domestic companies. Actions relating to registration of patents etc. are excluded because the principle of Art. 16(4) cannot be applied to allocate jurisdiction between courts in the United Kingdom since the registers of patents, trade marks and designs are all situated in London.[2] Actions concerned with registration or validity within the scope of Art. 16(4) are excluded from the operation of Sch. 4 (by Sch. 5, para. 2), but it would seem that actions for infringement would be within the other rules of Sch. 4, such as domicile of the defendant or place of the wrong;

(2) a number of the provisions of the 1968 Convention have no application to intra-United Kingdom allocation of jurisdiction, e.g. Arts. 2(2), 3(2) and 4: these have been omitted;

(3) in Art. 5(3) it has been made clear that it applies to the case of threatened torts by the addition of the words "or in the case of a threatened wrong is likely to occur";

(4) Art. 5(8) is additional and confers jurisdiction in the courts of the part of the United Kingdom in which property is situated in proceedings (a) concerning a debt secured on that property if it is immovable property[3] or (b) if the proceedings are brought to assert, declare or determine

---

[1] See 1982 Act, s. 17.
[2] Maxwell Report, paras 13.124–6.
[3] It seems that the action may be for an amount which exceeds the value of the property secured.

proprietary or possessory rights, or rights of security in or over, or to obtain authority to dispose of, that property if it is movable;

(5) a new Art. 5A confers jurisdiction in proceedings which have as their object a decision of an organ of a company or other legal person or of an association of natural or legal persons on the courts of the part of the United Kingdom in which that company, legal person or association has its seat. In the Convention (Art. 16(2)) *exclusive* jurisdiction is conferred on that place and not merely non-exclusive jurisdiction, and Art. 16(2) of the Convention also covers winding-up of solvent companies. Article 16 in Schedule 4 has been amended so as to delete the references to proceedings which have as their object a decision of an organ of a company, etc.;

(6) the provisions of Section 3 relating to jurisdiction in matters relating to insurance are entirely deleted. It would follow from this that, in proceedings between an insurer and an insured, they must be brought in the court of the defendant's domicile or under Art. 5(1) (the place of performance) or Art. 5(5) (branches etc). Section 4 (jurisdiction over consumer contracts) does not apply to insurance;[1]

(7) Article 16(4) in Schedule 1 does not appear in Schedule 4. Proceedings concerned with the registration or validity of patents, trade marks, designs or other similar rights are excluded by Schedule 5 from the operation of Schedule 4;[2]

(8) Article 17 has been altered in Sch. 4 to remove the requirement for writing and to make it clear that it does not apply if the choice of jurisdiction agreement would be otherwise ineffective (e.g. under the employment legislation). The provision of Art. 17(4) dealing with an agreement conferring jurisdiction having been concluded for the benefit of only one of the parties has been omitted;

(9) Articles 21 to 23, dealing with lis pendens and related actions have been omitted, because their subject matter is covered by s. 49 of the Act.

It is important to note that the adoption of the Convention scheme will have a far-reaching change on the rules of jurisdiction in actions between a plaintiff who sues in one part of the United Kingdom a defendant domiciled in another. For example, at present a plaintiff may obtain leave to serve an English writ on a defendant in Northern Ireland (but not one in Scotland) in a contract claim if the contract was made in England;[3] or he may sue a Scotsman temporarily in London. In each case, it is true, the court has a discretion, in the former case not to allow service out of the jurisdiction to stand[4] and in the latter case to stay the proceedings.[5] But under the scheme in Schedule 4 these heads of jurisdiction will disappear and if the defendant is domiciled in Scotland or Northern Ireland, and the contract was, although made in England, to be performed in Scotland or Northern Ireland, the English plaintiff will have to sue in the place of the defendant's domicile.[6]

---

[1] See amended Art. 13 in 1982 Act, Sch. 4.
[2] See p. 129, ante.
[3] RSC Ord. 11, r. 1(1)(*f*).
[4] Dicey & Morris, p. 197.
[5] P. 247.
[6] For the new RSC Ord. 11, r. 1(2) see Chapter 7 and Appendix 2, post.

Judgments

Section 18 of the 1982 Act is designed to replace the antiquated and limited procedure of the Judgments Extension Act 1868 and the Inferior Courts Judgments Extension Act 1882 with a more modern system of enforcement of judgments, and s. 19 is designed to provide a statutory basis for their recognition. The main defect of the dual system under the 1868 and 1882 Acts was that enforcement was limited to money judgments. An important difference between the 1868 Act and the 1920 and 1933 Acts is that, subject to one exception, under the 1868 Act the enforcing court is not entitled to investigate the jurisdiction of the original court and could not disregard its judgment on the ground that it lacked international jurisdiction. The exception was where a Scots judgment was founded on arrestment and entered in default. Under the 1882 Act there are stringent jurisdictional requirements. The 1982 Act makes the international jurisdiction of the original court irrelevant. If the judgment has been pronounced by a court in the United Kingdom, a court in another part of the United Kingdom cannot question the exercise of its jurisdiction. The extension of the enforcement system to non-money judgments is novel, and the differences in the types of orders granted by Scots and English courts will present obvious practical problems which will only be overcome when the nature of the orders involved is fully understood.[1]

Section 18 applies the provisions of Schedules 6 and 7 to the enforcement in one part of the United Kingdom of money and non-money judgments given by a court in another part. Judgment means[2] or includes[3] any of the following:

(a) a judgment or order given or made by a court of law in the United Kingdom;

(b) any other judgment or order which has been entered in England and Wales or Northern Ireland in the High Court or a county court;

(c) any document which in Scotland has been registered for execution in the books of Council and Session or in the sheriff court books kept for any sheriffdom;

(d) any award or order made by a tribunal in any part of the United Kingdom which is enforceable in that part without an order of a court of law;

(e) an arbitration award which has become enforceable in the part of the United Kingdom in which it was given in the same manner as a judgment by a court of law in that part;

(f) decrees issued under s. 13 of the Court of Exchequer (Scotland) Act 1856 (recovery of rent charges and penalties by process of the Court of Session); and

(g) orders relating to fines for contempt of court and forfeiture of recognisances under s. 16 of the Contempt of Court Act 1981 or s. 140 of the Supreme Court Act 1981.

Section 18 does not apply to the following classes of judgments:[4]

---

[1] For the procedure in the High Court see the new RSC Ord. 71, rr. 37 and 38, especially in the case of non-money judgments, the power of the court to direct the issue of a summons: Ord. 71, r. 38(1).

[2] 1982 Act, s. 18(2).

[3] 1982 Act, s. 18(4).

[4] 1982 Act, s. 18(3), (5)–(6).

(*a*) judgments given in proceedings in magistrates' courts in England or Northern Ireland;

(*b*) judgments given in proceedings other than civil proceedings;

(*c*) judgments given in proceedings relating to (i) bankruptcy, (ii) winding up or (iii) the obtaining of title to administer the estate of a deceased person;

(*d*) maintenance orders (which will continue to be enforced under the Maintenance Orders Act 1950);

(*e*) judgments concerning status or legal capacity of an individual, which include decrees of judicial separation or of separation and any provision relating to guardianship or custody;

(*f*) judgments relating to the management of the affairs of a person not capable of managing his own affairs;

(*g*) provisional (including protective) measures other than orders for the making of interim payments.

In addition, s. 18(7) in effect prevents "judgments on judgments" being enforced, at least where they are judgments registered under the statutory provisions for enforcement of foreign judgments, including the 1982 Act itself. So that if a French judgment is registered in England under the 1982 Act, it will be the French judgment which the judgment creditor will have to register in Scotland, and not the re-registered English registration. But it seems that judgments at common law on foreign judgments could be enforced under s. 18.

The procedure by way of registration is the exclusive procedure,[1] whereas under the previous system the right of action at common law was retained, subject to a costs sanction. Schedule 6 contains the procedure for the enforcement of money judgments and Schedule 7 of non-money judgments. In the case of money judgments the party who wishes to enforce applies for a certificate from the original court, and in the case of non-money judgments for a certified copy of the judgment. Once registered, the judgment of the original court has effect as a judgment of the court in which it is registered.[2] The application for a certificate or certified copy is made to an officer of the original court. A certificate (or certified copy) is not to be issued unless under the law of the part of the United Kingdom in which the judgment was given two conditions are fulfilled: first, either (i) the time for bringing an appeal against the judgment has expired, no such appeal having been brought within that time; or (ii) such an appeal having been brought within that time, that appeal has finally been disposed of; and, second, enforcement of the judgment is not for the time being stayed or suspended, and the time available for its enforcement has not expired. If the conditions are fulfilled, the officer of the court issues a certificate, in the case of a money judgment, stating the sum or aggregate of sums (including any costs or expenses) payable under the money provisions contained in the judgment, the rate of interest, if any, payable thereon and the date or time from which any such interest began to accrue; and stating that the conditions concerning the absence of an appeal or enforceability of a judgment are satisfied. In the case of a non-money judgment he issues a certified copy of the judgment. Where a certificate (or certified copy of a judgment) has been issued any interested party

---

[1] 1982 Act, s. 18(8).
[2] 1982 Act, Sch. 6, para. 6; Sch. 7, para. 6.

may, within six months from the date of its issue, in the case of money judgments (there is no time limit for non-money judgments) apply to the proper officer of the Superior Court in any other part of the United Kingdom for the certificate (or judgment) to be registered. Superior Court means in England and Wales or Northern Ireland the High Court, and in relation to Scotland, the Court of Session. Where an application is made to the proper officer, he registers the certificate in that court. Where a certificate or judgment is registered the reasonable costs or expenses of and incidental to the obtaining of the certificate and its registration are recoverable as if they were costs or expenses stated in the certificate to be payable under a money provision contained in the original judgment. In the case of money judgments, provision is made for interest from registration at the rate, if any, stated in the certificate on the date or time so stated. Provision may be made by Rules of Court as to the manner in which and the periods by reference to which any interest payable is to be calculated and paid, including provision for interest to cease to accrue as from a prescribed date. All sums recoverable as costs or expenses (in relation to both money and non-money judgments) carry interest as if they were the subject of an order for costs or expenses made by the registering court on the date of registration of the certificate.

The registering court may, if it is satisfied that any person against whom it sought to enforce the certificate is entitled and intends to apply under the law of the part of the United Kingdom in which the judgment was given for any remedy which would result in the setting aside or quashing of the judgment, stay proceedings for the enforcement of the certificate (or judgment) on such terms as it thinks fit, for such period as appears to the court to be reasonably sufficient to enable the application to be disposed of. A certificate or registered judgment must be set aside by the registering court if, on an application made by any interested party, it is satisfied that registration was contrary to the provisions of Schedule 6 or 7, as the case may be; and may set aside the registration if, on an application so made, it is satisfied that the matter in dispute in the proceedings in which the judgment in question was given had previously been the subject of a judgment by another court or tribunal having jurisdiction in the matter. But fraud is not a ground for setting registration aside.

Prior to the 1982 Act, recognition (as distinct from enforcement) in one part of the United Kingdom of judgments given in another part was regulated by the common law, where the ordinary rules as to jurisdiction of foreign courts were applicable.[1] Section 19 of the 1982 Act introduces a statutory scheme of recognition, which is not dependant on the international jurisdiction of the original court. It provides that a judgment to which it applies given in one part of the United Kingdom shall not be refused recognition in another part solely on the ground that, in relation to that judgment, the court which gave it was not a court of competent jurisdiction according to the rules of private international law in force in that other part. Section 19 applies to any judgment to which s. 18 applies except: (*a*) documents registered for execution in Scotland; (*b*) awards of tribunals and arbitral awards including those which have been registered; (*c*) the provisions relating to rent charges and penalties and to fines for contempt of court and forfeiture of recognisances.

---

[1] See Dicey & Morris, p. 1118.

Chapter 6

Jurisdiction in Scotland

The opportunity afforded by the 1982 Act to revise not only the jurisdictional rules in Convention cases and intra-United Kingdom cases but also in international cases has only partially been taken in England, where other cases will continue to come under the ordinary rules, including temporary presence within the jurisdiction and the provisions of RSC Ord. 11 as amended in 1983. But in Scotland a new code of jurisdiction has been introduced by Part III and Schedule 8 of the Act. These rules, which are based on the recommendations of the Maxwell Report,[1] are influenced by the Convention rules, but they retain in addition the traditional Scottish bases of jurisdiction, including arrestment of movable property, and ownership of immovable property. The Scottish rules are expressly subject to the Convention rules and the intra-United Kingdom rules when they are applicable.[2] To the extent that the rules are based on the Convention rules, in determining their meaning or effect regard may be had to the decisions of the European Court and the Jenard and Schlosser reports.[3] All of the rules in Schedule 8 are subject to the power of the Scots court to decline jurisdiction either on the ground of forum non conveniens, or on the ground that the parties have agreed to the jurisdiction of another court.[4] Certain categories of proceedings are excluded from the operation of the rules.[5] These include proceedings relating to status, bankruptcy and winding-up and admiralty actions in rem.

It follows that in determining whether any of the heads of jurisdiction in Schedule 8 can be exercised against defendants domiciled in other Contracting States or in other parts of the United Kingdom it will be necessary to consider whether the relevant Scottish rule is compatible with the Convention rules[6] and the intra-United Kingdom rules (in Schedule 4). Thus, for example, the jurisdiction in matters relating to a contract of the court of the place of performance of the obligation in question is common to the Convention, the intra-United Kingdom and the Scottish rules; the jurisdiction of the court of the place of a threatened wrong is common to the intra-United Kingdom and Scottish rules, and may (although this is not certain) be exercised under Art. 5(3) of the Convention; the jurisdiction in proceedings concerning a debt secured on immovable property in the courts where the property is situated is one which is common to the intra-United Kingdom rules and Scottish rules but cannot be exercised under the Convention unless the debt is payable or the defendant is domiciled in the place where the property is situate; the jurisdiction based on the arrestment of movable property or the ownership of immovable property cannot be exercised against domiciliaries of other Contracting States or of other parts of the United Kingdom.

Transitional Provisions

Parts II and III of the 1982 Act will come into force on a day to be appointed.[7] The intra-United Kingdom jurisdictional provisions in s. 16 and Schedule 4 will

---

[1] Chapters 13 and 14.
[2] 1982 Act, s. 20(1).
[3] 1982 Act, s. 20(5).
[4] 1982 Act, s. 22(1)–(2).
[5] 1982 Act, s. 21 and Sch. 9.
[6] 1982 Act, Sch. 1.
[7] 1982 Act, Sch. 13, Part I, para. 3.

only apply to proceedings begun after they come into force;[1] but even after they have come into force the courts of England and Northern Ireland will still be entitled to exercise jurisdiction in connection with a dispute concerning a contract if the parties have agreed before s. 16 comes into force that the contract was to be governed by the law of England or Northern Ireland, as the case may be.[2] The transitional provisions relating to intra-United Kingdom enforcement of judgments differ as between those concerned with money judgments and those concerned with non-money judgments. As regards money judgments, certificates registered under the 1868 or 1882 Acts before the repeal of those Acts come into force will continue to be effective, but once s. 18 and Schedule 6 come into force they may be applied to judgments given before they come into force unless they are already registered under the 1868 or 1882 Acts; but Schedule 7, which deals with non-money judgments, will only apply to judgments given after it comes into force.[3] The recognition provisions of s. 19 will apply only to judgments given after it comes into force.[4]

---

[1] As will the Scottish provisions in 1982 Act, Sch. 8.
[2] 1982 Act, Sch. 13, Part II, para. 1.
[3] Ibid., paras. 2 to 3.
[4] Ibid., para. 4.

CHAPTER 7

REFORMS OF THE GENERAL LAW RELATING TO JURISDICTION AND JUDGMENTS NEW RULES OF THE SUPREME COURT

Introduction

The opportunity has been taken in the 1982 Act to make changes in the law of jurisdiction and judgments, some of which are consequent upon the 1968 Convention (such as the introduction of a power to grant interim relief even though the substance of the case is being heard in another Contracting State) and others of which are the result of the unsatisfactory state of the previous law, especially that relating to what constitutes a submission to a foreign court. The changes cover the following areas: (1) jurisdiction is given to grant interim relief in cases of doubtful jurisdiction or in the absence of substantive proceedings (ss. 24 to 28); (2) the rule that English courts cannot entertain proceedings for trespass to foreign land is abolished except where the proceedings are principally concerned with title to or right to possession of the property (s. 30); (3) provision is made with regard to the enforcement in the United Kingdom of foreign judgments against foreign states (s. 31); (4) foreign judgments in proceedings brought in breach of jurisdiction and arbitration agreements are not to be enforceable (s. 32); (5) objecting to the jurisdiction of a foreign court is not to be regarded as a voluntary submission (s. 33); (6) the rule that a cause of action is not merged in a foreign judgment is abrogated (s. 34); (7) the Foreign Judgments (Reciprocal Enforcement) Act 1933 is amended so as to allow it to be applied to judgments of courts other than superior courts, to judgments providing for interim payments and to certain arbitration awards (s. 35 and Schedule 10); (8) the enactments relating to the enforcement of maintenance orders are amended to extend them to lump sum orders, to provide for the recovery of interest, and to extend the Maintenance Orders (Reciprocal Enforcement) Act 1972 to cases where the payer under the order is not resident within the jurisdiction but has assets there (s. 37); (9) a minor amendment to the Protection of Trading Interests Act 1980 (s. 38).

(1) *Interim relief*

Article 24 of the 1968 Convention allows national courts to grant provisional and protective measures even when, under the Convention, they do not have jurisdiction over the substance of the case. In English law, the position before 1982 was that such relief could not be granted where the court did not have jurisdiction over the main action, and the fact that an injunction was sought in relation to some relief in England was not sufficient to bring a case within Ord.

11 so as to confer jurisdiction over the substance of the case.[1] Where the jurisdiction was merely doubtful, rather than non-existent, injunctions were commonly granted in practice but there was sometimes reluctance to grant them.[2] Section 24 deals with cases where the jurisdiction of the court over the substance of the action is doubtful, and ss. 25 and 27 to 28 with cases where proceedings on the substance have been or are to be commenced in another Contracting State or in another part of the United Kingdom. The effect of s. 24 is that a court in England may grant interim relief pending trial, or pending the determination of an appeal, even in a case where (a) the issue to be tried, or which is the subject of the appeal, relates to the jurisdiction of the court to entertain the proceedings; or (b) the proceedings involve the reference of any matter to the European Court under the 1971 Protocol.[3] Section 25 deals with the power of the court to grant interim relief[4] where proceedings have been, or are to be commenced in another State (or in another part of the United Kingdom). It is designed both to give effect to Art. 24 of the Convention and also to reverse the effect of the decision in *The Siskina*.[5] As regards Convention and intra-United Kingdom cases, the High Court is to have power to grant interim relief where two conditions are fulfilled: the first is that proceedings have been or are to be commenced in a Contracting State other than the United Kingdom or in a part of the United Kingdom other than that in which the High Court exercises jurisdiction; the second is that the proceedings are or will be proceedings the subject matter of which is within the scope of the 1968 Convention as determined by Art. 1 (whether or not the Convention has effect in relation to the proceedings).[6] On any application for interim relief the court may refuse to grant that relief if, in the opinion of the court, the fact that the court has no jurisdiction apart from the Section in relation to the subject matter of the proceedings in question makes it inexpedient for the court to grant it.

As regards cases other than Convention and intra-United Kingdom, power is exercisable by Order in Council to extend the jurisdiction to grant interim relief[7] so as to make it exercisable in relation to proceedings of the following kinds:

(a) proceedings commenced, or to be commenced, otherwise than in a Contracting State (as in *The Siskina* itself);
(b) proceedings whose subject matter is not within the scope of the 1968 Convention as determined by Art. 1—i.e. proceedings in another Contracting State or in another part of the United Kingdom, but outside the scope of the 1968 Convention;

---

[1] See *The Siskina* [1979] AC 210, [1977] 3 All ER 803; *Perry v Zissis* [1977] 1 Lloyd's Rep. 607; Collins (1981) 1 Yb Eur Law 249, 251–8; pp. 98 to 102, ante; but cf. *Chief Constable of Kent v V* [1983] QB 34, [1982] 3 All ER 36, CA.

[2] As in *Evans Marshall & Co Ltd v Bertola SA* [1973] 1 WLR 349 at 357.

[3] 1982 Act, s. 24(2) makes similar provision with regard to protective relief in Scotland.

[4] Which means interim relief of any kind which that court has power to grant in proceedings relating to matters within its jurisdiction, other than (a) a warrant for the arrest of property or (b) provision for obtaining evidence: 1982 Act, s. 25(7).

[5] Ante.

[6] 1982 Act, s. 25(1). For Scotland see s. 27(1), and, for the special case of inspection or custody of property, s. 28.

[7] 1982 Act, ss. 25(3), 27(3).

(c) arbitration proceedings: at present the court may grant a *Mareva* injunction when there is an arbitration pending between the parties and even though there may have to be a mandatory stay of court proceedings under the Arbitration Act 1975[1] but there is no jurisdiction to grant it if the defendant is not amenable to the *in personam* jurisdiction of the Court.[2]

Section 26 deals with Admiralty proceedings. In particular it seeks to overcome a problem, which is akin to that thrown up by *The Siskina*. A & Co., charterers, have a claim against B & Co., a Panamanian ship-owning company; the charterparty contains a clause providing for arbitration in Hamburg; an action *in rem* must therefore be stayed under the Arbitration Act 1975 and A & Co. have no security for their claim.[3] Section 26 provides that where Admiralty proceedings have to be stayed or dismissed on the ground that the dispute in question should be submitted to arbitration or to the determination of the courts of another part of the United Kingdom, or of an overseas country, the court may, if in those proceedings property has been arrested or bail or other security has been given to prevent or obtain release from arrest, (a) order that the property arrested be retained as security for the satisfaction of any resulting award or judgment or (b) order that the stay or dismissal of those proceedings be conditional on the provision or equivalent security for the satisfaction of any such award or judgment. The court may attach such conditions to the order as it thinks fit, in particular conditions with respect to the institution or prosecution of the relevant arbitration or legal proceedings. Section 26 will not apply in relation to property arrested before its commencement; or in relation to security given before its commencement to prevent the arrest of property, or to obtain the release of property arrested before its commencement.[4]

(2) *Trespass to foreign land*

Section 30, which is already in force, reverses the much-criticised rule that actions for trespass to foreign land not involving questions of title fell within the rule in *British South Africa Co v Companhia de Mocambique*.[5] In *Hesperides Hotels Ltd v Aegean Turkish Holidays Ltd*[6] the House of Lords had the opportunity, which it did not take, to limit the *Mocambique* rule to cases not involving title. Lord Fraser said:[7]

"For these reasons I have serious doubt whether the law as laid down in the *Mocambique* case is either logical or satisfactory in its result. If the matter

---

[1] *The Rena K* [1979] QB 377, [1979] 1 All ER 397.
[2] See also Mustill & Boyd, p. 301; *Mantovani v Carapelli SpA* [1980] 1 Lloyd's Rep. 375 CA at 382. 1982 Act, s. 25(5) makes provision for repeal of s. 12(6) of the Arbitration Act 1950, which gives the High Court power to grant interim injunctions in the case of English arbitrations, to the extent that it may be superseded by an order made under s. 25(3).
[3] *The Golden Trader* [1975] QB 348, [1974] 2 All ER 686; but the position may be different where the stay is discretionary, or may not be final or where the arbitration is in England: *The Rena K* [1979] QB 377, [1979] 1 All ER 397; see Mustill & Boyd, pp. 298–300.
[4] 1982 Act, Sch. 13, Part II, para. 6.
[5] [1893] AC 602.
[6] [1979] AC 508, [1978] 2 All ER 1168.
[7] At 544.

were free from authority, there would be much to be said for what Mr. Kemp suggested was the true rule to be extracted from the *Mocambique* case, videlicet that the English court has jurisdiction to entertain an action for damages for trespass to foreign land against a person within the jurisdiction in a case where title is not in dispute and where there is no real dispute as to the plaintiff's right to possession of the land. But the matter is not free from authority and, in my opinion, this is not one on which it would be right for the House to depart from its earlier decisions. The main reason is that I do not think that the House in its judicial capacity has enough information to enable it to see the possible repercussions of making the suggested change in the law."

This invitation has been taken up by s. 30, the effect of which is that the courts in England and Northern Ireland will have jurisdiction to entertain proceedings for trespass to, or any other tort affecting, immovable property even in cases in which the property in question is situated outside the part of the United Kingdom in which it exercises jurisdiction, unless the proceedings are principally concerned with the question of the title to, or the right to possession of, that property. The exercise of this jurisdiction is subject to Art. 16(1) of the Convention and to the intra-United Kingdom jurisdiction rules. Thus it could not be exercised if the defendant is domiciled in another Contracting State or if the European Court should give an extended meaning to the expression "proceedings which have as their object rights *in rem* ... in immovable property" so as to make it cover some cases not involving title or right to possession. In any event, as Lord Fraser himself suggested,[1] the new power under s. 30 would have to be subject to the exercise of a discretion based on the principle of forum non conveniens, or a similar principle.[2]

(3) *Overseas judgments against foreign States*

Section 31, which is in force,[3] is designed to render foreign judgments against foreign States more easily enforceable in the United Kingdom. The position under the Foreign Judgments (Reciprocal Enforcement) Act 1933 is that for the purposes of that Act a foreign court has no jurisdiction to give a judgment capable of enforcement or recognition in England against a person who, under the rules of public international law, was entitled to immunity from jurisdiction of the courts of that country and did not submit thereto.[4] This is superseded by s. 31 of the 1982 Act in so far as it relates to foreign States, but will continue to operate with regard to judgments against diplomats or international organisations and also in relation to judgments rendered pursuant to certain international

---

[1] Ibid.

[2] See 1982 Act, s. 49.

[3] It does not apply to any judgment which was registered under the 1920 or 1933 Acts, or in respect of which proceedings at common law for its enforcement had been finally determined, before it came into force on 24 August 1982: 1982 Act, Sch. 13, Part II, para. 7.

[4] S. 4(3)(c).

agreements.[1] The broad effect of s. 31 is that a foreign judgment against a State, other than the United Kingdom or the State to which the court which pronounced the judgment belongs, shall be recognised and enforced in the United Kingdom if it would be so recognised and enforced if it had not been given against a State and the foreign court would have had jurisdiction in the matter if it had applied rules corresponding to those applicable to such matters in the United Kingdom in accordance with ss. 2 to 11 of the State Immunity Act 1978. For this purpose judgments against a State include judgments against a government, a department of the government, against the sovereign or head of State in his public capacity, but not judgments against an entity which is distinct from the executive organs or government, except in proceedings relating to anything done by it in the exercise of the sovereign authority of the State; in the case of a federal State, State includes any of its constituent territories.[2]

The consequence of s. 31 is that a foreign judgment against a State will be enforceable by way of execution in England, if both of the following conditions are fulfilled:

(1) first, that the foreign court would have had jurisdiction if it had applied the United Kingdom rules on sovereign immunity set out in ss. 2 to 11 of the State Immunity Act 1978, the effect of which is that a State is not immune (inter alia) where it submits to the jurisdiction or where the proceedings relate to a commercial transaction;[3]

(2) second, that under United Kingdom law the State is not immune from the process of execution. Section 31(4) of the 1982 Act gives to judgments against foreign States the benefit of (inter alia) the immunities from execution contained in ss. 13 and 14(3), (4) of the 1978 Act; their effect is that there can be no execution against sovereign property without the written consent of the foreign State unless the property is in use or intended for use for commercial purposes.[4]

(4) Overseas judgments given in proceedings brought in breach of agreement for settlement of disputes

Section 32, which is in force,[5] replaces s. 4(3)(b) of the Foriegn Judgments (Reciprocal Enforcement) Act 1933[6] and provides that a judgment given by a

---

[1] 1982 Act, s. 31(3) provides that s. 31 is not to affect the recognition or enforcement in the United Kingdom of judgments to which the 1933 Act applies by virtue of the Carriage of Goods by Road Act 1965, s. 4; Nuclear Installations Act 1965, s. 17(4); Merchant Shipping (Oil Pollution) Act 1971, s. 13(3); Carriage by Railway Act 1972, s. 5 (which will be replaced by International Transport Conventions Act 1983, s. 6, when it comes into force); Carriage of Passengers by Road Act 1974, s. 5.

[2] 1982 Act, s. 31(2), (5).

[3] See Dicey & Morris, pp. 156–171.

[4] 1978 Act, s. 13(3), (4). But property of a State's central bank or other monetary authority is not regarded as in use or intended for use for commercial purposes.

[5] It does not apply to any judgment which was registered under the 1920 Act or 1933 Acts or the Maintenance Orders (Reciprocal Enforcement) Act 1972, or in respect of which proceedings at common law for its enforcement had been finally determined, before it came into force on 24 August 1982: Sch. 13, Part II, para. 8.

[6] The position at common law was not covered by authority: see Dicey & Morris, p. 1061.

foreign court shall not be recognised or enforced in the United Kingdom if (*a*) the bringing of the proceedings in that court was contrary to an agreement under which the dispute in question was to be settled otherwise than proceedings in the courts of that country; and (*b*) those proceedings were not brought in that court by or with the agreement of, the person against whom the judgment was given; and (*c*) that person did not counterclaim in the proceedings or otherwise submit to the jurisdiction of that court. The principal object of s. 32 is to counteract those systems of law which disregard arbitration clauses or clauses providing for the jurisdiction of the English courts on the ground (for example) that an exchange of telexes or printed forms incorporating an arbitration or jurisdiction clause is not in "writing". Thus although the section does not apply where the agreement was illegal, void or unenforceable or was incapable of being performed for reasons not attributable to the fault of the party bringing the proceedings in which the judgment was given, nevertheless in determining whether a judgment given by the foreign court should be recognised or enforced a court in the United Kingdom is not bound by any decision of the overseas court relating to any of these matters.[1] The law of the relevant part of the United Kingdom (including its rules of the conflict of laws) would apply to determine whether the agreement was illegal, void or unenforceable, etc., without regard to the determination of the foreign court. Section 32 is not to affect the recognition or enforcement of a foreign judgment within the scope of the 1968 Convention.[2] It has already been seen that it is possible that s. 32 may be used to prevent the recognition or enforcement of judgments of courts of other Contracting States given in breach of arbitration clauses, but that it is unlikely that it would be used similarly where a jurisdiction clause has been overridden by the court of another Contracting State.[3]

Section 32 was applied in *Tracomin SA v Sudan Oil Seeds Co Ltd*[4] where a Swiss company had bought peanuts from a company connected with the Government of the Sudan. The contract incorporated a contract form which provided for English law to govern and for London arbitration. The buyers alleged that the peanuts were contaminated. In breach of the arbitration clause the Swiss buyers brought an action in the Swiss courts because the sellers had some assets there whereas they had none in England; the sellers applied to the Swiss court for the equivalent of a stay on the ground that the parties had agreed to arbitration in London; the Swiss court held that the arbitration clause was not incorporated in the contract, and its judgment was upheld by an appeal court. Meanwhile the sellers had appointed an arbitrator in the London arbitration. The buyers applied to the English court for an injunction to restrain the arbitration on the ground that, although by English law the arbitration clause formed part of the contract, the question whether it was incorporated in the contract had already been decided in the negative by the Swiss court and the sellers were bound by that determination. The question was therefore whether

---

[1] 1982 Act, s. 32(2), (3).
[2] 1982 Act, s. 32(4)(*a*). Nor does it apply to judgments within the scope of certain international agreements: see the statutory provisions at p. 141, n. 1, ante and Merchant Shipping Act 1974, s. 6(4): s. 32(4)(*b*).
[3] P. 112, ante.
[4] [1983] 1 All ER 404, [1983] 1 WLR 662, affd. (1983) Times, 2 July, CA.

the Swiss judgment should be *recognised* in England, rather than enforced. The Swiss judgment had been given in January 1982 and its decision on appeal affirmed in April 1982. The proceedings in England to restrain the arbitration were heard in June 1982 but the hearing was not concluded until September, by which time s. 32 of the 1982 Act had come into force. Staughton J. held that the Swiss judgment should not be recognised. His reasoning was as follows: (1) s. 32(1) provided that a foreign judgment should not be recognised if the bringing of the proceedings in the foreign court was contrary to an arbitration agreement; (2) by English law there was an arbitration agreement and s. 32(3) made the determination by the Swiss court on that question immaterial; (3) s. 32 did not apply if the person against whom the foreign judgment was given had submitted to the jurisdiction of the foreign court; (4) although there might have been what could be regarded as a submission at common law by the sellers in applying to the Swiss courts for a stay, s. 33 of the 1982 Act made it clear that an application to stay foreign proceedings on the ground that the dispute should be submitted to arbitration was not to be regarded as a submission; (5) on the basis that what was in issue was recognition of the Swiss judgment, there was nothing in the transitional provisions which required recognition of the Swiss judgment notwithstanding that it had been rendered before ss. 32 and 33 came into force.[1]

(5) *Abolition of the rule in Harris v Taylor [1915] 2 KB 580, CA and Henry v Geoprosco International Ltd [1976] QB 726, [1975] 2 All ER 702, CA*

The effect of s. 33, which is in force,[2] is to allow a defendant to object to the jurisdiction, or the exercise of jurisdiction, of a foreign court without running the risk of being regarded as having submitted to the jurisdiction of that court for the purposes of the enforcement of a subsequent judgment in default of appearance or defence if the objection to the jurisdiction of the foreign court should fail. Section 4(2)(*a*)(i) of the 1933 Act gave at least some protection by providing that intervention in proceedings for the purpose of protecting, or obtaining the release of, property seized, or threatened with seizure, in the proceedings or of contesting the jurisdiction of that court was not to be regarded as a voluntary appearance. But there was considerable doubt as to whether the common law gave similar protection, and it was held in *Henry v Geoprosco International Ltd*[3] that at common law there was a voluntary appearance where the defendant appeared before a foreign court to invite that court in its discretion not to exercise a jurisdiction which it had under its local law; and that there was also a voluntary appearance if the defendant merely protested against the jurisdiction of a foreign court if the protest took the form of a conditional appearance which was converted automatically by operation of law into an unconditional appearance if the decision on jurisdiction went against the

---

[1] Subsequently the Court of Appeal enjoined the continuance of the Swiss proceedings: (1983) Times, 2 July.

[2] It does not apply to any judgment which was registered under the 1920 or 1933 Acts, or in respect of which proceedings at common law for its enforcement had been finally determined before it came into force on 24 August 1982: Sch. 13, Part II, para. 9, on which see *Tracomin SA v Sudan Oil Seeds Co Ltd* [1983] 1 All ER 404, [1983] 1 WLR 662, affd. (1983) Times, 2 July, CA.

[3] [1976] QB 726, [1975] 2 All ER 702.

defendant; the Court of Appeal left open the question whether an appearance the sole purpose and effect of which was to protest against the jurisdiction of the foreign court would be a voluntary appearance. The decision was criticised on the ground that the distinctions between conditional appearances and appearances solely to protest the jurisdiction, and between protests against the existence of jurisdiction and protests against its exercise, were narrow and unsuited to questions of international jurisdiction,[1] and there was considerable pressure for the reversal of the decision by legislation.

The effect of s. 33[2] is that where a defendant with assets in England is sued abroad he may appear (conditionally or otherwise) to do any of the following things without laying his English assets open to the danger of execution on a resulting foreign judgment:

(a) to contest the jurisdiction of the court;
(b) to ask the court to dismiss or stay the proceedings on the ground that the dispute in question should be submitted to arbitration or to the determination of the courts of another country; or
(c) to protect, or obtain the release of, property seized or threatened with seizure in the proceedings.

But, if having lost on the jurisdictional issues, he goes on to defend the case on the merits he will be deemed to have submitted. A more difficult question arises when he has had to plead to the merits in the alternative to the plea on jurisdiction, as many systems of law require. At common law such a plea was regarded as a submission in *Boissière & Co v Brockner & Co*[3] but it should not now be so regarded, provided at least that having lost on the issue of jurisdiction the defendant does not put forward his case on the merits. In *Elefanten Schuh GmbH v Jacqmain*[4] the European Court held, in the context of Art. 18 of the Convention, that pleading to the merits as an alternative to jurisdiction would not be a submission, but this case is not directly relevant to the present problem because it does not concern the recognition and enforcement of foreign judgments. Under the Convention scheme the question of submission under Art. 18 is only relevant in the original court and not in the court in which enforcement is sought. It is for this reason that s. 33 cannot be used to prevent recognition and enforcement of judgments under the 1968 Convention, to which it is expressly made subject.[5] Section 33 was applied for the first time in *Tracomin SA v Sudan Oil Seeds Co Ltd*[6] where an application by a defendant to the Swiss courts for a stay on the ground that the claim was subject to arbitration in London was held not to be a submission to the jurisdiction of the Swiss court.

---

[1] See Dicey & Morris, pp. 1049–50; Collins (1976) 92 LQR 268.
[2] Which does not apply to Scotland, because "there has been no trace of such a doctrine in Scots law" (Anton, p. 579).
[3] (1889) 6 TLR 85.
[4] Case 150/80: [1981] ECR 1671, [1982] 3 CMLR 1.
[5] 1982 Act, s. 33(2).
[6] [1983] 1 All ER 404, [1983] 1 WLR 662, affd. (1983) Times, 2 July, CA discussed p. 142, ante.

(6) *Abolition of the non-merger rule*

Section 34, which is in force,[1] provides that no proceedings may be brought by a person on a cause of action in respect of which a judgment has been given in his favour in proceedings between the same parties, or their privies, in a court in another part of the United Kingdom or in a court of an overseas country, unless that judgment is not enforceable or entitled to recognition in England and Wales or, as the case may be, in Northern Ireland. This reverses, in part, the rule that a foreign judgment does not of itself extinguish the original cause of action in respect of which the judgment was given.[2] The original cause of action may however be sued upon if the foreign judgment is not enforceable in England. For example, if an Englishman obtains a judgment in California against a Californian resident on a cause of action based on a contract governed by English law, he cannot enforce the judgment in England unless the defendant can be served in England with a writ seeking enforcement of the foreign judgment at common law, even if the defendant has assets in England.[3] But the plaintiff may start again and obtain leave to serve a writ out of the jurisdiction, suing on the original contract as governed by English law, and then enforce any subsequent English judgment against the assets in England.

(7) *Minor amendments to the Administration of Justice Act 1920 and the Foreign Judgments (Reciprocal Enforcement) Act 1933*

Section 35 of the 1982 Act makes minor amendments to the 1920 and 1933 Acts, in conjunction with Schedule 10.[4]

1920 Act. Section 10 is amended so as to omit the requirement, in connection with the issue of certificates for the purposes of enforcement in Her Majesty's dominions outside the United Kingdom, of proof that the judgment debtor is resident in some part of those dominions. Section 14 is amended to allow an Order in Council to consolidate any Orders in Council made under the Section declaring to which territories the Act extends.

1933 Act. The 1933 Act is amended so that it can be applied to judgments of courts other than superior courts, to judgments providing for interim payments and to certain arbitration awards. The effect of the amendments in Schedules 10 and 14 is as follows:

(*a*) the Act may be applied to courts other than Superior Courts;
(*b*) the Act will apply to judgments ordering interim payments;
(*c*) the Act will not apply to foreign "judgments on judgments", i.e. "a

---

[1] It does not apply to judgments given before it came into force on 24 August 1982: Sch. 13, part II, para. 10. It does not apply to Scotland.
[2] See Dicey & Morris, p. 1077; *Carl Zeiss Stiftung v Rayner & Keeler Ltd (No 2)* [1967] 1 AC 853, esp. at 966 (a rule which "maintains a precarious foothold" and is "an illogical survival") per Lord Wilberforce.
[3] See *Perry v Zissis* [1977] 1 Lloyd's Rep 607. When the new RSC Ord. 11, r. 1(1)(*m*) comes into force, the original judgment will be enforceable
[4] There is some overlap between these provisions and 1982 Act, s. 54 and Sch. 14.

judgment or other instrument which is regarded for the purposes of its enforcement as a judgment of that court but which was given or made in another country" or "a judgment given by that court in proceedings founded on a judgment of a court in another country and having as their object the enforcement of that judgment."

(*d*) Section 4(2)(*a*)(i) is amended in consequence of s. 33 of the 1982 Act so as to omit all words relating to the exceptions to what constitutes a voluntary appearance.

(*e*) Section 4(3)(*b*) is repealed since it is replaced by s. 32.

(*f*) There is a new s. 10 providing that rules may make provision for enabling a judgment creditor to obtain copies and certificates in connection with U.K. judgments.

(*g*) A new s. 10A is added so that the Act will apply to all arbitration awards which have become enforceable in the countries to which it applies in the same manner as a judgment[1].

(8) *Maintenance orders*

Section 37 and Schedule 11 amend certain enactments relating to maintenance orders (*a*) to extend them to lump sum orders; (*b*) to provide for the recovery of interest according to the law of the country of origin in the case of maintenance orders made in other jurisdictions and registered in the High Court; and (*c*) to extend the Maintenance Orders (Reciprocal Enforcement) Act 1972 to cases where the payer under a maintenance order is not resident within the jurisdiction but has assets there. The enactments amended are the Maintenance Orders Act 1950; the Maintenance Orders Act 1958; the Maintenance and Affiliation Orders Act (Northern Ireland) 1966; and the Maintenance Orders (Reciprocal Enforcement) Act 1972.

(9) *Overseas Judgments counteracting an award of multiple damages*

Section 38 of the 1982 Act makes a minor amendment to s. 7 of the Protection of Trading Interests Act 1980. That section allows provision for the enforcement in the United Kingdom of judgments of courts of foreign countries counteracting awards of multiple damages on a reciprocal basis. The amendment relaxes the requirement of reciprocity by no longer requiring the foreign law to "correspond" to United Kingdom law within s. 6 of the 1980 Act: it will be sufficient now if the foreign law relates to the recovery of multiple damages within the meaning of the 1980 Act, whether or not the foreign law "corresponds" to the United Kingdom system of recovery.

New Rules of the Supreme Court

The amendments to the Rules of the Supreme Court made in July 1983[2] are designed to achieve two objects: the first is to make provision to deal with

---

[1] This replaces Administration of Justice Act 1956, s 51(*a*), which had applied the 1933 Act to awards of those Commonwealth countries to which it had been extended.

[2] S.I. 1983 No. 1181.

certain jurisdictional and enforcement aspects of the 1982 Act, both as regards Convention cases and intra-United Kingdom cases; the second is to make more general reforms in the operation of RSC Ord 11, r. 1 in non-Convention cases. The more important of the new Rules as amended are set out in Appendix 2 at the end of this book in the form which they will take when they are operation. Most of the major changes will not come into effect until s. 2 of the 1982 Act comes into force. The result is that the new Rules will only be fully effective when the Convention scheme comes into force in the United Kingdom.

Jurisdiction: Convention and intra-United Kingdom cases

When the English court has jurisdiction under the provisions of Schedule 1 to the 1982 Act in a Convention case, or under Schedule 4 in an intra-United Kingdom case, service out of the jurisdiction on a defendant will not normally be a matter of discretion (as under RSC Ord. 11, r. 1(1)) but a matter of right. The effect of certain provisions of the Convention is that the United Kingdom court must examine its jurisdiction "of its own motion".[1] Art. 19 of the Convention provides that where a court of a Contracting State is seised of a claim which is principally concerned with a matter over which the courts of another Contracting State have exclusive jurisdiction by virtue of Art. 16, it shall declare of its own motion that it has no jurisdiction; Art. 20(1) provides that where a defendant domiciled in one Contracting State is sued in a court of another Contracting State and does not enter an appearance, the court shall declare of its own motion that it has no jurisdiction unless its jurisdiction is derived from the provisions of the Convention, and shall stay its proceedings so long as it is not shown that the defendant has been able to receive the document instituting the proceedings in sufficient time to arrange for his defence; by Art. 21(1), where proceedings involving the same cause of action are brought in the courts of different Contracting States, any court other than the first seised shall of its own motion decline jurisdiction. Arts. 19 and 20 (but not 21) apply under Schedule 4 to intra-United Kingdom cases.

In order to give effect to these provisions the new Rules make three important changes relating to (1) service out of the jurisdiction; (2) issue of the writ; and (3) default judgments.

(1) *Service out of the jurisdiction*

By RSC Ord. 11, r. 1(2)(*a*) service of a writ out of the jurisdiction will be permissible without the leave of the court if each claim made by the writ is one which by virtue of the 1982 Act the court has power to hear and determine and the following conditions apply: first, no proceedings between the parties concerning the same cause of action are pending in the courts of any other part of the United Kingdom or in any other Contracting State; and second, either (i) the defendant is domiciled in any part of the United Kingdom or in any other

---

[1] See pp. 94–96, ante.

Contracting State, or (ii) the proceedings are within the exclusive jurisdiction of the court under Art. 16 of Schedule 1 or Schedule 4, or (iii) the defendant is a party to a jurisdiction agreement to which Art. 17 of Schedule 1 or Schedule 4 applies.[1]

(2) *Issue of the writ*

In order to prevent abuse of the right to serve a writ out of the jurisdiction under RSC Ord. 11, r. 1(2)(a) and in order to give the court an opportunity to verify its jurisdiction, RSC Ord. 6, rule 7 is amended so as to provide that no writ which is to be so served shall be issued without the leave of the court unless each claim made by the writ is one which, by virtue of the 1982 Act, the court has power to hear and determine and the writ is endorsed before it is issued with a statement (i) that the court has power under the 1982 Act to hear and determine the claim; and (ii) that no proceedings involving the same cause of action are pending between the parties in another part of the United Kingdom or in another Contracting State. The endorsement to the writ does not require the plaintiff to state what provision of the Convention or Schedule 4 gives the court jurisdiction.

(3) *Default judgments*

A new RSC Ord. 13, r. 7 provides that where a writ has been served out of the jurisdiction under RSC Ord. 11, r. 1(2)(a) (ie, where the 1982 Act purportedly applies) or has been served within the jurisdiction on a defendant domiciled in Scotland or Northern Ireland or in any Contracting State the plaintiff is not to be entitled to enter judgment for failure to give notice of intention to defend except with the leave of the court. In order for leave to be obtained, the application must be supported by an affidavit to the effect that (a) each claim made by the writ is one which by virtue of the 1982 Act the court has power to hear and determine; (b) no other court has exclusive jurisdiction within the meaning of Schedule 1 or under Schedule 4 to the 1982 Act to hear and determine such claim; and (c) where the writ is served out of the jurisdcition under RSC Ord. 11, r. 1(2)(a), such service satisfied the requirements of Schedule 1, or, as the case may require, of Art. 20 of Schedule 4 to the 1982 Act. Where, therefore, a plaintiff seeks to obtain a default judgment on a writ served out of the jurisdiction in a Convention case, he will have to show under what provision of the Convention the court has jurisdiction, so that the court can satisfy itself under Art. 20 of its jurisdiction and of due service if the defendant does not acknowledge service.

Jurisdiction: RSC Ord. 11, r. 1 and non-Convention cases

At the same time as the changes to give effect to the 1982 Act, the opportunity has been taken to make a number of important changes to RSC Ord. 11, r. 1 on

---

[1] See also amendments to RSC Ord. 10, r. 3, in relation to contractual provisions conferring jurisdiction on English courts.

service out of the jurisdiction in non-Convention cases. The details of the heads of jurisdiction under RSC Ord. 11, r. 1(1), where exercise is a matter of discretion, are outside the scope of this work,[1] but the main alterations call for a short comment:

Re-arrangement

The heads of jurisdiction have been grouped in a more logical order, and all sub-paragraphs of RSC Ord. 11, r. 1(1) have been re-lettered. The new sequence is as follows:

		New sub-paragraph	Previous sub-paragraph
General—	domicile	(a)	(c)
	injunctions	(b)	(i)
	necessary or proper party	(c)	(j)
Contract—	made in jurisdiction; made through agent in jurisdiction; governed by English law; provides for jurisdiction of English court	(d)	(f), Ord. 11, r. 2
	breach within jurisdiction	(e)	(g)
Tort		(f)	(h)
Property—	land	(g)	(a)
	deeds, wills, contracts etc. affecting land	(h)	(b)
	debt secured on immovable property; movable property	(i)	(k)
	trusts	(j)	(e)
	administration of estates	(k)	(d)
	probate	(l)	(m)
Judgments and awards		(m)	no equivalent
Revenue		(n)	(o)
Nuclear Installations Act 1965 and Social Security Act 1975		(o)	(l)
EEC Directive 76/308		(p)	(p)

Domicile

The new RSC Ord. 11, r. 1(1)(a) provides for jurisdiction in the case of action against "a person domiciled within the jurisdiction". The previous version gave jurisdiction in the case of a person "domiciled or ordinarily resident" within the jurisdiction. In the new version (which, like the old, applies to corporations as well as to natural persons) "domicile" is to have the same meaning as under the

---

[1] See Supreme Court Practice 1982, 11/1/1–21; Dicey & Morris, pp. 196–229.

Chapter 7

1982 Act,[1] as it is under the new sub-paragraph (*k*), which gives jurisdiction in administration actions in the case of the estates of persons who died domiciled within the jurisdiction, and is otherwise unchanged.

Necessary or proper party

The new sub-paragraph (*c*) confers jurisdiction over a person out of the jurisdiction who is a necessary or proper party to an action against a person duly served within or out of the jurisdiction. There are three important changes in the practice. First, the new version applies whether the defendant first served is served within the jurisdiction or outside the jurisdiction. It will be no longer be necessary for the defendant first served to have been served within the jurisdiction, so that now it will be possible for A to serve B out of the jurisdiction under one of the heads of RSC Ord. 11, r. 1(1) and subsequently join C as a necessary or proper party. Second, as a result of an amendment to RSC Ord. 16, r. 3(4), the new sub-paragraph (*c*) applies to third parties: it had been held previously that it did not apply to third party proceedings.[2] Thirdly, in order to prevent collusive actions between A and B designed to join C as an additional defendant or third party, RSC Ord. 11, r. 4(1)(*d*) requires the plaintiff to support his application to serve a necessary or proper party out of the jurisdiction with an affidavit showing that there is a real issue between him and the defendant first served.[3]

Jurisdiction clauses

The new sub-paragraph (*d*)(iv), replacing RSC Ord. 11, r. 2 (which is revoked), provides that leave to serve out of the jurisdiction may be granted in contract cases where the contract contains a term that the High Court is to have jurisdiction to hear and determine any action in respect of the contract. Where the contract provides for the method of service, the writ will be deemed to have been duly served on the defendant if that method is followed; but leave must still be obtained if the place of service is to be outside the jurisdiction.[4]

Place of Tort

The new sub-paragraph (*f*) provides that leave to serve out of the jurisdcition may be given where the claim is founded on a tort and "the damage was sustained, or resulted from an act committed, within the jurisdiction". This is designed to adopt for the purposes of RSC Ord. 11, r. 1(1) the dual test of place of the tort held by the European Court in *Handelswekerij GJ Bier BV v Mines de Potasse d'Alsace SA*[5] to be appropriate for Art. 5(3) of the Convention. The

---

[1] RSC Ord. 11, r. 1(4).

[2] See Dicey & Morris, p. 227.

[3] Cf. *Tyne Improvement Comrs v Armement Anversois SA, The Brabo* [1949] AC 326, [1949] 1 All ER 294; *Ellinger v Guinness, Mahon & Co* [1939] 4 All ER 16.

[4] RSC Ord. 10, r. 3(1), (2).

[5] Case 21/76: [1976] ECR 1735, [1977] 1 CMLR 284. See pp. 58–61, ante.

European Court held that jurisdiction could be exercised by the court of the place where the wrongful act occurred or of the place where the damage arose. Under the previous version it was not finally settled whether it was the place of acting or the place of harm which was appropriate, although the more recent tendency was to look at the place of the "substance" of the cause of action.[1] Under the new rule, the English court may take jurisdiction if either the wrongful act took place in England, or the injury occurred in England. But the exercise of the jurisdiction, by contrast with that under Art. 5(3) of the Convention, will continue to be discretionary.

Property

The new sub-paragraph (*i*) is considerably more extensive than the previous sub-paragraph (*k*), which applied principally to actions relating to security over movable property. The new version applies to the following claims: (*a*) for a debt secured on immovable property; (*b*) to assert, declare or determine proprietary or possessory rights, or rights of security, in or over movable property situate within the jurisdiction; (*c*) to obtain authority to dispose of movable property situate within the jurisdiction.

Trusts

The new sub-paragraph (*j*) confers jurisdiction in actions against trustees to execute a written trust governed by English law. Previously it also required that the trust property be situate within the jurisdiction, and it was held that it did not apply when by the time of the issue of the writ the trustee had absconded with the trust property.[2]

Judgments and awards

Sub-paragraph (*m*) provides a new head of jurisdiction to give jurisdiction in common law actions to enforce foreign judgments or awards against judgment debtors who have assets in England but who are neither resident in, or carry on business in, England. This is intended to fill a gap shown by a case such as *Perry v Zissis*,[3] where a judgment creditor on a United States judgment, otherwise entitled to recognition and enforcement, was not able to enforce it in England against the judgment debtor, who had assets in England but could not be served with the writ in England.[4]

---

[1] See *Castree v E R Squibb & Sons* [1980] 2 All ER 589, [1980] 1 WLR 1248, CA; *Multinational Gas v Multinational Gas Services Ltd* [1983] 2 All ER 563, [1983] 3 WLR 492, CA.

[2] *Winter v Winter* [1894] 1 Ch 421, criticised in *Official Solicitor v Stype Investments (Jersey) Ltd* [1983] 1 All ER 629, [1983] 1 WLR 214. A trustee absconding to a Contracting State could be sued in England under Art. 5(6) of the Convention, taken in conjunction with s. 45 of the 1982 Act.

[3] [1977] 1 Lloyd's Rep. 607, CA.

[4] For awards, see also the new RSC Ord. 73, r. 7(1A).

Tax

Sub-paragraph (*n*) has been widened so that it applies to all revenue claims. The previous version applied only to estate duty and capital transfer tax.

Jurisdiction: changes applying generally

Two miscellaneous changes are made which will be applicable in Convention cases, intra-United Kingdom cases, and other cases where the defendant is outside the jurisdiction.

(1) *Dispute as to jurisdiction*

RSC Ord. 12, r. 8 is amended so that the time by which a defendant who wishes to dispute the jurisdiction must apply to set aside service or apply for other similar relief, after acknowledging service and giving notice of intention to defend, is to be the time limited for service of defence, instead of the previous 14 day requirement; and the draconian provision that an application for extension must be made before the expiry of the time is deleted, thereby giving effect to the suggestion by Robert Goff J. in *Carmel Exporters (Sales) Ltd v Sea-Land Services Inc.*[1] Another reason for the change is that such a rigid requirement for disputing jurisdiction meant that a defendant would be regarded as having submitted to the jurisdiction even before the time-limit for putting in a defence: but it seems from the decisions of the European Court[2] that in Convention cases at least it is open to a defendant to wait until the defence is due before electing to contest the jurisdiction or submit to it.

(2) *Individual traders carrying on business within the jurisdiction*

RSC Ord. 81, r. 9 is amended so that an individual foreigner trading within the jurisdiction but resident outside may be served with a writ within the jurisdiction at the place of business within the jurisdiction. It had been held under the previous wording that the rules relating to service on a partnership (which allow service on a person having management or control of the partnership business within the jurisdiction) did not apply to an individual trading as a firm who resides out of the jurisdiction but who carries on business within the jurisdiction through a branch situated in the jurisdiction.[3] The change will not only remove an anomalous distinction between foreign partnerships and foreign individual traders, but will also make it easier for plaintiffs to make use of their rights in Convention cases under Art. 5(5) to sue foreign individual

---

[1] [1981] 1 All ER 984, [1981] 1 WLR 1068.
[2] Case 150/80: *Elefanten Schuh GmbH v Jacqmain* [1981] ECR 1671, [1982] 3 CMLR 1; Case 27/81: *Rohr SA v Ossberger* [1981] ECR 2431, [1982] 3 CMLR 29.
[3] *St Gobain, Chauny & Cirey Co v Hoyermann's Agency* [1893] 2 QB 96.

traders with branches in England in disputes arising out of the operations of such branches.

Enforcement of judgments: Convention cases

RSC Ord. 71 has been amended to contain detailed provisions for the procedure for enforcement of judgments in Convention cases. These follow the Convention closely.

Applications are reserved to the Queen's Bench Division. The initial application is made ex parte to a Master with the information and evidence required by Arts. 33, 46 and 47 of the Convention,[1] but the court has power to extend the time for production of documents, and to accept equivalent documents or dispense with them.[2] No security for costs may be required from the applicant on the ground that he is not domiciled or resident within the jurisdiction.[3] The judgment creditor, after registration, may apply to the judge in chambers for protective measures,[4] but execution is not to issue until expiration of the time for appeal against the order. Notice of registration is given to the judgment debtor, who may appeal by summons to the judge in chambers; the time for appeal will be one month for United Kingdom domiciliaries, and two months for persons domiciled in other Contracting States and in non-Contracting States: in the case of judgment debtors domiciled in non-Contracting States the time may be extended upon application, but not in the case of judgment debtors domiciled in Contracting States.[5] The applicant for registration may appeal to the judge in chambers against a master's refusal to authorise registration.[6]

Enforcement of judgments: intra-United Kingdom cases

RSC Ord. 71, rr. 37 and 38 set out respectively the procedure for obtaining of certificates or certified copies of judgments of, respectively, money and non-money judgments of courts of other parts of the United Kingdom. In the case of non-money judgments, although the application is initially ex parte, the court may direct a summons to be issued; and the person obliged under the non-money judgment may apply to have the registration set aside.[7]

---

[1] RSC Ord. 71, rr. 26–28.
[2] RSC Ord. 71, r. 28(2).
[3] RSC Ord. 71, r. 29. See p. 122, ante.
[4] RSC Ord. 71, r. 30(3). See p. 120, ante.
[5] RSC Ord. 71, r. 29(4), r. 33(3).
[6] RSC Ord. 71, r. 33(1).
[7] RSC Ord. 71, r. 38(4).

APPENDIX 1

THE CIVIL JURISDICTION AND JUDGMENTS ACT 1982

(1982 c 27)

ARRANGEMENT OF SECTIONS

PART I

IMPLEMENTATION OF THE CONVENTIONS

Main implementing provisions

Appendix 1

An Act to make further provision about the jurisdiction of courts and tribunals in the United Kingdom and certain other territories and about the recognition and enforcement of judgments given in the United Kingdom or elsewhere; to provide for the modification of certain provisions relating to legal aid; and for connected purposes [13th July 1982]

Part I

Implementation of the Conventions

Main implementing provisions

1. Interpretation of references to the Conventions and Contracting States

(1) In this Act—

"the 1968 Convention" means the Convention on jurisdiction and the enforcement of judgments in civil and commercial matters (including the Protocol annexed to that Convention), signed at Brussels on 27th September 1968;

"the 1971 Protocol" means the Protocol on the interpretation of the 1968 Convention by the European Court, signed at Luxembourg on 3rd June 1971;

"the Accession Convention" means the Convention on the accession to the 1968 Convention and the 1971 Protocol of Denmark, the Republic of Ireland and the United Kingdom, signed at Luxembourg on 9th October 1978;

"the Conventions" means the 1968 Convention, the 1971 Protocol and the Accession Convention.

(2) In this Act, unless the context otherwise requires—

(a) references to, or to any provision of, the 1968 Convention or the 1971 Protocol are references to that Convention, Protocol or provision as amended by the Accession Convention; and

(b) any reference to a numbered Article is a reference to the Article so numbered of the 1968 Convention, and any reference to a sub-division of a numbered Article shall be construed accordingly.

(3) In this Act "Contracting State" means—

(a) one of the original parties to the 1968 Convention (Belgium, the Federal Republic of Germany, France, Italy, Luxembourg and the Netherlands); or

(b) one of the parties acceding to that Convention under the Accession Convention (Denmark, the Republic of Ireland and the United Kingdom),

being a state in respect of which the Accession Convention has entered into force in accordance with Article 39 of that Convention.

157

2. The Conventions to have the force of law

(1) The Conventions shall have the force of law in the United Kingdom, and judicial notice shall be taken of them.

(2) For convenience of reference there are set out in Schedules 1, 2 and 3 respectively the English texts of—

   (a) the 1968 Convention as amended by Titles II and III of the Accession Convention;
   (b) the 1971 Protocol as amended by Title IV of the Accession Convention; and
   (c) Title V and VI of the Accession Convention (transitional and final provisions),

being texts prepared from the authentic English texts referred to in Articles 37 and 41 of the Accession Convention.

3. Interpretation of the Conventions

(1) Any question as to the meaning or effect of any provision of the Conventions shall, if not referred to the European Court in accordance with the 1971 Protocol, be determined in accordance with the principles laid down by and any relevant decision of the European Court.

(2) Judicial notice shall be taken of any decision of, or expression of opinion by, the European Court on any such question.

(3) Without prejudice to the generality of subsection (1), the following reports (which are reproduced in the Official Journal of the Communities), namely—

   (a) the reports by Mr P Jenard on the 1968 Convention and the 1971 Protocol;[1] and
   (b) the report by Professor Peter Schlosser on the Accession Convention,[2]

may be considered in ascertaining the meaning or effect of any provision of the Conventions and shall be given such weight as is appropriate in the circumstances.

Supplementary provisions as to recognition and enforcement of judgments

4. Enforcement of judgments other than maintenance orders

(1) A judgment, other than a maintenance order, which is the subject of an application under Article 31 for its enforcement in any part of the United Kingdom shall, to the extent that its enforcement is authorised by the appropriate court, be registered in the prescribed manner in that court.

In this subsection "the appropriate court" means the court to which the application is made in pursuance of Article 32 (that is to say, the High Court or the Court of Session).

(2) Where a judgment is registered under this section, the reasonable costs or expenses of and incidental to its registration shall be recoverable as if they were sums recoverable under the judgment.

(3) A judgment registered under this section shall, for the purposes of its enforcement, be of the same force and effect, the registering court shall have in relation to its enforcement the same powers, and proceedings for or with respect to its enforcement may be taken, as if the judgment had been originally given by the registering court and had (where relevant) been entered.

(4) Subsection (3) is subject to Article 39 (restriction on enforcement where appeal pending or time for appeal unexpired), to section 7 and to any provision made by rules of court as to the manner in which and conditions subject to which a judgment registered under this section may be enforced.

---

[1] OJ 1979 No. C59, pp 1, 66.
[2] OJ 1979 No. C59, p 71.

5. Recognition and enforcement of maintenance orders

(1) The function of transmitting to the appropriate court an application under Article 31 for the recognition or enforcement in the United Kingdom of a maintenance order shall be discharged—

    (a) as respects England and Wales and Scotland, by the Secretary of State;
    (b) as respects Northern Ireland, by the Lord Chancellor.

In this subsection "the appropriate court" means the magistrates' court or sheriff court having jurisdiction in the matter in accordance with the second paragraph of Article 32.

(2) Such an application shall be determined in the first instance by the prescribed officer of that court.

(3) Where on such an application the enforcement of the order is authorised to any extent, the order shall to that extent be registered in the prescribed manner in that court.

(4) A maintenance order registered under this section shall, for the purposes of its enforcement, be of the same force and effect, the registering court shall have in relation to its enforcement the same powers, and proceedings for or with respect to its enforcement may be taken, as if the order had been originally made by the registering court.

(5) Subsection (4) is subject to Article 39 (restriction on enforcement where appeal pending or time for appeal unexpired), to section 7 and to any provision made by rules of court as to the manner in which and conditions subject to which an order registered under this section may be enforced.

(6) A maintenance order which by virtue of this section is enforceable by a magistrates' court in England and Wales or Northern Ireland shall be enforceable in the same manner as an affiliation order made by that court.

(7) The payer under a maintenance order registered under this section in a magistrates' court in England and Wales or Northern Ireland shall give notice of any change of address to the clerk of that court.

A person who without reasonable excuse fails to comply with this subsection shall be guilty of an offence and liable on summary conviction to a fine not exceeding [level 2 on the standard scale].[1]

6. Appeals under Article 37, second paragraph and Article 41

(1) The single further appeal on a point of a law referred to in Article 37, second paragraph and Article 41 in relation to the recognition or enforcement of a judgment other than a maintenance order lies—

    (a) in England and Wales or Northern Ireland, to the Court of Appeal or to the House of Lords in accordance with Part II of the Administration of Justice Act 1969 (appeals direct from the High Court to the House of Lords);
    (b) In Scotland, to the Inner House of the Court of Session.

(2) Paragraph (a) of subsection (1) has effect notwithstanding section 15(2) of the Administration of Justice Act 1969 (exclusion of direct appeal to the House of Lords in cases where no appeal to that House lies from a decision of the Court of Appeal).

(3) The single further appeal on a point of law referred to in Article 37, second paragraph and Article 41 in relation to the recognition or enforcement of a maintenance order lies—

    (a) in England and Wales, to the High Court by way of case stated in accordance with section 111 of the Magistrates' Courts Act 1980;

---

[1] Amended by virtue of the Criminal Justice Act 1982, ss 37, 46.

(b) In Scotland, to the Inner House of the Court of Session;

(c) in Northern Ireland, to the Court of Appeal.

7. Interest on registered judgments

(1) Subject to subsection (4), where in connection with an application for registration of a judgment under section 4 or 5 the applicant shows—

(a) that the judgment provides for the payment of a sum of money; and

(b) that in accordance with the law of the Contracting State in which the judgment was given interest on that sum is recoverable under the judgment from a particular date or time,

the rate of interest and the date or time from which it is so recoverable shall be registered with the judgment and, subject to any provision made under subsection (2), the debt resulting, apart from section 4(2), from the registration of the judgment shall carry interest in accordance with the registered particulars.

(2) Provision may be made by rules of court as to the manner in which and the periods by reference to which any interest payable by virtue of subsection (1) is to be calculated and paid, including provision for such interest to cease to accrue as from a prescribed date.

(3) Costs or expenses recoverable by virtue of section 4(2) shall carry interest as if they were the subject of an order for the payment of costs or expenses made by the registering court on the date of registration.

(4) Interest on arrears of sums payable under a maintenance order registered under section 5 in a magistrates' court in England and Wales or Northern Ireland shall not be recoverable in that court, but without prejudice to the operation in relation to any such order of section 2A of the Maintenance Orders Acts 1958 or section 11A of the Maintenance and Affiliation Orders Act (Northern Ireland) 1966 (which enable interest to be recovered if the order is re-registered for enforcement in the High Court).

(5) Except as mentioned in subsection (4), debts under judgments registered under section 4 or 5 shall carry interest only as provided by this section.

8. Currency of payment under registered maintenance orders

(1) Sums payable in the United Kingdom under a maintenance order by virtue of its registration under section 5, including any arrears so payable, shall be paid in the currency of the United Kingdom.

(2) Where the order is expressed in any other currency, the amounts shall be converted on the basis of the exchange rate prevailing on the date of registration of the order.

(3) For the purposes of this section, a written certificate purporting to be signed by an officer of any bank in the United Kingdom and stating the exchange rate prevailing on a specified date shall be evidence, and in Scotland sufficient evidence, of the facts stated.

Other supplementary provisions

9. Provisions supplementary to Title VII of 1968 Convention

(1) The provisions of Title VII of the 1968 Convention (relationship between that convention and other conventions to which Contracting States are or may become parties) shall have effect in relation to—

(a) any statutory provision, whenever passed or made, implementing any such other convention in the United Kingdom; and

(b) any rule of law so far as it has the effect of so implementing any such other convention,

as they have effect in relation to that other convention itself.

(2) Her Majesty may by Order in Council declare a provision of a convention entered into by the United Kingdom to be a provision whereby the United Kingdom assumed an obligation of a kind provided for in Article 59 (which allows a Contracting State to agree with a third State to withhold recognition in certain cases from a judgment given by a court in another Contracting State which took jurisdiction on one of the grounds mentioned in the second paragraph of Article 3).

10. Allocation within UK of jurisdiction with respect to trusts and consumer contracts

(1) The provisions of this section have effect for the purpose of allocating within the United Kingdom jurisdiction in certain proceedings in respect of which the 1968 Convention confers jurisdiction on the courts of the United Kingdom generally and to which section 16 does not apply.

(2) Any proceedings which by virtue of Article 5(6) (trusts) are brought in the United Kingdom shall be brought in the courts of the part of the United Kingdom in which the trust is domiciled.

(3) Any proceedings which by virtue of the first paragraph of Article 14 (consumer contracts) are brought in the United Kingdom by a consumer on the ground that he is himself domiciled there shall be brought in the courts of the part of the United Kingdom in which he is domiciled.

11. Proof and admissibility of certain judgments and related documents

(1) For the purposes of the 1968 Convention—

(a) a document, duly authenticated, which purports to be a copy of a judgment given by a court of a Contracting State other than the United Kingdom shall without further proof be deemed to be a true copy, unless the contrary is shown; and

(b) the original or a copy of any such document as is mentioned in Article 46(2) or 47 (supporting documents to be produced by a party seeking recognition or enforcement of a judgment) shall be evidence, and in Scotland sufficient evidence, of any matter to which it relates.

(2) A document purporting to be a copy of a judgment given by any such court as is mentioned in subsection (1)(a) is duly authenticated for the purposes of this section if it purports—

(a) to bear the seal of that court; or

(b) to be certified by any person in his capacity as a judge or officer of that court to be a true copy of a judgment given by that court.

(3) Nothing in this section shall prejudice the admission in evidence of any document which is admissible apart from this section.

12. Provision for issue of copies of, and certificates in connection with, UK judgments

Rules of court may make provision for enabling any interested party wishing to secure under the 1968 Convention the recognition or enforcement in another

Contracting State of a judgment given by a court in the United Kingdom to obtain, subject to any conditions specified in the rules—

(a) a copy of the judgment; and

(b) a certificate giving particulars relating to the judgment and the proceedings in which it was given.

13. Modifications to cover authentic instruments and court settlements

(1) Her Majesty may by Order in Council provide that—

(a) any provision of this Act relating to the recognition or enforcement in the United Kingdom or elsewhere of judgments to which the 1968 Convention applies; and

(b) any other statutory provision, whenever passed or made, so relating,

shall apply, with such modifications as may be specified in the Order, in relation to documents and settlements within Title IV of the 1968 Convention (authentic instruments and court settlements enforceable in the same manner as judgments) as if they were judgments to which that Convention applies.

(2) An Order in Council under this section may make different provision in relation to different descriptions of documents and settlements.

(3) Any Order in Council under this section shall be subject to annulment in pursuance of a resolution of either House of Parliament.

14. Modifications consequential on revision of the Conventions

(1) If at any time it appears to Her Majesty in Council that Her Majesty's Government in the United Kingdom have agreed to a revision of any of the Conventions, including in particular any revision connected with the accession to the 1968 Convention of one or more further states, Her Majesty may by Order in Council make such modifications of this Act or any other statutory provision, whenever passed or made, as Her Majesty considers appropriate in consequence of the revision.

(2) An Order in Council under this section shall not be made unless a draft of the Order has been laid before Parliament and approved by a resolution of each House of Parliament.

(3) In this section "revision" means an omission from, addition to or alteration of any of the Conventions and includes replacement of any of the Conventions to any extent by another convention, protocol or other description of international agreement.

15. Interpretation of Part I and consequential amendments

(1) In this Part, unless the context otherwise requires—

"judgment" has the meaning given by Article 25;

"maintenance order" means a maintenance judgment within the meaning of the 1968 Convention;

"payer", in relation to a maintenance order, means the person liable to make the payments for which the order provides;

"prescribed" means prescribed by rules of court.

(2) References in this Part to a judgment registered under section 4 or 5 include, to the extent of its registration, references to a judgment so registered to a limited extent only.

(3) Anything authorised or required by the 1968 Convention or this Part to be done by, to or before a particular magistrates' court may be done by, to or before any

magistrates' court acting for the same petty sessions area (or, in Northern Ireland, petty sessions district) as that court.

(4) The enactments specified in Part I of Schedule 12 shall have effect with the amendments specified there, being amendments consequential on this Part.

PART II

JURISDICTION, AND RECOGNITION AND ENFORCEMENT OF JUDGMENTS, WITHIN UNITED KINGDOM

16. Allocation within UK of jurisdiction in certain civil proceedings

(1) The provisions set out in Schedule 4 (which contains a modified version of Title II of the 1968 Convention) shall have effect for determining, for each part of the United Kingdom, whether the courts of law of that part, or any particular court of law in that part, have or has jurisdiction in proceedings where—

- (a) the subject-matter of the proceedings is within the scope of the 1968 Convention as determined by Article 1 (whether or not the Convention has effect in relation to the proceedings); and
- (b) the defendant or defender is domiciled in the United Kingdom or the proceedings are of a kind mentioned in Article 16 (exclusive jurisdiction regardless of domicile).

(2) In Schedule 4 modifications of Title II of the 1968 Convention are indicated as follows—

- (a) modifications by way of omission are indicated by dots; and
- (b) within each Article words resulting from modifications by way of addition or substitution are printed in heavy type.

(3) In determining any question as to the meaning or effect of any provision contained in Schedule 4—

- (a) regard shall be had to any relevant principles laid down by the European Court in connection with Title II of the 1968 Convention and to any relevant decision of that court as to the meaning or effect of any provision of that Title; and
- (b) without prejudice to the generality of paragraph (a), the reports mentioned in section 3(3) may be considered and shall, so far as relevant, be given such weight as is appropriate in the circumstances.

(4) The provisions of this section and Schedule 4 shall have effect subject to the 1968 Convention and to the provisions of section 17.

(5) In section 15(1)(a) of the Maintenance Orders Act 1950 (domestic proceedings in which initial process may be served in another part of the United Kingdom), after sub-paragraph (v) there shall be added—

"(vi) Article 5(2) of Schedule 4 to the Civil Jurisdiction and Judgments Act 1982; or".

17. Exclusion of certain proceedings from Schedule 4

(1) Schedule 4 shall not apply to proceedings of any description listed in Schedule 5 or to proceedings in Scotland under any enactment which confers jurisdiction on a Scottish court in respect of a specific subject-matter on specific grounds.

(2) Her Majesty may by Order in Council—

- (a) add to the list in Schedule 5 any description of proceedings in any part of the United Kingdom; and

(b) remove from that list any description of proceedings in any part of the United Kingdom (whether included in the list as originally enacted or added by virtue of this subsection).

(3) An Order in Council under subsection (2)—

(a) may make different provisions for different descriptions of proceedings, for the same description of proceedings in different courts or for different parts of the United Kingdom; and

(b) may contain such transitional and other incidental provisions as appear to Her Majesty to be appropriate.

(4) An Order in Council under subsection (2) shall not be made unless a draft of the Order has been laid before Parliament and approved by a resolution of each House of Parliament.

18. Enforcement of UK judgments in other parts of UK

(1) In relation to any judgment to which this section applies—

(a) Schedule 6 shall have effect for the purpose of enabling any money provisions contained in the judgment to be enforced in a part of the United Kingdom other than the part in which the judgment was given; and

(b) Schedule 7 shall have effect for the purpose of enabling any non-money provisions so contained to be so enforced.

(2) In this section "judgment" means any of the following (references to the giving of a judgment being construed accordingly)—

(a) any judgment or order (by whatever name called) given or made by a court of law in the United Kingdom;

(b) any judgment or order not within paragraph (a) which has been entered in England and Wales or Northern Ireland in the High Court or a county court;

(c) any document which in Scotland has been registered for execution in the Books of Council and Session or in the sheriff court books kept for any sheriffdom;

(d) any award or order made by a tribunal in any part of the United Kingdom which is enforceable in that part without an order of a court of law;

(e) an arbitration award which has become enforceable in the part of the United Kingdom in which it was given in the same manner as a judgment given by a court of law in that part;

and, subject to the following provisions of this section, this section applies to all such judgments.

(3) Subject to subsection (4), this section does not apply to—

(a) a judgment given in proceedings in a magistrates' court in England and Wales or Northern Ireland;

(b) a judgment given in proceedings other than civil proceedings;

(c) a judgment given in proceedings relating to—

(i) bankruptcy; or

(ii) the winding up of a corporation or association; or

(iii) the obtaining of title to administer the estate of a deceased person.

(4) This section applies, whatever the nature of the proceedings in which it is made, to—

(a) a decree issued under section 13 of the Court of Exchequer (Scotland) Act 1856 (recovery of certain rentcharges and penalties by process of the Court of Session);

(b) an order which is enforceable in the same manner as a judgment of the High Court in England and Wales by virtue of section 16 of the Contempt of Court Act 1981 or section 140 of the Supreme Court Act 1981 (which relate to fines for contempt of court and forfeiture of recognisances).

(5) This section does not apply to so much of any judgment as—

(a) is an order to which section 16 of the Maintenance Orders Act 1950 applies (and is therefore an order for whose enforcement in another part of the United Kingdom provision is made by Part II of that Act);

(b) concerns the status or legal capacity of an individual;

(c) relates to the management of the affairs of a person not capable of managing his own affairs;

(d) is a provisional (including protective) measure other than an order for the making of an interim payment;

and except where otherwise stated references to a judgment to which this section applies are to such a judgment exclusive of any such provisions.

(6) The following are within subsection (5)(b), but without prejudice to the generality of that provision—

(a) a decree of judicial separation or of separation;

(b) any provision relating to guardianship or custody.

(7) This section does not apply to a judgment of a court outside the United Kingdom which falls to be treated for the purposes of its enforcement as a judgment of a court of law in the United Kingdom by virtue of registration under Part II of the Administration of Justice Act 1920, Part I of the Foreign Judgments (Reciprocal Enforcement) Act 1933, Part I of the Maintenance Orders (Reciprocal Enforcement) Act 1972 or section 4 or 5 of this Act.

(8) A judgment to which this section applies, other than a judgment within paragraph (e) of subsection (2), shall not be enforced in another part of the United Kingdom except by way of registration under Schedule 6 or 7.

19. Recognition of UK judgments in other parts of UK

(1) A judgment to which this section applies given in one part of the United Kingdom shall not be refused recognition in another part of the United Kingdom solely on the ground that, in relation to that judgment, the court which gave it was not a court of competent jurisdiction according to the rules of private international law in force in that other part.

(2) Subject to subsection (3), this section applies to any judgment to which section 18 applies.

(3) This section does not apply to—

(a) the documents mentioned in paragraph (c) of the definition of "judgment" in section 18(2);

(b) the awards and orders mentioned in paragraphs (d) and (e) of that definition;

(c) the decrees and orders referred to in section 18(4).

PART III

JURISDICTION IN SCOTLAND

20. Rules as to jurisdiction in Scotland

(1) Subject to Parts I and II and to the following provisions of this Part, Schedule 8 has effect to determine in what circumstances a person may be sued in civil proceedings in the Court of Session or in a sheriff court.

(2) Nothing in Schedule 8 affects the competence as respects subject-matter or value of the Court of Session or of the sheriff court.

(3) Section 6 of the Sheriff Courts (Scotland) Act 1907 shall cease to have effect to the extent that it determines jurisdiction in relation to any matter to which Schedule 8 applies.

(4) In Schedule 8—

    (a) words resulting from modifications of Title II of the 1968 Convention, by way of addition or substitution, and provisions not derived from that Title are printed in heavy type; and

    (b) the marginal notes show, where appropriate, of which provision of Title II a provision of Schedule 8 is a modified version.

(5) In determining any question as to the meaning or effect of any provision contained in Schedule 8 and derived to any extent from Title II of the 1968 Convention—

    (a) regard shall be had to any relevant principles laid down by the European Court in connection with Title II of the 1968 Convention and to any relevant decision of that court as to the meaning or effect of any provision of that Title; and

    (b) without prejudice to the generality of paragraph (a), the reports mentioned in section 3(3) may be considered and shall, so far as relevant, be given such weight as is appropriate in the circumstances.

21. Continuance of certain existing jurisdictions

(1) Schedule 8 does not affect—

    (a) the operation of any enactment which confers jurisdiction on a Scottish court in respect of a specific subject-matter on specific grounds;

    (b) without prejudice to the foregoing generality, the jurisdiction of any court in respect of any matter mentioned in Schedule 9.

(2) Her Majesty may by Order in Council—

    (a) add to the list in Schedule 9 any description of proceedings; and

    (b) remove from that list any description of proceedings (whether included in the list as originally enacted or added by virtue of this subsection).

(3) An Order in Council under subsection (2) may—

    (a) make different provision for different descriptions of proceedings or for the same description of proceedings in different courts; and

    (b) contain such transitional and other incidental provisions as appear to Her Majesty to be appropriate.

(4) An Order in Council under subsection (2) shall not be made unless a draft of the Order has been laid before Parliament and approved by a resolution of each House of Parliament.

22. Supplementary provisions

(1) Nothing in Schedule 8 shall prevent a court from declining jurisdiction on the grounds of *forum non conveniens.*

(2) Nothing in Schedule 8 affects the operation of any enactment or rule of law under which a court may decline to exercise jurisdiction because of the prorogation of parties of the jurisdiction of another court.

(3) For the avoidance of doubt, it is declared that nothing in Schedule 8 affects the *nobile officium* of the Court of Session.

(4) Where a court has jurisdiction in any proceedings by virtue of Schedule 8, that court shall also have jurisdiction to determine any matter which—

  (a) is ancillary or incidental to the proceedings; or
  (b) requires to be determined for the purposes of a decision in the proceedings.

23. Savings and consequential amendments

(1) Nothing in Schedule 8 shall affect—

  (a) the power of any court to vary or recall a maintenance order granted by that court;
  (b) the power of a sheriff court under section 22 of the Maintenance Orders Act 1950 (discharge and variation of maintenance orders registered in sheriff courts) to vary or discharge a maintenance order registered in that court under Part II of that Act; or
  (c) the power of a sheriff court under section 9 of the Maintenance Orders (Reciprocal Enforcement) Act 1972 (variation and revocation of maintenance orders registered in United Kingdom courts) to vary or revoke a registered order within the meaning of Part I of that Act.

(2) The enactments specified in Part II of Schedule 11 shall have effect with the amendments specified there, being amendments consequential on Schedule 8.

PART IV

MISCELLANEOUS PROVISIONS

Provisions relating to jurisdiction

24. Interim relief and protective measures in cases of doubtful jurisdiction

(1) Any power of a court in England and Wales or Northern Ireland to grant interim relief pending trial or pending the determination of an appeal shall extend to a case where—

  (a) the issue to be tried, or which is the subject of the appeal, relates to the jurisdiction of the court to entertain the proceedings; or
  (b) the proceedings involve the reference of any matter to the European Court under the 1971 Protocol.

(2) Any power of a court in Scotland to grant protective measures pending the decision of any hearing shall apply to a case where—

  (a) the subject of the proceedings includes a question as to the jurisdiction of the court to entertain them; or
  (b) the proceedings involve the reference of a matter to the European Court under the 1971 Protocol.

(3) Subsections (1) and (2) shall not be construed as restricting any power to grant interim relief or protective measures which a court may have apart from this section.

25. Interim relief in England and Wales and Northern Ireland in the absence of substantive proceedings

(1) The High Court in England and Wales or Northern Ireland shall have power to grant interim relief where—

(a) proceedings have been or are to be commenced in a Contracting State other than the United Kingdom or in a part of the United Kingdom other than that in which the High Court in question exercises jurisdiction; and

(b) they are or will be proceedings whose subject-matter is within the scope of the 1968 Convention as determined by Article 1 (whether or not the Convention has effect in relation to the proceedings).

(2) On an application for any interim relief under subsection (1) the court may refuse to grant that relief if, in the opinion of the court, the fact that the court has no jurisdiction apart from this section in relation to the subject-matter of the proceedings in question makes it inexpedient for the court to grant it.

(3) Her Majesty may by Order in Council extend the power to grant interim relief conferred by subsection (1) so as to make it exercisable in relation to proceedings of any of the following descriptions, namely—

(a) proceedings commenced or to be commenced otherwise than in a Contracting State;

(b) proceedings whose subject-matter is not within the scope of the 1968 Convention as determined by Article 1;

(c) arbitration proceedings.

(4) An Order in Council under subsection (3)—

(a) may confer power to grant only specified descriptions of interim relief;

(b) may make different provision for different classes of proceedings, for proceedings pending in different countries or courts outside the United Kingdom or in different parts of the United Kingdom, and for other different circumstances; and

(c) may impose conditions or restrictions on the exercise of any power conferred by the Order.

(5) An Order in Council under subsection (3) which confers power to grant interim relief in relation to arbitration proceedings may provide for the repeal of any provision of section 12(6) of the Arbitration Act 1950 or section 21(1) of the Arbitration Act (Northern Ireland) 1937 to the extent that it is superseded by the provisions of the Order.

(6) Any Order in Council under subsection (3) shall be subject to annulment in pursuance of a resolution of either House of Parliament.

(7) In this section "interim relief", in relation to the High Court in England and Wales or Northern Ireland, means interim relief of any kind which that court has power to grant in proceedings relating to matters within its jurisdiction, other than—

(a) a warrant for the arrest of property; or

(b) provision for obtaining evidence.

26. Security in Admiralty proceedings in England and Wales or Northern Ireland in case of stay, &c

(1) Where in England and Wales or Northern Ireland a court stays or dismisses Admiralty proceedings on the ground that the dispute in question should be submitted to arbitration or to the determination of the courts of another part of the United Kingdom or of an overseas country, the court may if in those proceedings property has been arrested or bail or other security has been given to prevent or obtain release from arrest—

(a) order that the property arrested be retained as security for the satisfaction of any award or judgment which—

   (i) is given in respect of the dispute in the arbitration or legal proceedings in
        favour of which those proceedings are stayed or dismissed; and
   (ii) is enforceable in England or Wales or, as the case may be, in Northern
        Ireland; or
  (b) order that the stay or dismissal of those proceedings be conditional on the
       provision of equivalent security for the satisfaction of any such award or
       judgment.

(2) Where a court makes an order under subsection (1), it may attach such conditions
to the order as it thinks fit, in particular conditions with respect to the institution or
prosecution of the relevant arbitration or legal proceedings.

(3) Subject to any provisions made by rules of court and to any necessary
modifications, the same law and practice shall apply in relation to property retained
in pursuance of an order made by a court under subsection (1) as would apply if it
were held for the purposes of proceedings in that court.

27. Provisional and protective measures in Scotland in the absence of substantive proceedings

(1) The Court of Session may, in any case to which this subsection applies—
  (a) subject to subsection (2)(c), grant a warrant for the arrestment of any assets
       situated in Scotland;
  (b) subject to subsection (2)(c), grant a warrant of inhibition over any property
       situated in Scotland; and
  (c) grant interim interdict.

(2) Subsection (1) applies to any case in which—
  (a) proceedings have been commenced but not concluded, or, in relation to
       paragraph (c) of that subsection, are to be commenced, in another Contracting
       State or in England and Wales or Northern Ireland;
  (b) the subject-matter of the proceedings is within the scope of the 1968 Convention
       as determined by Article 1; and
  (c) in relation to paragraphs (a) and (b) of subsection (1), such a warrant could
       competently have been granted in equivalent proceedings before a Scottish
       court;
but it shall not be necessary, in determining whether proceedings have been
commenced for the purpose of paragraph (a) of this subsection, to show that any
document has been served on or notice given to the defender.

(3) Her Majesty may by Order in Council confer on the Court of Session power to do
anything mentioned in subsection (1) or in section 28 in relation to proceedings of
any of the following descriptions, namely—
  (a) proceedings commenced otherwise than in a Contracting State;
  (b) proceedings whose subject-matter is not within the scope of the 1968
       Convention as determined by Article 1;
  (c) arbitration proceedings;
  (d) in relation to subsection (1)(c) or section 28, proceedings which are to be
       commenced otherwise than in a Contracting State.

(4) An Order in Council under subsection (3)—
  (a) may confer power to do only certain of the things mentioned in subsection (1)
       or in section 28;
  (b) may make different provision for different classes of proceedings, for
       proceedings pending in different countries or courts outside the United

Kingdom or in different parts of the United Kingdom, and for other different circumstances; and

(c) may impose conditions or restrictions on the exercise of any power conferred by the Order.

(5) Any Order in Council under subsection (3) shall be subject to annulment in pursuance of a resolution of either House of Parliament.

28. Application of s 1 of Administration of Justice (Scotland) Act 1972

When any proceedings have been brought, or are likely to be brought, in another Contracting State or in England and Wales or Northern Ireland in respect of any matter which is within the scope of the 1968 Convention as determined by Article 1, the Court of Session shall have the like power to make an order under section 1 of the Administration of Justice (Scotland) Act 1972 as if the proceedings in question had been brought, or were likely to be brought, in that court.

29. Service of county court process outside Northern Ireland

The County Court Rules Committee established by Article 46 of the County Courts (Northern Ireland) Order 1980 may make county court rules with respect to the service of process outside Northern Ireland and the conditions subject to which process may be so served; and accordingly in Article 48 of that Order (powers of Rules Committee), after paragraph (e) there shall be added—

"(f) the service of process outside Northern Ireland, and the conditions subject to which process may be so served.".

30. Proceedings in England and Wales or Northern Ireland for torts to immovable property

(1) The jurisdiction of any court in England and Wales or Northern Ireland to entertain proceedings for trespass to, or any other tort affecting, immovable property shall extend to cases in which the property in question is situated outside that part of the United Kingdom unless the proceedings are principally concerned with a question of the title to, or the right to possession of, that property.

(2) Subsection (1) has effect subject to the 1968 Convention and to the provisions set out in Schedule 4.

Provisions relating to recognition and enforcement of judgments

31. Overseas judgments given against states, etc

(1) A judgment given by a court of an overseas country against a state other than the United Kingdom or the state to which that court belongs shall be recognised and enforced in the United Kingdom if, and only if—

(a) it would be so recognised and enforced if it had not been given against a state; and

(b) that court would have had jurisdiction in the matter if it had applied rules corresponding to those applicable to such matters in the United Kingdom in accordance with sections 2 to 11 of the State Immunity Act 1978.

(2) References in subsection (1) to a judgment given against a state include references to judgments of any of the following descriptions given in relation to a state—

(a) judgments against the government, or a department of the government, of the state but not (except as mentioned in paragraph (c)) judgments against an entity which is distinct from the executive organs of government;

(b) judgments against the sovereign or head of state in his public capacity;
(c) judgments against any such separate entity as is mentioned in paragraph (a) given in proceedings relating to anything done by it in the exercise of the sovereign authority of the state.

(3) Nothing in subsection (1) shall affect the recognition or enforcement in the United Kingdom of a judgment to which Part I of the Foreign Judgments (Reciprocal Enforcement) Act 1933 applies by virtue of section 4 of the Carriage of Goods by Road Act 1965, section 17(4) of the Nuclear Installations Act 1965, section 13(3) of the Merchant Shipping (Oil Pollution) Act 1971, section 5 of the Carriage by Railway Act 1972[1] or section 5 of the Carriage of Passengers by Road Act 1974.

(4) Sections 12, 13 and 14(3) and (4) of the State Immunity Act 1978 (service of process and procedural privileges) shall apply to proceedings for the recognition or enforcement in the United Kingdom of a judgment given by a court of an overseas country (whether or not that judgment is within subsection (1) of this section) as they apply to other proceedings.

(5) In this section "state", in the case of a federal state, includes any of its constituent territories.

32. Overseas judgments given in breach of agreement for settlement of disputes

(1) Subject to the following provisions of this section, a judgment given by a court of an overseas country in any proceedings shall not be recognised or enforced in the United Kingdom if—

(a) the bringing of those proceedings in that court was contrary to an agreement under which the dispute in question was to be settled otherwise than by proceedings in the courts of that country; and
(b) those proceedings were not brought in that court by, or with the agreement of, the person against whom the judgment was given; and
(c) that person did not counterclaim in the proceedings or otherwise submit to the jurisdiction of that court.

(2) Subsection (1) does not apply where the agreement referred to in paragraph (a) of that subsection was illegal, void or unenforceable or was incapable of being performed for reasons not attributable to the fault of the party bringing the proceedings in which the judgment was given.

(3) In determining whether a judgment given by a court of an overseas country should be recognised or enforced in the United Kingdom, a court in the United Kingdom shall not be bound by any decision of the overseas court relating to any of the matters mentioned in subsection (1) or (2).

(4) Nothing in subsection (1) shall affect the recognition or enforcement in the United Kingdom of—

(a) a judgment which is required to be recognised or enforced there under the 1968 Convention;
(b) a judgment to which Part I of the Foreign Judgments (Reciprocal Enforcement) Act 1933 applies by virtue of section 4 of the Carriage of Goods by Road Act 1965, section 17(4) of the Nuclear Installations Act 1965, section 13(3) of the Merchant Shipping (Oil Pollution) Act 1971, section 5 of the Carriage by Railway Act 1972,[1] section 5 of the Carriage of Passengers by Road Act 1974 or section 6(4) of the Merchant Shipping Act 1974.

[1] When the International Transport Conventions Act 1983 comes into force, the reference to s 5 of the 1972 Act will be replaced by a reference to s 6 of the 1983 Act.

33. Certain steps not to amount to submission to jurisdiction of overseas court

(1) For the purposes of determining whether a judgment given by a court of an overseas country should be recognised or enforced in England and Wales or Northern Ireland, the person against whom the judgment was given shall not be treated as having submitted to the jurisdiction of the court by reason only of the fact that he appeared (conditionally or otherwise) in the proceedings for all or any one or more of the following purposes, namely—

    (a) to contest the jurisdiction of the court;

    (b) to ask the court to dismiss or stay the proceedings on the ground that the dispute in question should be submitted to arbitration or to the determination of the courts of another country;

    (c) to protect, or obtain the release of, property seized or threatened with seizure in the proceedings.

(2) Nothing in this section shall affect the recognition or enforcement in England and Wales or Northern Ireland of a judgment which is required to be recognised or enforced there under the 1968 Convention.

34. Certain judgments a bar to further proceedings on the same cause of action

(1) No proceedings may be brought by a person in England and Wales or Northern Ireland on a cause of action in respect of which a judgment has been given in his favour in proceedings between the same parties, or their privies, in a court in another part of the United Kingdom or in a court of an overseas country, unless that judgment is not enforceable or entitled to recognition in England and Wales or, as the case may be, in Northern Ireland.

35. Minor amendments relating to overseas judgments

(1) The Foreign Judgments (Reciprocal Enforcement) Act 1933 shall have effect with the amendments specified in Schedule 10, being amendments whose main purpose is to enable Part I of that Act to be applied to judgments of courts other than superior courts, to judgments providing for interim payments and to certain arbitration awards.

(2) For section 10 of the Administration of Justice Act 1920 (issue of certificates of judgments obtained in the United Kingdom) there shall be substituted—

    "10.—(1) Where—

        (a) a judgment has been obtained in the High Court in England or Northern Ireland, or in the Court of Session in Scotland, against any person; and

        (b) the judgment creditor wishes to secure the enforcement of the judgment in a part of Her Majesty's dominions outside the United Kingdom to which this Part of this Act extends,

    the court shall, on an application made by the judgment creditor, issue to him a certified copy of the judgment.

    (2) The reference in the preceding subsection to Her Majesty's dominions shall be construed as if that subsection had come into force in its present form at the commencement of this Act.".

(3) In section 14 of the Administration of Justice Act 1920 (extent of Part II of that Act), after subsection (2) there shall be inserted—

    "(3) Her Majesty may by Order in Council under this section consolidate any

Orders in Council under this section which are in force when the consolidating Order is made.".

36. Registration of maintenance orders in Northern Ireland

(1) Where—

(a) a High Court order or a Court of Session order has been registered in the High Court of Justice in Northern Ireland ("the Northern Ireland High Court") under Part II of the Maintenance Orders Act 1950; or

(b) a county court order, a magistrates' court order or a sheriff court order has been registered in a court of summary jurisdiction in Northern Ireland under that Part,

an application may be made to the original court for the registration of the order in, respectively, a court of summary jurisdiction in Northern Ireland or the Northern Ireland High Court.

(2) In subsection (1) "the original court", in relation to an order, means the court by which the order was made.

(3) Section 2 (except subsection (6A)) and section 2A of the Maintenance Orders Act 1958 shall have effect for the purposes of an application under subsection (1), and subsections (2), (3), (4) and (4A) of section 5 of that Act shall have effect for the purposes of the cancellation of a registration made on such an application, as if—

(a) "registration" in those provisions included registration in the appropriate Northern Ireland court ("registered" being construed accordingly);

(b) any reference in those provisions to a High Court order or a magistrates' court order included, respectively, a Court of Session order or a sheriff court order; and

(c) any other reference in those provisions to the High Court or a magistrates' court included the Northern Ireland High Court or a court of summary jurisdiction in Northern Ireland.

(4) Where an order is registered in Northern Ireland under this section, Part II of the Maintenance and Affiliation Orders Act (Northern Ireland) 1966, except sections 11, 11A and 14(2) and (3), shall apply as if the order had been registered in accordance with the provisions of that Part.

(5) A court of summary jurisdiction in Northern Ireland shall have jurisdiction to hear a complaint by or against a person residing outside Northern Ireland for the discharge or variation of an order registered in Northern Ireland under this section; and where such a complaint is made against a person residing outside Northern Ireland, then, if he resides in England and Wales or Scotland, section 15 of the Maintenance Orders Act 1950 (which relates to the service of process on persons residing in those countries) shall have effect in relation to the complaint as it has effect in relation to the proceedings therein mentioned.

(6) The enactments specified in Part III of Schedule 11 shall have effect with the amendments specified there, being amendments consequential on this section.

37. Minor amendments relating to maintenance orders

(1) The enactments specified in Schedule 11 shall have effect with the amendments specified there, being amendments whose main purpose is as follows—

Part I—to extend certain enforcement provisions to lump sum maintenance orders;

Part II—to provide for the recovery of interest according to the law of the country of origin in the case of maintenance orders made in other jurisdictions and registered in the High Court;

Part III—to extend the Maintenance Orders (Reciprocal Enforcement) Act 1972 to cases where the payer under a maintenance order is not resident within the jurisdiction but has assets there.

(2) In section 27(1) of the Maintenance Orders (Reciprocal Enforcement) Act 1972 (application by person in convention country for recovery of maintenance in England and Wales or Northern Ireland to be treated as a complaint), after "as if it were a complaint" there shall be inserted "made at the time when the application was received by the Secretary of State or the Lord Chancellor".

38. Overseas judgments counteracting an award of multiple damages

(1) Section 7 of the Protection of Trading Interests Act 1980 (which enables provision to be made by Order in Council for the enforcement in the United Kingdom on a reciprocal basis of overseas judgments directed to counteracting a judgment for multiple damages given in a third country) shall be amended as follows.

(2) In subsection (1) for "judgments given under any provision of the law of that country corresponding to that section" there shall be substituted "judgments of any description specified in the Order which are given under any provision of the law of that country relating to the recovery of sums paid or obtained pursuant to a judgment for multiple damages within the meaning of section 5(3) above, whether or not that provision corresponds to section 6 above".

(3) After subsection (1) there shall be inserted—

"(1A) Such an Order in Council may, as respects judgments to which it relates—

(a) make different provisions for different descriptions of judgment; and
(b) impose conditions or restrictions on the enforcement of judgments of any description.".

Jurisdiction, and recognition and enforcement of judgments, as between United Kingdom and certain territories

39. Application of provisions corresponding to 1968 Convention in relation to certain territories

(1) Her Majesty may by Order in Council make provision corresponding to the provision made by the 1968 Convention as between the Contracting States to that Convention, with such modifications as appear to Her Majesty to be appropriate, for regulating, as between the United Kingdom and any of the territories mentioned in subsection (2), the jurisdiction of courts and the recognition and enforcement of judgments.

(2) The territories referred to in subsection (1) are—

(a) the Isle of Man;
(b) any of the Channel Islands;
(c) Gibraltar;
(d) the Sovereign Base Areas of Akrotiri and Dhekelia (that is to say the areas mentioned in section 2(1) of the Cyprus Act 1960).

(3) An Order in Council under this section may contain such supplementary and incidental provisions as appear to Her Majesty to be necessary or expedient, including in particular provisions corresponding to or applying any of the provisions of Part I with such modifications as may be specified in the Order.

(4) Any Order in Council under this section shall be subject to annulment in pursuance of a resolution of either House of Parliament.

Legal aid

40. Power to modify enactments relating to legal aid etc

(1) In section 20 of the Legal Aid Act 1974 (power of Lord Chancellor to make regulations), after subsection (4) there shall be inserted as subsection (4A)—

"(4A) Without prejudice to the preceding provisions of this section or any other provision of this Part of this Act authorising the making of regulations, regulations may also modify the provisions of, or of any instrument having effect under, this Part of this Act (including so much of any of those provisions as specifies a sum of money) for the purposes of the application of those provisions—

(a) in cases where their modification appears to the Lord Chancellor necessary for the purpose of fulfilling any obligation imposed on the United Kingdom or Her Majesty's government therein by any international agreement; or

(b) in relation to proceedings for securing the recognition or enforcement in England and Wales of judgments given outside the United Kingdom for whose recognition or enforcement in the United Kingdom provision is made by any international agreement.".

(2) In section 15 of the Legal Aid (Scotland) Act 1967 (power of Secretary of State to make regulations), after subsection (4) there shall be inserted as subsection (4A)—

"(4A) Without prejudice to the preceding provisions of this section or any other provision of this Act authorising the making of regulations, regulations may also modify the provisions of, or of any instrument having effect under, this Act (including so much of any of those provisions as specifies a sum of money) for the purposes of the application of those provisions—

(a) in cases where their modification appears to the Secretary of State necessary for the purpose of fulfilling any obligation imposed on the United Kingdom or Her Majesty's government therein by any international agreement; or

(b) in relation to proceedings for securing the recognition or enforcement in Scotland of judgments given outside the United Kingdom for whose recognition or enforcement in the United Kingdom provision is made by any international agreement.".

(3) In Article 22 of the Legal Aid, Advice and Assistance (Northern Ireland) Order 1981 (power of Lord Chancellor to make regulations), after paragraph (4) there shall be inserted as paragraph (4A)—

"(4A) Without prejudice to the preceding provisions of this Article or any other provision of this Part authorising the making of regulations, regulations may also modify the provisions of, or of any instrument having effect under, this Part (including so much of any of those provisions as specifies a sum of money) for the purposes of the application of those provisions—

(a) in cases where their modification appears to the Lord Chancellor necessary for the purpose of fulfilling any obligation imposed on the United Kingdom or Her Majesty's government therein by any international agreement; or

(b) in relation to proceedings for securing the recognition or enforcement in Northern Ireland of judgments given outside the United Kingdom for whose recognition or enforcement in the United Kingdom provision is made by any international agreement.".

Part V

Supplementary and General Provisions

Domicile

41. Domicile of individuals

(1) Subject to Article 52 (which contains provisions for determining whether a party is domiciled in a Contracting State), the following provisions of this section determine, for the purposes of the 1968 Convention and this Act, whether an individual is domiciled in the United Kingdom or in a particular part of, or place in, the United Kingdom or in a state other than a Contracting State.

(2) An individual is domiciled in the United Kingdom if and only if—

    (a) he is resident in the United Kingdom; and

    (b) the nature and circumstances of his residence indicate that he has a substantial connection with the United Kingdom.

(3) Subject to subsection (5), an individual is domiciled in a particular part of the United Kingdom if and only if—

    (a) he is resident in that part; and

    (b) the nature and circumstances of his residence indicate that he has a substantial connection with that part.

(4) An individual is domiciled in a particular place in the United Kingdom if and only if he—

    (a) is domiciled in the part of the United Kingdom in which that place is situated; and

    (b) is resident in that place.

(5) An individual who is domiciled in the United Kingdom but in whose case the requirements of subsection (3)(b) are not satisfied in relation to any particular part of the United Kingdom shall be treated as domiciled in the part of the United Kingdom in which he is resident.

(6) In the case of an individual who—

    (a) is resident in the United Kingdom, or in a particular part of the United Kingdom; and

    (b) has been so resident for the last three months or more,

the requirements of subsection (2)(b) or, as the case may be, subsection (3)(b) shall be presumed to be fulfilled unless the contrary is proved.

(7) An individual is domiciled in a state other than a Contracting State if and only if—

    (a) he is resident in that state; and

    (b) the nature and circumstances of his residence indicate that he has a substantial connection with that state.

42. Domicile and seat of corporation or association

(1) For the purposes of this Act the seat of a corporation or association (as determined by this section) shall be treated as its domicile.

(2) The following provisions of this section determine where a corporation or association has its seat—

    (a) for the purpose of Article 53 (which for the purposes of the 1968 Convention equates the domicile of such a body with its seat); and

    (b) for the purposes of this Act other than the provisions mentioned in section 43(1)(b) and (c).

(3) A corporation or association has its seat in the United Kingdom if and only if—

    (a) it was incorporated or formed under the law of a part of the United Kingdom and has its registered office or some other official address in the United Kingdom; or

    (b) its central management and control is exercised in the United Kingdom.

(4) A corporation or association has its seat in a particular part of the United Kingdom if and only if it has its seat in the United Kingdom and—

    (a) it has its registered office or some other official address in that part; or

    (b) its central management and control is exercised in that part; or

    (c) it has a place of business in that part.

(5) A corporation or association has its seat in a particular place in the United Kingdom if and only if it has its seat in the part of the United Kingdom in which that place is situated and—

    (a) it has its registered office or some other official address in that place; or

    (b) its central management and control is exercised in that place; or

    (c) it has a place of business in that place.

(6) Subject to subsection (7), a corporation or association has its seat in a state other than the United Kingdom if and only if—

    (a) it was incorporated or formed under the law of that state and has its registered office or some other official address there; or

    (b) its central management and control is exercised in that state.

(7) A corporation or association shall not be regarded as having its seat in a Contracting State other than the United Kingdom if it is shown that the courts of that state would not regard it as having its seat there.

(8) In this section—

    "business" includes any activity carried on by a corporation or association, and "place of business" shall be construed accordingly;

    "official address", in relation to a corporation or association, means an address which it is required by law to register, notify or maintain for the purpose of receiving notices or other communications.

43. Seat of corporation or association for purposes of Article 16(2) and related provisions

(1) The following provisions of this section determine where a corporation or association has its seat for the purposes of—

    (a) Article 16(2) (which confers exclusive jurisdiction over proceedings relating to the formation or dissolution of such bodies, or to the decisions of their organs);

    (b) Articles 5A and 16(2) in Schedule 4; and

    (c) Rules 2(12) and 4(1)(b) in Schedule 8.

(2) A corporation or association has its seat in the United Kingdom if and only if—

    (a) it was incorporated or formed under the law of a part of the United Kingdom; or

    (b) its central management and control is exercised in the United Kingdom.

(3) A corporation or association has its seat in a particular part of the United Kingdom if and only if it has its seat in the United Kingdom and—

(a) subject to subsection (5), it was incorporated or formed under the law of that part; or

(b) being incorporated or formed under the law of a state other than the United Kingdom, its central management and control is exercised in that part.

(4) A corporation or association has its seat in a particular place in Scotland if and only if it has its seat in Scotland and—

(a) it has its registered office or some other official address in that place; or

(b) it has no registered office or other official address in Scotland, but its central management and control is exercised in that place.

(5) A corporation or association incorporated or formed under—

(a) an enactment forming part of the law of more than one part of the United Kingdom; or

(b) an instrument having effect in the domestic law of more than one part of the United Kingdom,

shall, if it has a registered office, be taken to have its seat in the part of the United Kingdom in which that office is situated, and not in any other part of the United Kingdom.

(6) Subject to subsection (7), a corporation or association has its seat in a Contracting State other than the United Kingdom if and only if—

(a) it was incorporated or formed under the law of that state; or

(b) its central management and control is exercised in that state.

(7) A corporation or association shall not be regarded as having its seat in a Contracting State other than the United Kingdom if—

(a) it has its seat in the United Kingdom by virtue of subsection (2)(a); or

(b) it is shown that the courts of that other state would not regard it for the purposes of Article 16(2) as having its seat there.

(8) In this section "official address" has the same meaning as in section 42.

44. Persons deemed to be domiciled in the United Kingdom for certain purposes

(1) This section applies to—

(a) proceedings within Section 3 of Title II of the 1968 Convention (insurance contracts), and

(b) proceedings within Section 4 of that Title (consumer contracts).

(2) A person who, for the purposes of proceedings to which this section applies arising out of the operations of a branch, agency or other establishment in the United Kingdom, is deemed for the purposes of the 1968 Convention to be domiciled in the United Kingdom by virtue of—

(a) Article 8, second paragraph (insurers); or

(b) Article 13, second paragraph (suppliers of goods, services or credit to consumers),

shall, for the purposes of those proceedings, be treated for the purposes of this Act as so domiciled and as domiciled in the part of the United Kingdom in which the branch, agency or establishment in question is situated.

45. Domicile of trusts

(1) The following provisions of this section determine, for the purposes of the 1968 Convention and this Act, where a trust is domiciled.

(2) A trust is domiciled in the United Kingdom if and only if it is by virtue of subsection (3) domiciled in a part of the United Kingdom.

(3) A trust is domiciled in a part of the United Kingdom if and only if the system of law of that part is the system of law with which the trust has its closest and most real connection.

46. Domicile and seat of the Crown

(1) For the purposes of this Act the seat of the Crown (as determined by this section) shall be treated as its domicile.

(2) The following provisions of this section determine where the Crown has its seat—

    (a) for the purposes of the 1968 Convention (in which Article 53 equates the domicile of a legal person with its seat); and

    (b) for the purposes of this Act.

(3) Subject to the provisions of any Order in Council for the time being in force under subsection (4)—

    (a) the Crown in right of Her Majesty's government in the United Kingdom has its seat in every part of, and every place in, the United Kingdom; and

    (b) the Crown in right of Her Majesty's government in Northern Ireland has its seat in, and in every place in, Northern Ireland.

(4) Her Majesty may by Order in Council provide that, in the case of proceedings of any specified description against the Crown in right of Her Majesty's government in the United Kingdom, the Crown shall be treated for the purposes of the 1968 Convention and this Act as having its seat in, and in every place in, a specified part of the United Kingdom and not in any other part of the United Kingdom.

(5) An Order in Council under subsection (4) may frame a description of proceedings in any way, and in particular may do so by reference to the government department or officer of the Crown against which or against whom they fall to be instituted.

(6) Any Order in Council made under this section shall be subject to annulment in pursuance of a resolution of either House of Parliament.

(7) Nothing in this section applies to the Crown otherwise than in right of Her Majesty's government in the United Kingdom or Her Majesty's government in Northern Ireland.

Other supplementary provisions

47. Modifications occasioned by decisions of European Court as to meaning or effect of Conventions

(1) Her Majesty may by Order in Council—

    (a) make such provision as Her Majesty considers appropriate for the purpose of bringing the law of any part of the United Kingdom into accord with the Conventions as affected by any principle laid down by the European Court in connection with the Conventions or by any decision of that court as to the meaning or effect of any provision of the Conventions; or

    (b) make such modifications of Schedule 4 or Schedule 8, or of any other statutory provision affected by any provision of either of those Schedules, as Her Majesty considers appropriate in view of any principle laid down by the European Court in connection with Title II of the 1968 Convention or of any decision of that court as to the meaning or effect of any provision of that Title.

(2) The provision which may be made by virtue of paragraph (a) of subsection (1)

includes such modifications of this Act or any other statutory provision, whenever passed or made, as Her Majesty considers appropriate for the purpose mentioned in that paragraph.

(3) The modifications which may be made by virtue of paragraph (b) of subsection (1) include modifications designed to produce divergence between any provision of Schedule 4 or Schedule 8 and a corresponding provision of Title II of the 1968 Convention as affected by any such principle or decision as is mentioned in that paragraph.

(4) An Order in Council under this section shall not be made unless a draft of the Order has been laid before Parliament and approved by a resolution of each House of Parliament.

48. Matters for which rules of court may provide

(1) Rules of court may make provision for regulating the procedure to be followed in any court in connection with any provision of this Act or the Conventions.

(2) Rules of court may make provision as to the manner in which and the conditions subject to which a certificate or judgment registered in any court under any provision of this Act may be enforced, including provision for enabling the court or, in Northern Ireland, the Enforcement of Judgments Office, subject to any conditions specified in the rules, to give directions about such matters.

(3) Without prejudice to the generality of subsections (1) and (2), the power to make rules of court for magistrates' courts, and in Northern Ireland the power to make Judgment Enforcement Rules, shall include power to make such provision as the rule-making authority considers necessary or expedient for the purposes of the provisions of the Conventions and this Act relating to maintenance proceedings and the recognition and enforcement of maintenance orders, and shall in particular include power to make provision as to any of the following matters—

  (a) authorising the service in another Contracting State of process issued by or for the purposes of a magistrates' court and the service and execution in England and Wales or Northern Ireland of process issued in another Contracting State;
  (b) requesting courts in other parts of the United Kingdom or in other Contracting States to take evidence there for the purposes of proceedings in England and Wales or Northern Ireland;
  (c) the taking of evidence in England and Wales or Northern Ireland in response to similar requests received from such courts;
  (d) the circumstances in which and the conditions subject to which any powers conferred under paragraphs (a) to (c) are to be exercised;
  (e) the admission in evidence, subject to such conditions as may be prescribed in the rules, of statements contained in documents purporting to be made or authenticated by a court in another part of the United Kingdom or in another Contracting State, or by a judge or official of such a court, which purport—
   (i) to set out or summarise evidence given in proceedings in that court or to be documents received in evidence in such proceedings or copies of such documents; or
   (ii) to set out or summarise evidence taken for the purposes of proceedings in England and Wales or Northern Ireland, whether or not in response to any such request as is mentioned in paragraph (b); or
   (iii) to record information relating to the payments made under an order of that court;
  (f) the circumstances and manner in which a magistrates' court may or must vary

or revoke a maintenance order registered in that court, cancel the registration of, or refrain from enforcing, such an order or transmit such an order for enforcement in another part of the United Kingdom;

(g) the cases and manner in which courts in other parts of the United Kingdom or in other Contracting States are to be informed of orders made, or other things done, by or for the purposes of a magistrates' court;

(h) the circumstances and manner in which a magistrates' court may communicate for other purposes with such courts;

(i) the giving of notice of such matters as may be prescribed in the rules to such persons as may be so prescribed and the manner in which such notice is to be given.

(4) Nothing in this section shall be taken as derogating from the generality of any power to make rules of court conferred by any other enactment.

49. Savings for powers to stay, sist, strike out or dismiss proceedings

Nothing in this Act shall prevent any court in the United Kingdom from staying, sisting, striking out or dismissing any proceedings before it, on the ground of *forum non conveniens* or otherwise, where to do so is not inconsistent with the 1968 Convention.

General

50. Interpretation: general

In this Act, unless the context otherwise requires—

"the Accession Convention" has the meaning given by section 1(1);

"Article" and references to sub-divisions of numbered Articles are to be construed in accordance with section 1(2)(b);

"association" means an unincorporated body of persons;

"Contracting State" has the meaning given by section 1(3);

"the 1968 Convention" has the meaning given by section 1(1), and references to that Convention and to provisions of it are to be construed in accordance with section 1(2)(a);

"the Conventions" has the meaning given by section 1(1);

"corporation" means a body corporate, and includes a partnership subsisting under the law of Scotland;

"court", without more, includes a tribunal;

"court of law", in relation to the United Kingdom, means any of the following courts, namely—

(a) the House of Lords,

(b) in England and Wales or Northern Ireland, the Court of Appeal, the High Court, the Crown Court, a county court and a magistrates' court,

(c) in Scotland, the Court of Session and a sheriff court;

"the Crown" is to be construed in accordance with section 51(2);

"enactment" includes an enactment comprised in Northern Ireland legislation;

"judgment", subject to sections 15(1) and 18(2) and to paragraph 1 of Schedules 6 and 7, means any judgment or order (by whatever name called) given or made by a court, in any civil proceedings;

"magistrates' court", in relation to Northern Ireland, means a court of summary jurisdiction;

"modifications" includes additions, omissions and alterations;

"overseas country" means any country or territory outside the United Kingdom;

"part of the United Kingdom" means England and Wales, Scotland or Northern Ireland;

"the 1971 Protocol" has the meaning given by section 1(1), and references to that Protocol and to provisions of it are to be construed in accordance with section 1(2)(a);

"rules of court", in relation to any court, means rules, orders or regulations made by the authority having power to make rules, orders or regulations regulating the procedure of that court, and includes—

    (a) in Scotland, Acts of Sederunt;

    (b) in Northern Ireland, Judgment Enforcement Rules;

"statutory provision" means any provision contained in an Act, or in any Northern Ireland legislation, or in—

    (a) subordinate legislation (as defined in section 21(1) of the Interpretation Act 1978); or

    (b) any instrument of a legislative character made under any Northern Ireland legislation;

"tribunal"—

    (a) means a tribunal of any description other than a court of law;

    (b) in relation to an overseas country, includes, as regards matters relating to maintenance within the meaning of the 1968 Convention, any authority having power to give, enforce, vary or revoke a maintenance order.

51. Application to Crown

(1) This Act binds the Crown.

(2) In this section and elsewhere in this Act references to the Crown do not include references to Her Majesty in Her private capacity or to Her Majesty in right of Her Duchy of Lancaster or to the Duke of Cornwall.

52. Extent

(1) This Act extends to Northern Ireland.

(2) Without prejudice to the power conferred by section 39, Her Majesty may by Order in Council direct that all or any of the provisions of this Act apart from that section shall extend, subject to such modifications as may be specified in the Order, to any of the following territories, that is to say—

    (a) the Isle of Man;

    (b) any of the Channel Islands;

    (c) Gibraltar;

    (d) the Sovereign Base Areas of Akrotiri and Dhekelia (that is to say the areas mentioned in section 2(1) of the Cyprus Act 1960).

53. Commencement, transitional provisions and savings

(1) This Act shall come into force in accordance with the provisions of Part I of Schedule 13.

(2) The transitional provisions and savings contained in Part II of that Schedule shall have effect in relation to the commencement of the provisions of this Act mentioned in that Part.

54. Repeals

The enactments mentioned in Schedule 14 are hereby repealed to the extent specified in the third column of that Schedule.

55. Short title

This Act may be cited as the Civil Jurisdiction and Judgments Act 1982.

SCHEDULES

SCHEDULE 1

Section 2(2)

TEXT OF 1968 CONVENTION, AS AMENDED

ARRANGEMENT OF PROVISIONS

CONVENTION ON JURISDICTION AND THE ENFORCEMENT OF JUDGMENTS IN CIVIL AND COMMERCIAL MATTERS

Preamble

The High Contracting Parties to the Treaty establishing the European Economic Community;

Desiring to implement the provisions of Article 220 of that Treaty by virtue of which they undertook to secure the simplification of formalities governing the reciprocal recognition and enforcement of judgments of courts or tribunals;

Anxious to strengthen in the Community the legal protection of persons therein established;

Considering that it is necessary for this purpose to determine the international jurisdiction of their courts, to facilitate recognition and to introduce an expeditious procedure for securing the enforcement of judgments, authentic instruments and court settlements;

Have decided to conclude this Convention and to this end have designated as their Plenipotentiaries:

183

(Designations of Plenipotentiaries of the original six Contracting States)

Who, meeting within the Council, having exchanged their Full Powers, found in good and due form;

Have agreed as follows:

TITLE I
SCOPE
ARTICLE 1

This Convention shall apply in civil and commercial matters whatever the nature of the court or tribunal. It shall not extend, in particular, to revenue, customs or administrative matters.

The Convention shall not apply to:

(1) the status or legal capacity of natural persons, rights in property arising out of a matrimonial relationship, wills and succession;
(2) bankruptcy, proceedings relating to the winding-up of insolvent companies or other legal persons, judicial arrangements, compositions and analogous proceedings;
(3) social security;
(4) arbitration.

TITLE II
JURISDICTION
Section 1
General provisions
ARTICLE 2

Subject to the provisions of this Convention, persons domiciled in a Contracting State shall, whatever their nationality, be sued in the courts of that State.

Persons who are not nationals of the State in which they are domiciled shall be governed by the rules of jurisdiction applicable to nationals of that State.

ARTICLE 3

Persons domiciled in a Contracting State may be sued in the courts of another Contracting State only by virtue of the rules set out in Sections 2 to 6 of this Title.

In particular the following provisions shall not be applicable as against them:

—in Belgium:	Article 15 of the civil code *(Code civil—Burgerlijk Wetboek)* and Article 638 of the Judicial code *(Code judiciaire—Gerechtelijk Wetboek)*;
—in Denmark:	Article 248(2) of the law on civil procedure *(Lov om rettens pleje)* and Chapter 3, Article 3 of the Greenland law on civil procedure *(Lov for Grønland om rettens pleje)*;
—in the Federal Republic of Germany:	Article 23 of the code of civil procedure *(Zivil-prozessordnung)*;
—in France:	Articles 14 and 15 of the civil code *(Code civil)*;
—in Ireland:	the rules which enable jurisdiction to be founded on the document instituting the proceedings having been served on the defendant during his temporary presence in Ireland:
—in Italy:	Article 2 and Article 4, Nos 1 and 2 of the code of civil procedure *(Codice di procedura civile)*;
—in Luxembourg:	Articles 14 and 15 of the civil code *(Code civil)*;

—in the Netherlands:

—in the United Kingdom:

Article 126(3) and Article 127 of the code of civil procedure (*Wetboek van Burgerlijke Rechtsvordering*);

the rules which enable jurisdiction to be founded on:

(a) the document instituting the proceedings having been served on the defendant during his temporary presence in the United Kingdom; or

(b) the presence within the United Kingdom of property belonging to the defendant; or

(c) the seizure by the plaintiff of property situated in the United Kingdom.

ARTICLE 4

If the defendant is not domiciled in a Contracting State, the jurisdiction of the courts of each Contracting State shall, subject to the provisions of Article 16, be determined by the law of that State.

As against such a defendant, any person domiciled in a Contracting State may, whatever his nationality, avail himself in that State of the rules of jurisdiction there in force, and in particular those specified in the second paragraph of Article 3, in the same way as the nationals of that State.

Section 2
Special jurisdiction
ARTICLE 5

A person domiciled in a Contracting State may, in another Contracting State, be sued:

(1) in matters relating to a contract, in the courts for the place of performance of the obligation in question;

(2) in matters relating to maintenance, in the courts for the place where the maintenance creditor is domiciled or habitually resident or, if the matter is ancillary to proceedings concerning the status of a person, in the court which, according to its own law, has jurisdiction to entertain those proceedings, unless that jurisdiction is based solely on the nationality of one of the parties;

(3) in matters relating to tort, delict or quasi-delict, in the courts for the place where the harmful event occurred;

(4) as regards a civil claim for damages or restitution which is based on an act giving rise to criminal proceedings, in the court seised of those proceedings, to the extent that that court has jurisdiction under its own law to entertain civil proceedings;

(5) as regards a dispute arising out of the operations of a branch, agency or other establishment, in the courts for the place in which the branch, agency or other establishment is situated;

(6) in his capacity as settlor, trustee or beneficiary of a trust created by the operation of a statute, or by a written instrument, or created orally and evidenced in writing, in the courts of the Contracting State in which the trust is domiciled;

(7) as regards a dispute concerning the payment of remuneration claimed in respect of the salvage of a cargo or freight, in the court under the authority of which the cargo or freight in question

(a) has been arrested to secure such payment, or

(b) could have been so arrested, but bail or other security has been given;

provided that this provision shall apply only if it claimed that the defendant has an interest in the cargo or freight or had such an interest at the time of salvage.

ARTICLE 6

A person domiciled in a Contracting State may also be sued:

(1) where he is one of a number of defendants, in the courts for the place where any one of them is domiciled;

(2) as a third party in an action on a warranty or guarantee or in any other third party

proceedings, in the court seised of the original proceedings, unless these were instituted solely with the object of removing him from the jurisdiction of the court which would be competent in his case;

(3) on a counterclaim arising from the same contract or facts on which the original claim was based, in the court in which the original claim is pending.

ARTICLE 6A

Where by virtue of this Convention a court of a Contracting State has jurisdiction in actions relating to liability arising from the use or operation of a ship, that court, or any other court substituted for this purpose by the internal law of that State, shall also have jurisdiction over claims for limitation of such liability.

Section 3

Jurisdiction in matters relating to insurance

ARTICLE 7

In matters relating to insurance, jurisdiction shall be determined by this Section, without prejudice to the provisions of Articles 4 and 5(5).

ARTICLE 8

An insurer domiciled in a Contracting State may be sued:

(1) in the courts of the State where he is domiciled, or

(2) in another Contracting State, in the courts for the place where the policy-holder is domiciled, or

(3) if he is a co-insurer, in the courts of a Contracting State in which proceedings are brought against the leading insurer.

An insurer who is not domiciled in a Contracting State but has a branch, agency or other establishment in one of the Contracting States shall, in disputes arising out of the operations of the branch, agency or establishment, be deemed to be domiciled in that State.

ARTICLE 9

In respect of liability insurance or insurance of immovable property, the insurer may in addition be sued in the courts for the place where the harmful event occurred. The same applies if movable and immovable property are covered by the same insurance policy and both are adversely affected by the same contingency.

ARTICLE 10

In respect of liability insurance, the insurer may also, if the law of the court permits it, be joined in proceedings which the injured party has brought against the insured.

The provisions of Articles 7, 8 and 9 shall apply to actions brought by the injured party directly against the insurer, where such direct actions are permitted.

If the law governing such direct actions provides that the policy-holder or the insured may be joined as a party to the action, the same court shall have jurisdiction over them.

ARTICLE 11

Without prejudice to the provisions of the third paragraph of Article 10, an insurer may bring proceedings only in the courts of the Contracting State in which the defendant is domiciled, irrespective of whether he is the policy-holder, the insured or a beneficiary.

The provisions of this Section shall not affect the right to bring a counterclaim in the court in which, in accordance with this Section, the original claim is pending.

ARTICLE 12

The provisions of this Section may be departed from only by an agreement on jurisdiction:

(1) which is entered into after the dispute has arisen, or

(2) which allows the policy-holder, the insured or a beneficiary to bring proceedings in courts other than those indicated in this Section, or

(3) which is concluded between a policy-holder and an insurer, both of whom are at the time of conclusion of the contract domiciled or habitually resident in the same Contracting State, and which has the effect of conferring jurisdiction on the courts of that State even if the harmful event were to occur abroad, provided that such an agreement is not contrary to the law of that State, or

(4) which is concluded with a policy-holder who is not domiciled in a Contracting State, except in so far as the insurance is compulsory or relates to immovable property in a Contracting State, or

(5) which relates to a contract of insurance in so far as it covers one or more of the risks set out in Article 12A.

ARTICLE 12A

The following are the risks referred to in Article 12(5):

(1) Any loss of or damage to

    (a) sea-going ships, installations situated offshore or on the high seas, or aircraft, arising from perils which relate to their use for commercial purposes,

    (b) goods in transit other than passengers' baggage where the transit consists of or includes carriage by such ships or aircraft;

(2) Any liability, other than for bodily injury to passengers or loss of or damage to their baggage,

    (a) arising out of the use or operation of ships, installations or aircraft as referred to in (1)(a) above in so far as the law of the Contracting State in which such aircraft are registered does not prohibit agreements on jurisdiction regarding insurance of such risks,

    (b) for loss or damage caused by goods in transit as described in (1)(b) above;

(3) Any financial loss connected with the use or operation of ships, installations or aircraft as referred to in (1)(a) above, in particular loss of freight or charter-hire;

(4) Any risk or interest connected with any of those referred to in (1) to (3) above.

Section 4

Jurisdiction over consumer contracts

ARTICLE 13

In proceedings concerning a contract concluded by a person for a purpose which can be regarded as being outside his trade or profession, hereinafter called the "consumer", jurisdiction shall be determined by this Section, without prejudice to the provisions of Articles 4 and 5(5), if it is:

(1) a contract for the sale of goods on instalment credit terms, or

(2) a contract for a loan repayable by instalments, or for any other form of credit, made to finance the sale of goods, or

(3) any other contract for the supply of goods or a contract for the supply of services and

    (a) in the State of the consumer's domicile the conclusion of the contract was preceded by a specific invitation addressed to him or by advertising, and

    (b) the consumer took in that State the steps necessary for the conclusion of the contract.

Where a consumer enters into a contract with a party who is not domiciled in a Contracting State but has a branch, agency or other establishment in one of the Contracting States, that party shall, in disputes arising out of the operations of the branch, agency or establishment, be deemed to be domiciled in that State.

This Section shall not apply to contracts of transport.

ARTICLE 14

A consumer may bring proceedings against the other party to a contract either in the courts of the Contracting State in which that party is domiciled or in the courts of the Contracting State in which he is himself domiciled.

Proceedings may be brought against a consumer by the other party to the contract only in the courts of the Contracting State in which the consumer is domiciled.

These provisions shall not affect the right to bring a counterclaim in the court in which, in accordance with this Section, the original claim is pending.

ARTICLE 15

The provisions of this Section may be departed from only by an agreement:

(1) which is entered into after the dispute has arisen, or
(2) which allows the consumer to bring proceedings in courts other than those indicated in this Section, or
(3) which is entered into by the consumer and the other party to the contract, both of whom are at the time of conclusion of the contract domiciled or habitually resident in the same Contracting State, and which confers jurisdiction on the courts of that State, provided that such an agreement is not contrary to the law of that State.

Section 5

Exclusive jurisdiction

ARTICLE 16

The following courts shall have exclusive jurisdiction, regardless of domicile:

(1) in proceedings which have as their object rights *in rem* in, or tenancies of, immovable property, the courts of the Contracting State in which the property is situated;
(2) in proceedings which have as their object the validity of the constitution, the nullity or the dissolution of companies or other legal persons or associations of natural or legal persons, or the decision of their organs, the courts of the Contracting State in which the company, legal person or association has its seat;
(3) in proceedings which have as their object the validity of entries in public registers, the courts of the Contracting State in which the register is kept;
(4) in proceedings concerned with the registration or validity of patents, trade marks, designs, or other similar rights required to be deposited or registered, the courts of the Contracting State in which the deposit or registration has been applied for, has taken place or is under the terms of an international convention deemed to have taken place;
(5) in proceedings concerned with the enforcement of judgments, the courts of the Contracting State in which the judgment has been or is to be enforced.

Section 6

Prorogation of jurisdiction

ARTICLE 17

If the parties, one or more of whom is domiciled in a Contracting State, have agreed that a court or the courts of a Contracting State are to have jurisdiction to settle any disputes which have arisen or which may arise in connection with a particular legal relationship, that court or those courts shall have exclusive jurisdiction. Such an agreement conferring jurisdiction shall be either in writing or evidenced in writing or, in international trade or commerce, in a form which accords with practices in that trade or commerce of which the parties are or ought to have been aware. Where such an agreement is concluded by parties, none of whom is domiciled in a Contracting State, the courts of other Contracting States shall have no jurisdiction over their disputes unless the court or courts chosen have declined jurisdiction.

The court or courts of a Contracting State on which a trust instrument has conferred jurisdiction shall have exclusive jurisdiction in any proceedings brought against a settlor, trustee or beneficiary, if relations between these persons or their rights or obligations under the trust are involved.

Agreements or provisions of a trust instrument conferring jurisdiction shall have no legal force if they are contrary to the provisions of Articles 12 or 15, or if the courts whose jurisdiction they purport to exclude have exclusive jurisdiction by virtue of Article 16.

If an agreement conferring jurisdiction was concluded for the benefit of only one of the parties, that party shall retain the right to bring proceedings in any other court which has jurisdiction by virtue of this Convention.

ARTICLE 18

Apart from jurisdiction derived from other provisions of this Convention, a court of a Contracting State before whom a defendant enters an appearance shall have jurisdiction. This rule shall not apply where appearance was entered solely to contest the jurisdiction, or where another court has exclusive jurisdiction by virtue of Article 16.

Section 7
Examination as to jurisdiction and admissibility
ARTICLE 19

Where a court of a Contracting State is seised of a claim which is principally concerned with a matter over which the courts of another Contracting State have exclusive jurisdiction by virtue of Article 16, it shall declare of its own motion that it has no jurisdiction.

ARTICLE 20

Where a defendant domiciled in one Contracting State is sued in a court of another Contracting State and does not enter an appearance, the court shall declare of its own motion that it has no jurisdiction unless its jurisdiction is derived from the provisions of this Convention.

The court shall stay the proceedings so long as it is not shown that the defendant has been able to receive the document instituting the proceedings or an equivalent document in sufficient time to enable him to arrange for his defence, or that all necessary steps have been taken to this end.

The provisions of the foregoing paragraph shall be replaced by those of Article 15 of the Hague Convention of 15 November 1965 on the Service Abroad of Judicial and Extrajudicial Documents in Civil or Commercial Matters, if the documents instituting the proceedings or notice thereof had to be transmitted abroad in accordance with that Convention.

Section 8
Lis Pendens—Related actions
ARTICLE 21

Where proceedings involving the same cause of action and between the same parties are brought in the courts of different Contracting States, any court other than the court first seised shall of its own motion decline jurisdiction in favour of that court.

A court which would be required to decline jurisdiction may stay its proceedings if the jurisdiction of the other court is contested.

ARTICLE 22

Where related actions are brought in the courts of different Contracting States, any court other than the court first seised may, while the actions are pending at first instance, stay its proceedings.

A court other than the court first seised may also, on the application of one of the parties, decline jurisdiction if the law of that court permits the consolidation of related actions and the court first seised has jurisdiction over both actions.

For the purposes of this Article, actions are deemed to be related where they are so closely connected that it is expedient to hear and determine them together to avoid the risk of irreconcilable judgments resulting from separate proceedings.

ARTICLE 23

Where actions come within the exclusive jurisdiction of several courts, any court other than the court first seised shall decline jurisdiction in favour of that court.

Section 9

Provisional, including protective, measures

ARTICLE 24

Application may be made to the courts of a Contracting State for such provisional, including protective, measures as may be available under the law of that State, even if, under this Convention, the courts of another Contracting State have jurisdiction as to the substance of the matter.

TITLE III

RECOGNITION AND ENFORCEMENT

ARTICLE 25

For the purposes of this Convention, "judgment" means any judgment given by a court or tribunal of a Contracting State, whatever the judgment may be called, including a decree, order, decision or writ of execution, as well as the determination of costs or expenses by an officer of the court.

Section 1

Recognition

ARTICLE 26

A judgment given in a Contracting State shall be recognised in the other Contracting States without any special procedure being required.

Any interested party who raises the recognition of a judgment as the principal issue in a dispute may, in accordance with the procedures provided for in Sections 2 and 3 of this Title, apply for a decision that the judgment be recognised.

If the outcome of proceedings in a court of a Contracting State depends on the determination of an incidental question of recognition that court shall have jurisdiction over that question.

ARTICLE 27

A judgment shall not be recognised:
(1) if such recognition is contrary to public policy in the State in which recognition is sought;
(2) where it was given in default of appearance, if the defendant was not duly served with the document which instituted the proceedings or with an equivalent document in sufficient time to enable him to arrange for his defence;
(3) if the judgment is irreconcilable with a judgment given in a dispute between the same parties in the State in which recognition is sought;
(4) if the court of the State in which the judgment was given, in order to arrive at its judgment, has decided a preliminary question concerning the status or legal capacity of natural persons, rights in property arising out of a matrimonial relationship, wills or succession in a way that conflicts with a rule of the private international law of the State in which the recognition is sought, unless the same result would have been reached by the application of the rules of private international law of that State;
(5) if the judgment is irreconcilable with an earlier judgment given in a non-Contracting State involving the same cause of action and between the same parties, provided that this latter judgment fulfils the conditions necessary for its recognition in the State addressed.

ARTICLE 28

Moreover, a judgment shall not be recognised if it conflicts with the provisions of Sections 3, 4 or 5 of Title II, or in a case provided for in Article 59.

In its examination of the grounds of jurisdiction referred to in the foregoing paragraph, the court or authority applied to shall be bound by the findings of fact on which the court of the State in which the judgment was given based its jurisdiction.

Subject to the provisions of the first paragraph, the jurisdiction of the court of the State in which the judgment was given may not be reviewed; the test of public policy referred to in Article 27(1) may not be applied to the rules relating to jurisdiction.

ARTICLE 29

Under no circumstances may a foreign judgment be reviewed as to its substance.

ARTICLE 30

A court of a Contracting State in which recognition is sought of a judgment given in another Contracting State may stay the proceedings if an ordinary appeal against the judgment has been lodged.

A court of a Contracting State in which recognition is sought of a judgment given in Ireland or the United Kingdom may stay the proceedings if enforcement is suspended in the State in which the judgment was given by reason of an appeal.

Section 2

Enforcement

ARTICLE 31

A judgment given in a Contracting State and enforceable in that State shall be enforced in another Contracting State when, on the application of any interested party, the order for its enforcement has been issued there.

However, in the United Kingdom, such a judgment shall be enforced in England and Wales, in Scotland, or in Northern Ireland when, on the application of any interested party, it has been registered for enforcement in that part of the United Kingdom.

ARTICLE 32

The application shall be submitted:

—in Belgium, to the *tribunal de première instance* or *rechtbank van eerste aanleg*;
—in Denmark, to the *underret*;
—in the Federal Republic of Germany, to the presiding judge of a chamber of the *Landgericht*;
—in France, to the presiding judge of the *tribunal de grande instance*;
—in Ireland, to the High Court;
—in Italy, to the *corte d'appello*;
—in Luxembourg, to the presiding judge of the *tribunal d'arrondissement*;
—in the Netherlands, to the presiding judge of the *arrondissementsrechtbank*;
—in the United Kingdom;

(1) in England and Wales, to the High Court of Justice, or in the case of a maintenance judgment to the Magistrates' Court on transmission by the Secretary of State;
(2) in Scotland, to the Court of Session, or in the case of a maintenance judgment to the Sheriff Court on transmission by the Secretary of State;
(3) in Northern Ireland, to the High Court of Justice, or in the case of a maintenance judgment to the Magistrates' Court on transmission by the Secretary of State.

The jurisdiction of local courts shall be determined by reference to the place of domicile of the party against whom enforcement is sought. If he is not domiciled in the State in which enforcement is sought, it shall be determined by reference to the place of enforcement.

ARTICLE 33

The procedure for making the application shall be governed by the law of the State in which enforcement is sought.

The applicant must give an address for service of process within the area of jurisdiction of the court applied to. However, if the law of the State in which enforcement is sought does not provide for the furnishing of such an address, the applicant shall appoint a representative *ad litem*.

The documents referred to in Articles 46 and 47 shall be attached to the application.

ARTICLE 34

The court applied to shall give its decision without delay; the party against whom enforcement is sought shall not at this stage of the proceedings be entitled to make any submissions on the application.

The application may be refused only for one of the reasons specified in Articles 27 and 28.

Under no circumstances may the foreign judgment be reviewed as to its substance.

ARTICLE 35

The appropriate officer of the court shall without delay bring the decision given on the application to the notice of the applicant in accordance with the procedure laid down by the law of the State in which enforcement is sought.

ARTICLE 36

If enforcement is authorised, the party against whom enforcement is sought may appeal against the decision within one month of service thereof.

If that party is domiciled in a Contracting State other than that in which the decision authorising enforcement was given, the time for appealing shall be two months and shall run from the date of service, either on him in person or at his residence. No extension of time may be granted on account of distance.

ARTICLE 37

An appeal against the decision authorising enforcement shall be lodged in accordance with the rules governing procedure in contentious matters:

—in Belgium, with the *tribunal de première instance* or *rechtbank van eerste aanleg*;
—in Denmark, with the *landsret*;
—in the Federal Republic of Germany, with the *Oberlandesgericht*;
—in France, with the *cour d'appel*;
—in Ireland, with the High Court;
—in Italy, with the *corte d'appello*;
—in Luxembourg, with the *Cour supérieure de Justice* sitting as a court of civil appeal;
—in the Netherlands, with the *arrondissementsrechtbank*;
—in the United Kingdom:

(1) in England and Wales, with the High Court of Justice, or in the case of a maintenance judgment with the Magistrates' Court;
(2) in Scotland, with the Court of Session, or in the case of a maintenance judgment with the Sheriff Court;
(3) in Northern Ireland, with the High Court of Justice, or in the case of a maintenance judgment with the Magistrates' Court.

The judgment given on the appeal may be contested only:

—in Belgium, France, Italy, Luxembourg and the Netherlands, by an appeal in cassation;
—in Denmark, by an appeal to the *højesteret*, with the leave of the Minister of Justice;
—in the Federal Republic of Germany, by a *Rechtsbeschwerde*;
—in Ireland, by an appeal on a point of law to the Supreme Court;
—in the United Kingdom, by a single further appeal on a point of law.

ARTICLE 38

The court with which the appeal under the first paragraph of Article 37 is lodged may, on the application of the appellant, stay the proceedings if an ordinary appeal has been lodged against the judgment in the State in which that judgment was given or if the time for such an appeal has not yet expired; in the latter case, the court may specify the time within which such an appeal is to be lodged.

Where the judgment was given in Ireland or the United Kingdom, any form of appeal available in the State in which it was given shall be treated as an ordinary appeal for the purposes of the first paragraph.

The court may also make enforcement conditional on the provision of such security as it shall determine.

ARTICLE 39

During the time specified for an appeal pursuant to Article 36 and until any such appeal has been determined, no measures of enforcement may be taken other than protective measures taken against the property of the party against whom enforcement is sought.

The decision authorising enforcement shall carry with it the power to proceed to any such protective measures.

ARTICLE 40

If the application for enforcement is refused, the applicant may appeal:

—in Belgium, to the *cour d'appel* or *hof van beroep*;
—in Denmark, to the *landsret*;
—in the Federal Republic of Germany, to the *Oberlandesgericht*;
—in France, to the *cour d'appel*;
—in Ireland, to the High Court;
—in Italy, to the *corte d'appello*;
—in Luxembourg, to the *Cour supérieure de Justice* sitting as a court of civil appeal;
—in the Netherlands, to the *gerechtshof*;
—in the United Kingdom:

(1) in England and Wales, to the High Court of Justice, or in the case of a maintenance judgment to the Magistrates' Court;
(2) in Scotland, to the Court of Session, or in the case of a maintenance judgment to the Sheriff Court;
(3) in Northern Ireland, to the High Court of Justice, or in the case of a maintenance judgment to the Magistrates' Court.

The party against whom enforcement is sought shall be summoned to appear before the appellate court. If he fails to appear, the provisions of the second and third paragraphs of Article 20 shall apply even where he is not domiciled in any of the Contracting States.

ARTICLE 41

A judgment given on an appeal provided for in Article 40 may be contested only:

—in Belgium, France, Italy, Luxembourg and the Netherlands, by an appeal in cassation;
—in Denmark, by an appeal to the *højesteret*, with the leave of the Minister of Justice;
—in the Federal Republic of Germany, by a *Rechtsbeschwerde*;
—in Ireland, by an appeal on a point of law to the Supreme Court;
—in the United Kingdom, by a single further appeal on a point of law.

ARTICLE 42

Where a foreign judgment has been given in respect of several matters and enforcement cannot be authorised for all of them the court shall authorise enforcement for one or more of them.

An applicant may request partial enforcement of a judgment.

ARTICLE 43

A foreign judgment which orders a periodic payment by way of a penalty shall be enforceable in the State in which enforcement is sought only if the amount of the payment has been finally determined by the courts of the State in which the judgment was given.

ARTICLE 44

An applicant who, in the State in which the judgment was given, has benefited from complete or partial legal aid or exemption from costs or expenses, shall be entitled, in the procedures provided for in Articles 32 to 35, to benefit from the most favourable legal aid or the most extensive exemption from costs or expenses provided for by the law of the State addressed.

An applicant who requests the enforcement of a decision given by an administrative authority in Denmark in respect of a maintenance order may, in the State addressed, claim the benefits referred to in the first paragraph if he presents a statement from the Danish Ministry of Justice to the effect that he fulfils the economic requirements to qualify for the grant of complete or partial legal aid or exemption from costs or expenses.

ARTICLE 45

No security, bond or deposit, however described, shall be required of a party who in one Contracting State applies for enforcement of a judgment given in another Contracting State on the ground that he is a foreign national or that he is not domiciled or resident in the State in which enforcement is sought.

Section 3

Common provisions

ARTICLE 46

A party seeking recognition or applying for enforcement of a judgment shall produce:

(1) a copy of the judgment which satisfies the conditions necessary to establish its authenticity;

(2) in the case of a judgment given in default, the original or a certified true copy of the document which establishes that the party in default was served with the document instituting the proceedings or with an equivalent document.

ARTICLE 47

A party applying for enforcement shall also produce:

(1) documents which establish that, according to the law of the State in which it has been given, the judgment is enforceable and has been served;

(2) where appropriate, a document showing that the applicant is in receipt of legal aid in the State in which the judgment was given.

ARTICLE 48

If the documents specified in Article 46(2) and Article 47(2) are not produced, the court may specify a time for their production, accept equivalent documents or, if it considers that it has sufficient information before it, dispense with their production.

If the court so requires, a translation of the documents shall be produced; the translation shall be certified by a person qualified to do so in one of the Contracting States.

ARTICLE 49

No legalisation or other similar formality shall be required in respect of the documents referred to in Articles 46 or 47 or the second paragraph of Article 48, or in respect of a document appointing a representative *ad litem*.

TITLE IV

AUTHENTIC INSTRUMENTS AND COURT SETTLEMENTS

ARTICLE 50

A document which has been formally drawn up or registered as an authentic instrument and is enforceable in one Contracting State shall, in another Contracting State, have an order for its enforcement issued there, on application made in accordance with the procedures provided for in Article 31 *et seq.* The application may be refused only if enforcement of the instrument is contrary to public policy in the State in which enforcement is sought.

The instrument produced must satisfy the conditions necessary to establish its authenticity in the State of origin.

The provisions of Section 3 of Title III shall apply as appropriate.

ARTICLE 51

A settlement which has been approved by a court in the course of proceedings and is enforceable in the State in which it was concluded shall be enforceable in the State in which enforcement is sought under the same conditions as authentic instruments.

TITLE V
GENERAL PROVISIONS
ARTICLE 52

In order to determine whether a party is domiciled in the Contracting State whose courts are seised of the matter, the court shall apply its internal law.

If a party is not domiciled in the State whose courts are seised of the matter, then, in order to determine whether the party is domiciled in another Contracting State, the court shall apply the law of that State.

The domicile of a party shall, however, be determined in accordance with his national law if, by that law, his domicile depends on that of another person or on the seat of an authority.

ARTICLE 53

For the purposes of this Convention, the seat of a company or other legal person or association of natural or legal persons shall be treated as its domicile. However, in order to determine that seat, the court shall apply its rules of private international law.

In order to determine whether a trust is domiciled in the Contracting State whose courts are seised of the matter, the court shall apply its rules of private international law.

TITLE VI
TRANSITIONAL PROVISIONS
ARTICLE 54

The provisions of this Convention shall apply only to legal proceedings instituted and to documents formally drawn up or registered as authentic instruments after its entry into force.

However, judgments given after the date of entry into force of this Convention in proceedings instituted before that date shall be recognised and enforced in accordance with the provisions of Title III if jurisdiction was founded upon rules which accorded with those provided for either in Title II of this Convention or in a convention concluded between the State or origin and the State addressed which was in force when the proceedings were instituted.

TITLE VII
RELATIONSHIP TO OTHER CONVENTIONS
ARTICLE 55

Subject to the provisions of the second paragraph of Article 54, and of Article 56, this Convention shall, for the States which are parties to it, supersede the following conventions concluded between two or more of them:

—the Convention between Belgium and France on Jurisdiction and the Validity and Enforcement of Judgments, Arbitration Awards and Authentic Instruments, signed at Paris on 8 July 1899;
—the Convention between Belgium and the Netherlands on Jurisdiction, Bankruptcy, and the Validity and Enforcement of Judgments, Arbitration Awards and Authentic Instruments, signed at Brussels on 28 March 1925;

—the Convention between France and Italy on the Enforcement of Judgments in Civil and Commercial Matters, signed at Rome on 3 June 1930;

—the Convention between the United Kingdom and the French Republic providing for the Reciprocal Enforcement of Judgments in Civil and Commercial Matters, with Protocol, signed at Paris on 18 January 1934;

—the Convention between the United Kingdom and the Kingdom of Belgium providing for the Reciprocal Enforcement of Judgments in Civil and Commercial Matters, with Protocol, signed at Brussels on 2 May 1934;

—the Convention between Germany and Italy on the Recognition and Enforcement of Judgments in Civil and Commercial matters, signed at Rome on 9 March 1936;

—the Convention between the Federal Republic of Germany and the Kingdom of Belgium on the Mutual Recognition and Enforcement of Judgments, Arbitration Awards and Authentic Instruments in Civil and Commercial Matters, signed at Bonn on 30 June 1958;

—the Convention between the Kingdom of the Netherlands and the Italian Republic on the Recognition and Enforcement of Judgments in Civil and Commercial Matters, signed at Rome on 17 April 1959;

—the Convention between the United Kingdom and the Federal Republic of Germany for the Reciprocal Recognition and Enforcement of Judgments in Civil and Commercial Matters, signed at Bonn on 14 July 1960;

—the Convention between the Kingdom of Belgium and the Italian Republic on the Recognition and Enforcement of Judgments and other Enforceable Instruments in Civil and Commercial Matters, signed at Rome on 6 April 1962;

—the Convention between the Kingdom of the Netherlands and the Federal Republic of Germany on the Mutual Recognition and Enforcement of Judgments and other Enforceable Instruments in Civil and Commercial Matters, signed at The Hague on 30 August 1962;

—the Convention between the United Kingdom and the Republic of Italy for the Reciprocal Recognition and Enforcement of Judgments in Civil and Commercial Matters, signed at Rome on 7 February 1964, with amending Protocol signed at Rome on 14 July 1970;

—the Convention between the United Kingdom and the Kingdom of the Netherlands providing for the Reciprocal Recognition and Enforcement of Judgments in Civil Matters, signed at The Hague on 17 November 1967,

and, in so far as it is in force:

—the Treaty between Belgium, the Netherlands and Luxembourg on Jurisdiction, Bankruptcy, and the Validity and Enforcement of Judgments, Arbitration Awards and Authentic Instruments, signed at Brussels on 24 November 1961.

ARTICLE 56

The Treaty and the conventions referred to in Article 55 shall continue to have effect in relation to matters to which this Convention does not apply.

They shall continue to have effect in respect of judgments given and documents formally drawn up or registered as authentic instruments before the entry into force of this Convention.

ARTICLE 57

This Convention shall not affect any conventions to which the Contracting States are or will be parties and which, in relation to particular matters, govern jurisdiction or the recognition or enforcement of judgments.

This Convention shall not affect the application of provisions which, in relation to particular matters, govern jurisdiction or the recognition or enforcement of judgments and which are or will be contained in acts of the Institutions of the European Communities or in national laws harmonised in implementation of such acts.

(Article 25(2) of the Accession Convention provides:
"With a view to its uniform interpretation, paragraph 1 of Article 57 shall be applied in the following manner:

(a) The 1968 Convention as amended shall not prevent a court of a Contracting State which is a party to a convention on a particular matter from assuming jurisdiction in accordance

with that convention, even where the defendant is domiciled in another Contracting State which is not a party to that convention. The court shall, in any event, apply Article 20 of the 1968 Convention as amended.
(b) A judgment given in a Contracting State in the exercise of jurisdiction provided for in a convention on a particular matter shall be recognised and enforced in the other Contracting States in accordance with the 1968 Convention as amended.

Where a convention on a particular matter to which both the State of origin and the State addressed are parties lays down conditions for the recognition or enforcement of judgments, those conditions shall apply. In any event, the provisions of the 1968 Convention as amended which concerned the procedures for recognition and enforcement of judgments may be applied.")

ARTICLE 58

This Convention shall not affect the rights granted to Swiss nationals by the Convention concluded on 15 June 1869 between France and the Swiss Confederation on Jurisdiction and the Enforcement of Judgments in Civil Matters.

ARTICLE 59

This Convention shall not prevent a Contracting State from assuming, in a convention on the recognition and enforcement of judgments, an obligation towards a third State not to recognise judgments given in other Contracting States against defendants domiciled or habitually resident in the third State where, in cases provided for in Article 4, the judgment could only be founded on a ground of jurisdiction specified in the second paragraph of Article 3.

However, a Contracting State may not assume an obligation towards a third State not to recognise a judgment given in another Contracting State by a court basing its jurisdiction on the presence within that State of property belonging to the defendant, or the seizure by the plaintiff of property situated there:

(1) if the action is brought to assert or declare proprietary or possessory rights in that property, seeks to obtain authority to dispose of it, or arises from another issue relating to such property, or,
(2) if the property constitutes the security for a debt which is the subject-matter of the action.

TITLE VIII
FINAL PROVISIONS
ARTICLE 60

This Convention shall apply to the European territories of the Contracting States, including Greenland, to the French overseas departments and territories, and to Mayotte.

The Kingdom of the Netherlands may declare at the time of signing or ratifying this Convention or at any later time, by notifying the Secretary-General of the Council of the European Communities, that this Convention shall be applicable to the Netherlands Antilles. In the absence of such declaration, proceedings taking place in the European territory of the Kingdom as a result of an appeal in cassation from the judgment of a court in the Netherlands Antilles shall be deemed to be proceedings taking place in the latter court.

Notwithstanding the first paragraph, this Convention shall not apply to:

(1) the Faroe Islands, unless the Kingdom of Denmark makes a declaration to the contrary,
(2) any European territory situated outside the United Kingdom for the international relations of which the United Kingdom is responsible, unless the United Kingdom makes a declaration to the contrary in respect of any such territory.

Such declarations may be made at any time by notifying the Secretary-General of the Council of the European Communities.

Proceedings brought in the United Kingdom on appeal from courts in one of the territories referred to in subparagraph (2) of the third paragraph shall be deemed to be proceedings taking place in those courts.

Appendix 1

Proceedings which in the Kingdom of Denmark are dealt with under the law on civil procedure for the Faroe Islands (*lov for Faerøerne om rettens pleje*) shall be deemed to be proceedings taking place in the courts of the Faroe Islands.

ARTICLE 61

This Convention shall be ratified by the signatory States. The instruments of ratification shall be deposited with the Secretary-General of the Council of the European Communities.

ARTICLE 62

This Convention shall enter into force on the first day of the third month following the deposit of the instrument of ratification by the last signatory State to take this step.

ARTICLE 63

The Contracting States recognise that any State which becomes a member of the European Economic Community shall be required to accept this Convention as a basis for the negotiations between the Contracting States and that State necessary to ensure the implementation of the last paragraph of Article 220 of the Treaty establishing the European Economic Community.

The necessary adjustments may be the subject of a special convention between the Contracting States of the one part and the new Member State of the other part.

ARTICLE 64

The Secretary-General of the Council of the European Communities shall notify the signatory States of:

(a) the deposit of each instrument of ratification;
(b) the date of entry into force of this Convention;
(c) any declaration received pursuant to Article 60;
(d) any declaration received pursuant to Article IV of the Protocol;
(e) any communication made pursuant to Article VI of the Protocol.

ARTICLE 65

The Protocol annexed to this Convention by common accord of the Contracting States shall form an integral part thereof.

ARTICLE 66

This Convention is concluded for an unlimited period.

ARTICLE 67

Any Contracting State may request the revision of this Convention. In this event, a revision conference shall be convened by the President of the Council of the European Communities.

ARTICLE 68

This Convention, drawn up in a single original in the Dutch, French, German and Italian languages, all four texts being equally authentic, shall be deposited in the archives of the Secretariat of the Council of the European Communities. The Secretary-General shall transmit a certified copy to the Government of each signatory State.

(Signatures of Plenipotentiaries of the original six Contracting States)

ANNEXED PROTOCOL

ARTICLE I

Any person domiciled in Luxembourg who is sued in a court of another Contracting State pursuant to Article 5(1) may refuse to submit to the jurisdiction of that court. If the defendant does not enter an appearance the court shall declare of its own motion that it has no jurisdiction.

An agreement conferring jurisdiction, within the meaning of Article 17, shall be valid with respect to a person domiciled in Luxembourg only if that persons has expressly and specifically so agreed.

ARTICLE II

Without prejudice to any more favourable provisions of national laws, persons domiciled in a Contracting State who are being prosecuted in the criminal courts of another Contracting State of which they are not nationals for an offence which was not intentionally committed may be defended by persons qualified to do so, even if they do not appear in person.

However, the court seised of the matter may order appearance in person; in the case of failure to appear, a judgment given in the civil action without the person concerned having had the opportunity to arrange for his defence need not be recognised or enforced in the other Contracting States.

ARTICLE III

In proceedings for the issue of an order for enforcement, no charge, duty or fee calculated by reference to the value of the matter in issue may be levied in the State in which enforcement is sought.

ARTICLE IV

Judicial and extrajudicial documents drawn up in one Contracting State which have to be served on persons in another Contracting State shall be transmitted in accordance with the procedures laid down in the conventions and agreements concluded between the Contracting States.

Unless the State in which service is to take place objects by declaration to the Secretary-General of the Council of the European Communities, such documents may also be sent by the appropriate public officers of the State in which the document has been drawn up directly to the appropriate public officers of the State in which the addressee is to be found. In this case the officer of the State of origin shall send a copy of the document to the officer of the State addressed who is competent to forward it to the addressee. The document shall be forwarded in the manner specified by the law of the State addressed. The forwarding shall be recorded by a certificate sent directly to the officer of the State of origin.

ARTICLE V

The jurisdiction specified in Article 6(2) and Article 10 in actions on a warranty or guarantee or in any other third party proceedings may not be resorted to in the Federal Republic of Germany. In that State, any person domiciled in another Contracting State may be sued in the courts in pursuance of Articles 68, 72, 73 and 74 of the code of civil procedure (*Zivilprozessordnung*) concerning third-party notices.

Judgments given in the other Contracting States by virtue of Article 6(2) or Article 10 shall be recognised and enforced in the Federal Republic of Germany in accordance with Title III. Any effects which judgments given in that State may have on third parties by application of Articles 68, 72, 73 and 74 of the code of civil procedure (*Zivilprozessordnung*) shall also be recognised in the other Contracting States.

ARTICLE V A

In matters relating to maintenance, the expression "court" includes the Danish administrative authorities.

ARTICLE V B

In proceedings involving a dispute between the master and a member of the crew of a sea-going ship registered in Denmark or in Ireland, concerning remuneration or other conditions of service, a court in a Contracting State shall establish whether the diplomatic or consular officer responsible for the ship has been notified of the dispute. It shall stay the proceedings so long as he has not been notified. It shall of its own motion decline jurisdiction if the officer, having been duly notified, has exercised the powers accorded to him in the matter by a consular convention, or in the absence of such a convention has, within the time allowed, raised any objection to the exercise of such jurisdiction.

ARTICLE V C

Articles 52 and 53 of this Convention shall, when applied by Article 69(5) of the Convention for the European Patent for the Common Market, signed at Luxembourg on 15 December 1975, to the provisions relating to "residence" in the English text of that Convention, operate as if "residence" in that text were the same as "domicile" in Articles 52 and 53.

ARTICLE V D

Without prejudice to the jurisdiction of the European Patent Office under the Convention on the Grant of European Patents, signed at Munich on 5 October 1973, the courts of each Contracting State shall have exclusive jurisdiction, regardless of domicile, in proceedings concerned with the registration or validity of any European patent granted for that State which is not a Community patent by virtue of the provisions of Article 86 of the Convention for the European Patent for the Common Market, signed at Luxembourg on 15 December 1975.

ARTICLE VI

The Contracting States shall communicate to the Secretary-General of the Council of the European Communities the text of any provisions of their laws which amend either those articles of their laws mentioned in the Convention or the lists of courts specified in Section 2 of Title III of the Convention.

SCHEDULE 2

Section 2(2)

TEXT OF 1971 PROTOCOL, AS AMENDED

ARTICLE 1

The Court of Justice of the European Communities shall have jurisdiction to give rulings on the interpretation of the Convention on Jurisdiction and the Enforcement of Judgments in Civil and Commercial Matters and of the Protocol annexed to that Convention, signed at Brussels on 27 September 1968, and also on the interpretation of the present Protocol.

The Court of Justice of the European Communities shall also have jurisdiction to give rulings on the interpretation of the Convention on the Accession of the Kingdom of Denmark, Ireland and the United Kingdom of Great Britain and Northern Ireland to the Convention of 27 September 1968 and to this Protocol.

ARTICLE 2

The following courts may request the Court of Justice to give preliminary rulings on questions of interpretation:

(1) —in Belgium: *la Cour de Cassation—het Hof van Cassatie* and *le Conseil d'Etat—de Raad van State,*
—in Demark: *højesteret,*
—in the Federal Republic of Germany: *die obersten Gerichtshöfe des Bundes,*
—in France: *la Cour de Cassation* and *le Conseil d'Etat,*
—in Ireland: the Supreme Court,
—in Italy: *la Corte Suprema di Cassazione,*
—in Luxembourg: *la Cour supérieure de Justice* when sitting as *Cour de Cassation,*
—in the Netherlands: *de Hoge Raad,*
—in the United Kingdom: the House of Lords and courts to which application has been made under the second paragraph of Article 37 or under Article 41 of the Convention;

(2) the courts of the Contracting States when they are sitting in an appellate capacity;
(3) in the cases provided for in Article 37 of the Convention, the courts referred to in that Article.

ARTICLE 3

(1) Where a question of the interpretation of the Convention or of one of the other instruments referred to in Article 1 is raised in a case pending before one of the courts listed in Article 2(1), that court shall, if it considers that a decision on the question is necessary to enable it to give judgment, request the Court of Justice to give a ruling thereon.

(2) Where such a question is raised before any court referred to in Article 2(2) or (3), that court may, under the conditions laid down in paragraph (1), request the Court of Justice to give a ruling thereon.

ARTICLE 4

(1) The competent authority of a Contracting State may request the Court of Justice to give a ruling on a question of interpretation of the Convention or of one of the other instruments referred to in Article 1 if judgments given by courts of that State conflict with the interpretation given either by the Court of Justice or in a judgment of one of the courts of another Contracting State referred to in Article 2(1) or (2). The provisions of this paragraph shall apply only to judgments which have become *res judicata*.

(2) The interpretation given by the Court of Justice in response to such a request shall not affect the judgments which gave rise to the request for interpretation.

(3) The Procurators-General of the Courts of Cassation of the Contracting States, or any other authority designated by a Contracting State, shall be entitled to request the Court of Justice for a ruling on interpretation in accordance with paragraph (1).

(4) The Registrar of the Court of Justice shall give notice of the request to the Contracting States, to the Commission and to the Council of the European Communities; they shall then be entitled within two months of the notification to submit statements of case or written observations to the Court.

(5) No fees shall be levied or any costs or expenses awarded in respect of the proceedings provided for in this Article.

ARTICLE 5

(1) Except where this Protocol otherwise provides, the provisions of the Treaty establishing the European Economic Community and those of the Protocol on the Statute of the Court of Justice annexed thereto, which are applicable when the Court is requested to give a preliminary ruling, shall also apply to any proceedings for the interpretation of the Convention and the other instruments referred to in Article 1.

(2) The Rules of Procedure of the Court of Justice shall, if necessary, be adjusted and supplemented in accordance with Article 188 of the Treaty establishing the European Economic Community.

ARTICLE 6

This Protocol shall apply to the European territories of the Contracting States, including Greenland, to the French overseas departments and territories, and to Mayotte.

The Kingdom of the Netherlands may declare at the time of signing or ratifying this Protocol or at any later time, by notifying the Secretary-General of the Council of the European Communities, that this Protocol shall be applicable to the Netherlands Antilles.

Notwithstanding the first paragraph, this Protocol shall not apply to:

(1) the Faroe Islands, unless the Kingdom of Denmark makes a declaration to the contrary,
(2) any European territory situated outside the United Kingdom for the international relations of which the United Kingdom is responsible, unless the United Kingdom makes a declaration to the contrary in respect of any such territory.

Such declarations may be made at any time by notifying the Secretary-General of the Council of the European Communities.

Appendix 1

ARTICLE 7

This protocol shall be ratified by the signatory States. The instruments of ratification shall be deposited with the Secretary-General of the Council of the European Communities

ARTICLE 8

This Protocol shall enter into force on the first day of the third month following the deposit of the instrument of ratification by the last signatory State to take this step; provided that it shall at the earliest enter into force at the same time as the Convention of 27 September 1968 on Jurisdiction and the Enforcement of Judgments in Civil and Commercial Matters.

ARTICLE 9

The Contracting States recognise that any State which becomes a member of the European Economic Community, and to which Article 63 of the Convention on Jurisdiction and the Enforcement of Judgments in Civil and Commercial Matters applies, must accept the provisions of this Protocol, subject to such adjustments as may be required.

ARTICLE 10

The Secretary-General of the Council of the European Communities shall notify the signatory States of:
   (a) the deposit of each instrument of ratification;
   (b) the date of entry into force of this Protocol;
   (c) any designation received pursuant to Article 4(3);
   (d) any declaration received pursuant to Article 6.

ARTICLE 11

The Contracting States shall communicate to the Secretary-General of the Council of the European Communities the texts of any provisions of their laws which necessitate an amendment to the list of courts in Article 2(1).

ARTICLE 12

This Protocol is concluded for an unlimited period.

ARTICLE 13

Any Contracting State may request the revision of this Protocol. In this event, a revision conference shall be convened by the President of the Council of the European Communities.

ARTICLE 14

This Protocol, drawn up in a single original in the Dutch, French, German and Italian languages, all four texts being equally authentic, shall be deposited in the archives of the Secretariat of the Council of the European Communities. The Secretary-General shall transmit a certified copy to the Government of each signatory State.

SCHEDULE 3

Section 2(2)

TEXT OF TITLES V AND VI OF ACCESSION CONVENTION

TITLE V

TRANSITIONAL PROVISIONS

ARTICLE 34

(1) The 1968 Convention and the 1971 Protocol, with the amendments made by this Convention, shall apply only to legal proceedings instituted and to authentic instruments formally drawn up or registered after the entry into force of this Convention in the State of origin and, where recognition or enforcement of a judgment or authentic instrument is sought, in the State addressed.

(2) However, as between the six Contracting States to the 1968 Convention, judgments given after the date of entry into force of this Convention in proceedings instituted before that date shall be recognised and enforced in accordance with the provisions of Title III of the 1968 Convention as amended.

(3) Moreover, as between the six Contracting States to the 1968 Convention and the three States mentioned in Article 1 of this Convention, and as between those three States, judgments given after the date of entry into force of this Convention between the State of origin and the State addressed in proceedings instituted before that date shall also be recognised and enforced in accordance with the provisions of Title III of the 1968 Convention as amended if jurisdiction was founded upon rules which accorded with the provisions of Title II, as amended, or with provisions of a convention concluded between the State of origin and the State addressed which was in force when the proceedings were instituted.

ARTICLE 35

If the parties to a dispute concerning a contract had agreed in writing before the entry into force of this Convention that the contract was to be governed by the law of Ireland or of a part of the United Kingdom, the courts of Ireland or of that part of the United Kingdom shall retain the right to exercise jurisdiction in the dispute.

ARTICLE 36

For a period of three years from the entry into force of the 1968 Convention for the Kingdom of Denmark and Ireland respectively, jurisdiction in maritime matters shall be determined in these States not only in accordance with the provisions of that Convention but also in accordance with the provisions of paragraphs (1) to (6) following. However, upon the entry into force of the International Convention relating to the Arrest of Sea-going Ships, signed at Brussels on 10th May 1952, for one of these States, these provisions shall cease to have effect for that State.

(1) A person who is domiciled in a Contracting State may be sued in the courts of one of the States mentioned above in respect of a maritime claim if the ship to which the claim relates or any other ship owned by him has been arrested by judicial process within the territory of the latter State to secure the claim, or could have been so arrested there but bail or other security has been given, and either:

  (a) the claimant is domiciled in the latter State; or
  (b) the claim arose in the latter State; or
  (c) the claim concerns the voyage during which the arrest was made or could have been made; or
  (d) the claim arises out of a collision or out of damage caused by a ship to another ship or to goods or persons on board either ship, either by the execution or non-execution of a manoeuvre or by the non-observance of regulations; or
  (e) the claim is for salvage; or
  (f) the claim is in respect of a mortgage or hypothecation of the ship arrested.

(2) A claimant may arrest either the particular ship to which the maritime claim relates, or any other ship which is owned by the person who was, at the time when the maritime claim arose, the owner of the particular ship. However, only the particular ship to which the maritime claim relates may be arrested in respect of the maritime claims set out in subparagraphs (o), (p) or (q) of paragraph (5) of this Article.

(3) Ships shall be deemed to be in the same ownership when all the shares therein are owned by the same person or persons.

(4) When in the case of a charter by demise of a ship the charterer alone is liable in respect of a maritime claim relating to that ship, the claimant may arrest that ship or any other ship owned by the charterer, but no other ship owned by the owner may be arrested in respect of such claim. The same shall apply to any case in which a person other than the owner of a ship is liable in respect of a maritime claim relating to that ship.

(5) The expression "maritime claim" means a claim arising out of one or more of the following:

  (a) damage caused by any ship either in collision or otherwise;

(b) loss of life or personal injury caused by any ship or occurring in connection with the operation of any ship;

(c) salvage;

(d) agreement relating to the use or hire of any ship whether by charterparty or otherwise;

(e) agreement relating to the carriage of goods in any ship whether by charterparty or otherwise;

(f) loss of or damage to goods including baggage carried in any ship;

(g) general average;

(h) bottomry;

(i) towage;

(j) pilotage;

(k) goods or materials wherever supplied to a ship for her operation or maintenance;

(l) construction, repair or equipment of any ship or dock charges and dues;

(m) wages of masters, officers or crew;

(n) master's disbursements, including disbursements made by shippers, charterers or agents on behalf of a ship or her owner;

(o) dispute as to the title to or ownership of any ship;

(p) disputes between co-owners of any ship as to the ownership, possession, employment or earnings of that ship;

(q) the mortgage or hypothecation of any ship.

(6) In Denmark, the expression "arrest" shall be deemed as regards the maritime claims referred to in subparagraphs (o) and (p) of paragraph (5) of this Article, to include a *forbud*, where that is the only procedure allowed in respect of such a claim under Articles 646 to 653 of the law on civil procedure (*lov om rettens pleje*).

TITLE VI
FINAL PROVISIONS
ARTICLE 37

The Secretary-General of the Council of the European Communities shall transmit a certified copy of the 1968 Convention and of the 1971 Protocol in the Dutch, French, German and Italian languages to the Governments of the Kingdom of Denmark, Ireland and the United Kingdom of Great Britain and Northern Ireland.

The texts of the 1968 Convention and the 1971 Protocol, drawn up in the Danish, English and Irish languages, shall be annexed to this Convention. The texts drawn up in the Danish, English and Irish languages shall be authentic under the same conditions as the original texts of the 1968 Convention and the 1971 Protocol.

ARTICLE 38

This Convention shall be ratified by the signatory States. The instruments of ratification shall be deposited with the Secretary-General of the Council of the European Communities.

ARTICLE 39

This Convention shall enter into force, as between the States which shall have ratified it, on the first day of the third month following the deposit of the last instrument of ratification by the original Member States of the Community and one new Member State.

It shall enter into force for each new Member State which subsequently ratifies it on the first day of the third month following the deposit of its instrument of ratification.

ARTICLE 40

The Secretary-General of the Council of the European Communities shall notify the signatory States of:

(a) the deposit of each instrument of ratification,

(b) the dates of entry into force of this Convention for the Contracting States.

ARTICLE 41

This Convention, drawn up in a single original in the Danish, Dutch, English, French, German, Irish and Italian languages, all seven texts being equally authentic, shall be deposited in the archives of the Secretariat of the Council of the European Communities. The Secretary-General shall transmit a certified copy to the Government of each signatory State.

SCHEDULE 4

Section 16

TITLE II OF 1968 CONVENTION AS MODIFIED FOR ALLOCATION OF JURISDICTION WITHIN UK

TITLE II

JURISDICTION

Section 1

General Provisions

ARTICLE 2

Subject to the provisions of this **Title,** persons domiciled in a **part of the United Kingdom** shall . . . be sued in the courts of that **part.**

. . . .

ARTICLE 3

Persons domiciled in a **part of the United Kingdom** may be sued in the courts of another **part of the United Kingdom** only by virtue of the rules set out in Sections 2, **4, 5 and** 6 of this Title.

. . . .

Section 2

Special jurisdiction

ARTICLE 5

A person domiciled in a **part of the United Kingdom** may, in another **part of the United Kingdom,** be sued:

(1) in matters relating to a contract, in the courts for the place of performance of the obligation in question;

(2) in matters relating to maintenance, in the courts for the place where the maintenance creditor is domiciled or habitually resident or, if the matter is ancillary to proceedings concerning the status of a person, in the court which, according to its own law, has jurisdiction to entertain those proceedings, unless that jurisdiction is based solely on the nationality of one of the parties;

(3) in matters relating to tort, delict or quasi-delict, in the courts for the place where the harmful event occurred **or in the case of a threatened wrong is likely to occur**;

(4) as regards a civil claim for damages or restitution which is based on an act giving rise to criminal proceedings, in the court seised of those proceedings, to the extent that that court has jurisdiction under its own law to entertain civil proceedings;

(5) as regards a dispute arising out of the operations of a branch, agency or other establishment, in the courts for the place in which the branch, agency or other establishment is situated;

(6) in his capacity as a settlor, trustee or beneficiary of a trust created by the operation of a

statute, or by a written instrument, or created orally and evidenced in writing, in the courts of the **part of the United Kingdom** in which the trust is domiciled;

(7) as regards a dispute concerning the payment of remuneration claimed in respect of the salvage of a cargo or freight, in the court under the authority of which the cargo or freight in question

    (a) has been arrested to secure such payment, or

    (b) could have been so arrested, but bail or other security has been given;

provided that this provision shall apply only if it is claimed that the defendant has an interest in the cargo or freight or had such an interest at the time of salvage;

(8) in proceedings—

    (a) concerning a debt secured on immovable property ; or

    (b) which are brought to assert, declare or determine proprietary or possessory rights, or rights of security, in or over movable property, or to obtain authority to dispose of movable property,

in the courts of the part of the United Kingdom in which the property is situated.

ARTICLE 5A

Proceedings which have as their object a decision of an organ of a company or other legal person or of an association of natural or legal persons may, without prejudice to the other provisions of this Title, be brought in the courts of the part of the United Kingdom in which that company, legal person or association has its seat.

ARTICLE 6

A person domiciled in a **part of the United Kingdom** may, **in another part of the United Kingdom,** also be sued:

(1) where he is one of a number of defendants, in the courts for the place where any one of them is domiciled;

(2) as a third party in an action on a warranty or guarantee or in any other third party proceedings, in the court seised of the original proceedings, unless these were instituted solely with the object of removing him from the jurisdiction of the court which would be competent in his case;

(3) on a counterclaim arising from the same contract or facts on which the original claim was based, in the court in which the original claim is pending.

ARTICLE 6A

Where by virtue of this **Title** a court of a **part of the United Kingdom** has jurisdiction in actions relating to liability arising from the use or operation of a ship, that court, or any other court substituted for this purpose by the internal law of that **part,** shall also have jurisdiction over claims for limitation of such liability.

. . . .

Section 4

Jurisdiction over consumer contracts

ARTICLE 13

In proceedings concerning a contract concluded by a person for a purpose which can be regarded as being outside his trade or profession, hereinafter called "the consumer", jurisdiction shall be determined by this Section, without prejudice to the provisions of Articles . . . 5(5) **and (8)(b),** if it is:

(1) a contract for the sale of goods on instalment credit terms, or

(2) a contract for a loan repayable by instalments, or for any other form of credit, made to finance the sale of goods, or

(3) any other contract for the supply of goods or a contract for the supply of services and ...
the consumer took in **the part of the United Kingdom in which he is domiciled** the
steps necessary for the conclusion of the contract.

. . . .

This Section shall not apply to contracts of transport **or insurance.**

ARTICLE 14

A consumer may bring proceedings against the other party to a contract either in the courts of
the **part of the United Kingdom** in which that party is domiciled or in the courts of the **part
of the United Kingdom** in which he is himself domiciled.
Proceedings may be brought against a consumer by the other party to the contract only in
the courts of the **part of the United Kingdom** in which the consumer is domiciled.
These provisions shall not affect the right to bring a counterclaim in the court in which, in
accordance with this Section, the original claim is pending.

ARTICLE 15

The provisions of this Section may be departed from only by an agreement:
  (1) which is entered into after the dispute has arisen, or
  (2) which allows the consumer to bring proceedings in courts other than those indicated in
this Section, or
  (3) which is entered into by the consumer and the other party to the contract, both of whom
are at the time of conclusion of the contract domiciled or habitually resident in the same
part of the United Kingdom, and which confers jurisdiction on the courts of that **part,**
provided that such an agreement is not contrary to the law of that **part.**

Section 5

Exclusive jurisdiction

ARTICLE 16

The following courts shall have exclusive jurisdiction, regardless of domicile:
  (1) in proceedings which have as their object rights *in rem* in, or tenancies of, immovable
property, the courts of the **part of the United Kingdom** in which the property is
situated;
  (2) in proceedings which have as their object the validity of the constitution, the nullity or
the dissolution of companies or other legal persons or associations of natural or legal
persons ... the courts of the **part of the United Kingdom** in which the company, legal
person or association has its seat;
  (3) in proceedings which have as their object the validity of entries in public registers, the
courts of the **part of the United Kingdom** in which the register is kept;

. . . .

  (5) in proceedings concerned with the enforcement of judgments, the courts of the **part of
the United Kingdom** in which the judgment has been or is to be enforced.

Section 6

Prorogation of jurisdiction

ARTICLE 17

If the parties ... have agreed that a court or the courts of a **part of the United Kingdom** are
to have jurisdiction to settle any disputes which have arisen or which may arise in connection
with a particular legal relationship, **and, apart from this Schedule, the agreement would**

be effective to confer jurisdiction under the law of that part, that court or those courts shall have ... jurisdiction ...

The court or courts of a **part of the United Kingdom** on which a trust instrument has conferred jurisdiction shall have ... jurisdiction in any proceedings brought against a settlor, trustee or beneficiary, if relations between these persons or their rights or obligations under the trust are involved.

Agreements or provisions of a trust instrument conferring jurisdiction shall have no legal force if they are contrary to the provisions of Article ... 15, or if the courts whose jurisdiction they purport to exclude have exclusive jurisdiction by virtue of Article 16.

. . . .

ARTICLE 18

Apart from jurisdiction derived from other provisions of this **Title**, a court of a **part of the United Kingdom** before whom a defendant enters an appearance shall have jurisdiction. This rule shall not apply where appearance was entered solely to contest the jurisdiction, or where another court has exclusive jurisdiction by virtue of Article 16.

Section 7

Examination as to jurisdiction and admissibility

ARTICLE 19

Where a court of a **part of the United Kingdom** is seised of a claim which is principally concerned with a matter over which the courts of another **part of the United Kingdom** have exclusive jurisdiction by virtue of Article 16, it shall declare of its own motion that it has no jurisdiction.

ARTICLE 20

Where a defendant domiciled in one **part of the United Kingdom** is sued in a court of another **part of the United Kingdom** and does not enter an appearance, the court shall declare of its own motion that it has no jurisdiction unless its jurisdiction is derived from the provisions of this **Title**.

The court shall stay the proceedings so long as it is not shown that the defendant has been able to receive the document instituting the proceedings or an equivalent document in sufficient time to enable him to arrange for his defence, or that all necessary steps have been taken to this end.

. . . .

Section 9

Provisional, including protective, measures

ARTICLE 24

Application may be made to the courts of a **part of the United Kingdom** for such provisional, including protective, measures as may be available under the law of that **part**, even if, under this **Title**, the courts of another **part of the United Kingdom** have jurisdiction as to the substance of the matter.

SCHEDULE 5

Section 17

PROCEEDINGS EXCLUDED FROM SCHEDULE 4

Proceedings under the Companies Acts

1. Proceedings for the winding up of a company under the Companies Act 1948 or the Companies Act (Northern Ireland) 1960, or proceedings relating to a company as respects

which jurisdiction is conferred on the court having winding up jurisdiction under either of those Acts.

Patents, trade marks, designs and similar rights

2. Proceedings concerned with the registration or validity of patents, trade marks, designs or other similar rights required to be deposited or registered.

Protection of Trading Interests Act 1980

3. Proceedings under section 6 of the Protection of Trading Interests Act 1980 (recovery of sums paid or obtained pursuant to a judgment for multiple damages).

Appeals etc from tribunals

4. Proceedings on appeal from, or for review of, decisions of tribunals.

Maintenance and similar payments to local and other public authorities

5. Proceedings for, or otherwise relating to, an order under any of the following provisions—

(a) section 47 or 51 of the Child Care Act 1980, section 80 of the Social Work (Scotland) Act 1968 or section 156 of the Children and Young Persons Act (Northern Ireland) 1968 (contributions in respect of children in care, etc);

(b) section 49 or 50 of the Child Care Act 1980, section 81 of the Social Work (Scotland) Act 1968 or section 159 of the Children and Young Persons Act (Northern Ireland) 1968 (applications for, or for variation of, affiliation orders in respect of children in care, etc);

(c) section 43 of the National Assistance Act 1948, section 18 of the Supplementary Benefits Act 1976, Article 101 of the Health and Personal Social Services (Northern Ireland) Order 1972 or Article 23 of the Supplementary Benefits (Northern Ireland) Order 1977 (recovery of cost of assistance or benefit from person liable to maintain the assisted person);

(d) section 44 of the National Assistance Act 1948, section 19 of the Supplementary Benefits Act 1976, Article 102 of the Health and Personal Social Services (Northern Ireland) Order 1972 or Article 24 of the Supplementary Benefits (Northern Ireland) Order 1977 (applications for, or for variation of, affiliation orders in respect of children for whom assistance or benefit provided).

Proceedings under certain conventions, etc

6. Proceedings brought in any court in pursuance of—

(a) any statutory provision which, in the case of any convention to which Article 57 applies (conventions relating to specific matters which override the general rules in the 1968 Convention), implements the convention or makes provision with respect to jurisdiction in any field to which the convention relates; and

(b) any rule of law so far as it has the effect of implementing any such convention.

Certain Admiralty proceedings in Scotland

7. Proceedings in Scotland in an Admiralty cause where the jurisdiction of the Court of Session or, as the case may be, of the sheriff is based on arrestment *in rem* or *ad fundandam jurisdictionem* of a ship, cargo or freight.

Register of aircraft mortgages

8. Proceedings for the rectification of the Register of Aircraft Mortgages kept by the Civil Aviation Authority.

Continental Shelf Act 1964

9. Proceedings brought in any court in pursuance of an order under section 3 of the Continental Shelf Act 1964.

Appendix 1

SCHEDULE 6

Section 18

ENFORCEMENT OF UK JUDGMENTS (MONEY PROVISIONS)

Preliminary

1. In this Schedule—

"judgment" means any judgment to which section 18 applies and references to the giving of a judgment shall be construed accordingly;
"money provision" means a provision for the payment of one or more sums of money;
"prescribed" means prescribed by rules of court.

Certificates in respect of judgments

2.—(1) Any interested party who wishes to secure the enforcement in another part of the United Kingdom of any money provisions contained in a judgment may apply for a certificate under this Schedule.

(2) The application shall be made in the prescribed manner to the proper officer of the original court, that is to say—

    (a) in relation to a judgment within paragraph (a) of the definition of "judgment" in section 18(2), the court by which the judgment or order was given or made;
    (b) in relation to a judgment within paragraph (b) of that definition, the court in which the judgment or order is entered;
    (c) in relation to a judgment within paragraph (c) of that definition, the court in whose books the document is registered;
    (d) in relation to a judgment within paragraph (d) of that definition, the tribunal by which the award or order was made;
    (e) in relation to a judgment within paragraph (e) of that definition, the court which gave the judgment or made the order by virtue of which the award has become enforceable as mentioned in that paragraph.

3. A certificate shall not be issued under this Schedule in respect of a judgment unless under the law of the part of the United Kingdom in which the judgment was given—

    (a) either—

        (i) the time for bringing an appeal against the judgment has expired, no such appeal having been brought within that time; or
        (ii) such an appeal having been brought within that time, that appeal has been finally disposed of; and

    (b) enforcement of the judgment is not for the time being stayed or suspended, and the time available for its enforcement has not expired.

4.—(1) Subject to paragraph 3, on an application under paragraph 2 the proper officer shall issue to the applicant a certificate in the prescribed form—

    (a) stating the sum or aggregate of the sums (including any costs or expenses) payable under the money provisions contained in the judgment, the rate of interest, if any, payable thereon and the date or time from which any such interest began to accrue;
    (b) stating that the conditions specified in paragraph 3(a) and (b) are satisfied in relation to the judgment; and
    (c) containing such other particulars as may be prescribed.

(2) More than one certificate may be issued under this Schedule (simultaneously or at different times) in respect of the same judgment.

Registration of certificates

5.—(1) Where a certificate has been issued under this Schedule in any part of the United Kingdom, any interested party may, within six months from the date of its issue, apply in the prescribed manner to the proper officer of the superior court in any other part of the United Kingdom for the certificate to be registered in that court.

(2) In this paragraph "superior court" means, in relation to England and Wales or Northern Ireland, the High Court and, in relation to Scotland, the Court of Session.

(3) Where an application is duly made under this paragraph to the proper officer of a superior court, he shall register the certificate in that court in the prescribed manner.

General effect of registration

6.—(1) A certificate registered under this Schedule shall, for the purposes of its enforcement, be of the same force and effect, the registering court shall have in relation to its enforcement the same powers, and proceedings for or with respect to its enforcement may be taken, as if the certificate had been a judgment originally given in the registering court and had (where relevant) been entered.

(2) Sub-paragraph (1) is subject to the following provisions of this Schedule and to any provision made by rules of court as to the manner in which and the conditions subject to which a certificate registered under this Schedule may be enforced.

Costs or expenses

7. Where a certificate is registered under this Schedule, the reasonable costs or expenses of and incidental to the obtaining of the certificate and its registration shall be recoverable as if they were costs or expenses stated in the certificate to be payable under a money provision contained in the original judgment.

Interest

8.—(1) Subject to any provision made under sub-paragraph (2), the debt resulting, apart from paragraph 7, from the registration of the certificate shall carry interest at the rate, if any, stated in the certificate from the date or time so stated.

(2) Provision may be made by rules of court as to the manner in which and the periods by reference to which any interest payable by virtue of sub-paragraph (1) is to be calculated and paid, including provision for such interest to cease to accrue as from a prescribed date.

(3) All such sums as are recoverable by virtue of paragraph 7 carry interest as if they were the subject of an order for costs or expenses made by the registering court on the date of registration of the certificate.

(4) Except as provided by this paragraph sums payable by virtue of the registration of a certificate under this Schedule shall not carry interest.

Stay or sisting of enforcement in certain cases

9. Where a certificate in respect of a judgment has been registered under this Schedule, the registering court may, if it is satisfied that any person against whom it is sought to enforce the certificate is entitled and intends to apply under the law of the part of the United Kingdom in which the judgment was given for any remedy which would result in the setting aside or quashing of the judgment, stay (or, in Scotland, sist) proceedings for the enforcement of the certificate, on such terms as it thinks fit, for such period as appears to the court to be reasonably sufficient to enable the application to be disposed of.

Cases in which registration of a certificate must or may be set aside

10. Where a certificate has been registered under this Schedule, the registering court—

    (a) shall set aside the registration if, on an application made by any interested party, it is satisfied that the registration was contrary to the provisions of this Schedule;

    (b) may set aside the registration if, on an application so made, it is satisfied that the matter in dispute in the proceedings in which the judgment in question was given had previously been the subject of a judgment by another court or tribunal having jurisdiction in the matter.

SCHEDULE 7

Section 18

ENFORCEMENT OF UK JUDGMENTS (NON-MONEY PROVISIONS)

Preliminary

1. In this Schedule—

"judgment" means any judgment to which section 18 applies and references to the giving of a judgment shall be construed accordingly;

"non-money provision" means a provision for any relief or remedy not requiring payment of a sum of money;

"prescribed" means prescribed by rules of court.

Certified copies of judgments

2.—(1) Any interested party who wishes to secure the enforcement in another part of the United Kingdom of any non-money provisions contained in a judgment may apply for a certified copy of the judgment.

(2) The application shall be made in the prescribed manner to the proper officer of the original court, that is to say—

    (a) in relation to a judgment within paragraph (a) of the definition of "judgment" in section 18(2), the court by which the judgment or order was given or made;

    (b) in relation to a judgment within paragraph (b) of that definition, the court in which the judgment or order is entered;

    (c) in relation to a judgment within paragraph (c) of that definition, the court in whose books the document is registered;

    (d) in relation to a judgment within paragraph (d) of that definition, the tribunal by which the award or order was made;

    (e) in relation to a judgment within paragraph (e) of that definition, the court which gave the judgment or made the order by virtue of which the award has become enforceable as mentioned in that paragraph.

3. A certified copy of a judgment shall not be issued under this Schedule unless under the law of the part of the United Kingdom in which the judgment was given—

    (a) either—

        (i) the time for bringing an appeal against the judgment has expired, no such appeal having been brought within that time; or

        (ii) such an appeal having been brought within that time, that appeal has been finally disposed of; and

    (b) enforcement of the judgment is not for the time being stayed or suspended, and the time available for its enforcement has not expired.

4.—(1) Subject to paragraph 3, on an application under paragraph 2 the proper officer shall issue to the applicant—

    (a) a certified copy of the judgment (including any money provisions or excepted provisions which it may contain); and

    (b) a certificate stating that the conditions specified in paragraph 3(a) and (b) are satisfied in relation to the judgment.

(2) In sub-paragraph (1)(a) "excepted provision" means any provision of a judgment which is excepted from the application of section 18 by subsection (5) of that section.

(3) There may be issued under this Schedule (simultaneously or at different times)—

    (a) more than one certified copy of the same judgment; and

    (b) more than one certificate in respect of the same judgment.

Registration of judgments

5.—(1) Where a certified copy of a judgment has been issued under this Schedule in any part of the United Kingdom, any interested party may apply in the prescribed manner to the superior court in any other part of the United Kingdom for the judgment to be registered in that court.

(2) In this paragraph "superior court" means, in relation to England and Wales or Northern Ireland, the High Court and, in relation to Scotland, the Court of Session.

(3) An application under this paragraph for the registration of a judgment must be accompanied by—

    (a) a certified copy of the judgment issued under this Schedule; and
    (b) a certificate issued under paragraph 4(1)(b) in respect of the judgment not more than six months before the date of the application.

(4) Subject to sub-paragraph (5), where an application under this paragraph is duly made to a superior court, the court shall order the whole of the judgment as set out in the certified copy to be registered in that court in the prescribed manner.

(5) A judgment shall not be registered under this Schedule by the superior court in any part of the United Kingdom if compliance with the non-money provisions contained in the judgment would involve a breach of the law of that part of the United Kingdom.

General effect of registration

6.—(1) The non-money provisions contained in a judgment registered under this Schedule shall, for the purposes of their enforcement, be of the same force and effect, the registering court shall have in relation to their enforcement the same powers, and proceedings for or with respect to their enforcement may be taken, as if the judgment containing them had been originally given in the registering court and had (where relevant) been entered.

(2) Sub-paragraph (1) is subject to the following provisions of this Schedule and to any provision made by rules of court as to the manner in which and conditions subject to which the non-money provisions contained in a judgment registered under this Schedule may be enforced.

Costs or expenses

7.—(1) Where a judgment is registered under this Schedule, the reasonable costs or expenses of and incidental to—

    (a) the obtaining of the certified copy of the judgment and of the necessary certificate under paragraph 4(1)(b) in respect of it; and
    (b) the registration of the judgment,

shall be recoverable as if on the date of registration there had also been registered in the registering court a certificate under Schedule 6 in respect of the judgment and as if those costs or expenses were costs or expenses stated in that certificate to be payable under a money provisions contained in the judgment.

(2) All such sums as are recoverable by virtue of sub-paragraph (1) shall carry interest as if they were the subject of an order for costs or expenses made by the registering court on the date of registration of the judgment.

Stay or sisting of enforcement in certain cases

8. Where a judgment has been registered under this Schedule, the registering court may, if it is satisfied that any person against whom it is sought to enforce the judgment is entitled and intends to apply under the law of the part of the United Kingdom in which the judgment was given for any remedy which would result in the setting aside or quashing of the judgment, stay (or, in Scotland, sist) proceedings for the enforcement of the judgment, on such terms as it thinks fit, for such period as appears to the court to be reasonably sufficient to enable the application to be disposed of.

Cases in which registered judgment must or may be set aside

9. Where a judgment has been registered under this Schedule, the registering court—

    (a) shall set aside the registration if, on an application made by any interested party, it is satisfied that the registration was contrary to the provisions of this Schedule;

(b) may set aside the registration if, on an application so made, it is satisfied that the matter in dispute in the proceedings in which the judgment was given had previously been the subject of a judgment by another court or tribunal having jurisdiction in the matter.

SCHEDULE 8

Section 20.

RULES AS TO JURISDICTION IN SCOTLAND

General

[Art. 2]   1. Subject to the **following Rules,** persons shall be sued in the courts **for the place where they are domiciled.**

Special jurisdiction

[Art. 5]   2. **Subject to Rules 3 (jurisdiction over consumer contracts), 4 (exclusive jurisdiction and 5 (prorogation)** a person may **also** be sued—

(1) **where he has no fixed residence, in a court within whose jurisdiction he is personaly cited;**

[Art. 5(1)]   (2) in matters relating to a contract, in the courts for the place of performance of the obligation in question;

[Art. 5(3)]   (3) in matters relating to delict or quasi-delict, in the courts for the place where the harmful event occurred;

[Art. 5(4)]   (4) as regards a civil claim for damages or restitution which is based on an act giving rise to criminal proceedings, in the court seised of those procedings to the extent that that court has jurisdiction to entertain civil proceedings;

[Art. 5(2)]   (5) in matters relating to maintenance, in the courts for the place where the maintenance creditor is domiciled or habitually resident or, if the matter is ancillary to proceedings concerning the status of a person, in the court which has jurisdiction to entertain those proceedings, **provided that as action for adherence and aliment or of affiliation and aliment shall be treated as a matter relating to maintenance which is not ancillary to proceedings concerning the status of a person, and provided also that—**

(a) **where a local authority exercises its power to raise an action under section 44(7)(a) of the National Assistance Act 1948 or under section 81(1) of the Social Work (Scotland) Act 1968; and**

(b) **where the Secretary of State exercises his power to raise an action under section 19(8)(a) of the Supplementary Benefits Act 1976;**

this Rule shall apply as if the reference to the maintenance creditor were a reference to the mother of the child;

[Art. 5(5)]   (6) as regards a dispute arising out of the operations of a branch, agency or other establishment, in the courts for the place in which the branch, agency or other establishment is situated;

[Art. 5(6)]   (7) **in his capacity as settlor, trustee or beneficiary of a trust domiciled in Scotland** created by the operation of a statute, or by a written instrument, or created orally and evidenced in writing, in the **Court of Session, or the appropriate sheriff court within the meaning of section 24A of the Trusts (Scotland) Act 1921;**

(8) **where he is not domiciled in the United Kindgom, in the courts for any place where—**

(a) **any moveable property belonging to him has been arrested; or**

(b) **any immoveable property in which he has any beneficial interest is situated;**

(9) **in proceedings which are brought to assert, declare or determine proprietary or possessory rights, or rights of security, in or over moveable property, or to obtain authority to dispose of moveable property, in the courts for the place where the property is situated;**

214

(10) **in proceedings for interdict, in the courts for the place where it is alleged that the wrong is likely to be committed;**

(11) **in proceedings concerning a debt secured over immoveable property, in the courts for the place where the property is situated;**

(12) **in proceedings which have as their object a decision of an organ of a company or other legal person or of an association of natural or legal persons, in the courts for the place where that company, legal person or association has its seat;**

(13) **in proceedings concerning an arbitration which is conducted in Scotland or in which the procedure is governed by Scots law, in the Courts of Session;**

(14) **in proceedings principally concerned with the registration in the United Kingdom or the validity in the United Kingdom of patents, trade marks, designs or other similar rights required to be deposited or registered, in the Court of Session;**

(15)(a) where he is one of a number of **defenders,** in the courts for the place [Art. 6] where any one of them is domiciled;

(b) as a third party in an action on a warranty or guarantee or in any other third party proceedings, in the court seised of the original proceedings, unless these were instituted solely with the object of removing him from the jurisdiction of the court which would be competent in his case;

(c) on a counterclaim arising from the same contract or facts on which the original claim was based, in the court in which the original claim is pending.

Jurisdiction over consumer contracts

3.—(1) In proceedings concerning a contract concluded by a person for a purpose [Art. 13] which can be regarded as being outside his trade or profession, hereinafter called the "consumer", **subject to Rule 4 (exclusive jurisdiction),** jurisdiction shall be determined by this **Rule** if it is—

(a) a contract for the sale of goods on instalment credit terms; or

(b) a contract for a loan repayable by instalments, or for any other form of credit, made to finance the sale of goods; or

(c) any other contract for the supply of goods or a contract for the supply of services, **if—**

(i) the consumer took in **Scotland** the steps necessary for the conclusion of the contract; **or**

(ii) **proceedings are brought in Scotland by virtue of section 10(3).**

(2) This **Rule** shall not apply to contracts of transport **or contracts of insurance**.

(3) A consumer may bring proceedings against the other party to a contract **only** [Art. 14] in—

(a) the courts **for the place** in which that party is domiciled;

(b) the courts **for the place** in which he is himself domiciled; **or**

(c) **any court having jurisdiction by virtue of Rule 2(6) or (9)**.

(4) Proceedings may be brought against a consumer by the other party to the contract only in the courts **for the place where** the consumer is domiciled **or any court having jurisdiction under Rule 2(9)**.

(5) **Nothing in this rule** shall affect the right to bring a counter-claim in the court in which, **in accordance with this Rule**, the original claim is pending.

(6) The provisions of this **Rule** may be departed from only by an agreement— [Art. 15(1) and (2)]

(a) which is entered into after the dispute has arisen; or

(b) which allows the consumer to bring proceedings in **a court** other than **a court** indicated in this **Rule**.

Appendix 1

Exclusive jurisdiction

[Art. 16]   4.—(1) **Notwithstanding anything contained in any of Rules 1 to 3 above or 5 to 8 below**, the following courts shall have exclusive jurisdiction—

[Art. 16(1)]   (a) in proceedings which have as their rights *in rem* in, or tenancies of, immoveable property, the courts **for the place where** the property is situated;

[Art. 16(2)]   (b) in proceedings which have as their object the validity of the constitution, the nullity or the dissolution of companies or other legal persons or associations of natural or legal persons, the courts **for the place where** the company, legal person or association has its seat;

[Art. 16(3)]   (c) in proceedings which have as their object the validity of entries in public registers, the courts **for the place where** the register is kept;

[Art. 16(5)]   (d) in proceedings concerned with the enforcement of judgments, the courts **for the place where** the judgment has been or is to be enforced.

(2) **Nothing in paragraph (1)(c) above affects jurisdiction in any proceedings concerning the validity of entries in registers of patents, trade marks, designs, or other similar rights required to be deposited or registered.**

(3) **No court shall exercise jurisdiction in a case where immoveable property, the seat of a body mentioned in paragraph (1)(b) above, a public register or the place where a judgment has been or is to be enforced is situated outside Scotland and where paragraph (1) above would apply if the property, seat, register or, as the case may be, place of enforcement were situated in Scotland.**

Prorogation of jurisdiction

[Art. 17(1)]   5.—(1) If the parties have agreed that a court is to have jurisdiction to settle any disputes which have arisen or which may arise in connection with a particular legal relationship, that court shall have exclusive jurisdiction.

[Art. 17(1)]   (2) Such an agreement conferring jurisdiction shall be either in writing or evidenced in writing or, in trade or commerce, in a form which accords with practices in that trade or commerce of which the parties are or ought to have been aware.

[Art. 17(2)]   (3) The court on which a trust instrument has conferred jurisdiction shall have exclusive jurisdiction in any proceedings brought against a settlor, trustee or beneficiary, if relations between these persons or their rights or obligations under the trust are involved.

(4) **Where an agreement or a trust instrument confers jurisdiction on the courts of the United Kingdom or of Scotland, proceedings to which paragraph (1) or, as the case may be, (3) above applies may be brought in any court in Scotland.**

[Art. 17(3)]   (5) Agreement or provisions of a trust instrument conferring jurisdiction shall have no legal force if the courts whose jurisdiction they purport to exclude have exclusive jurisdiction by virtue of **Rule 4 or where Rule 4(3) applies**.

[Art. 18]   6.—(1) Apart from jurisdiction derived from other provisions of this **Schedule**, a court before whom a defender enters an appearance shall have jurisdiction.

(2) This Rule shall not apply where appearance was entered solely to contest jurisdiction, or where another court has exclusive jurisdiction by virtue of **Rule 4 or where Rule 4(3) applies**.

Examination as to jurisdiction and admissibility

7. Where a court is seised of a claim which is principally concerned with a matter [Art. 19]
over which **another court has** exclusive jurisdiction by virtue of **Rule 4, where
it is precluded from exercising jurisdiction by Rule 4(3)**, it shall declare of
its own motion that it has no jurisdiction.

8. Where **in any case a court has no jurisdiction which is compatible with** [Art. 20]
this Act, and the defender does not enter an appearance, the court shall declare
of its own motion that it has no jurisdiction.

SCHEDULE 9

Section 21

Proceedings Excluded From Schedule 8

1. Proceedings concerning the status or legal capacity of natural persons (including proceedings for separation) other than proceedings which consists solely of proceedings for adherence and aliment or of affiliation and aliment.

2. Proceedings for regulating the custody of children.

3. Proceedings relating to tutory and curatory and all proceedings relating to the management of the affairs of persons who are incapable of managing their own affairs.

4. Proceedings in respect of sequestration in bankruptcy; or the winding up of a company or other legal person; or proceedings in respect of a judicial arrangement or judicial composition with creditors.

5. Proceedings relating to a company where, by any enactment, jurisdiction in respect of those proceedings is conferred on the court having jurisdiction to wind it up.

6. Admiralty causes in so far as the jurisdiction is based on arrestment *in rem* or *ad fundandam jurisdictionem* of a ship, cargo or freight.

7. Commissary proceedings.

8. Proceedings for the rectification of the register of aircraft mortgages kept by the Civil Aviation Authority.

9. Proceedings under section 7(3) of the Civil Aviation (Euro-control) Act 1962 (recovery of charges for air navigation services and proceedings for damages against Eurocontrol).

10. Proceedings brought in pursuance of an order under section 3 of the Continental Shelf Act 1964.

11. Proceedings under section 6 of the Protection of Trading Interests Act 1980 (recovery of sums paid or obtained pursuant to a judgment for multiple damages).

12. Appeals from or review of decisions of tribunals.

13. Proceedings which are not in substance proceedings in which a decree against any person is sought.

14. Proceedings brought in any court in pursuance of—

(a) any statutory provision which, in the case of any convention to which Article 57 applies (conventions relating to specific matters which override the general rules in the 1968 Convention), implements the convention; and

(b) any rule of law so far as it has the effect of implementing any such convention.

SCHEDULE 10

Section 35(1)

Amendments of Foreign Judgments (Reciprocal Enforcement) Act 1933

1.—(1) Section 1 (power to extend Part I to foreign countries giving reciprocal treatment) is amended as follows.

(2) For subsections (1) and (2) substitute—

"(1) If, in the case of any foreign country, Her Majesty is satisfied that, in the event of the benefits conferred by this Part of this Act being extended to, or to any particular class of, judgments given in the courts of that country or in any particular class of those courts, substantial reciprocity of treatment will be assured as regards the enforcement in that country of similar judgments given in similar courts of the United Kingdom, She may by Order in Council direct—

  (a) that this Part of this Act shall extend to that country;
  (b) that such courts of that country as are specified in the Order shall be recognised courts of that country for the purposes of this Part of this Act; and
  (c) that judgments of any such recognised court, or such judgments of any class so specified, shall, if within subsection (2) of this section, be judgments to which this Part of this Act applies.

(2) Subject to subsection (2A) of this section, a judgment of a recognised court is within this subsection if it satisfies the following conditions, namely—

  (a) it is either final and conclusive as between the judgment debtor and the judgment creditor or requires the former to make an interim payment to the latter; and
  (b) there is payable under it a sum of money, not being a sum payable in respect of taxes or other charges of a like nature or in respect of a fine or other penalty; and
  (c) it is given after the coming into force of the Order in Council which made that court a recognised court.

(2A) The following judgments of a recognised court are not within subsection (2) of this section —

  (a) a judgment given by that court on appeal from a court which is not a recognised court;
  (b) a judgment or other instrument which is regarded for the purposes of its enforcement as a judgment of that court but which was given or made in another country;
  (c) a judgment given by that court in proceedings founded on a judgment of a court in another country and having as their object the enforcement of that judgment.".

(3) After subsection (4) add—

"(5) Any Order in Council made under this section before its amendment by the Civil Jurisdiction and Judgments Act 1982 which deems any court of a foreign country to be a superior court of that country for the purposes of this Part of this Act shall (without prejudice to subsection (4) of this section) have effect from the time of that amendment as if it provided for that court to be a recognised court of that country for those purposes, and for any final and conclusive judgment of that court, if within subsection (2) of this section, to be a judgment to which this Part of this Act applies.".

2. In section 9 (power to make foreign judgments unenforceable in United Kingdom if no reciprocity), in subsection (1) omit "superior" in both places where it occurs.

3. For section 10 (issue of certificates of judgments obtained in the United Kingdom) substitute—

"10. Provision for issue of copies of, and certificates in connection with, UK judgments

(1) Rules may make provision for enabling any judgment creditor wishing to secure the enforcement in a foreign country to which Part I of this Act extends of a judgment to which this subsection applies, to obtain, subject to any conditions specified in the rules—

  (a) a copy of the judgment; and
  (b) a certificate giving particulars relating to the judgment and the proceedings in which it was given.

(2) Subsection (1) applies to any judgment given by a court or tribunal in the United Kingdom under which a sum of money is payable, not being a sum payable in respect of taxes or other charges of a like nature or in respect of a fine or other penalty.

(3) In this section 'rules'—

  (a) in relation to judgments given by a court, means rules of court;
  (b) in relation to judgments given by any other tribunal, means rules or regulations made

by the authority having power to make rules or regulations regulating the procedure of that tribunal.".

4. After section 10 insert—

"10A. Arbitration awards

The provisions of this Act, except sections 1(5) and 6, shall apply, as they apply to a judgment, in relation to an award in proceedings on an arbitration which has, in pursuance of the law in force in the place where it was made, become enforceable in the same manner as a judgment given by a court in that place.".

5.—(1) Section 11(1) (interpretation) is amended as follows.

(2) After the definition of "Country of the original court" insert—

"'Court', except in section 10 of this Act, includes a tribunal;".

(3) Omit the definition of "Judgments given in the superior courts of the United Kingdom".

SCHEDULE 11

Section 37(1)

MINOR AMENDMENTS RELATING TO MAINTENANCE ORDERS
PART I
ENFORCEMENT OF LUMP SUM ORDERS

Maintenance Orders Act 1950 (c 37)

1. In section 18(3A) of the Maintenance Orders Act 1950 (order not to be enforced by registering court under that Act if re-registered for enforcement in another court), for "whilst it is registered" substitute "to the extent that it is for the time being registered".

Maintenance Orders Act 1958 (c 39)

2.—(1) Section 2 of the Maintenance Orders Act 1958 (registration of orders) is amended as follows.

(2) In subsection (3) (registration of magistrates' court order for enforcement in the High Court), for the words from "shall" onwards (which require the court to be satisfied that not less than a certain number of periodical payments are in arrears) substitute "may, if it thinks fit, grant the application".

(3) After subsection (3) insert—

"(3A) Without prejudice to subsection (3) of this section, where a magistrates' court order provides both for the payment of a lump sum and for the making of periodical payments, a person entitled to receive a lump sum under the order who considers that, so far as it relates to that sum, the order could be more effectively enforced if it were registered may apply to the original court for the registration of the order so far as it so relates, and the court may, if it thinks fit, grant the application.

(3B) Where an application under subsection (3A) of this section is granted in the case of a magistrates' court order, the provisions of this Part of this Act shall have effect in relation to that order as if so far as it relates to the payment of a lump sum it were a separate order."

Maintenance and Affiliation Orders Act (Northern Ireland) 1966 (c 35) (NI)

3.—(1) Section 11 of the Maintenance and Affiliation Orders Act (Northern Ireland) 1966 (registration of orders) is amended as follows.

(2) In subsection (3) (registration of order made by court of summary jurisdiction for enforcement in the High Court), for the words from "shall" onwards (which require the court to be satisfied that not less than a certain number of periodical payments are in arrears) substitute "may, if it thinks fit, grant the application".

(3) After subsection (3) insert—

"(3A) Without prejudice to subsection (3), where an order made by a court of summary jurisdiction provides both for the payment of a lump sum and for the making of periodical payments, a person entitled to receive a lump sum under the order who considers that, so far as it relates to that sum the order could be more effectively enforced if it were registered may apply to the original court for the registration of the order so far as it so relates, and the court may, if it thinks fit, grant the application.

(3B) Where an application under subsection (3A) is granted in the case of an order made by a court of summary jurisdiction, the provisions of this Part shall have effect in relation to that order as if so far as it relates to the payment of a lump sum it were a separate order.".

Maintenance Orders (Reciprocal Enforcement) Act 1972 (c 18)

4.—(1) In section 9 of the Maintenance Orders (Reciprocal Enforcement) Act 1972 (variation and revocation of orders), after subsection (1) insert—

"(1A) The powers conferred by subsection (1) above are not exercisable in relation to so much of a registered order as provides for the payment of a lump sum.".

(2) In section 21 of that Act (interpretation of Part I)—

    (a) in paragraph (a) of the definition of "maintenance order" in subsection (1); and
    (b) in subsection (2),

for "periodical payment of sums of money" substitute "payment of a lump sum or the making of periodical payments".

Part II
Recovery of Interest on Arrears
Maintenance Orders Act 1950 (c 37)

5. In section 18 of the Maintenance Orders Act 1950 (enforcement of registered orders), after subsection (1) (orders to be enforced in the same manner as orders made by the court of registration), insert—

"(1A) A maintenance order registered under this Part of this Act in a court of summary jurisdiction in England or Northern Ireland shall not carry interest; but where a maintenance order so registered is registered in the High Court under Part I of the Maintenance Orders Act 1958 or section 36 of the Civil Jurisdiction and Judgments Act 1982, this subsection shall not prevent any sum for whose payment the order provides from carrying interest in accordance with section 2A of the said Act of 1958 or section 11A of the Maintenance and Affiliation Orders Act (Northern Ireland) 1966.

(1B) A maintenance order made in Scotland which is registered under this Part of this Act in the Supreme Court in England or Northern Ireland shall, if interest is by the law of Scotland recoverable under the order, carry the like interest in accordance with subsection (1) of this section.".

Maintenance Orders Act 1958 (c 39)

6.—(1) The Maintenance Orders Act 1958 is amended as follows.

(2) After section 2 insert—

"2A. Interest on sums recoverable under certain orders registered in the High Court

(1) Where, in connection with an application under secton 2(3) of this Act for the registration of a magistrates' court order, the applicant shows in accordance with rules of court—

    (a) that the order, though deemed for the purposes of section 1 of this Act to have been made by a magistrates' court in England, was in fact made in another part of the United Kingdom or in a country or territory outside the United Kingdom; and
    (b) that, as regards any sum for whose payment the order provides, interest on that sum at a particular rate is, by the law of that part or of that country or territory, recoverable under the order from a particular date or time,

then, if the original court grants the application and causes a certified copy of the order to be sent to the prescribed officer of the High Court under section 2(4)(c) of this Act, it shall also cause to be sent to him a certificate in the prescribed form showing, as regards that sum, the rate of interest so recoverable and the date or time from which it is so recoverable.

(2) The officer of the court who receives a certificate sent to him under the preceding subsection shall cause the certificate to be registered in that court together with the order to which it relates.

(3) Where an order is registered together with a certificate under this section, then, subject to any provision made under the next following subsection, sums payable under the order shall carry interest at the rate specified in the certificate from the date or time so specified.

(4) Provision may be made by rules of court as to the manner in which and the periods by reference to which any interest payable by virtue of subsection (3) is to be calculated and paid, including provision for such interest to cease to accrue as from a prescribed date.

(5) Except as provided by this section sums payable under registered orders shall not carry interest.".

(3) In section 3(1) of that Act (enforcement of registered orders), after "Subject to the provisions of" insert "section 2A of this Act and".

Maintenance and Affiliation Orders Act (Northern Ireland) 1966 (c 35) (NI)

7.—(1) The Maintenance and Affiliation Orders Act (Northern Ireland) 1966 is amended as follows.

(2) After section 11 insert—

"11A. Interest on sums recoverable under certain orders registered in the High Court

(1) Where, in connection with an application under section 11(3) for the registration of an order made by a court of summary jurisdiction, the applicant shows in accordance with rules of court—

(a) that the order, though deemed for the purposes of this Part to have been made by a court of summary jurisdiction in Northern Ireland, was in fact made in a country or territory outside the United Kingdom; and

(b) that, as regards any sum for whose payment the order provides, interest on that sum at a particular rate is, by the law of that country or territory, recoverable under the order from a particular date or time,

then, if the original court grants the application and causes a certified copy of the order to be sent to the prescribed officer of the High Court under section 11(4)(c) it shall also cause to be sent to him a certificate in the prescribed form showing, as regards that sum, the rate of interest so recoverable and the date or time from which it is so recoverable.

(2) The officer of a court who receives a certificate sent to him under subsection (1) shall cause the certificate to be registered in that court together with the order to which it relates.

(3) Where an order is registered together with a certificate under this section, then, subject to any provision made under subsection (4), sums payable under the order shall carry interest at the rate specified in the certificate from the date or time so specified.

(4) Provision may be made by rules of court as to the manner in which and the periods by reference to which any interest payable by virtue of subsection (3) is to be calculated and paid, including provision for such interest to cease to accrue as from a prescribed date.

(5) Except as provided by this section sums payable under registered orders shall not carry interest.".

(3) In section 12(1) (enforcement of registered orders), after "Subject to the provisions of" insert "section 11A and".

(4) In section 16(2) of that Act (construction of "rules of court") at the end add "and in section 11A(4) shall be construed as including a reference to Judgment Enforcement Rules made under Article 141 of the Judgments Enforcement (Northern Ireland) Order 1981".

Part III

Reciprocal Enforcement Founded on Presence of Assets

Maintenance Orders (Reciprocal Enforcement) Act 1972 (c 18)

8. The Maintenance Orders (Reciprocal Enforcement) Act 1972 is amended as follows.

9. In section 2 (transmission of United Kingdom order for enforcement in reciprocating country—

    (a) in subsections (1) and (4), after "residing" insert "or has assets"; and

    (b) in subsection (4), after "whereabouts of the payer", in both places where it occurrs, insert "and the nature and location of his assets in that country".

10. In section 6 (registration in United Kingdom of order made in reciprocating country)—

    (a) in subsection (2), after "residing" insert "or has assets"; and

    (b) in subsection (4)—

        (i) after "is residing" insert "or has assets";

        (ii) for "so residing" substitute "residing and has no assets within the jurisdiction of the court"; and

        (iii) at the end insert "and the nature and location of his assets".

11. In section 8(5) (duty of magistrates' court and its officers to take prescribed steps for enforcing registered orders), after "enforcing" insert "or facilitating the enforcement of".

12. In section 9 (variation and revocation of orders), after the subsection (1A) inserted by paragraph 4(1) of this Schedule, insert—

"(1B) The registering court shall not vary or revoke a registered order if neither the payer nor the payee under the order is resident in the United Kingdom.".

13.—(1) Section 10 (cancellation of registration and transfer of orders) is amended as follows.

(2) In subsection (2), for "has ceased to reside within the jurisdiction of that court", substitute "is not residing within the jurisdiction of that court and has no assets within that jurisdiction against which the order can be effectively enforced,".

(3) In subsection (3), after "residing" insert "or has assets".

(4) In subsection (5), for "still residing" substitute "residing or has assets".

(5) In subsection (6)—

    (a) after "is residing" insert "or has assets"; and

    (b) for "so residing" insert "residing and has no assets within the jurisdiction of the court".

(6) In subsection (7)(b), after "payer" insert "and the nature and location of his assets".

14. In section 11(1) (steps to be taken where payer is not residing in the United Kingdom)—

    (a) before "it appears" insert "at any time";

    (b) for the words from "in the United Kingdom" to "therein," substitute "and has no assets in the United Kingdom,"; and

    (c) after "payer" in paragraph (c) insert "and the nature and location of his assets".

15. In section 21(1) (interpretation of Part I), in the definition of "the appropriate court"—

        (i) after "residing", in the first and second places where it occurs, insert "or having assets";

        (ii) for "the sheriff court" substitute "a sheriff court"; and

        (iii) after "residing", where it last occurs, insert "or has assets".

16. In section 24 (application of Part I to certain orders and proceedings under Maintenance Orders (Facilities for Enforcement) Act 1920), in paragraph (a)(i) and (ii), after "residing" insert "or having assets".

17. In section 40 (power to apply Act with modifications by Order in Council)—

    (a) in paragraph (a), omit "against persons in that country or territory"; and

    (b) in paragraph (b), omit "against persons in the United Kingdom".

18. In section 47 (interpretation), in subsection (3) (construction of references to a court's

jurisdiction), after "the reference is" insert "to assets being located or" and omit the words "or having ceased to reside".

SCHEDULE 12

Sections 15(4), 23(2) and 36(6)

CONSEQUENTIAL AMENDMENTS

PART I

AMENDMENTS CONSEQUENTIAL ON
PART I OF THIS ACT

Army Act 1955 (c 18) and Air Force Act 1955 (c 19)

1. In section 150 of the Army Act 1955 and in section 150 of the Air Force Act 1955 (enforcement of maintenance and other orders by deduction from pay), in subsection (5), after "Part I of the Maintenance Orders (Reciprocal Enforcement) Act 1972" insert "or Part I of the Civil Jurisdiction and Judgments Act 1982".

Naval Discipline Act 1957 (c 53)

2. In section 101 of the Naval Discipline Act 1957 (service of process in maintenance and other proceedings), in subsection (5), after "Part I of the Maintenance Orders (Reciprocal Enforcement) Act 1972" insert "or Part I of the Civil Jurisdiction and Judgments Act 1982".

Maintenance Orders Act 1958 (c 39)

3. In section 1 of the Maintenance Orders Act 1958 (scope of application of Part I), in subsection (4), for the words from "within the meaning" to "the said Part I" substitute "which is registered in a magistrates' court under Part I of the Maintenance Orders (Reciprocal Enforcement) Act 1972 or Part I of the Civil Jurisdiction and Judgments Act 1982".

Maintenance and Affiliation Orders Act (Northern Ireland) 1966 (c 35) (NI)

4. In section 10 of the Maintenance and Affiliation Orders Act (Northern Ireland) 1966 (orders to which Part II of that Act applies), in subsections (2) and (5), after "Part I of the Maintenance Orders (Reciprocal Enforcement) Act 1972" insert "or Part I of the Civil Jurisdiction and Judgments Act 1982".

Administration of Justice Act 1970 (c 31)

5. In Schedule 8 to the Administration of Justice Act 1970 (orders which are "maintenance orders" for the purposes of Part II of that Act and Part II of the Maintenance Orders Act 1958), after paragraph 12 insert—

"13. A maintenance order within the meaning of Part I of the Civil Jurisdiction and Judgments Act 1982 which is registered in a magistrates' court under that Part.".

Attachment of Earnings Act 1971 (c 32)

6. In Schedule 1 to the Attachment of Earnings Act 1971 (orders which are "maintenance orders" for the purposes of that Act), after paragraph 12 insert—

"13. A maintenance order within the meaning of Part I of the Civil Jurisdiction and Judgments Act 1982 which is registered in a magistrates' court under that Part.".

Magistrates' Courts Act 1980 (c 43)

7. In section 65 of the Magistrates' Courts Act 1980 (definition of "domestic proceedings" for the purposes of that Act)—

(a) in subsection (1), after paragraph (l) insert—

"(m) Part I of the Civil Jurisdiction and Judgments Act 1982, so far as that Part relates to the recognition or enforcement of maintenance orders;";

(b) in subsection (2)(a), after "(k)" insert "and (m)".

223

Appendix 1

Magistrates' Courts (Northern Ireland) Order 1981 (SI 1981/1675 (NI 26))

8.—(1) In Article 88 of the Magistrates' Courts (Northern Ireland) Order 1981 (definition of "domestic proceedings" for the purposes of that Order), in paragraph (a), after "Part I of the Maintenance Orders (Reciprocal Enforcement) Act 1972" insert "or under Part I of the Civil Jurisdiction and Judgments Act 1982 so far as that Part relates to the recognition and enforcement of maintenance orders".

(2) In Article 98 of that Order (enforcement of orders for periodical payment of money), in sub-paragraph (b) of paragraph (11), after "Part I of the Maintenance Orders (Reciprocal Enforcement) Act 1972" insert "or Part I of the Civil Jurisdiction and Judgments Act 1982".

PART II

AMENDMENTS CONSEQUENTIAL ON SCHEDULE 8

Law Reform (Miscellaneous Provisions) (Scotland) Act 1940 (c 42)

1. In the Law Reform (Miscellaneous Provisions) (Scotland) Act 1940 after section 4(2) there shall be inserted the following subsection—

"(3) This section does not apply—

(a) in the case of an agreement entered into after the dispute in respect of which the agreement is intended to have effect has arisen; or
(b) where the contract is one referred to in Rule 3 of Schedule 8 to the Civil Jurisdiction and Judgments Act 1982.".

Maintenance Orders Act 1950 (c 37)

2. In section 15(1)(b) of the Maintenance Orders Act 1950 for the words "for separation and aliment" there shall be substituted the words "which contains a conclusion for aliment not falling within the scope of paragraph (a)(i) above".

Maintenance Orders (Reciprocal Enforcement) Act 1972 (c 18)

3.—(1) In section 4 of the Maintenance Orders (Reciprocal Enforcement) Act 1972 (power of the sheriff to make a provisional maintenance order against a person residing in a reciprocating country) the following subsection shall be substituted for subsections (1) and (2)—

"(1) In any action where the sheriff has jurisdiction by virtue of Rule 2(5) of Schedule 8 to the Civil Jurisdiction and Judgments Act 1982 and the defender resides in a reciprocating country, any maintenance order granted by the sheriff shall be a provisional order.".

(2) In subsections (3), (4) and (5) of that section for the words "in which the sheriff has jurisdiction by virtue of" there shall be substituted in each place where they occur the words "referred to in".

Consumer Credit Act 1974 (c 39)

4. In section 141 of the Consumer Credit Act 1974 the following subsections shall be substituted for subsection (3)—

"(3) In Scotland the sheriff court shall have jurisdiction to hear and determine any action referred to in subsection (1) and such an action shall not be brought in any other court.

(3A) Subject to subsection (3B) an action which is brought in the sheriff court by virtue of subsection (3) shall be brought only in one of the following courts, namely—

(a) the court for the place where the debtor or hirer is domiciled (within the meaning of section 41 or 42 of the Civil Jurisdiction and Judgments Act 1982);
(b) the court for the place where the debtor or hirer carries on business; and
(c) where the purpose of the action is to assert, declare or determine proprietary or possessory rights, or rights of security, in or over moveable property, or to obtain authority to dispose of moveable property, the court for the place where the property is situated.

(3B) Subsection (3A) shall not apply—

(a) where Rule 3 of Schedule 8 to the said Act of 1982 applies; or
(b) where the jurisdiction of another court has been prorogated by an agreement entered into after the dispute has arisen.".

PART III

AMENDMENTS CONSEQUENTIAL ON SECTION 36

Maintenance Orders Act 1950 (c 37)

1.—(1) The Maintenance Orders Act 1950 is amended as follows.

(2) In section 18 (enforcement of registered orders), after subsection (3A) insert—

"(3B) Notwithstanding subsection (1) above, no court in Northern Ireland in which a maintenance order is registered under this Part of this Act shall enforce that order to the extent that it is for the time being registered in another court in Northern Ireland under section 36 of the Civil Jurisdiction and Judgments Act 1982.".

(3) In section 21(2) (evidence admissible before court where order registered)—

(a) in paragraph (a) after "1958" insert "or under section 36 of the Civil Jurisdiction and Judgments Act 1982";
(b) after "that Act" (twice) insert "of 1958";
(c) after paragraph (b) insert—

"(c) registered in a court in Northern Ireland under section 36 of the Civil Jurisdiction and Judgments Act 1982".

(4) In section 24(3) (notice of cancellation of order to be given to other courts interested), after "Part I of the Maintenance Orders Act 1958" insert "or section 36 of the Civil Jurisdiction and Judgments Act 1982".

Maintenance Orders Act 1958 (c 39)

2. In section 23(2) of the Maintenance Orders Act 1958 (provisions which extend to Scotland and Northern Ireland) after "section 2" insert "section 2A".

Maintenance and Affiliation Orders Act (Northern Ireland) 1966 (c 35) (NI)

3.—(1) The Maintenance and Affiliation Orders Act (Northern Ireland) 1966 is amended as follows.

(2) At the beginning of section 9 (introductory provisions relating to registration in one court of maintenance order made by another) insert "Without prejudice to section 36 of the Civil Jurisdiction and Judgments Act 1982,".

(3) In section 10 (orders to which Part II applies), after subsection (1) insert—

"(1A) This Part, except sections 11, 11A and 14(2) and (3), also applies in accordance with section 36 of the Civil Jurisdiction and Judgments Act 1982 to maintenance orders made by a court in England and Wales or Scotland and registered in Northern Ireland under Part II of the Maintenance Orders Act 1950.".

(4) In section 13 (variation of orders registered in courts of summary jurisdiction), after subsection (7) insert—

"(7A) No application for any variation in respect of a registered order shall be made to any court in respect of an order made by the High Court of Justice in England or the Court of Session and registered in that court under section 36 of the Civil Jurisdiction and Judgments Act 1982.".

Judgments Enforcement (Northern Ireland) Order 1981 (SI 1981/226 (NI 6))

4. In Article 98 of the Judgments Enforcement (Northern Ireland) Order 1981, (powers of courts to make attachment of earnings orders), in sub-paragraph (iv) of paragraph (a) at the end add "but not subsequently registered in a court of summary jurisdiction under section 36 of the Civil Jurisdiction and Judgments Act 1982".

Appendix 1

Magistrates' Courts (Northern Ireland) Order 1981 (SI 1981/1675 (NI 26))

5.—(1) In Article 88 of the Magistrates' Courts (Northern Ireland) Order 1981 (definition of "domestic proceedings" for the purposes of that Order)—

    (a) in paragraph (a), delete the words "or the Maintenance Orders Act 1950";
    (b) after paragraph (a) insert—

       "(aa) in relation to maintenance orders registered in a court of summary jurisdiction under the Maintenance Orders Acts 1950 or Part II of the Maintenance and Affiliation Orders Act (Northern Ireland) 1966 or section 36 of the Civil Jurisdiction and Judgments Act 1982, under that Act of 1950 or Part II of that Act of 1966".

(2) In Article 98 of that Order (enforcement of orders for periodical payment of money), in sub-paragraph (d) of paragraph (11), at the end add—

    "or under section 36 of the Civil Jurisdiction and Judgments Act 1982".

SCHEDULE 13

Section 53

COMMENCEMENT, TRANSITIONAL PROVISIONS AND SAVINGS

PART I

COMMENCEMENT

Provisions coming into force on Royal Assent

1.—The following provisions come into force on Royal Assent:

Provision	Subject-matter
section 53(1) and Part I of this Schedule	Commencement.
section 55	Short title.

Provisions coming into force six weeks after Royal Assent

2. The following provisions come into force at the end of the period of six weeks beginning with the day on which this Act is passed:

Provision	Subject-matter
section 24(1)(a), (2)(a) and (3)	Interim relief and protective measures in cases of doubtful jurisdiction.
section 29	Service of county court process outside Northern Ireland.
section 30	Proceedings in England and Wales or Northern Ireland for torts to immovable property.
section 31	Overseas judgments given against states.
section 32	Overseas judgments given in breach of agreement for settlement of disputes.
section 33	Certain steps not to amount to submission to jurisdiction of overseas court.
section 34	Certain judgments a bar to further proceedings on the same cause of action.
section 35(3)	Consolidation of Orders in Council under section 14 of the Administration of Justice Act 1920.
section 38	Overseas judgments counteracting an award of multiple damages.
section 40	Power to modify enactments relating to legal aid, etc.
section 49	Saving for powers to stay, sist, strike out or dismiss proceedings.
section 50	Interpretation: general.

Provision	Subject-matter
section 51	Application to Crown.
section 52	Extent.
paragraphs 7 to 10 of Part II of this Schedule and section 53(2) so far as relates to those paragraphs	Transitional provisions and savings.
section 54 and Schedule 14 so far as relating to the repeal of provisions in section 4 of the Foreign Judgments (Reciprocal Enforcement) Act 1933.	Repeals consequential on sections 32 and 33.

Provisions coming into force on a day to be appointed

3.—(1) The other provisions of this Act come into force on such day as the Lord Chancellor and the Lord Advocate may appoint by order made by statutory instrument.

(2) Different days may be appointed under this paragraph for different purposes.

PART II

TRANSITIONAL PROVISIONS AND SAVINGS

Section 16 and Schedule 4

1.—(1) Section 16 and Schedule 4 shall not apply to any proceedings begun before the commencement of that section.

(2) Nothing in section 16 or Schedule 4 shall preclude the bringing of proceedings in any part of the United Kingdom in connection with a dispute concerning a contract if the parties to the dispute had agreed before the commencement of that section that the contract was to be governed by the law of that part of the United Kingdom.

Section 18 and Schedule 6 and associated repeals

2.—(1) In relation to a judgment a certificate whereof has been registered under the 1868 Act or the 1882 Act before the repeal of that Act by this Act, the 1868 Act or, as the case may be, the 1882 Act shall continue to have effect notwithstanding its repeal.

(2) Where by virtue of sub-paragraph (1) the 1882 Act continues to have effect in relation to an order to which section 47 of the Fair Employment (Northern Ireland) Act 1976 (damages etc for unfair discrimination) applies, that section shall continue to have effect in relation to that order notwithstanding the repeal of that section by this Act.

(3) A certificate issued under Schedule 6 shall not be registered under that Schedule in a part of the United Kingdom if the judgment to which that certificate relates is the subject of a certificate registered in that part under the 1868 Act or the 1882 Act.

(4) In this paragraph—

  "the 1868 Act" means the Judgments Extension Act 1868;
  "the 1882 Act" means the Inferior Courts Judgments Extension Act 1882;
  "judgment" has the same meaning as in section 18.

Section 18 and Schedule 7

3. Schedule 7 and, so far as it relates to that Schedule, section 18 shall not apply to judgments given before the coming into force of that section.

Section 19

4. Section 19 shall not apply to judgments given before the commencement of that section.

Section 20 and Schedule 8

5. Section 20 and Schedule 8 shall not apply to any proceedings begun before the commencement of that section.

Section 26

6. The power conferred by section 26 shall not be exercisable in relation to property arrested before the commencement of that section or in relation to bail or other security given—

    (a) before the commencement of that section to prevent the arrest of property; or

    (b) to obtain the release of property arrested before the commencement of that section; or

    (c) in substitution (whether directly or indirectly) for security given as mentioned in paragraph (a) or (b).".

Section 31

7. Section 31 shall not apply to any judgment—

    (a) which has been registered under Part II of the Administration of Justice Act 1920 or Part I of the Foreign Judgments (Reciprocal Enforcement) Act 1933 before the time when that section comes into force; or

    (b) in respect of which proceedings at common law for its enforcement have been finally determined before that time.

Section 32 and associated repeal

8.—(1) Section 32 shall not apply to any judgment—

    (a) which has been registered under Part II of the Administration of Justice Act 1920, Part I of the Foreign Judgments (Reciprocal Enforcement) Act 1933 or Part I of the Maintenance Orders (Reciprocal Enforcement) Act 1972 before the time when that section comes into force; or

    (b) in respect of which proceedings at common law for its enforcement have been finally determined before that time.

(2) Section 4(3)(b) of the Foreign Judgments (Reciprocal Enforcement) Act 1933 shall continue to have effect, notwithstanding its repeal by this Act, in relation to a judgment registered under Part I of that Act before the commencement of section 32.

Section 33 and associated repeal

9.—(1) Section 33 shall not apply to any judgment—

    (a) which has been registered under Part II of the Administration of Justice Act 1920 or Part I of the Foreign Judgments (Reciprocal Enforcement) Act 1933 before the time when that section comes into force; or

    (b) in respect of which proceedings at common law for its enforcement have been finally determined before that time.

(2) The repeal by this Act of words in section 4(2)(a)(i) of the Foreign Judgments (Reciprocal Enforcement) Act 1933 shall not affect the operation of that provision in relation to a judgment registered under Part I of that Act before the commencement of section 33.

Section 34

10. Section 34 shall not apply to judgments given before the commencement of that section.

SCHEDULE 14

Section 54

REPEALS

Chapter	Short title	Extent of repeal
41 Geo 3 c 90	Crown Debts Act 1801	The preamble. Sections 1 to 8.
5 Geo 4 c 111	Crown Debts Act 1824	The whole Act.
22 & 23 Vict c 21	Queen's Remembrancer Act 1859	Section 24.
31 & 32 Vict c 54	Judgments Extension Act 1868	The whole Act.

Chapter	Short title	Extent of repeal
31 & 32 Vict c 96	Ecclesiastical Buildings and Glebes (Scotland) Act 1868	In section 4, the words "of the county in which the parish concerned is situated" and the words from "provided" to the end.
45 & 46 Vict c 31	Inferior Courts Judgments Extension Act 1882	The whole Act.
7 Edw 7 c 51	Sheriff Courts (Scotland) Act 1907	In section 5, the words from the first "Provided"[1] to "that jurisdiction".
14 & 15 Geo 5 c 27	Conveyancing (Scotland) Act 1924	In section 23(6) the words from "of the county" to "is situated".
23 & 24 Geo 5 c 13	Foreign Judgments (Reciprocal Enforcement) Act 1933	In section 4(2)(a)(i), the words from "otherwise" to "that court". Section 4(3)(b). In section 9(1), the word "superior" in both places where it occurs. In section 11(1), the definition of "Judgments given in the superior courts of the United Kingdom". In section 12, in paragraph (a) the words from "(except" to "this Act)", and paragraph (d). In section 13(b), the words "and section two hundred and thirteen", "respectively" and "and 116".
14 Geo 6 c 37	Maintenance Orders Act 1950	Section 6. Section 8. Section 9(1)(a). In section 16(2)(b)(v), the words from the beginning to "or".
4 & 5 Eliz 2 c 46	Administration of Justice Act 1956	Section 51(a).
1963 c 22	Sheriff Courts (Civil Jurisdiction and Procedure) (Scotland) Act 1963	Section 3(2).
1965 c 2	Administration of Justice Act 1965	In Schedule 1, the entry relating to the Crown Debts Act 1801.
1971 c 55	Law Reform (Jurisdiction in Delict) (Scotland) Act 1971	The whole Act.
1972 c 18	Maintenance Orders (Reciprocal Enforcement) Act 1972	In section 40— (a) in paragraph (a), the words "against persons in that country or territory"; and (b) in paragraph (b), the words "against persons in the United Kingdom".

[1] When the Divorce Jurisdiction, Court Fees and Legal Aid (Scotland) Act 1983, s 6(1), Sch 1, para 24, comes into force, the words "the first "provided"" will be replaced by the words ""Provided that actions"".

Chapter	Short title	Extent of repeal
1972 c 18	Maintenance Orders (Reciprocal Enforcement) Act 1972—*cont.*	In section 47(3), the words "or having ceased to reside". In the Schedule, paragraph 4.
1976 c 25	Fair Employment (Northern Ireland) Act 1976	Section 47.
1978 c 23	Judicature (Northern Ireland) Act 1978	In Part II of Schedule 5— (a) the entry relating to the Crown Debts Act 1801; and (b) in the entry relating to the Foreign Judgments (Reciprocal Enforcement) Act 1933, the word "respectively", where last occurring, and the words "and 116".
1981 c 54	Supreme Court Act 1981	In Schedule 5, paragraph 2 of the entry relating to the Foreign Judgments (Reciprocal Enforcement) Act 1933.

APPENDIX 2

THE NEW RULES OF THE SUPREME COURT

This Appendix collects together some of the more important Rules of the Supreme Court relating to jurisdiction and the enforcement of judgments in the form which they will take when the Rules of the Supreme Court (Amendment No. 2) 1983 (S.I. 1983 No. 1181) come fully into operation. The amendments to Ord. 6, r. 7, Ord. 10, r. 3, Ord. 11, rr. 1, 4 and 9 and the new Ord. 13, r. 7B and Ord. 71, rr. 25 to 39 will come into operation when section 2 of the 1982 Act comes into force. The amendments to Ord. 12, r. 8 came into force on 1st October 1983.

ORDER 6

Writs of Summons: General Provisions

Issue of writ (Ord. 6, r. 7)

(1) No writ which is to be served out of the jurisdiction shall be issued without the leave of the court unless it complies with the following conditions, that is to say—

    (a) each claim made by the writ is either—

        (i) one which by virtue of the Civil Jurisdiction and Judgments Act 1982 the Court has power to hear and determine, or

        (ii) one which by virtue of any other enactment the Court has power to hear and determine notwithstanding that the person against whom the claim is made is not within the jurisdiction of the Court or that the wrongful act, neglect or default giving rise to the claim did not take place within its jurisdiction;

    and

    (b) where a claim made by the writ is one which the Court has power to hear and determine by virtue of the Civil Jurisdiction and Judgments Act 1982, the writ is indorsed before it is issued with a statement that the Court has power under that Act to hear and determine the claim, and that no proceedings involving the same cause of action are pending between the parties in Scotland, Northern Ireland or another Convention territory.

(2) Except where otherwise expressly provided by these Rules, a writ may be issued out of—

    (a) the Central Office if it relates to proceedings intended to be conducted in the Queen's Bench Division; or

(b) Chancery Chambers if it relates to proceedings intended to be conducted in the Chancery Division; or

(c) a district registry.

(3) Issue of a writ takes place upon its being sealed by an officer of the office out of which it is issued.

(4) the officer by whom a concurrent writ is sealed must mark it as a concurrent writ with an official stamp.

(5) No writ shall be sealed unless at the time of tender thereof for sealing the person tendering it leaves at the office at which it is tendered a copy thereof signed, where the plaintiff sues in person, by him or, where he does not so sue, by or on behalf of his solicitor.

(6) For the purposes of this rule, "Convention territory" means the territory or territories of any Contracting State, as defined by section 1(3) of that Act, to which the Conventions as defined in section 1(1) of that Act apply.

Note. Rule 7(1) substituted, and r. 7(6) added, by S.I. 1983 No. 1181, rr. 3, 4.

ORDER 10

SERVICE OF ORIGINATING PROCESS: GENERAL PROVISIONS

Service of writ on agent of oversea principal (Ord. 10, r. 2)

(1) Where the Court is satisfied on an *ex parte* application that—

(a) a contract has been entered into within the jurisdiction with or through an agent who is either an individual residing or carrying on business within the jurisdiction or a body corporate having a registered office or a place of business within the jurisdiction, and

(b) the principal for whom the agent was acting was at the time the contract was entered into and is at the time of the application neither such an individual nor such a body corporate, and

(c) at the time of the application either the agent's authority has not been determined or he is still in business relations with his principal,

the Court may authorise service of a writ beginning an action relating to the contract to be effected on the agent instead of the principal.

(2) An order under this Rule authorising service of a writ on a defendant's agent must limit a time within which the defendant must acknowledge service.

(3) Where an order is made under this Rule authorising service of a writ on a defendant's agent, a copy of the order and of the writ must be sent by post to the defendant at his address out of the jurisdiction.

Service of writ in pursuance of contract (Ord. 10, r. 3)

(1) Where—

(a) a contract contains a term to the effect that the High Court shall have jurisdiction to hear and determine any action in respect of a contract or, apart from any such term, the High Court has jurisdiction to hear and determine any such action, and

(b) the contract provides that, in the event of any action in respect of the contract being begun, the process by which it is begun may be served on the defendant, or on such other person on his behalf as may be specified in the contract, in such manner, or at such place (whether within or out of the jurisdiction), as may be so specified, then, if an action in respect of the contract is begun in the High Court and the writ by which it is begun is served in accordance with the contract, the writ shall, subject to paragraph (2), be deemed to have been duly served on the defendant.

(2) A writ which is served out of the jurisdiction in accordance with a contract shall not be deemed to have been duly served on the defendant by virtue of paragraph (1) unless leave to serve the writ, or notice thereof, out of the jurisdiction has been granted under Order 11, rule 1(1) or service of the writ is permitted without leave under Order 11, rule 1(2).

(3) Where a contract contains an agreement conferring jurisdiction to which Article 17 of Schedule 1 or of Schedule 4 to the Civil Jurisdiction and Judgments Act 1982 applies and the writ is served under Order 11, rule 1(2) the writ shall be deemed to have been duly served on the defendant.

Note. In r. 3(2), words from "has been granted" to the end of the paragraph substituted, and r. 3(3) added, by S.I. 1983 No. 1181, rr. 5, 6.

ORDER 11

SERVICE OF PROCESS ETC. OUT OF THE JURISDICTION

Principal cases in which service of writ out of jurisdiction is permissible (Ord. 11, r. 1)

(1) Provided that the writ does not contain any claim mentioned in Order 75, rule 2(1) and is not a writ to which paragraph (2) of this rule applies, service of a writ out of the jurisdiction is permissible with the leave of the Court if in the action begun by the writ—

(a) relief is sought against a person domiciled within the jurisdiction;
(b) an injunction is sought ordering the defendant to do or refrain from doing anything within the jurisdiction (whether or not damages are also claimed in respect of a failure to do or the doing of that thing);
(c) the claim is brought against a person duly served within or out of the jurisdiction and a person out of the jurisdiction is a necessary or proper party thereto;
(d) the claim is brought to enforce, rescind, dissolve, annul or otherwise affect a contract, or to recover damages or obtain other relief in respect of the breach of a contract, being (in either case) a contract which—
  (i) was made within the jurisdiction, or
  (ii) was made by or through an agent trading or residing within the jurisdiction on behalf of a principal trading or residing out of the jurisdiction, or
  (iii) is by its terms, or by implication, governed by English law, or
  (iv) contains a term to the effect that the High Court shall have jurisdiction to hear and determine any action in respect of the contract;
(e) the claim is brought in respect of a breach committed within the jurisdiction of a contract made within or out of the jurisdiction, and irrespective of the fact, if such be the case, that the breach was preceded or accompanied by a breach committed out of the jurisdiction that rendered impossible the performance of so much of the contract as ought to have been performed within the jurisdiction;
(f) the claim is founded on a tort and the damage was sustained, or resulted from an act committed, within the jurisdiction;
(g) the whole subject-matter of the action is land situate within the jurisdiction (with or without rents or profits) or the perpetuation of testimony relating to land so situate;

(*h*) the claim is brought to construe, rectify, set aside or enforce an act, deed, will, contract, obligation or liability affecting land situate within the jurisdiction;

(*i*) the claim is made for a debt secured on immovable property or is made to assert, declare or determine proprietary or possessory rights, or rights of security, in or over movable property, or to obtain authority to dispose of movable property, situate within the jurisdiction;

(*j*) the claim is brought to execute the trusts of a written instrument being trusts that ought to be executed according to English law and of which the person to be served with the writ is a trustee, or for any relief or remedy which might be obtained in any such action;

(*k*) the claim is made for the administration of the estate of a person who died domiciled within the jurisdiction or for any relief or remedy which might be obtained in any such action;

(*l*) the claim is brought in a probate action within the meaning of Order 76;

(*m*) the claim is brought to enforce any judgment or arbitral award;

(*n*) the claim is brought against a defendant not domiciled in Scotland or Northern Ireland in respect of a claim by the Commissioners of Inland Revenue for or in relation to any of the duties or taxes which have been, or are for the time being, placed under their care and management;

(*o*) the claim is brought under the Nuclear Installations Act 1965 or in respect of contributions under the Social Security Act 1975;

(*p*) the claim is made for a sum to which the Directive of the Council of the European Communities dated 15th March 1976 No. 76/308/EEC applies, and service is to be effected in a country which is a member State of the European Economic Community.

(2) Service of a writ out of the jurisdiction is permissible without the leave of the Court provided that each claim made by the writ is either:—

(*a*) a claim which by virtue of the Civil Jurisdiction and Judgments Act 1982 the Court has power to hear and determine, made in proceedings to which the following conditions apply—

   (i) no proceedings between the parties concerning the same cause of action are pending in the courts of any other part of the United Kingdom or of any other Convention territory, and

   (ii) either—

the defendant is domiciled in any part of the United Kingdom or in any other Convention territory, or

the proceedings begun by the writ are proceedings to which Article 16 of Schedule 1 or of Schedule 4 refers, or

the defendant is a party to an agreement conferring jurisdiction to which Article 17 of Schedule 1 or of Schedule 4 to that Act applies,

or

(*b*) a claim which by virtue of any other enactment the High Court has power to hear and determine notwithstanding that the person against whom the claim is made is not within the jurisdiction of the Court or that the wrongful act, neglect or default giving rise to the claim did not take place within its jurisdiction.

(3) Where a writ is to be served out of the jurisdiction under paragraph (2), the time to be inserted in the writ within which the defendant served therewith must acknowledge service shall be—

(*a*) 21 days where the writ is to be served out of the jurisdiction under paragraph (2)(*a*) in Scotland, Northern Ireland or in the European territory of another Contracting State, or

(b) 31 days where the writ is to be served under paragraph (2)(a) in any other territory of a Contracting State, or

(c) limited in accordance with the practice adopted under rule 4(4) where the writ is to be served under paragraph (2)(a) in a country not referred to in sub-paragraphs (a) or (b) or under paragraph (2)(b).

(4) For the purposes of this rule, and of rule 9 of this Order, domicile is to be determined in accordance with the provisions of sections 41 to 46 of the Civil Jurisdiction and Judgments Act 1982 and "Convention territory" means the territory or territories of any Contracting State, as defined by section 1(3) of that Act, to which the Conventions as defined in section 1(1) of that Act apply.

Note. Rule 1 substituted by S.I. 1983 No. 1181, r. 7.

Service out of jurisdiction in certain actions of contract (Ord. 11, r. 2)

Note. Rule 2 revoked by S.I. 1983 No. 1181, r. 8.

Leave for service of notice of writ (Ord. 11, r. 3)

Note. Rule 3 revoked by S.I. 1980 No. 2000, r. 17.

Application for, and grant of, leave to serve writ out of jurisdiction (Ord. 11, r. 4)

(1) An application for the grant of leave under rule 1(1) must be supported by an affidavit stating—

(a) the grounds on which the application is made,

(b) that in the deponent's belief the plaintiff has a good cause of action,

(c) in what place or country the defendant is, or probably may be found, and

(d) where the application is made under rule 1(1)(c), the grounds for the deponent's belief that there is between the plaintiff and the person on whom a writ has been served a real issue which the plaintiff may reasonably ask the Court to try.

(2) No such leave shall be granted unless it shall be made sufficiently to appear to the Court that the case is a proper one for service out of the jurisdiction under this Order.

(3) Where the application is for the grant of leave under Rule 1 to serve a writ in Scotland or Northern Ireland, if it appears to the Court that there may be a concurrent remedy there, the Court, in deciding whether to grant leave, shall have regard to the comparative cost and convenience of proceeding there or in England, and (where that is relevant) to the powers and jurisdiction of the sheriff court in Scotland or the county courts or courts of summary jurisdiction in Northern Ireland.

(4) An order granting under Rule 1 leave to serve a writ out of the jurisdiction must limit a time within which the defendant to be served must acknowledge service.

Note. Rule 4(1) substituted, and in r. 4(4) words "or 2" revoked, by S.I. 1983 No. 1181, r. 9.

Service of writ abroad: general (Ord. 11, r. 5)

(1) Subject to the following provisions of this Rule, Order 10, Rule 1 (1), (4), (5) and (6) and Order 65, Rule 4, shall apply in relation to the service of a writ, notwithstanding that the writ is to be served out of the jurisdiction, save that the accompanying form of acknowledgment of service shall be modified in such manner as may be appropriate.

(2) Nothing in this Rule or in any order or direction of the Court made by virtue of it shall authorise or require the doing of anything in a country in which service is to be effected which is contrary to the law of that country.

(3) A writ which is to be served out of the jurisdiction—

(*a*) need not be served personally on the person required to be served so long as it is served on him in accordance with the law of the country in which service is effected; and

(*b*) need not be served by the plaintiff or his agent if it is served by a method provided for by Rule 6 or Rule 7.

(4) (*Revoked by S.I. 1979 No. 402.*)

(5) An official certificate stating that a writ as regards which Rule 6 has been complied with has been served on a person personally, or in accordance with the law of the country in which service was effected, on a specified date, being a certificate—

(*a*) by a British consular authority in that country, or

(*b*) by the government or judicial authorities of that country, or

(*c*) by any other authority designated in respect of that country under the Hague Convention,

shall be evidence of the facts so stated.

(6) An official certificate by the Secretary of State stating that a writ has been duly served on a specified date in accordance with a request made under Rule 7 shall be evidence of that fact.

(7) A document purporting to be such a certificate as is mentioned in paragraph (5) or (6) shall, until the contrary is proved, be deemed to be such a certificate.

(8) In this rule and rule 6 "the Hague Convention" means the Convention on the service abroad of judicial and extra-judicial documents in civil or commercial matters signed at the Hague on November 15, 1965.

Service of writ abroad through foreign government, judicial authorities and British consuls (Ord. 11, r. 6)

(1) Save where a writ is to be served pursuant to paragraph (2A), this Rule does not apply to service in—

(*a*) Scotland, Northern Ireland, the Isle of Man or the Channel Islands;

(*b*) any independent Commonwealth country;

(*c*) any associated state;

(*d*) any colony;

(*e*) the Republic of Ireland.

(2) Where in accordance with these Rules a writ is to be served on a defendant in any country with respect to which there subsists a Civil Procedure Convention (other than the Hague Convention) providing for service in that country of process of the High Court, the writ may be served—

(*a*) through the judicial authorities of that country; or

(*b*) through a British consular authority in that country (subject to any provision of the convention as to the nationality of persons who may be so served).

(2A) Where in accordance with these Rules, a writ is to be served on a defendant in any country which is a party to the Hague Convention, the writ may be served—

(*a*) through the authority designated under the Convention in respect of that country; or

(*b*) if the law of that country permits—

(i) through the judicial authorities of that country, or

(ii) through a British consular authority in that country.

(3) Where in accordance with these Rules a writ is to be served on a defendant in any country with respect to which there does not subsist a Civil Procedure Convention providing for service in that country of process of the High Court, the writ may be served—

(*a*) through the government of that country, where that government is willing to effect service; or

(*b*) through a British consular authority in that country, except where service through such an authority is contrary to the law of that country.

(4) A person who wishes to serve a writ by a method specified in paragraph (2) (2A) or (3) must lodge in the Central Office a request for service of the writ by that method, together with a copy of the writ and an additional copy thereof for each person to be served.

(5) Every copy of a writ lodged under paragraph (4) must be accompanied by a translation of the writ in the official language of the country in which service is to be effected or, if there is more than one official language of that country, in any one of those languages which is appropriate to the place in that country where service is to be effected:

Provided that this paragraph shall not apply in relation to a copy of a writ which is to be served in a country the official language of which is, or the official languages of which include, English, or is to be served in any country by a British consular authority on a British subject, unless the service is to be effected under paragraph (2) and the Civil Procedure Convention with respect to that country expressly requires the copy to be accompanied by a translation.

(6) Every translation lodged under paragraph (5) must be certified by the person making it to be a correct translation; and the certificate must contain a statement of that person's full name, of his address and of his qualifications for making the translation.

(7) Documents duly lodged under paragraph (4) shall be sent by the Senior Master to the Parliamentary Under-Secretary of State to the Foreign Office with a request that he arrange the writ to be served by the method indicated in the request lodged under paragraph (4) or, where alternative methods are so indicated, by such one of those methods as is most convenient.

Service of writ in certain actions under certain Acts (Ord. 11, r. 7)

(1) Subject to paragraph (4) where a person to whom leave has been granted under rule 1 to serve a writ on a State, as defined in section 14 of the State Immunity Act 1978, wishes to have the writ served on that State, he must lodge in the Central Office—

(*a*) a request for service to be arranged by the Secretary of State; and

(*b*) a copy of the writ; and

(*c*) Except where the official language of the State is, or the official languages of that Party include, English, a translation of the writ in the official language or one of the official languages of the State.

(2) Rule 6(6) shall apply in relation to a translation lodged under paragraph (1) of this Rule as it applies in relation to a translation lodged under paragraph (5) of that Rule.

(3) Documents duly lodged under this Rule shall be sent by the Senior Master to the Secretary of State with a request that the Secretary of State arrange for the writ to be served on the State or the government in question, as the case may be.

(4) Where section 12(6) of the State Immunity Act 1978 applies and the State has agreed to a method of service other than that provided by the preceding paragraphs, the writ may be served either by the method agreed or in accordance with the preceding paragraphs of this rule.

Undertaking to pay expenses of service by Secretary of State (Ord. 11, r. 8)

Every request lodged under Rule 6(4) or Rule 7 must contain an undertaking by the person making the request to be responsible personally for all expenses incurred by the Secretary of State in respect of the service requested and, on receiving due notification of the amount of those expenses, to pay that amount to the Finance Officer of the office of the Secretary of State and to produce a receipt for the payment to the proper officer of the High Court.

Service of originating summons, petition, notice of motion, etc. (Ord. 11, r. 9)

(1) Subject to Order 73, rule 7, rule 1 of this Order shall apply to the service out of the jurisdiction of an originating summons, notice of motion or petition as it applies to service of a writ.

(4) Subject to Order 73, Rule 7, service out of the jurisdiction of any summons, notice or order issued, given or made in any proceedings is permissible with the leave of the Court, but leave shall not be required for such service in any proceedings in which the writ, originating summons, motion or petition may by these rules or under any Act be served out of the jurisdiction without leave.

(5) Rule 4(1), (2) and (3) shall, so far as applicable, apply in relation to an application for the grant of leave under this Rule as they apply in relation to an application for the grant of leave under Rule 1.

(6) An order granting under this Rule leave to serve out of the jurisdiction an originating summons must limit a time within which the defendant to be served with the summons must acknowledge service.

(7) Rules 5, 6 and 8 shall apply in relation to any document for the service of which out of the jurisdiction leave has been granted under this Rule as they apply in relation to a writ.

Note. Rule 9(1) substituted, rr. 9(2) and 9(3) revoked, in r 9(4) words following "permissible with the leave of the court" added, and in r. 9(5) words "or 2" revoked, by S.I. 1983 No. 1181, rr. 10, 11.

Service abroad of county court process (Ord. 11, r. 10)

Rule 6(7) shall apply, with the necessary modifications, to any county court documents sent to the senior master for service abroad in accordance with the County Court Rules, and every certificate or declaration of service received by the senior master in respect of such service shall be transmitted by him to the registrar of the county court concerned.

ORDER 12

ACKNOWLEDGMENT OF SERVICE TO WRIT OR ORIGINATING SUMMONS

Acknowledgment not to constitute waiver (Ord. 12, r. 7)

The acknowledgment by a defendant of service of a writ shall not be treated as a waiver by him of any irregularity in the writ or service thereof or in any order giving leave to serve the writ out of the jurisdiction or extending the validity of the writ for the purpose of service.

Dispute as to jurisdiction (Ord. 12, r. 8)

(1) A defendant who wishes to dispute the jurisdiction of the court in the proceedings by reason of any such irregularity as is mentioned in rule 7 or on any other ground shall give

notice of intention to defend the proceedings and shall, within the time limited for service of a defence, apply to the Court for—

(*a*) an order setting aside the writ or service of the writ on him, or
(*b*) an order declaring that the writ has not been duly served on him, or
(*c*) the discharge of any order giving leave to serve the writ on him out of the jurisdiction, or
(*d*) the discharge of any order extending the validity of the writ for the purpose of service, or
(*e*) the protection or release of any property of the defendant seized or threatened with seizure in the proceedings, or
(*f*) the discharge of any order made to prevent any dealing with any property of the defendant, or
(*g*) a declaration that in the circumstances of the case the court has no jurisdiction over the defendant in respect of the subject matter of the claim or the relief or remedy sought in the action, or
(*h*) such other relief as may be appropriate.

(3) An application under paragraph (1) must be made—

(*a*) in an Admiralty action in rem, by motion;
(*b*) in any other action in the Queen's bench Division, by summons;
(*c*) in any other action, by summons or motion,

and the notice of motion or summons must state the grounds of the application.

(4) An application under paragraph (1) must be supported by an affidavit verifying the facts on which the application is based and a copy of the affidavit must be served with the notice of motion or summons by which the application is made.

(5) Upon hearing an application under paragraph (1), the Court, if it does not dispose of the matter in dispute, may give such directions for its disposal as may be appropriate, including directions for the trial thereof as a preliminary issue.

(6) A defendant who makes an application under paragraph (1) shall not be treated as having submitted to the jurisdiction of the court by reason of his having given notice of intention to defend the action; and if the Court makes no order on the application or dismisses it, the notice shall cease to have effect, but the defendant may, subject to rule 6(1), lodge a further acknowledgment of service and in that case paragraph (7) shall apply as if the defendant had not made any such application.

(7) Except where the defendant makes an application in accordance with paragraph (1), the acknowledgment by a defendant of service of a writ shall, unless the acknowledgment is withdrawn by leave of the Court under Order 21, rule 1, be treated as a submission by the defendant to the jurisdiction of the Court in the proceedings.

Note. In r. 8(1) words "within the time limited for service of a defence" substituted, and r 8(2) revoked, by S.I. 1983 No. 1181, r. 12.

ORDER 13

FAILURE TO GIVE NOTICE OF INTENTION TO DEFEND

Judgments under the Civil Jurisdiction and Judgments Act 1982 (Ord. 13, r. 7B)
(1) Where a writ has been served out of the jurisdiction under Order 11, rule 1(2)(*a*) or has been served within the jurisdiction on a defendant domiciled in Scotland or Northern

Ireland or in any other Convention territory the plaintiff shall not be entitled to enter judgment under this Order except with the leave of the Court.

(2) An application for leave to enter judgment may be made ex parte and shall be supported by an affidavit stating that in the deponent's belief—

(a) each claim made by the writ is one which by virtue of the Civil Jurisdiction and Judgments Act 1982 the Court has power to hear and determine,

(b) no other court has exclusive jurisdiction within the meaning of Schedule 1 or under Schedule 4 to that Act to hear and determine such claim, and

(c) where the writ is served out of the jurisdiction under Order 11, rule 1(2)(a), such service satisfied the requirements of Schedule 1 or, as the case may require, of Article 20 of Schedule 4 to that Act,

and giving in each case the sources and grounds of such belief.

(3) For the purposes of this rule, domicile is to be determined in accordance with the provisions of sections 41 to 46 of the Civil Jurisdiction and Judgments Act 1982 and "Convention territory" means the territory or territories of any Contracting State, as defined by section 1(3) of that Act, to which the Conventions as defined in section 1(1) of that Act apply.

Note. New r. 7B added by S.I. 1983 No. 1181, r. 13.

ORDER 71

RECIPROCAL ENFORCEMENT OF JUDGMENTS AND ENFORCEMENT OF EUROPEAN COMMUNITY JUDGMENTS

I. RECIPROCAL ENFORCEMENT: THE ADMINISTRATION OF JUSTICE ACT 1920 AND THE FOREIGN JUDGMENTS (RECIPROCAL ENFORCEMENT) ACT 1933

Note. Heading above substituted by S.I. 1983 No. 1181, r. 19.

Powers under the relevant Acts exercisable by judge or master (Ord. 71, r. 1)

The powers conferred on the High Court by Part II of the Administration of Justice Act, 1920 (in this Order referred to as the "Act of 1920"), or Part I of the Foreign Judgments (Reciprocal Enforcement) Act, 1933 (in this Order referred to as the "Act of 1933"), may be exercised by a judge in chambers and a master of the Queen's Bench Division.

Application for registration (Ord. 71, r. 2)

(1) An application—

(a) under section 9 of the Act of 1920, in respect of a judgment obtained in a superior court in any part of Her Majesty's dominions or other territory to which Part II of that Act applies, or

(b) under section 2 of the Act of 1933, in respect of a judgment to which Part I of that Act applies,

to have the judgment registered in the High Court may be made ex parte, but the Court hearing the application may direct a summons to be issued.

(2) If the Court directs a summons to be issued, the summons shall be an originating summons.

(3) An originating summons under this rule shall be in Form No. 10 in Appendix A.

Evidence in support of application (Ord. 71, r. 3)

(1) An application for registration must be supported by an affidavit—

(a) exhibiting the judgment or a verified or certified or otherwise duly authenticated copy thereof, and where the judgment is not in the English language, a translation thereof in that language certified by a notary public or authenticated by affidavit;

(b) stating the name, trade or business and the usual or last known place of abode or business of the judgment creditor and the judgment debtor respectively, so far as known to the deponent;

(c) stating to the best of the information or belief of the deponent—

(i) that the judgment creditor is entitled to enforce the judgment;

(ii) as the case may require, either that at the date of the application the judgment has not been satisfied, or the amount in respect of which it remains unsatisfied;

(iii) where the application is made under the Act of 1920, that the judgment does not fall within any of the cases in which a judgment may not be ordered to be registered under section 9 of that Act;

(iv) where the application is made under the Act of 1933, that at the date of the application the judgment can be enforced by execution in the country of the original court and that, if it were registered, the registration would not be, or be liable to be, set aside under section 4 of that Act;

(d) specifying, where the application is made under the Act of 1933, the amount of the interest, if any, which under the law of the country of the original court has become due under the judgment up to the time of registration;

(e) verifying that the judgment is not a judgment to which section 5 of the Protection of Trading Interests Act 1980 applies.

(2) Where a judgment sought to be registered under the Act of 1933 is in respect of different matters, and some, but not all, of the provisions of the judgment are such that if those provisions had been contained in separate judgments, those judgments could properly have been registered, the affidavit must state the provisions in respect of which it is sought to register the judgment.

(3) In the case of an application under the Act of 1933, the affidavit must be accompanied by such other evidence with respect to the enforceability of the judgment by execution in the country of the original court, and of the law of that country under which any interest has become due under the judgment, as may be required having regard to the provisions of the Order in Council extending that Act to that country.

Security for costs (Ord. 71, r. 4)

Save as otherwise provided by any relevant Order in Council, the Court may order the judgment creditor to give security for the costs of the application for registration and of any proceedings which may be brought to set aside the registration.

Order for registration (Ord. 71, r. 5)

(1) An order giving leave to register a judgment must be drawn up by, or on behalf of, the judgment creditor.

(2) Except where the order is made on summons, no such order need be served on the judgment debtor.

(3) Every such order shall state the period within which an application may be made to set aside the registration and shall contain a notification that execution on the judgment will not issue until after the expiration of that period.

(4) The Court may, on an application made at any time while it remains competent for any party to apply to have the registration set aside, extend the period (either as originally

fixed or as subsequently extended) within which an application to have the registration set aside may be made.

Register of judgments (Ord. 71, r. 6)

(1) There shall be kept in the Central Office under the direction of the senior master a register of the judgments ordered to be registered under the Act of 1920 and a register of the judgments ordered to be registered under the Act of 1933.

(2) There shall be included in each such register particulars of any execution issued on a judgment ordered to be so registered.

Notice of registration (Ord. 71, r. 7)

(1) Notice of registration of a judgment must be served on the judgment debtor by delivering it to him personally or by sending it to him at his usual or last known place of abode or business or in such other manner as the Court may direct.

(2) Service of such a notice out of the jurisdiction is permissible without leave, and Order 11, rules 5, 6 and 8, shall apply in relation to such a notice as they apply in relation to a writ.

(3) The notice of registration must state—

(a) full particulars of the judgment registered and the order for registration,

(b) the name and address of the judgment creditor or of his solicitor or agent on whom, and at which, any summons issued by the judgment debtor may be served,

(c) the right of the judgment debtor to apply to have the registration set aside, and

(d) the period within which an application to set aside the registration may be made.

Indorsement of service (Ord. 71, r. 8)

Note. Rule 8 revoked by S.I. 1979 No. 402.

Application to set aside registration (Ord. 71, r. 9)

(1) An application to set aside the registration of a judgment must be made by summons supported by affidavit.

(2) The Court hearing such application may order any issue between the judgment creditor and the judgment debtor to be tried in any manner in which an issue in an action may be ordered to be tried.

(3) Where the Court hearing an application to set aside the registration of a judgment registered under the Act of 1920 is satisfied that the judgment falls within any of the cases in which a judgment may not be ordered to be registered under section 9 of that Act or that it is not just or convenient that the judgment should be enforced in England or Wales or that there is some other sufficient reason for setting aside the registration, it may order the registration of the judgment to be set aside on such terms as it thinks fit.

Issue of execution (Ord. 71, r. 10)

(1) Execution shall not issue on a judgment registered under the Act of 1920 or the Act of 1933 until after the expiration of the period which, in accordance with rule 5(3), is specified in the order for registration as the period within which an application may be made to set aside the registration or, if that period has been extended by the Court, until after the expiration of that period as so extended.

(2) If an application is made to set aside the registration of a judgment, execution on the judgment shall not issue until after such application is finally determined.

(3) Any party wishing to issue execution on a judgment registered under the Act of 1920 or the Act of 1933 must produce to the proper officer an affidavit of service of the notice of registration of the judgment and any order made by the Court in relation to the judgment.

Determination of certain questions (Ord. 71, r. 11)

If, in any case under the Act of 1933, any question arises whether a foreign judgment can be enforced by execution in the country of the original court, or what interest is payable under a foreign judgment under the law of the original court, that question shall be determined in accordance with the provisions in that behalf contained in the Order in Council extending Part I of that Act to that country.

Rules to have effect subject to Orders in Council (Ord. 71, r. 12)

The foregoing rules shall, in relation to any judgment registered or sought to be registered under the Act of 1933, have effect subject to any such provisions contained in the Order in Council extending Part I of that Act to the country of the original court as are declared by the Order to be necessary for giving effect to the agreement made between Her Majesty and that country in relation to matters with respect to which there is power to make those rules.

Certified copy of High Court judgment (Ord. 71, r. 13)

(1) An application under section 10 of the Act of 1920 or section 10 of the Act of 1933 for a certified copy of a judgment entered in the High Court must be made ex parte on affidavit to a master or in the case of a judgment given in a cause or matter proceeding in the Family Division, to a registrar of that Division.

(2) An affidavit by which an application under section 10 of the Act of 1920 is made must give particulars of the judgment, show that the judgment debtor is resident in some (stating which) part of Her Majesty's dominions or other territory to which Part II of that Act extends and state the name, trade or business and the usual or last known place of abode of the judgment creditor and the judgment debtor respectively, so far as known to the deponent.

(3) An affidavit by which an application under section 10 of the Act of 1933 is made must—

(a) give particulars of the proceedings in which the judgment was obtained;

(b) have annexed to it a copy of the writ originating summons or other process by which the proceedings were begun, the evidence of service thereof on, or appearance by, the defendant, copies of the pleadings, if any, and a statement of the grounds on which the judgment was based;

(c) state whether the defendant did or did not object to the jurisdiction, and, if so, on what grounds;

(d) show that the judgment is not subject to any stay of execution;

(e) state that the time for appealing has expired or, as the case may be, the date on which it will expire and in either case whether notice of appeal against the judgment has been entered; and

(f) state the rate at which the judgment carries interest.

(4) The certified copy of the judgment shall be an office copy sealed with the seal of the Supreme Court and indorsed with a certificate signed by a master or, where appropriate, a registrar certifying that the copy is a true copy of a judgment obtained in the High Court of England and that it is issued in accordance with section 10 of the Act of 1920 or section 10 of the Act of 1933, as the case may be.

(5) Where the application is made under section 10 of the Act of 1933 there shall also be issued a certificate (signed by a master or, where appropriate, a registrar and sealed with the seal of the Supreme Court) having annexed to it a copy of the writ originating summons or other process by which the proceedings were begun, and stating—

    (*a*) the manner in which the writ, or such summons or other process was served on the defendant or that the defendant acknowledged service thereof;

    (*b*) what objections, if any, were made to the jurisdiction,

    (*c*) what pleadings, if any, were served,

    (*d*) the grounds on which the judgment was based,

    (*e*) that the time for appealing has expired or, as the case may be, the date on which it will expire,

    (*f*) whether notice of appeal against the judgment has been entered, and

    (*g*) such other particulars as it may be necessary to give to the court in the foreign country in which it is sought to obtain execution of the judgment,

and a certificate (signed and sealed as aforesaid) stating the rate at which the judgment carries interest.

Registration of certificates under Judgments Extension Act 1868 (Ord. 71, r. 14)

Note. Rule 14 revoked by S.I. 1983 No. 1181, r. 20.

II. ENFORCEMENT OF EUROPEAN COMMUNITY JUDGMENTS

Note. Heading above substituted by S.I. 1983 No. 1181, r. 19.

Interpretation (Ord. 71, r. 15)

In this Part of this Order, "the Order in Council" means the European Communities (Enforcement of Community Judgments) Order 1972, and expressions used in the Order in Council shall, unless the context otherwise requires, have the same meanings as in that Order.

Functions under Order in Council exercisable by judge or master (Ord. 71, r. 16)

The functions assigned to the High Court by the Order in Council may be exercised by a judge in chambers and a master of the Queen's Bench Division.

Application for registration of Community judgments, etc. (Ord. 71, r. 17)

An application for the registration in the High Court of a Community judgment or Euratom inspection order may be made *ex parte*.

Evidence in support of application (Ord. 71, r. 18)

(1) An application for registration must be supported by an affidavit exhibiting—

    (*a*) the Community judgment and the order for its enforcement or, as the case may be, the Euratom inspection order or, in either case, a duly authenticated copy thereof, and

    (*b*) where the Community judgment or Euratom inspection order is not in the English language, a translation into English certified by a notary public or authenticated by affidavit.

(2) Where the application is for registration of a Community judgment under which a sum of money is payable, the affidavit shall also state—

(*a*) the name and occupation and the usual or last known place of abode or business of the judgment debtor, so far as known to the deponent; and

(*b*) to the best of the deponent's information and belief that at the date of the application the European Court has not suspended enforcement of the judgment and that the judgment is unsatisfied or, as the case may be, the amount in respect of which it remains unsatisfied.

Register of judgments and orders (Ord. 71, r. 19)

(1) There shall be kept in the Central Office under the direction of the Senior Master a register of the Community judgments and Euratom inspection orders registered under the Order in Council.

(2) There shall be included in the register particulars of any execution issued on a judgment so registered.

Notice of registration (Ord. 71, r. 20)

(1) Upon registering a Community judgment or Euratom inspection order, the proper officer of the Court shall forthwith send notice of the registration to every person against whom the judgment was given or the order was made.

(2) The notice of registration shall have annexed to it a copy of the registered Community judgment and the order for its enforcement or, as the case may be, a copy of the Euratom inspection order, and shall state the name and address of the person on whose application the judgment or order was registered or of his solicitor or agent on whom process may be served.

(3) Where the notice relates to a Community judgment under which a sum of money is payable, it shall also state that the judgment debtor may apply within 28 days of the date of the notice, or thereafter with the leave of the Court, for the variation or cancellation of the registration on the ground that the judgment had been partly or wholly satisfied at the date of registration.

Issue of execution (Ord. 71, r. 21)

Execution shall not issue without the leave of the Court on a Community judgment under which a sum of money is payable until the expiration of 28 days after the date of notice of registration of the judgment or, as the case may be, until any application made within that period for the variation or cancellation of the registration has been determined.

Application to vary or cancel registration (Ord. 71, r. 22)

An application for the variation or cancellation of the registration of a Community judgment on the ground that the judgment had been wholly or partly satisfied at the date of registration shall be made by summons supported by affidavit.

Application for registration of suspension order (Ord. 71, r. 23)

An application for the registration in the High Court of an order of the European Court that enforcement of a registered Community judgment be suspended may be made *ex parte* by lodging a copy of the order in the Central Office.

Application for enforcement of Euratom inspection order (Ord. 71, r. 24)

An application for an order under Article 6 of the Order in Council for the purpose of ensuring that effect is given to a Euratom inspection order may, in case of urgency, be made *ex parte* on affidavit but, except as aforesaid, shall be made by motion or summons.

III. Reciprocal Enforcement: The Civil Jurisdiction and Judgments Act 1982

Note. Heading above and rr. 25–39 added by S.I. 1983 No. 1181, r. 20.

Interpretation (Ord. 71, r. 25)

(1) In this Part of this Order—

"the Act of 1982" means the Civil Jurisdiction and Judgments Act 1982;

"Convention territory" means the territory or territories of any Contracting State, as defined by section 1(3) of the Act of 1982, to which the Conventions as defined in section 1(1) of the Act of 1982 apply;

"judgment" is to be construed in accordance with the definition of "judgment" in section 50 of the Act of 1982;

"money provision" means a provision for the payment of one or more sums of money;

"non-money provision" means a provision for any relief or remedy not requiring payment of a sum of money;

"protective measures" means the protective measures referred to in Article 39 of Schedule 1 to the Act of 1982.

(2) For the purposes of this Part of this Order domicile is to be determined in accordance with the provisions of sections 41 to 46 of the Act of 1982.

Assignment of business and exercise of powers (Ord. 71, r. 26)

Any application to the High Court under the Act of 1982 shall be assigned to the Queen's Bench Division and the powers conferred on the Court by that Act shall be exercised in accordance with the provisions of Order 32, rule 11.

Application for registration (Ord. 71, r. 27)

An application for registration of a judgment under section 4 of the Act of 1982 shall be made ex parte.

Evidence in support of application (Ord. 71, r. 28)

(1) An application for registration under section 4 of the Act of 1982 must be supported by an affidavit—

  (a) exhibiting—

    (i) the judgment or a verified or certified or otherwise duly authenticated copy thereof together with such other document or documents as may be requisite to show that, according to the law of the State in which it has been given, the judgment is enforceable and has been served;

    (ii) in the case of a judgment given in default, the original or a certified true copy of the document which establishes that the party in default was served with the document instituting the proceedings or with an equivalent document;

    (iii) where it is the case, a document showing that the party making the application is in receipt of legal aid in the State in which the judgment was given;

    (iv) where the judgment or document is not in the English language, a translation thereof into English certified by a notary public or a person qualified for the purpose in one of the Contracting States or authenticated by affidavit;

  (b) stating—

    (i) whether the judgment provides for the payment of a sum or sums of money;

(ii) whether interest is recoverable on the judgment or part thereof in accordance with the law of the State in which the judgment was given, and if such be the case, the rate of interest, the date from which interest is recoverable, and the date on which interest ceases to accrue;

(c) giving an address within the jurisdiction of the Court for service of process on the party making the application and stating, so far as is known to the deponent, the name and the usual or last known address or place of business of the person against whom judgment was given;

(d) stating to the best of the information or belief of the deponent—

(i) the grounds on which the right to enforce the judgment is vested in the party making the application;

(ii) as the case may require, either that at the date of the application the judgment has not been satisfied, or the part or amount in respect of which it remains unsatisfied.

(2) Where the party making the application does not produce the documents referred to in paragraphs (1)(a)(ii) and (iii) of this rule, the Court may—

(a) fix a time within which the documents are to be produced; or
(b) accept equivalent documents; or
(c) dispense with production of the documents.

Security for costs (Ord. 71, r. 29)

Notwithstanding the provisions of Order 23 a party making an application for registration under section 4 of the Act of 1982 shall not be required solely on the ground that he is not domiciled or resident within the jurisdiction, to give security for costs of the application.

Order for registration (Ord. 71, r. 30)

(1) An order giving leave to register a judgment under section 4 of the Act of 1982 must be drawn up by or on behalf of the party making the application for registration.

(2) Every such order shall state the period within which an appeal may be made against the order for registration and shall contain a notification that execution on the judgment will not issue until after the expiration of that period.

(3) The notification referred to in paragraph (2) shall not prevent any application for protective measures pending final determination of any issue relating to enforcement of the judgment.

Register of judgments registered under s. 4 of the Act of 1982 (Ord. 71, r. 31)

There shall be kept in the Central Office under the direction of the senior master a register of the judgments ordered to be registered under section 4 of the Act of 1982.

Notice of registration (Ord. 71, r. 32)

(1) Notice of the registration of a judgment must be served on the person against whom judgment was given by delivering it to him personally or by sending it to him at his usual or last known address or place of business or in such other manner as the Court may direct.

(2) Service of such a notice out of the jurisdiction is permissible without leave, and Order 11, rules 5, 6 and 8, shall apply in relation to such a notice as they apply in relation to a writ.

(3) The notice of registration must state—

(*a*) full particulars of the judgment registered and the order for registration,

(*b*) the name of the party making the application and his address for service within the jurisdiction,

(*c*) the right of the person against whom judgment was given to appeal against the order for registration, and

(*d*) the period within which an appeal against the order for registration may be made.

Appeals (Ord. 71, r. 33)

(1) An appeal under Article 37 or Article 40 of Schedule 1 to the Act of 1982 must be made by summons to a judge.

(2) A summons in an appeal to which this rule applies must be served—

(*a*) in the case of an appeal under the said Article 37 of Schedule 1, within one month of service of notice of registration of the judgment, or two months of service of such notice where that notice was served on a party not domiciled within the jurisdiction;

(*b*) in the case of an appeal under the said Article 40 of Schedule 1, within one month of the determination of the application under rule 27.

(3) If the party against whom judgment was given is not domiciled in a Convention territory and an application is made within two months of service of notice of registration, the Court may extend the period within which an appeal may be made against the order for registration.

Issue of execution (Ord. 71, r. 34)

(1) Execution shall not issue on a judgment registered under section 4 of the Act of 1982 until after the expiration of the period specified in accordance with rule 30(2) or, if that period has been extended by the Court, until after the expiration of the period so extended.

(2) If an appeal is made under rule 33(1), execution on the judgment shall not issue until after such appeal is determined.

(3) Any party wishing to issue execution on a judgment registered under section 4 of the Act of 1982 must produce to the proper officer an affidavit of service of the notice of registration of the judgment and of any order made by the Court in relation to the judgment.

(4) Nothing in this rule shall prevent the Court from granting protective measures pending final determination of any issue relating to enforcement of the judgment.

Application for recognition (Ord. 71, r. 35)

(1) Registration of the judgment under these rules shall serve for the purposes of the second paragraph of Article 26 of Schedule 1 to the Act of 1982 as a decision that the judgment is recognised.

(2) Where it is sought to apply for recognition of a judgment, the foregoing rules of this Order shall apply to such application as they apply to an application for registration under section 4 of the Act, with the exception that the applicant shall not be required to produce a document or documents which establish that according to the law of the State in which it has been given the judgment is enforceable and has been served, or the document referred to in rule 28(1)(*a*)(iii).

Enforcement of High Court judgments in other Contracting States (Ord. 71, r. 36)

(1) An application under section 12 of the Act of 1982 for a certified copy of a judgment entered in the High Court must made ex parte on affidavit to the Court.

(2) An affidavit by which an application under section 12 of the Act of 1982 is made must—

(a) give particulars of the proceedings in which the judgment was obtained;

(b) have annexed to it a copy of the writ, originating summons or other process by which the proceedings were begun, the evidence of service thereof on the defendant, copies of the pleadings, if any, and a statement of the grounds on which the judgment was based together, where appropriate, with any document under which the applicant is entitled to legal aid or assistance by way of representation for the purposes of the proceedings;

(c) state whether the defendant did or did not object to the jurisdiction, and, if so, on what grounds;

(d) show that the judgment has been served in accordance with Order 65, rule 5 and is not subject to any stay of execution;

(e) state that the time for appealing has expired, or, as the case may be, the date on which it will expire and in either case whether notice of appeal against the judgment has been given; and

(f) state—

  (i) whether the judgment provides for the payment of a sum or sums of money;

  (ii) whether interest is recoverable on the judgment or part thereof and if such be the case, the rate of interest, the date from which interest is recoverable, and the date on which interest ceases to accrue.

(3) The certified copy of the judgment shall be an office copy sealed with the seal of the Supreme Court and there shall be issued with the copy of the judgment a certificate in Form 110, signed by one of the persons referred to in Order 1, rule 4(2) and sealed with the seal of the Supreme Court, having annexed to it a copy of the writ, originating summons or other process by which the proceedings were begun.

Enforcement of United Kingdom judgments in other parts of the United Kingdom: money provisions (Ord. 71, r. 37)

(1) An application for registration in the High Court of a certificate in respect of any money provisions contained in a judgment given in another part of the United Kingdom to which section 18 of the Act of 1982 applies may be made by producing at the Central Office, within six months from the date of its issue, a certificate in the appropriate form prescribed under that Act together with a copy thereof certified by the applicant's solicitor to be a true copy.

(2) A certificate under paragraph (1) must be filed in the Central Office and the certified copy thereof, sealed by an officer of the office in which the certificate is filed, shall be returned to the applicant's solicitor.

(3) A certificate in respect of any money provisions contained in a judgment of the High Court to which section 18 of the Act of 1982 applies may be obtained by producing the form of certificate prescribed in Form 111 at the office in which the judgment is entered, together with an affidavit made by the party entitled to enforce the judgment—

(a) giving particulars of the judgment, stating the sum or aggregate of the sums (including any costs or expenses) payable and unsatisfied under the money provisions contained in the judgment, the rate of interest, if any, payable thereon and the date or time from which any such interest began to accrue;

(b) verifying that the time for appealing against the judgment has expired, or that any appeal brought has been finally disposed of and that enforcement of the judgment is not stayed or suspended; and

(c) stating to the best of the information or belief of the deponent the usual or last known address of the party entitled to enforce the judgment and of the party liable to execution on it.

Enforcement of United Kingdom judgments in other parts of the United Kingdom: non-money provisions (Ord. 71, r. 38)

(1) An application for registration in the High Court of a judgment which contains non-money provisions, being a judgment given in another part of the United Kingdom to which section 18 of the Act of 1982 applies, may be made ex parte, but the Court hearing the application may direct the issue of a summons to which paragraphs (2) and (3) of rule 2 shall apply.

(2) An application under paragraph (1) must be accompanied by a certified copy of the judgment issued under Schedule 7 to the Act of 1982 and a certificate in Form 112 issued not more than six months before the date of application.

(3) Rules 30 and 32 of this Order shall apply to judgments registered under Schedule 7 to the Act of 1982 as they apply to judgments registered under section 4 of that Act.

(4) Paragraphs (1) and (2) of rule 9 shall apply to applications to set aside registration of a judgment under Schedule 7 to the Act of 1982 as they apply to judgments registered under the Administration of Justice Act 1920 and the Foreign Judgments (Reciprocal Enforcements) Act 1933.

(5) A certified copy of a judgment of the High Court to which section 18 of the Act of 1982 applies and which contains any non-money provision may be obtained by an ex parte application on affidavit to the Court.

(6) The requirements in paragraph (3) of rule 37 shall apply with the necessary modifications to an affidavit made in an application under paragraph (5) of this rule.

(7) A certified copy of a judgment shall be an office copy sealed with the seal of the Supreme Court and indorsed with a certificate signed by a master or, where appropriate, a registrar certifying—

(a) that the copy is a true copy of a judgment obtained in the High Court;
(b) that it is issued in accordance with section 18 of the Act of 1982; and
(c) that the conditions specified in paragraphs 3(a) and (b) of Schedule 7 to that Act are satisfied in relation to the judgment.

Register of United Kingdom judgments (Ord 71, r. 39)

There shall be kept in the Central Office under the direction of the senior master a register of the certificates in respect of judgments and of the judgments ordered to be registered in the Central Office under Schedule 6, or, as the case may be, Schedule 7 to the Act.

APPENDIX 3

THE GREEK ACCESSION CONVENTION

CONVENTION[1]
on the accession of the Hellenic Republic to the Convention on jurisdiction and enforcement of judgments in civil and commercial matters and to the Protocol on its interpretation by the Court of Justice with the adjustments made to them by the Convention on the accession of the Kingdom of Denmark, of Ireland and of the United Kingdom of Great Britain and Northern Ireland

(82/972/EEC)

TITLE I

General provisions

Article 1

1. The Hellenic Republic hereby accedes to the Convention on jurisdiction and enforcement of judgments in civil and commercial matters, signed at Brussels on 27 September 1968 (hereinafter called "the 1968 Convention"), and to the Protocol on its interpretation by the Court of Justice, signed at Luxembourg on 3 June 1971 (hereinafter called "the 1971 Protocol"), with the adjustments made to them by the Convention on the accession of the Kingdom of Denmark, of Ireland and of the United Kingdom of Great Britain and Northern Ireland to the Convention on jurisdiction and enforcement of judgments in civil and commercial matters and to the Protocol on its interpretation by the Court of Justice, signed at Luxembourg on 9 October 1978 (hereinafter called "the 1978 Convention").

2. The accession of the Hellenic Republic extends, in particular, to Articles 25(2), 35 and 36 of the 1978 Convention.

Article 2

The adjustments made by this Convention to the 1968 Convention and the 1971 Protocol, as adjusted by the 1978 Convention, are set out in Titles II to IV.

TITLE II

Adjustments to the 1968 Convention

Article 3

The following shall be inserted between the third and fourth indents in the second subparagraph of Article 3 of the 1968 Convention, as amended by Article 4 of the 1978 Convention:

"—in Greece, Article 40 of the code of civil procedure (Κώδικας Πολιτικῆς Δικονομίας),".

---

[1] Signed on 25 October 1982: see Official Journal of the European Communities OJ L388, 31 December 1982.

Appendix 3

Article 4

The following shall be inserted between the third and fourth indents in the first subparagraph of Article 32 of the 1968 Convention, as amended by Article 16 of the 1978 Convention:

"—in Greece, to the μονομελές πρωτοδικεῖο,".[1]

Article 5

1. The following shall be inserted between the third and fourth indents of the first subparagraph of Article 37 of the 1968 Convention, as amended by Article 17 of the 1978 Convention:

"—in Greece, with the ἐφετεῖο,".[2]

2. The following shall be substituted for the first indent of the second subparagraph of Article 37 of the 1968 Convention, as amended by Article 17 of the 1978 Convention:

"—in Belgium, Greece, France, Italy, Luxembourg and in the Netherlands, by an appeal in cassation,".

Article 6

The following shall be inserted between the third and fourth indents of the first subparagraph of Article 40 of the 1968 Convention, as amended by Article 19 of the 1978 Convention:

"—in Greece, to the ἐφετεῖο,".[2]

Article 7

The following shall be substituted for the first indent of Article 41 of the 1968 Convention, as amended by Article 20 of the 1978 Convention:

"—in Belgium, Greece, France, Italy, Luxembourg and in the Netherlands, by an appeal in cassation,".

Article 8

The following shall be inserted at the appropriate place in chronological order in the list of Conventions set out in Article 55 of the 1968 Convention, as amended by Article 24 of the 1978 Convention:

"—the Convention between the Kingdom of Greece and the Federal Republic of Germany for the reciprocal recognition and enforcement of judgments, settlements and authentic instruments in civil and commercial matters, signed in Athens on 4 November 1961,".

TITLE III

Adjustment to the Protocol annexed to the 1968 Convention

Article 9

In the first sentence of the Article Vb added to the Protocol annexed to the 1968 Convention by Article 29 of the 1978 Convention there shall be added after the word "Denmark" a comma and the words "in Greece".

---

[1] Single first instance judge.
[2] Court of Appeal.

TITLE IV

Adjustments to the 1971 Protocol

Article 10

The following subparagraph shall be added to Article 1 of the 1971 Protocol, as amended by Article 30 of the 1978 Convention:

"The Court of Justice of the European Communities shall also have jurisdiction to give rulings on the interpretation of the Convention on the accession of the Hellenic Republic to the Convention of 27 September 1968 and to this Protocol, as adjusted by the 1978 Convention."

Article 11

The following shall be inserted between the third and fourth indents of point 1 of Article 2 of the 1971 Protocol, as amended by Article 31 of the 1978 Convention:

"—in Greece: the ἀνώτατα δικαστήρια,".[3]

TITLE V

Transitional provisions

Article 12

1. The 1968 Convention and the 1971 Protocol, as amended by the 1978 Convention and this Convention, shall apply only to legal proceedings instituted and to authentic instruments formally drawn up or registered after the entry into force of this Convention in the State of origin and, where recognition or enforcement of a judgment or authentic instrument is sought, in the State addressed.

2. However, judgments given after the date of entry into force of this Convention between the State of origin and the State addressed in proceedings instituted before that date shall be recognised and enforced in accordance with the provisions of Title III of the 1968 Convention, as amended by the 1978 Convention and this Convention, if jurisdiction was founded upon rules which accorded with the provisions of Title II of the 1968 Convention, as amended, or with the provisions of a convention which was in force between the State of origin and the State addressed when the proceedings were instituted.

TITLE VI

Final provisions

Article 13

The Secretary-General of the Council of the European Communities shall transmit a certified copy of the 1968 Convention, of the 1971 Protocol and of the 1978 Convention in the Danish, Dutch, English, French, German, Irish and Italian languages to the Government of the Hellenic Republic.

The texts of the 1968 Convention, of the 1971 Protocol and of the 1978 Convention, drawn up in the Greek language, shall be annexed to this Convention. The texts drawn up in the Greek language shall be authentic under the same conditions as the other texts of the 1968 Convention, the 1971 Protocol and the 1978 Convention.

---

[3] Supreme Court.

Appendix 3

Article 14

This Convention shall be ratified by the signatory States. The instruments of ratification shall be deposited with the Secretary-General of the Council of the European Communities.

Article 15

This Convention shall enter into force, as between the States which have ratified it, on the first day of the third month following the deposit of the last instrument of ratification by the Hellenic Republic and those States which have put into force the 1978 Convention in accordance with Article 39 of that Convention.

It shall enter into force for each Member State which subsequently ratifies it on the first day of the third month following the deposit of its instrument of ratification.

Article 16

The Secretary-General of the Council of the European Communities shall notify the signatory States of:

(a) the deposit of each instrument of ratification;
(b) the dates of entry into force of this Convention for the Contracting States.

Article 17

This Convention, drawn up in a single original in the Danish, Dutch, English, French, German, Greek, Irish and Italian languages, all eight texts being equally authentic, shall be deposited in the archives of the General Secretariat of the Council of the European Communities. The Secretary-General shall transmit a certified copy of the Government of each signatory State.

INDEX

257

Index